Motor Development During Childhood and Adolescence

Edited by

Jerry R. Thomas

Louisiana State University
Baton Rouge, Louisiana

Burgess Publishing Company
Minneapolis, Minnesota

Consulting editor: Robert D. Clayton
Acquisitions editor: Wayne Schotanus
Assistant editor: Sharon Harrington
Production editor: Anne Heller
Copy editor: Pamela A. White
Art coordinator: Priscilla Heimann
Composition: Comset Typesetting
Cover design: Catherine Cleary

Printed in the United States of America

Library of Congress Cataloging in Publication Data

Motor development during childhood and adolescence

Includes bibliographies and index.
1. Motor ability in children. I. Thomas, Jerry R.
BF723.M6M64 1984 155.4'12 83-15358
ISBN 0-8087-3637-X

Burgess Publishing Company
7108 Ohms Lane
Minneapolis, Minnesota 55435

J I H G F E D C B

Contents

List of Authors

Dr. CRYSTAL BRANTA is assistant professor and a member of the Youth Sport Institute at Michigan State University, East Lansing.

Dr. JERE D. GALLAGHER is assistant professor in the Department of Health, Physical and Recreation Education at the University of Pittsburgh, Pittsburgh.

Dr. DANIEL GOULD is associate professor in the Department of Health, Physical Education and Recreation at Kansas State University, Manhattan.

Dr. JACQUELINE HERKOWITZ is associate professor in the School of Health, Physical Education and Recreation at Ohio State University, Columbus.

Dr. ROBERT M. MALINA is professor in the Department of Anthropology and Department of Health and Physical Education at the University of Texas, Austin.

Dr. KARL M. NEWELL is associate professor in the Institute for Child Behavior and Development at the University of Illinois, Champaign.

Dr. SCOTT K. POWERS is assistant professor in the School of Health, Physical Education, Recreation and Dance at Louisiana State University, Baton Rouge.

Dr. MARY ANN ROBERTON is associate professor in the Department of Physical Education and Dance at the University of Wisconsin–Madison.

Dr. VERN SEEFELDT is professor and director of the Youth Sport Institute at Michigan State University, East Lansing.

Dr. RONALD E. SMITH is professor of psychology at the University of Washington, Seattle.

Dr. FRANK L. SMOLL is associate professor in the Department of Kinesiology at the University of Washington, Seattle.

Dr. JERRY R. THOMAS is professor in the School of Health, Physical Education, Recreation and Dance and Department of Psychology at Louisiana State University, Baton Rouge.

Dr. KATHERINE T. THOMAS is assistant professor in the Division of Health, Physical Education and Recreation at Southern University, Baton Rouge.

Preface

This book is intended to provide basic knowledge of motor development in children and suggest ways to apply this knowledge to physical education and sport programs. It should serve as a text for the first course in motor development. Also, this book, used with an elementary physical education methods book, will enhance methods courses.

The material in the book covers development from ages 4 to 15 years and is organized into four major sections. Part I reviews and summarizes basic motor development knowledge. Included are chapters on physical growth, effects of exercise on children, fundamental motor patterns, developmental skill acquisition, and physical constraints on learning. Each chapter traces development over childhood and adolescence, with appropriate figures and tables to present important data. In addition to the references at the end are suggested readings grouped separately for undergraduate and graduate students.

Part II provides a link for the book with elementary physical education, suggesting how knowledge of motor development can be used in structuring and evaluating programs for nonretarded and retarded children, in planning equipment and playgrounds that are developmentally appropriate, and in evaluation. The intent of this section is twofold:

1. If the book is used in a motor development course, Part II suggests potential applications of the knowledge from Part I.
2. If the book is used in an elementary physical education methods course with a methods book, Part II provides the transition between basic knowledge and program planning.

Part III covers one of the most popular topics today—children's sport—which probably falls between motor development and sport psychology. The three chapters in this section introduce and provide an overview of the area. This may be the only coverage of this topic that the undergraduate receives, and may encourage the interested graduate student to make more detailed study of this important subject. The three chapters cover patterns of participation in children's sport, psychosocial development and children's sport, and the coach-player relationship. All chapters in Part I have application to youth sport. Part III provides a more detailed example of the approach used in Part II—the application of knowledge of motor development to children's sport programs.

Part IV is designed for use with graduate students. This section, together with the graduate reading list at the end of each chapter, will aid further study for the beginning graduate student as well as the undergraduate student. The first chapter presents a number of important methodological issues for motor development research. The second chapter provides laboratory experiences that I have found useful in teaching my motor development course. These five laboratories are designed to be used with Chapters 1, 2, 3, 4, and 12.

The book should be useful for three different groups. First, an increasing number of undergraduate courses are offered in motor development. If a survey reported in the October 1979 issue of the *Journal of Physical Education and Recreation* (pp. 79-80) can be generalized to all major universities, 45% offer an undergraduate motor development course. Second, this same survey reports that 67% of the universities (again generalizing to all universities) were offering a graduate course in motor development. Third, teachers of elementary physical education methods increasingly are using motor development information in these courses. I believe a substantial number will find this book of value in connection with their methods book. Frequently, this methods course is the only course elementary education majors get in physical education, so information on the content of motor development as well as teaching methodology is needed.

Finally, if we are ever to be successful in teaching children motor skills, teachers must understand how children grow, respond to exercise, develop motor patterns, acquire skills, and develop psychosocially. Thus, in planning physical education programs, the curriculum and methodology must be based on knowledge of motor development. Otherwise, teachers only use approaches that have been handed down to them (from their teacher education programs or from other teachers) because these approaches have enjoyed some success. This is truly *teacher training*. To *educate teachers*, students must be able to understand the development of cognitive, motor, and affective processes in children and to plan programs at appropriate developmental levels rather than just to teach to the class average.

I hope you find this book as useful to read as I did to put together. If you love kids, you *will* find the book of value, as each of us authors conducts research with kids because we love them and want to help children realize the fulfillment to be obtained in sport, physical activity, and regular exercise.

Jerry R. Thomas

PART I

Knowledge Base in Motor Development

Part I of this text is designed to present knowledge in the subdiscipline of human movement called motor development. While motor development involves the changes in human movement associated with aging and covers the human life span, the emphasis in this part is on changes in children from 4 to 15 years of age.

Chapter 1 describes a number of changes during the childhood years that are important to skillful motor performance, including size, body proportions, body composition, and functional complexity, as well as the effects of puberty and gender similarities and differences.

Since physical educators have the development of physical fitness as a major program objective, Chapter 2 provides a careful overview of the effects of exercise on humans. It also describes how physiological development proceeds during childhood and adolescence, the acute and chronic effects of exercise, and some practical ideas for assessing physical fitness in children.

Chapter 3 covers primitive reflexes in infants through the mature forms of various motor patterns (as in throwing, catching, and running), the motor milestones in development, intertask and intratask development, a component approach to motor pattern development, age and sex differences in outcomes of the motor patterns, and the interaction of motor pattern (form) and motor performance (outcome).

Chapter 4 explains how the child's memory operations influence motor skill development and the changes in memory function that occur across childhood and into adolescence.

Chapter 5 discusses the problems that arise when motor skill development is viewed from different levels of analysis (e.g., biochemical, anatomical, physiological, behavioral).

1

Physical Growth and Maturation

Robert M. Malina

Between conception and adulthood, the biological activities of growth, maturation, and development are dominant activities of the individual. During roughly the first two decades of life (not overlooking the significance of the prenatal period), a child increases in size, changes in body proportions and composition, changes in functional complexity, sexually matures, and improves in performance capacities. These dynamic functions characterize the growing years to the extent that the individual is constantly striving for the mature or adult state. Thus, growth, maturation, and development are essentially purposive processes, implying progress or movement toward the mature or adult state.

The three terms used in the preceding paragraph merit more specific definition, as they are often treated synonymously. *Growth* implies changes in size that are the outcomes of the underlying processes of increase in cellular number (hyperplasia), cell size (hypertrophy), and intercellular materials (accretion). *Maturation*, specifically biological maturation, is an important corollary of growth and refers to the child's inborn chronometer or biological clock, which regulates progress toward the mature state. The mature state, however, is variously defined and in most studies of growth and development refers to the attainment of sexual maturity (or mature reproductive function) or to adult stature (i.e., structural maturity). *Development* is a more commonly used term that has a broader meaning. In physiological terms, it often refers to the specialization and differentiation of cells into different functional units. In behavioral terms, it refers to a number of different activities (e.g., cognitive development, development of social competence, or motor development).

The focus of this chapter is on biological growth and maturation. These are biological processes. However, we ordinarily do not study these processes per se; rather, we observe or measure the outcomes of the underlying processes. For example, we measure size attained but not the activities at the growth plate of specific long bones. We measure a stage of skeletal maturation but not the process of ossification occurring in a particular bone.

Growth and maturation operate over a time framework, that is, the outcomes are measured at a single point in time or over time. The point of reference for time is the child's chronological age, which is measured relative to the birthday (e.g., all children born on 21 May 1967 were 10 years of age on 21 May 1977). Although chronological age is the point of reference, it should be emphasized that biological processes have their own clocks, that is, biological time does not necessarily proceed in concert with the calendar. Hence, children of the same chronological age may differ by several years in biological age.

AGE PERIODS

Postnatal growth and maturation generally comprise the first two decades of life. This span can be divided into three age periods. *Infancy* comprises the first year of life and is a period of rapid growth in most bodily systems. *Childhood* covers the span from one year until adolescence. It is often divided into *early childhood*, which includes the preschool years, and *middle childhood*, which includes approximately the elementary school years in our culture. Childhood is a period of relatively steady progress in growth and maturation. Approximate ages for the two periods of childhood are one through five, and six through the beginning of adolescence. *Adolescence* is a variously defined age period due to variation in the time of its onset and termination. The age ranges—from 8 to 19 years in females and from 10 to 22 years in males—are often given as limits for normal variation in the onset and termination of adolescence in the human species. Most bodily systems become adult or mature both structurally and functionally during this period. Structurally, an acceleration in the rate of growth in stature represents the beginning of the adolescent growth spurt. The rate of statural growth then merges into a slowing or decelerating phase, and finally terminates with the attainment of adult stature. Functionally, adolescence usually is viewed in terms of sexual maturation, which begins with the initial development of the secondary sex characteristics (i.e., breasts and pubic hair in girls, genitalia and pubic hair in boys), and terminates with the attainment of mature reproductive function. Although menarche or the first menstrual flow is perhaps the most commonly used indicator of sexual maturity in girls, it does not necessarily mean reproductive maturity (fertility). The latter may not be achieved until the late teens or early 20s.

METHODS FOR THE STUDY OF GROWTH AND MATURATION

The study of growth and maturation implies measurement and observation of the outcomes of these processes. Several more commonly used methods are summarized subsequently.

Anthropometry refers to a systematized set of techniques for taking measurements, and is perhaps the basic tool in growth studies. Anthropometric procedures involve special equipment and the use of carefully defined landmarks for specific measurements. The number of measurements that can be taken on an individual is almost limitless. For simplicity, selected measurements of overall body size and of several specific parts and tissues are presented.

Weight and *stature* (height) are the two most often used measurements of growth. *Body weight* is a measure of body mass, a composite of independently varying tissues. Although weight should be measured with the child nude, frequently the individual is attired in ordinary indoor clothing (e.g., gym shorts) without shoes. *Stature*, or standing height, is a linear measurement of the distance from the floor or standing surface to the vertex of the skull that is made with the subject in a standard erect posture, without shoes. Stature is a composite of linear dimensions contributed by the lower extremities, the trunk, the neck, and the head. From birth to age two or three, an individual's stature is measured as *recumbent length* (i.e., the length of the child's body while lying in a standardized position). As a rule, people are longer lying down than when standing erect.

Sitting height, as the name implies, is the height of the child while sitting. The distance is measured from the sitting surface to the top of the head when the child is seated in a standard position. This measurement is especially of value when used with stature. Stature minus sitting height provides an estimate of the length of the lower extremities (*subischial length*). When sitting height is expressed as a percentage of stature, the sitting height/stature ratio provides an estimate of relative leg length. Two children, for example, can have the same stature, yet one has a sitting-height/standing-height ratio of 54% while the other has a ratio of 51%. In the former, sitting height accounts for 54% of stature, and by subtraction, the lower extremities account for 46%. This individual is said to be relatively short legged. In contrast, the other child's sitting height accounts for 51% of the standing height, and by subtraction, the legs account for 49% (i.e., this child is relatively long legged compared with the other child).

Breadth or width measurements are usually taken across specific bony landmarks and therefore provide an index of skeletal robustness. Four breadth measurements are often used in growth studies, although any number of others can be measured. *Biacromial breadth* measures the distance across the right and left acromial processes of the scapulae, and thus provides an indication of bony breadth across the shoulders. *Bicristal breadth* measures the maximum distance between the iliac crests, and thus provides an indication of the bony breadth across the hips. These two breadth measurements provide information on the dimensions of the upper and lower trunk and are commonly used in the form of a ratio (biacromial breadth/bicristal breadth × 100) to illustrate proportional changes in shoulder-hip relationships during growth. Breadths across the bony condyles of the femur (*bicondylar breadth*) and across the epicondyles of the humerus (*biepicondylar breadth*) provide general information on the skeletal robustness of the extremities. The former is a measure of bony breadth across the knee, while the latter is a measure of bony breadth across the elbow.

Limb circumferences are indicators of relative muscularity. Note, however, that a circumference includes bone in the center, surrounded by a mass of muscle that is ringed by a layer of subcutaneous fat. The two more commonly used circumference measurements are the *arm* and *calf circumferences*. Arm circumference is measured with the arm hanging loosely at the side at the point midway between the acromial (see above) and olecranon (tip of the elbow) processes. Calf circumference is measured at the maximum circumference of the calf, most often with the subject in a standing position and the weight distributed evenly on both legs.

Skinfold thicknesses are used as indicators of subcutaneous fat (i.e., body fat immediately beneath the skin). This thickness, in the form of a double fold of skin and underlying subcutaneous tissue, can be easily determined with calipers. The resultant measurement is a skinfold thickness, which can be taken at any number of sites on the body. Most often, skinfolds are measured on the extremities and on the trunk, as body fat shows a differential pattern of distribution. Two of the more commonly used sites in growth studies are the *triceps skinfold* on the back of the arm over the triceps muscle and the *subscapular skinfold* on the back just beneath the inferior angle of the scapula.

The triceps skinfold is measured at the same level of the arm as is arm circumference. Since the arm is a cylinder, the principles of circle geometry apply. When the arm circumference is corrected for the thickness of the outer perimeter of fat, an estimation of the midarm muscle and fat areas and of midarm muscle circumference can be derived. The latter is estimated as follows:

$$c_2 = c_1 - \pi s_t$$

where c_2 is the estimated midarm muscle circumference, c_1 is arm circumference, and s_t is the triceps skinfold. This estimated muscle measurement is used widely in studies of nutritional status, especially of preschool children.

The selection of measurements described above provides information about the size of the child and on specific parts and tissues. More specific study of body tissues falls within the area labeled *body composition*, which attempts to partition the body mass (i.e., weight) into its basic tissue components. Most often, body mass is partitioned into lean tissue (often called lean body mass) and fat tissue. A variety of techniques are available for such estimates. Many of them require specialized equipment and procedures. In addition, many of the procedures are not amenable to use over the entire growth period (i.e., infancy through adolescence). The procedures provide information for the body as a whole (that is, total body fat or lean body mass), but do not provide information on changes in specific tissues or changes in specific regions of the body that accompany growth. Nevertheless, they provide important growth data. The following discussion of changes in body composition during growth is based first on both total body composition estimates and then on data for limb circumferences and skinfolds, estimates of muscularity (the major component of lean body mass), and subcutaneous fatness (a major percentage of the body's fat).

The concept of *physique* or body build is important in studies of growth. Physique refers to the general configuration of the body as a whole. Assessment of body form or physique has a long history that goes back to the time of Hippocrates. Since then, numerous attempts have been made to classify physique, most derived from studies of adults and all eventually describing physique in two or three types of components. Sheldon's (1954) approach to assessment of physique has influenced the direction of studies in the United States.

Sheldon's method is built on the premise that there is continuous variation in physique based on the contribution of varying components to the conformation of the entire body. These components are termed *endomorphy*, referring to a relative preponderance of the digestive organs and of softness and roundness of contour throughout the body, as in an individual who tends toward fatness and obesity; *mesomorphy*, referring to a predominance of muscle, bone, and connective tissue so that muscles are prominent with sharp contours, as in a muscular individual; and *ectomorphy*, referring to a general linearity and fragility, poor muscle development, and a preponderance of surface area over body mass, as in an extremely thin individual. A clear-cut dominance of one of these three components defines the individual's physique, which is called a *somatotype*. In Sheldon's approach, the method used in assessing physique is basically photographic, visual (anthroposcopic), and subjective, although stature and weight measurements are used in the form of a weight/stature ratio. Note that the anthroposcopic method is basically observational and subjective, while the anthropometric method is mensurable and more objective.

Each of the three components making up an individual's physique is assessed individually from three standardized photographs. Rating is based on a 7-point scale, with 1 representing the least expression and 7 the fullest expression of the specific component. Emphasis is placed on the contribution of each component to total physique, which can be extreme or balanced. The ratings of each component comprise the individual's somatotype, which is expressed by three numerals that represent the strength or weakness of the three somatotype components. The first numeral always refers to endomorphy, the second to mesomorphy, and the third to ectomorphy. Thus, the extreme somatotypes are 711 (extreme endomorphy), 171 (extreme mesomorphy), and 117 (extreme ectomorphy). An individual with the somatotype 251 is low in endomorphy and ectomorphy but moderately high in mesomorphy. Since the dominant component is mesomorphy, this individual's somatotype is basically mesomorphic. An individual with the somatotype 344 has a balanced physique with no clear-cut dominance of any component. Possible somatotype component combinations are numerous (e.g., 352, 551, 461), but some are simply impossible (e.g., 717, 666).

The basic principles underlying Sheldon's approach to the assessment of physique have been modified. Heath and Carter (Carter 1980), for example, use both the anthroposcopic procedures (if photos are available) and anthropometric procedures to estimate an individual's somatotype, which is expressed as three digits as noted above. In practice, however, the anthropometric procedures of the Heath-Carter method are most often used. The anthropometric estimate of somatotype is derived from the sum of three skinfolds—triceps, subscapular, and suprailiac—to estimate endomorphy; stature is adjusted for biepicondylar and bicondylar breadths and for arm and calf circumferences corrected for the triceps and medial calf skinfolds, respectively, to estimate mesomorphy; and a height/weight ratio (height divided by the cube root of weight) is used to estimate ectomorphy.

Two types of maturity assessments are generally used in growth studies. Sexual maturation refers to the state of development of the primary and secondary sex characteristics (e.g., breast development and menarche in females, penis and testes growth in males, and pubic hair development in both sexes). Scales are available for the assessment of sexual maturation using these criteria (Tanner 1962). However, outside the clinical setting, such assessments are extremely difficult to use for primary social and cultural reasons. Age at menarche is the most commonly reported maturational event and is often used to classify girls into maturational categories for comparison. However, considerable error in reported ages at menarche may be found, and extreme care must be used in obtaining such information. In addition to practical difficulties in obtaining sexual maturity information, these maturity indicators are basically time limited, and thus are useful only during the adolescent years.

Skeletal maturation is perhaps the best method for the assessment of biological age or maturity status of a child. The skeleton is an ideal indicator of maturity in that its development spans the entire period of active growth and maturation. All children start with a skeleton of cartilage and have a fully developed bony skeleton in early adulthood. In other words, both the beginning and end points of the maturation process are known, since the skeletal structure of all individuals progresses from cartilage to bone.

The primary limitation in using skeletal maturation as an indicator of a child's maturity status at present is that it requires the use of an X ray of the hand and wrist. This area contains many separate centers of bone growth and maturation. Although some variation is apparent, the hand-wrist area is fairly typical of the remainder of the skeleton. Two procedures are commonly used to assess skeletal maturity—the Greulich-Pyle method (Greulich and Pyle 1959) and the Tanner-Whitehouse method (Tanner et al. 1975). Both methods involve the comparison of the X ray of a child with skeletal maturity reference criteria for American (in the case of the Greulich-Pyle system) or for British (in the case of Tanner-Whitehouse method) children. Both methods provide a bone age or skeletal age, which is expressed relative to the child's chronological age. Thus, a child may be 10.5 years of age chronologically but may be 12.3 years of age skeletally. Details of assessment procedures are given in the primary references to the methods.

AGE CHANGES AND SEX DIFFERENCES IN SIZE AND PROPORTIONS

The general course of growth in stature and weight from birth to 18 years is shown in Figure 1.1. From birth to early adulthood, both stature and weight generally follow a four-phase growth

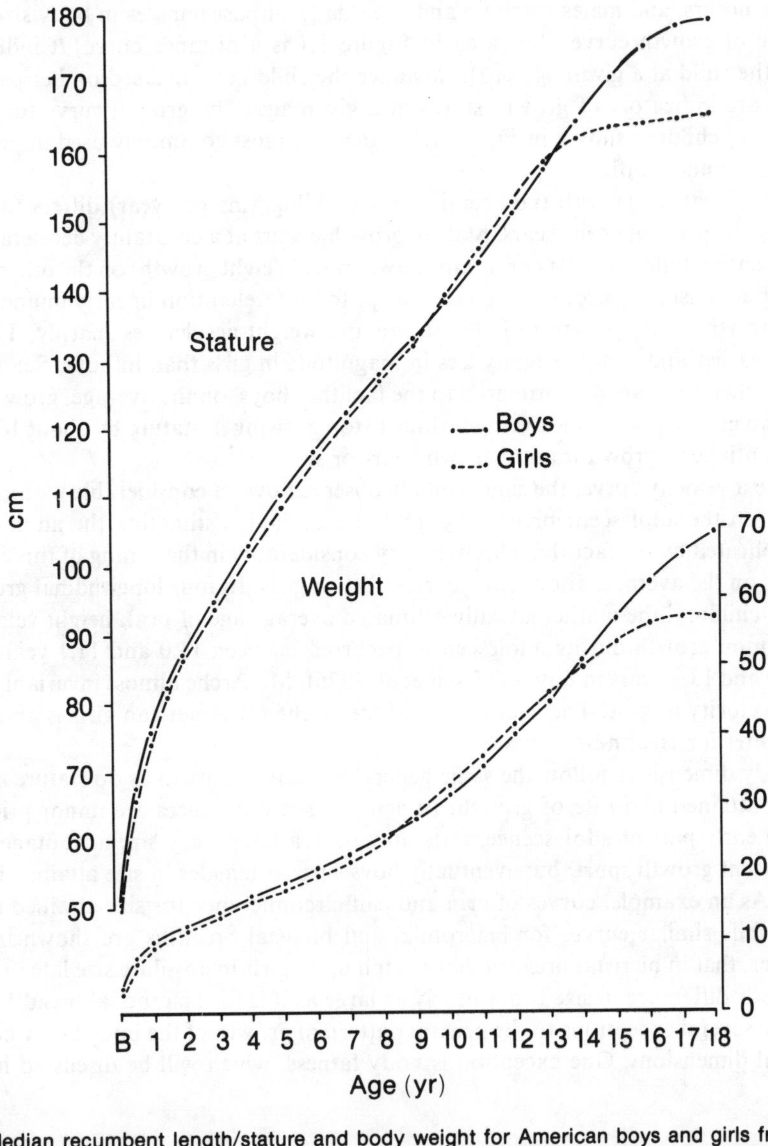

Figure 1.1. Median recumbent length/stature and body weight for American boys and girls from birth to 18 years of age. Recumbent length from birth to two years and then stature. (Based on data from the National Center for Health Statistics 1977.)

pattern: rapid gain in infancy and early childhood, rather steady gain during middle childhood, rapid gain during adolescence, and slow increase and eventual cessation of growth at the attainment of adult stature. Note, however, that body weight usually continues to increase into adult life. Both sexes follow the same course of growth. Sex differences before the adolescent growth spurt are consistent though minor. Boys, on the average, tend to be slightly longer or taller and heavier than girls. During the early part of adolescence, girls are temporarily taller and heavier than boys, which indicates their earlier adolescent spurt. Girls soon lose the size advantage as the adolescent spurt of boys occurs, and males catch up and eventually surpass females in body size.

The type of growth curve illustrated in Figure 1.1 is a distance curve. It indicates the size attained by the child at a given age or the distance the child has traversed on her path of growth. Such curves are indicators of growth status at a given age. The growth curve for assessing the growth status of children shown in Figure 1.1 is the type most commonly used in pediatric clinics or in the school nurse's office.

Rate or velocity of growth (i.e., centimeters or kilograms per year) differs for stature and weight during the preadolescent years. Stature growth occurs at a constantly decelerating rate. The youngster is getting taller but at a constantly slower rate. Weight growth, on the other hand, occurs at a slightly but constantly accelerating rate except for a deceleration in early infancy. During the adolescent growth spurt, growth in both stature and weight accelerates sharply. The adolescent spurt occurs earlier and is only slightly less in magnitude in girls than in boys. Sex differences in adult stature, therefore, are due primarily to the fact that boys, on the average, grow over a longer period than do girls. Girls, on the average, almost stop growing in stature by about 16 years of age, while boys continue to grow for another two years or so.

To derive a velocity curve, the same child is observed over a considerable period, especially if observations on the adolescent phase of growth are desired. Estimating the adolescent spurt is further complicated by the fact that children vary considerably in the timing of this event, and the event occurs, on the average, about two years earlier in girls. In four longitudinal growth studies[1] of American children, the mathematically estimated average age of peak height velocity (i.e., the age of maximum growth during adolescence) occurred between 11.0 and 11.1 years in girls and between 12.9 and 13.3 years in boys (Thissen et al. 1976). Menarche almost invariably occurs after peak height velocity in girls. The average age at menarche for American girls is about 12.8 years (National Center for Health Statistics 1973).

Most body dimensions follow the same general pattern of growth as do stature and weight in terms of size attained and rate of growth. In general, sex differences are minor prior to adolescence. In the early part of adolescence, girls may have a temporary size advantage due to their earlier adolescent growth spurt, but eventually boys surpass females in size attained in most body dimensions. As an example, curves of arm and calf circumference for size attained are shown in Figure 1.2, while similar curves for biacromial and bicristal breadths are shown in Figure 1.3. Note, however, that in bicristal breadth, boys catch up to girls in absolute size late in adolescence, and that the sex difference in size is not nearly as large as it is for biacromial breadth.

There are several exceptions to the general pattern of growth of the body as a whole and most of its external dimensions. One exception is body fatness, which will be discussed in the section

1. A longitudinal growth study is one in which the same child or children are observed at regular intervals over a considerable period of time.

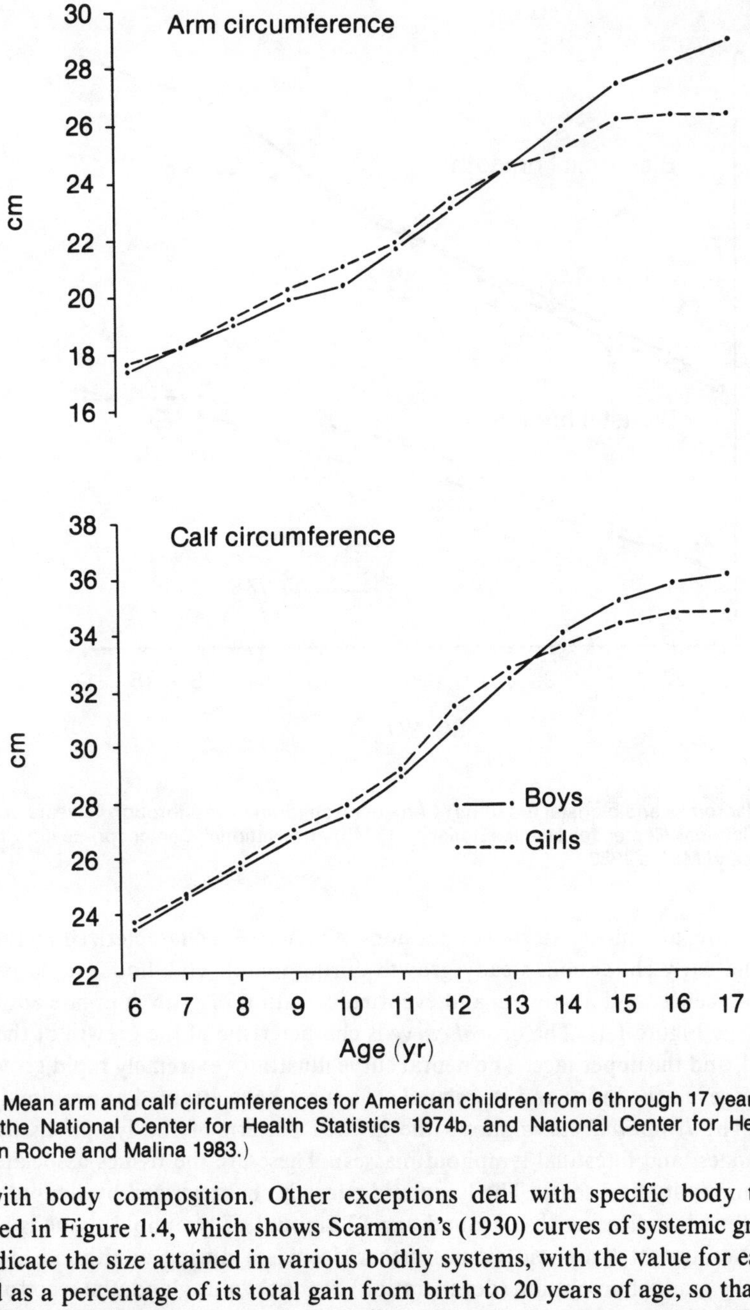

Figure 1.2. Mean arm and calf circumferences for American children from 6 through 17 years of age. (Based on data from the National Center for Health Statistics 1974b, and National Center for Health Statistics data published in Roche and Malina 1983.)

dealing with body composition. Other exceptions deal with specific body tissues; these are summarized in Figure 1.4, which shows Scammon's (1930) curves of systemic growth. The curves simply indicate the size attained in various bodily systems, with the value for each measurement calculated as a percentage of its total gain from birth to 20 years of age, so that size at age 20 is 100% on the vertical scale.

Scammon noted that the growth of most body tissues, organs, and systems followed one of four patterns. The *general curve* is characteristic of the body as a whole, including stature, weight,

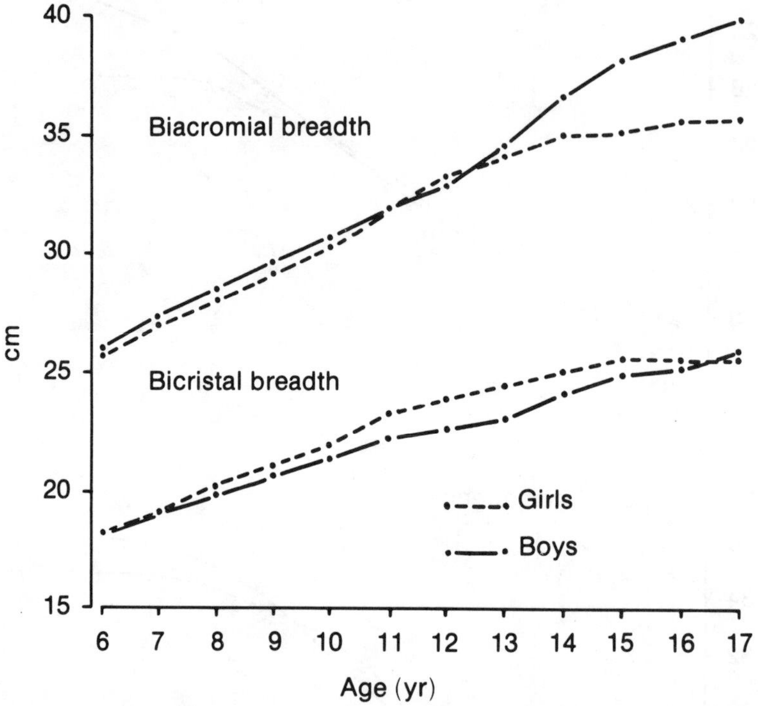

Figure 1.3. Mean biacromial and bicristal breadths of American children from 6 through 17 years of age. (Based on data from the National Center for Health Statistics 1974b, and National Center for Health Statistics data published in Roche and Malina 1983.)

skeleton, musculature, and most external dimensions. This curve is characterized by rapid growth during infancy and early childhood, steady growth during middle childhood, rapid growth once again during adolescence, and a slowing and eventual cessation of growth in late adolescence or early adulthood (see Figure 1.1). The *neural curve* is characteristic of the growth of the brain and its parts, the head, and the upper face. The neural curve illustrates extremely rapid growth early in life so that by age seven the brain and its related structures have attained approximately 95% of their adult size. The *lymphoid curve* shows the growth pattern of the lymph tissues (i.e., the thymus, lymph nodes, and intestinal lymphoid masses). These are the tissues associated, in part, with the body's immunity to disease. The lymphoid curve is characterized by a rapid rise during infancy and childhood, indicating that around age 12 amount of lymphoid tissue is about twice that at age 20. Amount of lymphoid tissue further decreases during adulthood. This relative decrease reflects the gradual involution (degeneration) of the thymus gland, the secretory function of which is considerably reduced. The *genital curve* is the pattern characteristic of the reproductive system and related structures (e.g., testes, penis, ovaries, uterus, prostate). Genital tissues show a

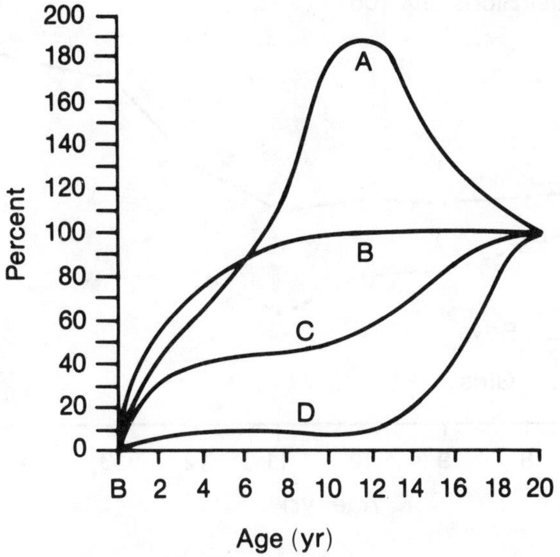

Figure 1.4. Scammon's curves of systemic growth: A, lymphoid; B, neural; C, general body; D, genital. (Adapted from Scammon 1930.)

slight increase early in postnatal life, followed by a latent period through childhood, and then an extremely rapid growth spurt during adolescence.

Although Scammon's curves of systemic growth are generalized and simplified, they do serve to indicate the differential but orderly nature of postnatal growth. Note the rapid growth of the nervous system early in life, the generally quiescent state of the reproductive system until the teen years, the sharp acceleration in growth of the lymphoid system early in life followed by a sharp deceleration, and the *S*-shaped curve of general body growth that is characteristic of most body dimensions used in studies of growth and motor performance.

A consideration of the relationship between specific measurements permits an examination of body proportions, that is, the size of one part of the body relative to another. Proportions are ordinarily viewed in terms of ratios, and two in particular contribute to the understanding of sex differences in body build and the impact of the adolescent growth spurt on body proportions.

The obvious broadening of the shoulders relative to the hips is characteristic of male adolescence, while the broadening of the hips relative to the shoulders and waist is characteristic of female adolescence. The development of these proportional differences is shown in the ratio of biacromial to bicristal breadths in Figure 1.5. From ages 6 to 11, the ratio is almost constant in boys and then shows a marked increase from ages 11 to 16. The rise in the ratio is due to the fact that biacromial breadth is getting larger at a faster rate than bicristal breadth during male adolescence (i.e., the numerator in the ratio increases at a faster rate than the denominator). (See also Figure 1.3. The data in this figure was used to calculate the ratios shown in Figure 1.5.) In girls, on the other hand, the ratio declines slightly but consistently from ages 7 through 17. Note

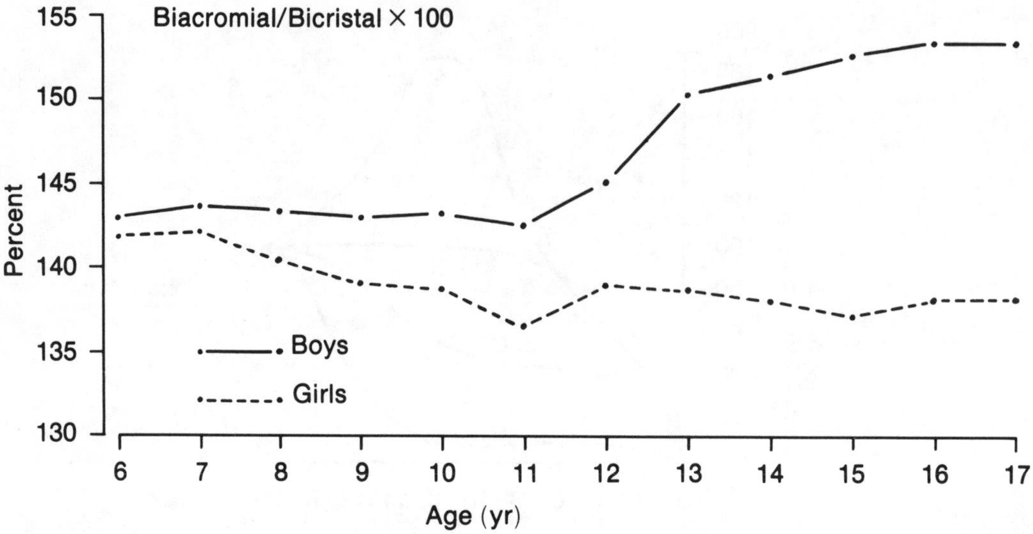

Figure 1.5. Biacromial/bicristal breadth ratio for American children from 6 through 17 years of age. (Drawn from the mean values plotted in Figure 1.3.)

that these ratios are derived from cross-sectional[2] data so that the curve is not necessarily smooth, as different children are represented at each age. Since girls are developing broader hips relative to their shoulders, the ratio declines as the denominator (bicristal breadth) increases at a faster rate than the numerator (biacromial breadth).

The sex difference in the biacromial/bicristal ratio is especially apparent in longitudinal data over adolescence. In growth studies, the ratio is ordinarily calculated annually before adolescence, and at three- or six-month intervals during the adolescent phase of growth. In a study of British children, the estimated adolescent gain in biacromial breadth was 8.5 cm in boys and 6.2 cm in girls. The estimated adolescent gain in bicristal breadth was only 4.8 cm in boys and 6.0 cm in girls (Tanner et al. 1976). Thus, boys on the average gain more in shoulder breadth, while girls gain more in hip breadth during adolescence, and this differential magnitude of gains during adolescence contributes to the sex differences in proportions observed at this time.

Similar proportional differences are apparent in the relative length of the extremities. Illustrations of this are seen in growth studies that use the ratio of sitting height to stature, thus giving an index of the contributions of the trunk and legs to stature. The growth curve for this proportion is shown in Figure 1.6. The ratio is highest in infancy and declines throughout childhood into adolescence. The ratio is lowest during the midst of adolescence—12 to 13 years of age in girls and 13 to 15 years of age in boys—and is then followed by an increase. This illustrates that during infancy and childhood the legs are growing faster than the trunk; as a result, sitting height

2. A cross-sectional growth study is one in which each child is represented only *once* in contrast with the longitudinal study in which a child is assessed over time at regular intervals.

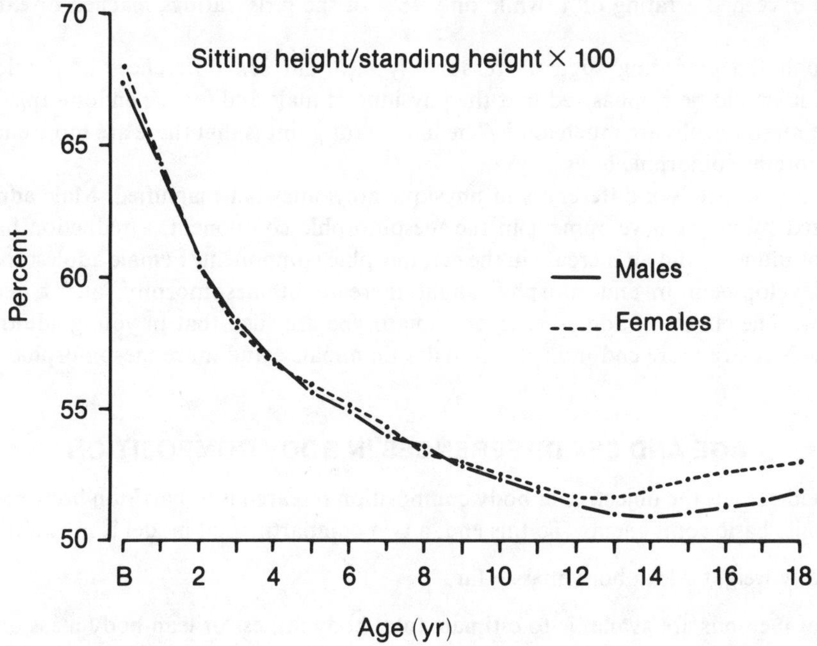

Figure 1.6. Sitting height/stature ratio of Denver children from birth to 18 years of age. (Based on data from Hansman 1970.)

contributes progressively less to stature with age, and the ratio declines. The ratio then reaches its lowest point during adolescence, earlier in girls than in boys, because during this time the legs experience their growth spurt earlier than the trunk. In British girls, for example, the age of peak velocity (maximum growth) for leg length is 11.6 years, while that for sitting height is 12.2 years. Corresponding ages for boys are 13.6 years and 14.3 years, respectively (Tanner et al. 1976). The slight increase in the ratio in later adolescence indicates the adolescent growth in trunk length at a time when growth in the lower extremities has already ceased.

The sitting height/stature ratio is identical for boys and girls until about age 12, when it becomes slightly higher in girls and remains so through adolescence and into adulthood. Thus, prior to adolescence, both boys and girls are proportionately similar in terms of relative leg length or relative trunk length. However, during adolescence and in adulthood, females have, for an equal stature, relatively shorter legs than males.

Changing body proportions during growth and maturation contribute to age- and sex-associated variation in physique. When the traditional three-component somatotype formula is used, the following summarizes changes in physique during growth and maturation: During childhood, girls have, on the average, higher endomorphy and boys have higher mesomorphy. The sexes differ little in ectomorphy. The distributions of individual somatotypes within a sample of boys and girls show the sex difference in physique somewhat more clearly. For example, in a study of preschool children, Walker (1962) noted that only 25% of the boys' somatotype ratings reached or exceeded a value of 4 for endomorphy, while more than 50% of the girls' ratings reached or exceeded this value for endomorphy. In mesomorphy, on the other hand, over 50% of the boys reached or exceeded a rating of 4, while only 16% of the girls' ratings reached or exceeded this value.

Although the preceding suggests reasonably clear-cut sex differences in physique during childhood, it should be emphasized that the physique of male and female endomorphs or of male and female mesomorphs are much alike. The important point is that there are more endomorphic girls and more mesomorphic boys.

Over adolescence, sex differences in physique are somewhat magnified. Male adolescence is characterized by major development in the mesomorphic component, a reduction in the endomorphic component, and an increase in the ectomorphic component. Female adolescence involves primary development in endomorphy, slight increase in mesomorphy, and a reduction in ectomorphy. The effects of adolescence on somatotype are such that in young adulthood, as in childhood, there are more endomorphic females than males, and more mesomorphic males than females.

AGE AND SEX DIFFERENCES IN BODY COMPOSITION

As noted earlier, the objective of body composition research is to partition body mass or body weight into its basic components. To this end, a two-compartmental model is most often used:

Body weight = lean body mass + fat

A variety of methods are available to estimate total body fatness or lean body mass or both. Age trends and sex differences in lean body mass and fatness as derived from measurements of potassium-40 (a naturally occurring radioisotope in the body) are shown in Figure 1.7. At all ages from 6 through 17 years, boys have, on the average, a greater lean body mass than girls. Note that the difference between the sexes is reduced during early adolescence. However, in contrast to the growth curve for body weight (see Figure 1.1), which shows a temporary female size advantage, the growth curve for lean body mass does not show an advantage. By inference, the temporary body weight advantage of females during early adolescence is most likely due to greater fatness in females, as illustrated in the middle and lower parts of Figure 1.7. On the average, girls exceed boys in absolute and relative amounts of fat during growth. The differences are not great during childhood, but as adolescence approaches, the differences are magnified and persist through adolescence and into adulthood.

Estimates of total lean body mass and fatness treat the body as a whole and do not illustrate changes in different areas of the body. Compositional changes in the upper arm are shown in Figure 1.8. In early childhood, sex differences in the triceps skinfold are negligible, but soon become larger in girls and remain so throughout growth. With age, the triceps skinfold increases in thickness from middle childhood through adolescence in girls. In boys, on the other hand, the triceps skinfold remains rather constant in thickness during most of childhood, increases slightly somewhat before adolescence, and then decreases in thickness during the adolescent growth spurt. Longitudinal data for children observed through adolescence indicate that the male adolescent fat loss, especially on the arm, coincides with the timing of the peak height velocity. At peak height velocity in girls, on the other hand, the rate of fat accumulation slows down (although one study indicates fat loss at peak height velocity—Tanner et al. 1981).

Estimated midarm muscle circumference shows the same growth pattern as lean body mass. At all ages, boys have a larger estimated midarm musculature, but the sex difference is exaggerated

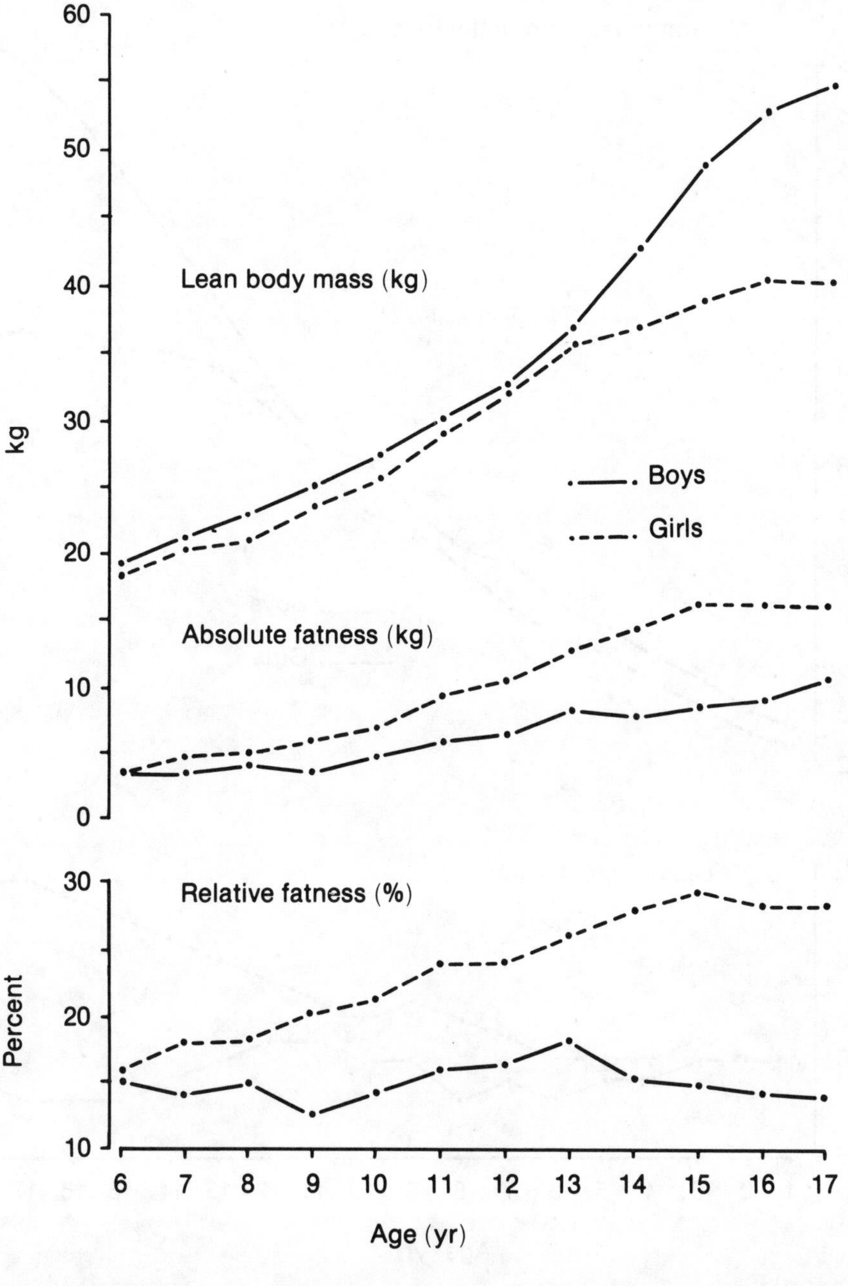

Figure 1.7. Median lean body mass (determined from potassium-40), absolute amount of fat, and percentage of body weight as fat in German children from 6 through 17 years of age. (Based on data from Burmeister 1965.)

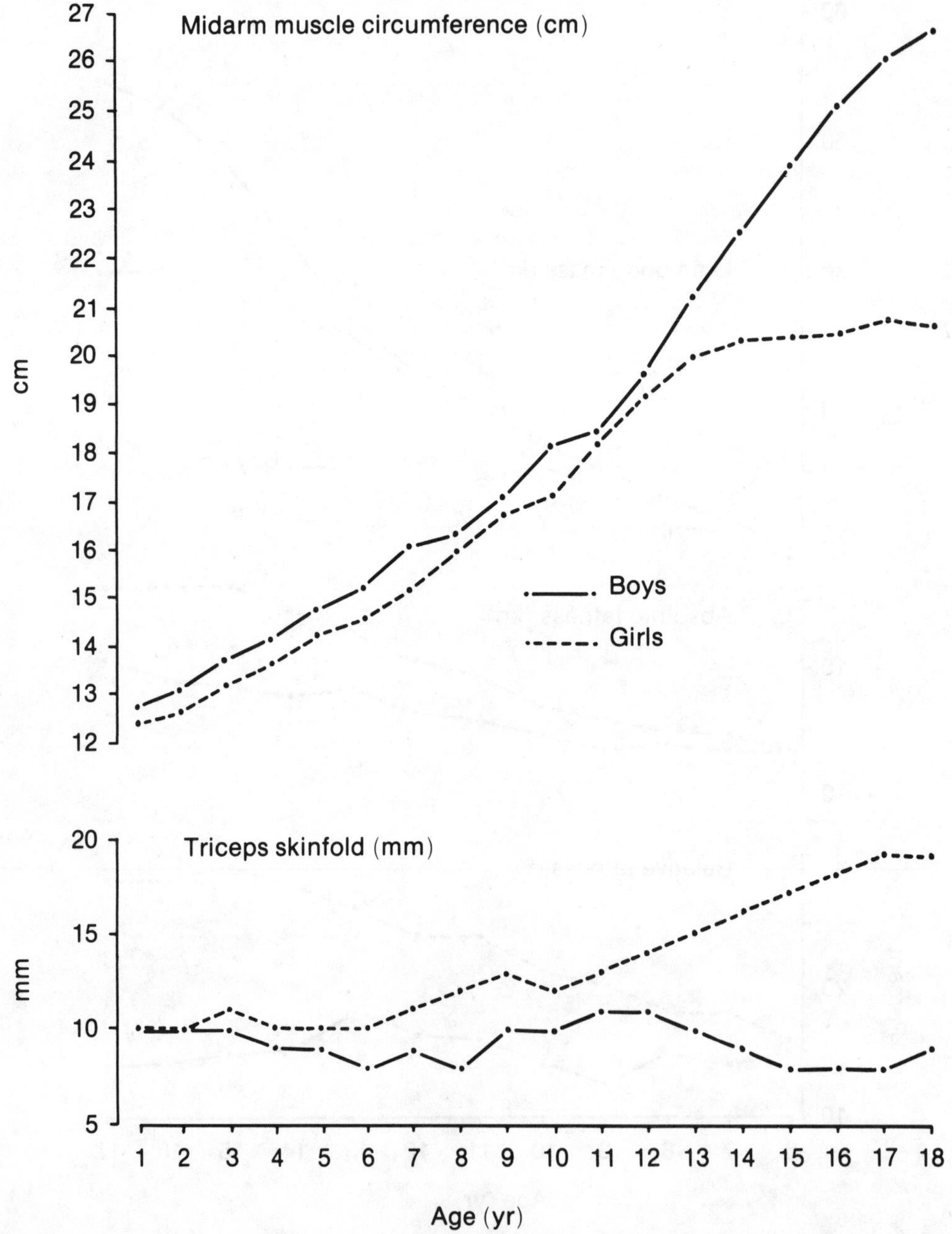

Figure 1.8. Median estimated midarm muscle circumference and triceps skinfold of American children from 1 through 18 years of age. (Based on data from Frisancho 1981.)

during adolescence. The growth curve for estimated midarm muscle circumference should be related to that for arm circumference in Figure 1.2. During middle childhood and into early adolescence, arm circumference is slightly larger in girls than in boys. This difference is related to the thicker triceps skinfold in girls.

Regional changes in subcutaneous fatness during growth are shown in Figure 1.9, which illustrates age- and sex-associated variation in the triceps (an extremity fat site) and subscapular (a trunk fat site) skinfolds. In girls both skinfolds are thicker and increase with age. By contrast, in boys the subscapular skinfold increases with age, while the triceps skinfold shows a decrease in thickness during adolescence. Thus, adolescent sex differences are more apparent for the extremities than for the trunk, which in turn suggests differential fat patterning of subcutaneous fat on the extremities and on the trunk.

MATURITY-ASSOCIATED VARIATION

In the preceding discussion, the child's chronological age is used as the point of reference. As noted earlier, children also have an inborn biological clock, which sets the pace of their growth rate and maturation. Hence, a youngster may not necessarily proceed in tempo with his biological clock. The net result is a considerable degree of maturity-associated variation in size, physique, and body composition during growth. Such maturity-associated variation is best observed when grouping children either by their skeletal age or by the state of development of secondary sex characteristics.

Children are generally grouped into maturity categories as early, average, and late maturers. Early maturing children are those in whom the maturity indicators are in advance of their chronological age. For example, a child with a chronological age of 9 and a skeletal age of 11 would be early maturing, as would a girl experiencing menarche at a chronological age of 11. In contrast, late-maturing children are those in whom the maturity indicators lag relative to chronological age. For example, a child having a chronological age of 9 years and a skeletal age of 7 years would be late maturing, as would a girl experiencing menarche at 15 years of age.

Maturity variations are especially apparent at the extremes. Average-maturing children comprise the broad middle range of normal variation, with normal variation in growth studies often defined as plus or minus one year of an individual's chronological age. This, however, is an arbitrary cutoff. In clinical studies of children with growth problems, for example, a broader range of normal variation is used, and commonly incorporates two or three years on either side of the child's chronological age.

Maturity-associated variation in size, physique, and composition, though apparent prior to adolescence, is most pronounced during this period of accelerated growth and sexual maturation. Early maturing children are generally taller and heavier for their age from early childhood through adolescence than their late-maturing peers. Late maturers, however, catch up to early maturers in stature in late adolescence or early adulthood, but they do not catch up in body weight. Early maturers thus have more weight for their stature than late maturers. This can be translated into differences in physique; early maturing boys are stockier and more mesomorphic and early maturing girls are stockier and more endomorphic. On the other hand, late maturers of both sexes tend to have less weight for height and tend to be extremely ectomorphic or linear in build. Such maturity-associated differences in physique can be extended to body composition. Early maturing children of both sexes compared with late-maturing children generally have larger amounts of fat

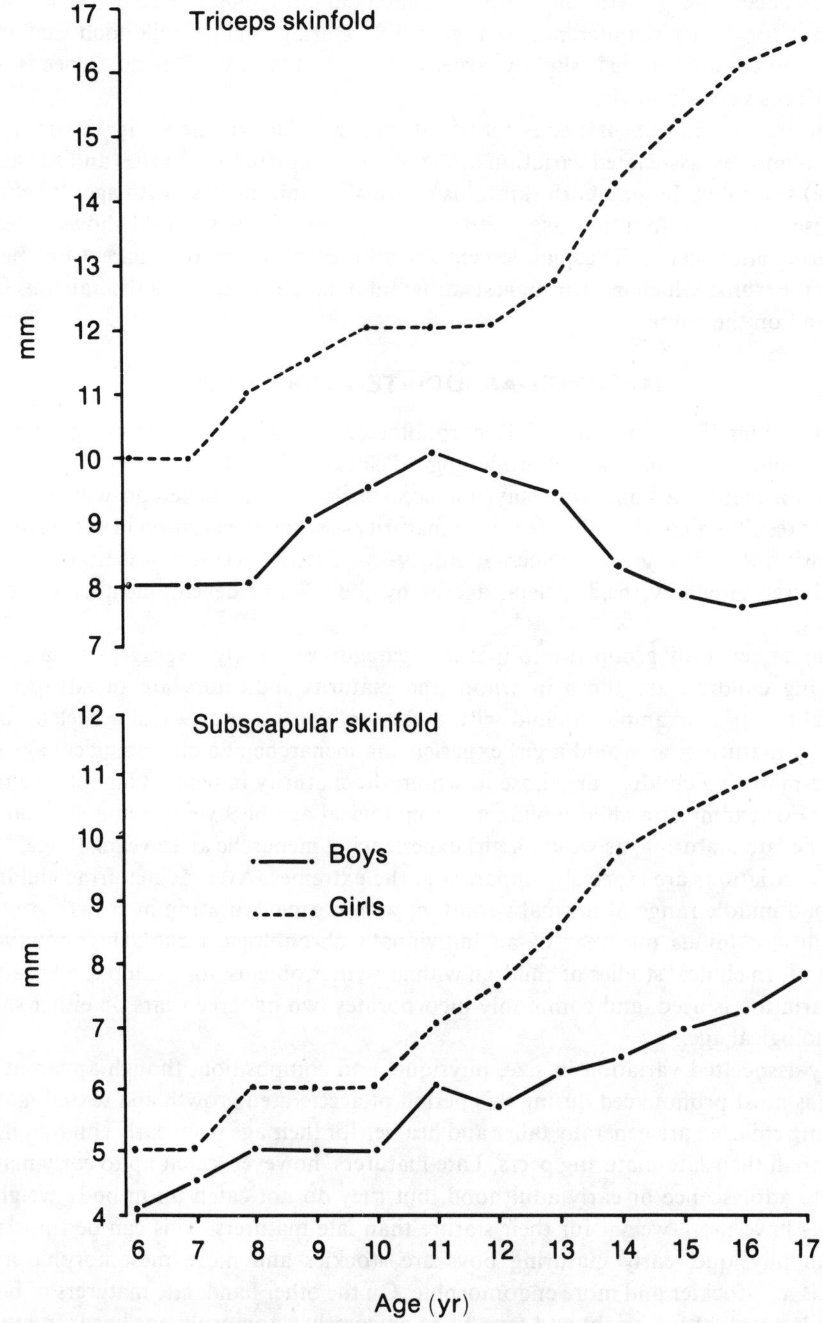

Figure 1.9. Median triceps and subscapular skinfolds for American children from 6 through 17 years of age. (Based on data from the National Center for Health Statistics 1972, 1974a.)

and lean tissue, reflecting to a great extent their overall larger body size. On a relative basis (i.e., when expressed as a percentage of body weight), early maturing children are fatter and not as lean as late maturers. Differences between late-maturing children and those in the average category of the maturity continuum are generally not as apparent as differences between early maturing and average-maturing children, and between early maturing and late-maturing children. This suggests that marked maturity-associated variations in physique and body composition are more often associated with early maturation.

FACTORS INFLUENCING GROWTH AND MATURATION

The integrated nature of growth and maturation is maintained by the interaction of genes, hormones, nutrients, and the environments in which the individual lives. This complex interaction regulates the organism's growth, sexual maturation, and in general, its physical metamorphosis. An individual's genotype (i.e., his genetic endowment) can be viewed as representing potential. Whether a child attains this growth potential, for example, depends on the environments in which she is reared. In a growth study or in the classroom, the child is observed in phenotypic form (i.e., his physical appearance, which is a product of genotype and environments). The partitioning of genotypic and environmental components in growth and maturation is important to understanding these processes.

Linear body measurements (e.g., stature, leg length) tend to have a higher genetic influence than breadths or circumferences. Circumferences, skinfolds, and body weight have a lower genetic influence than bone dimensions because the former are subject to short-term changes with the environment (e.g., training or nutritional stress). However, the pattern of fat distribution on the body is highly influenced by heredity, as are indices of biological maturity (i.e., menarche), skeletal age, and development of secondary sex characteristics. Hence, the genetic contribution to individual differences in growth and maturation is significant.

Endocrine secretions are basically regulatory and play an important function in growth and maturation processes. Some growth, however, occurs in the absence of growth-promoting hormones, emphasizing the organism's inherent tendency to grow. Endocrine secretions are themselves strongly influenced by genetic mechanisms. These hormones are essential for the full expression of the intrinsic, genetically determined growth and maturation patterns of tissues and systems, and thus the growth of the individual. The nervous system, in turn, is intimately involved in regulating endocrine secretions, and since the nervous system mediates interactions between individuals and their environment, the sources for potential variation among individuals are many.

Interacting with the child's genotype and endocrine secretions is his nutritional status. Nutrient requirements are many, and from the developmental perspective, can be viewed in terms of energy and proteins for growth, maintenance, and repair. Nutrient requirements vary considerably with age, sex, body size, and stages of growth. Energy needs that support growth processes are greatest during infancy and decline progressively with age. The energy needs for maintenance, on the other hand, increase during growth. In other words, as the individual gets bigger, more energy is necessary to support this size. However, with age, the rate of growth declines so that the amount of energy necessary to support growth is progressively reduced.

EXERCISE, GROWTH, AND MATURATION

The preceding has provided an overview of the major factors influencing growth and maturation of a child. In addition, other factors influencing growth exist, the direct effects of which are more difficult to identify or are of less overall importance. Of these, the role of physical activity is often viewed as a favorable influence on the growth and maturation of a child. Physical activity, however, is only one of many factors that may affect growth and maturation so that the precise role of properly graded activity programs in influencing these processes is not completely understood.

Physical activity has no apparent effect on stature in growing individuals and on maturation as commonly assessed (i.e., skeletal and sexual maturation). On the other hand, regular physical activity is a significant factor influencing the growth and integrity of specific tissues such as bone, muscle, and fat. Activity enhances skeletal mineralization and density and stimulates bone growth in width. Regular physical activity results in muscular hypertrophy, an increase in contractile proteins, and enhanced oxidative enzyme activity. Some evidence indicates a significant increase in the deoxyribonucleic acid (DNA) content of muscle tissue in growing animals above that expected with normal growth, suggesting that training during growth may be a significant factor in determining adult levels of DNA in muscle tissue.

Physical activity is an important factor in the regulation and maintenance of body weight. Regular activity generally results in an increase in lean body mass and a corresponding decrease in body weight, quite frequently without any appreciable change in body weight.

The preceding generalizations on changes associated with regular physical activity during growth are a function of the intensity and duration of training and continued activity. In growing individuals, separating the variations associated with maturity and growth from those attributed to an activity program is essential, especially during adolescence. Further, some changes associated with training are specific to the type of training program, as in endurance versus strength training.

Perhaps just as important as the effects of regular activity on the growing organism is the question of the persistence of changes associated with training. Changes in response to short-term training are generally not permanent, and vary with the quantity and type of training. This is especially clear in fluctuating levels of fatness commonly observed in young athletes. When they are in training for competition, fat levels generally decrease. However, as they begin to taper and go into the off season, fat levels slowly increase, only to decrease once again when training begins. Whether such changes occur in muscle and bone tissue is not known with certainty. Growth is an ongoing process, and separating growth effects from training effects in bone and muscle tissues is difficult.

The effects of regular training on maturation are less well known, but limited evidence suggests little if any effects. Three studies in Czechoslovakia, two on boys between 11 and 15 years of age and one on girls between 12 and 17 years of age, indicate virtually no effects of regular training on skeletal maturation of the hand and wrist, the most commonly used index of biological maturity status in growth studies (Cerny 1969, Kotulan et al. 1980, Novotny 1981). Frisch and colleagues (1981) have concluded on the basis of limited data that training before menarche functions to delay the onset of menarche. In addition to an extremely small sample (12 swimmers and 6 runners who began training before menarche), Frisch's conclusion is based on correlation, and correlation does not imply a cause-effect sequence. In other words, just because two variables are statistically related does not imply that one causes the other. The girls could well have taken up training because they were late maturers, and not because the training caused late maturation.

In this regard, note that a moderately high correlation exists between age at menarche and skeletal maturity, and a reduced variance exists in skeletal ages at the time of menarche. Further, both skeletal maturation and sexual maturation are under the influence of the same hormones, so that if training influences circulating hormonal levels, it should influence both maturational systems. Much of the data on hormonal changes with training, however, are derived from women who have already attained sexual maturity, so that inferences to youngsters who have not yet attained menarche or who are approaching menarche are questionable.

GROWTH, MATURITY, STRENGTH, AND MOTOR PERFORMANCE

Size, physique, body composition, and maturity are related to strength and motor performance during childhood and adolescence. The association of these factors with motor development during infancy and early childhood is not simple and is most apparent at the extremes of the size and physique continuum (i.e., very linear and very heavy infants). Analyses of physique and body composition relative to motor development during the preschool years are lacking. Subcutaneous fat, for example, decreases between three and six years of age (Figure 1.8 shows this trend for the triceps skinfold), the years when many basic motor skills are developing at a rapid rate. Unfortunately, little is known about the impact of the body's changing composition on the acquisition and refinement of motor skills in early childhood.

At the school ages, most studies of the association of growth and maturity status and strength and motor performance are correlational or involve comparisons between groups with extreme maturity variations. Correlations between stature and various strength measurements, and between weight and strength, for example, tend to be moderate, suggesting that the bigger child tends also to be stronger. In contrast, correlations between stature and weight and motor performance in a variety of motor tasks during childhood and adolescence are generally low. The relationships vary, however, as a function of the kind of performance tested. The direction of the correlations points to negative effects of excess body weight, presumably fatness, on running and jumping items, tasks in which the body is propelled or projected. On the other hand, tasks in which an object other than the body is projected (e.g., a ball) show positive correlations with body size. The overall contribution of age, height, and weight to variation in motor performance is generally low. For example, Espenschade (1963) estimated that the multiple relationship of age, stature, and weight accounts for only 25% of the variance in running, jumping, and throwing performance of boys 12 to 15 years of age and accounts for only 15% of the variance in jumping and 10% of the variance in throwing performance of boys 15 to 19 years of age. A similar pattern of age, stature, and weight relationships was not apparent in girls, suggesting the significance of factors other than age and body size in performance, especially during adolescence (see Chapter 3).

Somatotype components vary in their relationships with strength during childhood and adolescence. Data, however, are more available for boys than for girls, and correlations are generally low to moderate. Among preadolescents, both endomorphy and mesomorphy are related positively to muscular strength, while ectomorphy is related negatively to strength. The fact that endomorphy correlates with strength to the same extent as mesomorphy during childhood indicates the significant contribution of muscularity to endomorphic ratings and the importance of overall body size in strength tests.

During male adolescence, correlations between endomorphy and mesomorphy and strength are also positive. However, the relationship between mesomorphy and strength is slightly higher than between endomorphy and strength. As expected, correlations between ectomorphy and strength are consistently negative. Thus, ectomorphy is associated with strength deficiency, while mesomorphy is related to strength proficiency during male adolescence.

Studies of strength and physique in female adolescents are lacking. Some observations indicate consistently greater scores for adolescent girls having lateral physiques compared with those having linear builds, as derived from the ratio of hip width to stature. Strength differences between girls of lateral and linear physiques are generally most marked during early adolescence (11 to 13 years of age) but tend to persist into late adolescence (at least to 17 years of age).

Relationships between somatotype and motor performance during childhood and adolescence indicate consistently negative correlations (low to moderate in magnitude) between endomorphy and performance, especially in those activities in which the body is projected or in those requiring agility. Correlations between mesomorphy and performance are generally positive, but low. Those between ectomorphy and performance vary considerably, but are generally low. These general observations are derived primarily from studies of males. Data relating physique and motor performance of girls are lacking. Girls who excel in performance during adolescence have generally more slender physiques than those who perform poorly. The latter tend to be overweight and have broad physiques.

Relationships of body composition, strength, and performance during childhood and adolescence can be inferred from the preceding discussion of physique. Nevertheless, data relating body composition to strength and performance are limited, especially for females. As might be anticipated, strength is significantly related to lean body mass and muscle mass. The correlation between estimated lean body mass and grip strength is high for boys 9 to 18 years old. Correlations between measurements of muscle breadth in the arms and legs and strength of the respective muscle groups are lower, but generally moderate in both sexes during childhood, adolescence, and young adulthood. This suggests that there is more to the expression of muscular strength than the absolute size of the muscle mass.

Correlations between skinfold thicknesses (fatness) and performance in a variety of motor tasks are consistently negative, and are low to moderate in magnitude during both childhood and adolescence. The direction of the relationship emphasizes the negative effects of fatness on performance. Interestingly, the correlations between skinfold thicknesses and performance are reasonably similar in magnitude and direction as those between endomorphy and performance.

Data on the contribution of absolute[3] and relative lean body mass to motor performance are not extensive. However, among boys 10 to 12 years old, both absolute and relative lean body mass are similarly related to the performance of items in which the body is projected or moved. In contrast, in tasks involving the projection of an object rather than the body (e.g., throwing or kicking a ball), absolute lean body mass is more significant than relative lean body mass. Thus, activities in which the body or an object other than the body is projected are related differently to absolute and relative lean body mass in preadolescent boys. Further, the observations emphasize the importance of absolute body size and mass in the performance of growing youngsters in events requiring dynamic expressions of power. On the other hand, excessive amounts of body fat can function as a handicapping factor in that the fat represents dead weight that must be moved.

Size, physique, and body composition vary considerably with the maturity status of the developing individual. Such effects are evident during childhood, but are most apparent during adolescence.

3. Absolute lean body mass refers to its absolute size or weight, while relative lean body mass refers to lean body mass as a percentage of body weight.

Correlations between strength and skeletal maturity are moderate in primary grade boys, thus suggesting that the more mature boys are generally stronger. However, when the effects of body size are controlled, correlations between skeletal maturity and strength are considerably reduced. When boys are divided into the skeletally mature and immature, the former are stronger, taller, and heavier (Rarick and Oyster 1964). Thus, strength differences among young boys primarily reflect size differences.

During adolescence, maturity relationships with strength are more apparent for boys than girls. Early maturing boys are stronger than their average- and late-maturing peers from preadolescence through adolescence (Jones 1949, Carron and Bailey 1974, Clarke 1971). Strength differences between early and late maturers are especially apparent between 13 and 16 years of age, and the strength advantage for the early maturing boys reflects their larger body size and muscle mass. When the effects of body weight are removed in comparing early and late-maturing boys, strength differences between the maturity groups are eliminated (Carron and Bailey 1974).

Early maturing girls are stronger than their late-maturing peers during early adolescence. They do not, however, maintain this advantage as adolescence progresses (Jones 1949). Early and late-maturing girls attain comparable strength levels in later adolescence by apparently different routes. The early maturer shows rapid strength development through 13 years of age and then improves only slightly thereafter. The later maturer, however, improves in strength gradually between 11 and 16 years of age.

The correlation between skeletal maturity and motor performance in primary grade children is in the same direction, but of lesser magnitude, as that for muscular strength. In general, maturationally advanced children perform slightly better on a variety of motor tasks. This probably reflects their larger size and greater muscular strength.

Motor performance of adolescent boys is positively related to indices of skeletal and physiological maturity (Espenschade 1940, Clarke 1971). Between 12 and 17 years, boys who are maturationally advanced perform more proficiently in a variety of motor tasks than do less mature boys. This is related in part to the greater muscularity and strength of the more mature boy. In girls, motor performance during adolescence is not related to measures of skeletal and physiological maturity (Espenschade 1940). In fact, late maturation is commonly associated with outstanding motor performance of adolescent girls.

In summary, the correlations between size, physique, composition, and maturity status on the one hand, and strength and performance on the other, are generally low and at best moderate. Thus, the correlations are not meaningful for predictive purposes. Size, physique, composition, and maturity status seem to influence the strength and performance of children and adolescents moreso at the extremes of these parameters than within the broad, middle ranges considered to be average. Strength and motor performance involve more than the biological characteristics of the youngster, although these characteristics do enter into the matrix of factors influencing strength and performance.

REFERENCES

Burmeister, W. Body cell mass as the basis of allometric growth functions. *Annales Paediatrici*, 1965, **204**, 65-72.

Carron, A. V., & Bailey, D. A. Strength development in boys from 10 through 16 years. *Monographs of the Society for Research in Child Development*, 1974, Serial No. 157.

Carter, J. E. L. *The Heath-Carter somatotype method.* (Rev. ed.) San Diego: San Diego State University, 1980.

Cerny, L. The results of an evaluation of skeletal age of boys 11-15 years old with different regimes of physical activity. In *Physical fitness assessment*. Prague: Charles University Press, 1969.

Clarke, H. H. *Physical and motor tests in the Medford boy's growth study*. Englewood Cliffs, New Jersey: Prentice-Hall, 1971.

Espenschade, A. Motor performance in adolescence. *Monographs of the Society for Research in Child Development*, 1940, Serial No. 24.

Espenschade, A. Restudy of relationships between physical performances of school children and age, height, and weight. *Research Quarterly*, 1963, **34**, 144-153.

Frisancho, A. R. New norms of upper limb fat and muscle areas for assessment of nutritional status. *American Journal of Clinical Nutrition*, 1981, **34**, 2540-2545.

Frisch, R. E., Gotz-Welbergen, A. V., McArthur, J. W., Albright, T., Witschi, J., Bullen, B., Birnholz, J., Reed, R. B., & Hermann, H. Delayed menarche and amenorrhea of college athletes in relation to age of onset of training. *Journal of the American Medical Association*, 1981, **246**, 1559-1563.

Greulich, W. W., & Pyle, S. I. *Radiographic atlas of skeletal development of the hand and wrist.* (2nd ed.) Stanford: Stanford University Press, 1959.

Hansman, C. Anthropometry and related data. In R. W. McCammon (Ed.), *Human growth and development*. Springfield, Illinois: Charles C Thomas, 1970.

Jones, H. E. *Motor performance and growth*. Berkeley: University of California Press, 1949.

Kotulan, J., Řezničkova, M., & Placheta, Z. Exercise and growth. In Z. Placheta (Ed.), *Youth and physical activity*. Brno: Purkyne University Medical Faculty, 1980.

National Center for Health Statistics. Skinfold thickness of children 6-11 years, United States. *Vital and Health Statistics*, 1972, Series 11, No. 120.

National Center for Health Statistics. Age at menarche, United States. *Vital and Health Statistics*, 1973, Series 11, No. 133.

National Center for Health Statistics. Skinfold thickness of youths 12-17 years, United States. *Vital and Health Statistics*, 1974a, Series 11, No. 132.

National Center for Health Statistics. Body dimensions and proportions, White and Negro children 6-11 years, United States. *Vital and Health Statistics*, 1974b, Series 11, No. 143.

National Center for Health Statistics. NCHS growth curves for children birth-18 years, United States. *Vital and Health Statistics*, 1977, Series 11, No. 165.

Novotny, V. Veränderungen des Knochenalters im Verlauf einer mehrjährigen sportlichen Belastung. *Medizin und Sport*, 1981, **21**, 44-47.

Rarick, G. L., & Oyster, N. Physical maturity, muscular strength, and motor performance of young school-age boys. *Research Quarterly*, 1974, **35**, 523-531.

Roche, A. F., & Malina, R. M. (Eds.) *Manual of physical status and performance in childhood.* Vol. 1. New York: Plenum, 1983.

Scammon, R. E. The measurement of the body in childhood. In J. A. Harris, C. M. Jackson, D. G. Paterson, & R. E. Scammon (Eds.), *The measurement of man.* Minneapolis: University of Minnesota Press, 1930.

Sheldon, W. H., Dupertuis, C. W., & McDermott, E. *Atlas of men: A guide for somatotyping the adult male of all ages*. New York: Harper, 1954.

Tanner, J. M. *Growth at adolescence*. (2nd ed.) Oxford: Blackwell Scientific Publications, 1962.

Tanner, J. M., Hughes, P. C. R., & Whitehouse, R. H. Radiographically determined widths of bone, muscle and fat in the upper arm and calf from age 3-18 years. *Annals of Human Biology*, 1981, **8**, 495-517.

Tanner, J. M., Whitehouse, R. H., Marshall, W. A., Healy, M. J. P., & Goldstein, H. *Assessment of skeletal maturity and prediction of adult height*. New York: Academic Press, 1975.

Tanner, J. M., Whitehouse, R. H., Marubini, E., & Resele, L. F. The adolescent growth spurt of boys and girls of the Harpenden growth study. *Annals of Human Biology*, 1976, **3**, 109-126.

Thissen, D., Bock, D. R., Wainer, H., & Roche, A. F. Individual growth in stature: A comparison of four growth studies in the U.S.A. *Annals of Human Biology*, 1976, **3**, 529-542.

Walker, R. M. Body build and behavior in young children. I. Body build and nursery school teachers' ratings. *Monographs of the Society for Research in Child Development*, 1962, Serial No. 34.

SUGGESTED READINGS

Undergraduate Students

Clarke, H. H. *Physical and motor tests in the Medford boy's growth study*. Englewood Cliffs, New Jersey: Prentice-Hall, 1971.

Krogman, W. M. *Child growth*. Ann Arbor: University of Michigan Press, 1972.

Meredith, H. W. *Human body growth in the first ten years of life*. Columbia, South Carolina: State Printing Company, 1978.

Sinclair, D. *Human growth after birth*. (3rd ed.) London: Oxford University Press, 1978.

Tanner, J. M. *Fetus into man: Physical growth from conception to maturity*. Cambridge, Massachusetts: Harvard University Press, 1978.

Graduate Students

Acheson, R. M. Maturation of the skeleton. In F. Falkner (Ed.), *Human development*. Philadelphia: Saunders, 1966.

Bouchard, C., Thibault, M. C., & Jobin, J. Advances in selected areas of human work physiology. *Yearbook of Physical Anthropology*, 1981, **24**, 1-36.

Bouchard, C., & Malina, R. M. Genetics of physiological fitness and motor performance. *Exercise and Sport Sciences Reviews*, 1983, in press.

Brooks, G. A. (Ed.) *Perspectives on the academic discipline of physical education*. Champaign, Illinois: Human Kinetics, 1981. The following papers are of relevance to this chapter:
Rarick, G. L. The emergence of the study of human motor development.
Malina, R. M. Growth, maturation, and human performance.

Eveleth, P. B., & Tanner, J. M. *Worldwide variation in human growth*. Cambridge: Cambridge University Press, 1976.

Falkner, F., & Tanner, J. M. (Eds.) *Human growth*. Vol. 2. Postnatal growth. New York: Plenum, 1978. The following papers are of relevance to this chapter:
Cameron, N. The methods of auxological anthropometry.
Johnston, F. E. The somatic growth of the infant and preschool child.
Marshall, W. A. Puberty.
Forbes, G. B. Body composition in adolescence.
Malina, R. M. Growth of muscle tissue and muscle mass.
Roche, A. F. Bone growth and maturation.

Johnston, F. E., Roche, A. F., & Susanne, C. (Eds.) *Human physical growth and maturation: Methodologies and factors*. New York: Plenum, 1980. The following papers are of relevance to this chapter:
Malina, R. M. The measurement of body composition.
Roche, A. F. The measurement of skeletal maturation.
Susanne, C. Developmental genetics of Man.
Johnston, F. E. Nutrition and growth.
Malina, R. M. Physical activity, growth, and functional capacity.

Malina, R. M. Anthropometric correlates of strength and motor performance. *Exercise and Sport Sciences Reviews*, 1975, **3**, 249-274.

Malina, R. M. Adolescent growth and maturation: Selected aspects of current research. *Yearbook of Physical Anthropology*, 1978, **21**, 63-94.

Malina, R. M. The effects of exercise on specific tissues, dimensions and functions during growth. *Studies in Physical Anthropology*, 1979, **5**, 21-52.

Malina, R. M. Biosocial correlates of motor development during infancy and early childhood. In L. S. Greene & F. E. Johnston (Eds.), *Social and biological predictors of nutritional status, physical growth, and neurological development*. New York: Academic Press, 1980.

Malina, R. M. Menarche in athletes: A synthesis and hypothesis. *Annals of Human Biology*, 1983, **10**, 1-24.

Malina, R. M. Physical growth and maturity characteristics of young athletes. In R. A. Magill, M. J. Ash, & F. L. Smoll (Eds.), *Children in sport* (2nd ed.). Champaign, Illinois: Human Kinetics, 1982.

Rarick, G. L. (Ed.) *Physical activity: Human growth and development*. New York: Academic Press, 1973. The following papers are of relevance to this chapter.

Asmussen, E. Growth in muscular strength and power.

Parizkova, J. Body composition and exercise during growth and development.

Malina, R. M. and Rarick, G. L. Growth, physique, and motor performance.

Eckert, H. M. Age changes in motor skills.

Rarick, G. L. Stability and change in motor ability.

Malina, R. M. Ethnic and cultural factors in the development of motor abilities and strength in American children.

Tanner, J. M. *Growth at adolescence*. (2nd ed.) Oxford: Blackwell Scientific Publications, 1962.

Laboratory 1 from Chapter 14 should be used at the completion of this chapter.

2
Children and Exercise

Scott K. Powers

The child's physiological response to exercise is not merely of interest to the physiologist but also has wider implications. For example, the physical educator, parent, or physician can benefit from information on the effects of exercise training on a child's performance in a variety of skills. Despite the significance of physical activity in the physiological makeup of the preadolescent child, little attention has been given to this subject in textbooks on the physiology of exercise or in writings on growth and development. To date, published research on exercise and pediatric physiology is rather limited when compared with work completed using adults as subjects.

The purpose of this chapter is to provide a brief overview of the physiological responses of children to both acute and chronic exercise. Further, the chapter looks at both genetic and environmental factors that affect performance in children at all ages.

DEFINITIONS

This chapter is written with the assumption that upper level undergraduate students and graduate students will have had at least one survey course in exercise physiology. However, no background in physiology is required to read and comprehend most sections. The following definitions are offered as a form of review or to aid those students with little knowledge in the physiology of exercise.

Maximal aerobic power—Sometimes referred to as maximal oxygen uptake ($\dot{V}O_2$ max); defined as the maximum amount of oxygen that an individual can use per unit of time, usually expressed as liters or milliliters of oxygen per minute.

Cardiac output—The amount of blood pumped by the heart per minute, expressed as liters or milliliters per minute.

Stroke volume—The amount of blood expelled by the left ventricle during contraction of the heart, expressed as milliliters per heartbeat.

Adenosine triphosphate (ATP)—The chemical molecule in the body most available for energy release; synthesized and stored in small quantities in the cell.

Aerobic metabolism—The synthesis of ATP using oxygen in the mitochondria of the cell.

Anaerobic metabolism—Bioenergetic production of ATP either by rephosphorylation of adenosine diphosphate (ADP) via creatine phosphate or by anaerobic glycolysis in the cytoplasm of the cell.

Motor unit—An alpha motor neuron and all the muscle fibers that it innervates.

ACUTE EFFECTS OF EXERCISE

Before discussing the dynamic circulatory and respiratory responses to exercise, a few circulatory changes that take place in children as a function of increasing age are worthy of mention. The resting heart rate in both males and females declines from age 6 to approximately ages 12 to 14. Figure 2.1 shows that the resting heart rate tends to be 5 to 10 beats/min^{-1} higher at all ages in girls than in boys. Also, maximal heart rate declines with age in both sexes. Finally, a slight increase in both systolic and diastolic blood pressure from age six continues throughout life. Note in Figure 2.1 that both systolic and diastolic blood pressure tends to be 5 to 10 mm Hg lower in girls than in boys (Shaver 1981).

Cardiorespiratory Response to Graded Exercise

Figure 2.2 describes the changes in heart rate, stroke volume, and cardiac output that take place in an incremental dynamic exercise test (e.g., walking on a treadmill). Note that heart rate increases as a linear function of the intensity of the exercise. Stroke volume increases up to approximately 40% of $\dot{V}O_2$ max and then reaches a plateau or may even decline at maximal heart rates due to a decrease in end-diastolic ventricular volume. Cardiac output increases in a linear fashion up to 40% of $\dot{V}O_2$ max, after which the slope decreases because stroke volume is no longer increasing. Thus, at exercise intensities above 40% of $\dot{V}O_2$ max, cardiac output can be increased only by an increase in heart rate.

The absolute values for heart rate, stroke volume, and cardiac output during exercise in children vary as a function of size, sex, age, and the state of training. In general, maximum stroke volume and maximum cardiac output increase gradually across age in both sexes during maturation of the cardiovascular system. This increase in cardiac output in growing children must account for at least part of the increase in absolute maximum oxygen uptake seen in both sexes (more will be said about this later in the chapter).

Note that in Figure 2.3 the mean arterial pressure (MAP) increases as a linear function of the exercise intensity. This increase in MAP results from the increase in systolic blood pressure (SBP), with little change in diastolic blood pressure (DBP) occurring during isotonic work. Some children exhibit rapid increases in both SBP and DBP during even mild dynamic exercise. This is referred to as "labile hypertension," and it exists only in a small number of children and adults. The cause or causes of labile hypertension are obscure and remain under intense study.

Pulmonary ventilation increases in linear fashion (Figure 2.4) with a rise in the intensity of the exercise to approximately 50% to 65% of $\dot{V}O_2$ max, after which ventilation increases in an exponential fashion. This break in ventilation during graded exercise has been termed the *anaerobic threshold* and may represent a transition from aerobic to anaerobic metabolism (Wasserman

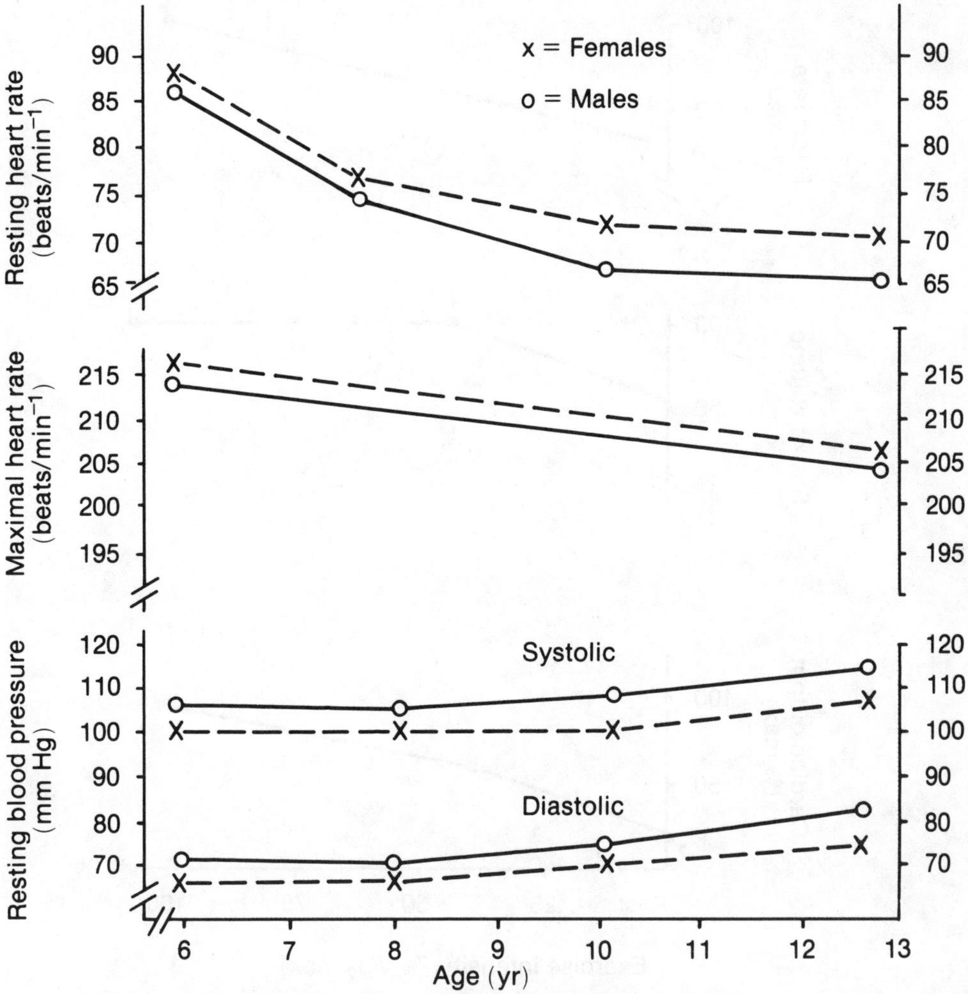

Figure 2.1. Changes in resting heart rate, maximal heart rate, and resting blood pressure as a function of age in children. (Based on data from Astrand 1952, and Astrand and Rodahl 1977.)

et al. 1973). This increase in anaerobic metabolism in the muscle results in an increase in both muscle and blood concentration of lactic acid. In near maximal work (e.g., working above 75% to 80% $\dot{V}O_2$ max), lactic acid (which may lower intracellular *p*H) is a prime suspect as a cause of muscle fatigue. The anaerobic threshold is known to occur at a lower work load (relative to $\dot{V}O_2$ max) in untrained subjects when compared with trained subjects. This finding has generated some interest and may have applications to endurance training (see Sady et al. 1980).

In general, the responses of females to exercise and training are basically no different than the responses observed in males. After all, the cellular mechanisms controlling most physiological responses to exercise are the same for both sexes. However, some clear differences in work capacity exist between boys and girls and will be discussed later in the chapter.

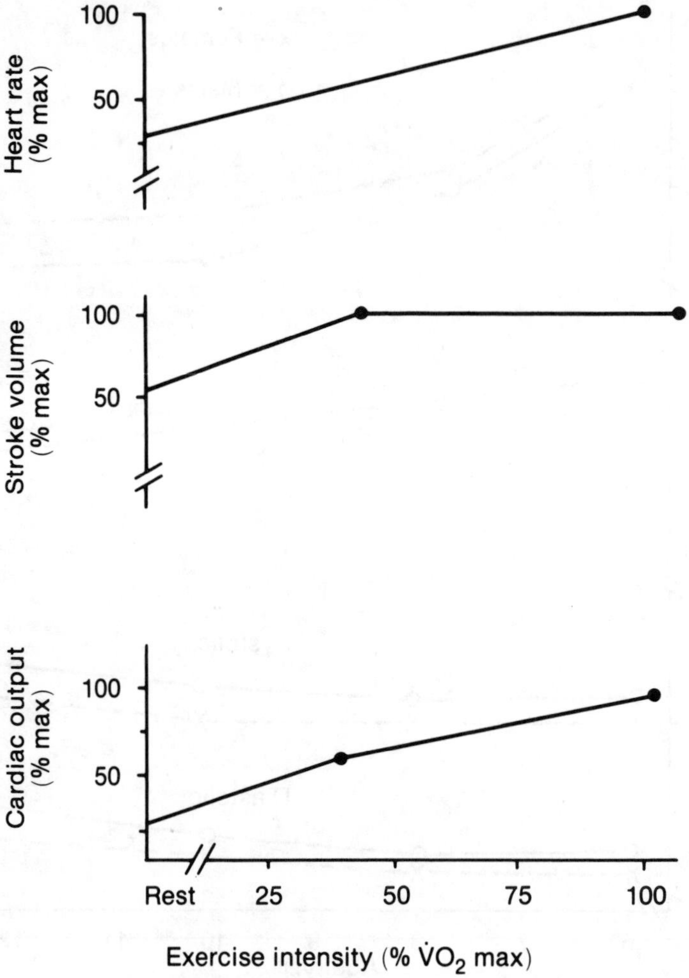

Figure 2.2 Circulatory response to graded exercise. (Based on data from Astrand and Rodahl 1977.)

In summary, sex differences in the cardiorespiratory response or responses to acute exercise are minimal. However, the magnitude of the cardiorespiratory response (e.g., stroke volume, cardiac output) is affected by age, sex, state of physical training, and the size of the child. Heart rate increases as a linear function of exercise intensity. Stroke volume increases until approximately 40% of $\dot{V}O_2$ max, while cardiac output increases until $\dot{V}O_2$ max is reached. Systolic and mean arterial blood pressures rise during graded dynamic work, while diastolic blood pressure remains relatively constant. Finally, pulmonary ventilation increases in linear fashion until approximately 50% to 65% of $\dot{V}O_2$ max. This abrupt and nonlinear increase in ventilation is termed the anaerobic threshold.

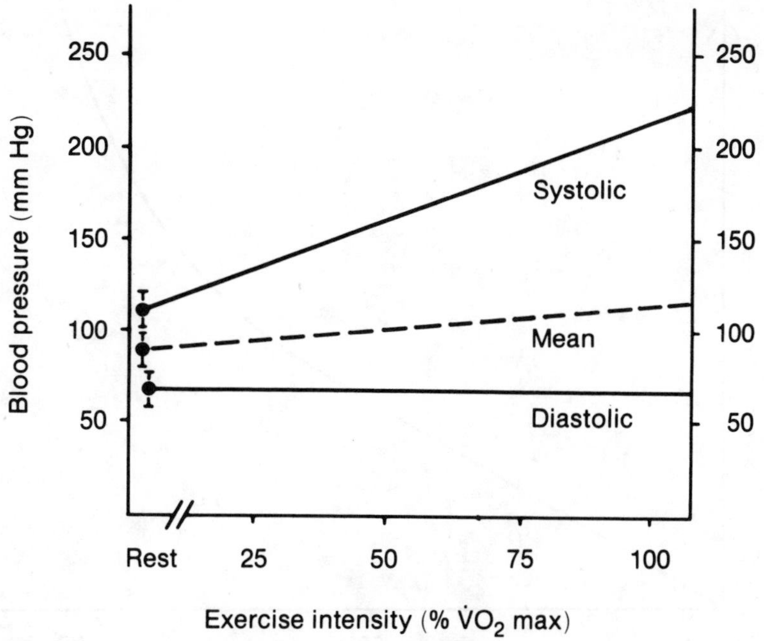

Figure 2.3. Changes in blood pressure as a result of an incremental exercise test. (Based on data from Fox and Mathews 1981.)

EFFECTS OF CHRONIC EXERCISE

Over the past decade, much has been written in both popular and scientific journals about the pros and cons of exercise, and especially about the effects of competitive sports on children's development. Extensive physiological studies have centered on the systemic and cellular adaptations that result from regular aerobic exercise, but unfortunately much of this work has involved only adult populations. Many questions on children remain concerning the long-term effects of chronic exercise on physical development and changes in working capacity. At present, sufficient data does not exist to make conclusive assessments of the long-term effects of competitive sports on the growth and development of the adolescent athlete. However, recent work has provided a data base to begin making reasonable decisions concerning the hazards and benefits of regular exercise on the physiological makeup of young children.

Growth and Body Composition

Longitudinal research provides no solid evidence that prolonged exercise training or sports participation adversely affect children's normal physical growth. In fact, documentation is available to demonstrate that young athletes of both elementary and middle school age are superior to nonathletes of similar age in the following measures (Parizkova 1977; Gutin, Trinidad, Norton, Giles, Giles, and Steward 1978; Clarke and Vaccaro 1979; Shaver 1981): (1) skeletal maturity (skeletal age as related to chronological age), (2) height and weight, (3) muscular strength and

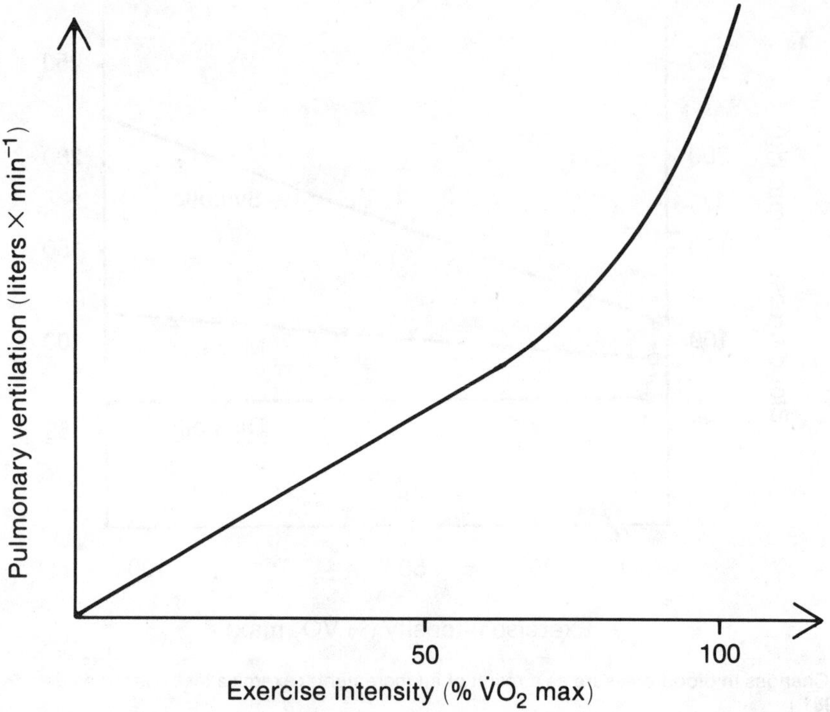

Figure 2.4. Changes in pulmonary ventilation as a function of exercise intensity.

power, and (4) percentage of body fat (lower than nonathletes). Thus, little reason exists to believe that the physical stress of regular exercise modifies the regular growth patterns of children in a negative manner. In fact, the large majority of evidence suggests that physical activity promotes growth and reduces body fat.

What the optimum level of exercise is that the young athlete can endure without undue stress or injury is a question that remains. Before addressing this, researchers must base their evaluations on long-term observations and consider factors such as the type of sport involved, the intensity and duration of the training program, the nature and frequency of the athletic event, the number of years of participation, and the age at which the child entered the sport. The need for research in this area is great.

Due to the increasing problem of pediatric obesity in the United States, further discussion of the effects of exercise on adipose cellularity is warranted. Obesity is usually defined as an excessive quantity of body fat in an individual. The standards for determining obesity in younger adults are as follows (McArdle, Katch, and Katch 1981):

Boys ≥ 20% body fat
Girls ≥ 30% body fat

Regular exercise during childhood is effective in significantly reducing the rate of fat cell accumulation and may result in a significant reduction of body fat in later life. Thus, exercise during this period of life not only influences body composition immediately but also may have a long-term influence (Parizkova 1977). Dietary reduction in the total number of calories consumed (resulting in a caloric deficit) may also reduce body fat over time. However, a severe reduction in diet has been shown to reduce normal growth in both young animals and humans (Parizkova 1977). Therefore, dietary reduction is not a recommended method for fat loss in growing children. Many researchers favor a combination of controlled diet and exercise to facilitate a healthier, more permanent weight loss than would result from a total reliance on caloric restriction.

Maximal Aerobic Power

Studies designed to measure the effects of training on cardiorespiratory function in both children and adults often have a number of problems in research design. Failure to provide control groups and to regulate the total work performed during training studies often makes the results of many reports difficult to interpret. While intensive training programs will increase adult circulatory and respiratory capacities (Ribisl 1963; Holmgren and Astrand 1966; Magel and Anderson 1969; Fox, Bartels, Billings, et al. 1975), studies on intensive training in children are few and at best equivocal with regard to these effects. For example, numerous authors (Ekblom 1969; Vaccaro and Clark 1978; Gatch and Byrd 1979) report that physical training in children improves the functional components of maximal aerobic power, while others (Spryranova 1966, Daniels and Oldridge 1971, Bar-Or and Zwiren 1973) report that training in preadolescents fails to produce any further increase in aerobic power beyond the increase mediated by growth. Sheperd (1971) has suggested that the lack of training adaptation reported in prepubescent children may be due to the high levels of physical activity in which preadolescents are normally engaged. In other words, due to habitual physical activity, many preadolescent children may already be trained, and exposure to additional training therefore does not improve maximal aerobic power.

In dated literature, some question exists about the effect that endurance training has on maximal aerobic power in children, while newer evidence indicates that high-intensity aerobic training increases $\dot{V}O_2$ max in children. Recently, several well-controlled studies have shown that when untrained preadolescents are exposed to high-intensity endurance training ($\geq$ 8 weeks' duration), a significant increase in both working capacity and $\dot{V}O_2$ max results beyond the increase occasioned by growth (Vaccaro and Clarke 1978, Gatch and Byrd 1979).

In adults, the increase in maximal aerobic power seen after endurance training results from an increase in both cardiac output ($\dot{Q}$) and the arteriovenous oxygen difference (A-V O_2 diff).[1] However, in preadolescent children, the increase in $\dot{V}O_2$ max after training appears to come only from an increase in $\dot{Q}$ due to an increase in stroke volume (i.e., $\dot{Q} = HR \times SV$) (Eriksson and Koch 1973). Little change in A-V O_2 diff in children after training might be explained by the low hemoglobin concentration (13 gm/100 ml of blood), which, incidentally, is normal for this age group. Thus, due to the lower oxygen-carrying capacity of the blood in preadolescent children, their A-V O_2 diff might be near the maximal level attainable even before training. After puberty, the hemoglobin concentration in the blood will increase to 14–15 gm/100 ml of blood (Figure 2.5). This increase in the oxygen-carrying capacity of the blood allows A-V O_2 diff changes with training normally seen in adults after several weeks of endurance exercise.

1. An increase in either $\dot{Q}$ or the A-V O_2 diff could increase $\dot{V}O_2$ max, since $\dot{V}O_2 = \dot{Q} \times$ A-V O_2 diff.

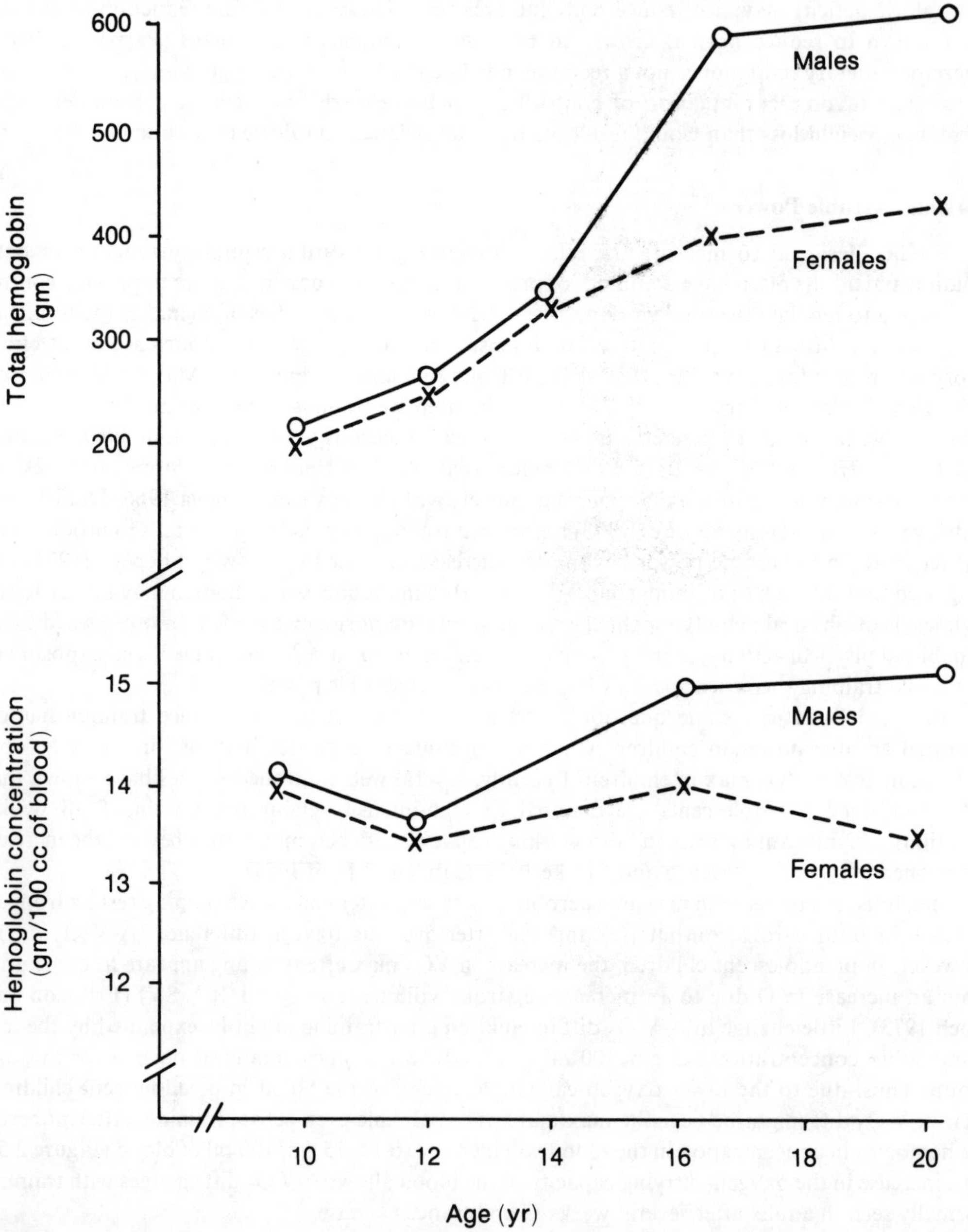

Figure 2.5. Total hemoglobin and hemoglobin concentrations in blood as a function of age and sex. (Based on data from Astrand 1952.)

In conclusion, recent literature suggests that children respond to high-intensity aerobic training in a manner that is similar to adults (a 10% to 20% increase in $\dot{V}O_2$ max). However, the circulatory responses of preadolescent children to physical training differ from those of adults, since the A-V O_2 diff does not increase during maximal exercise.

Anaerobic Power

Some physical activities rely chiefly on the cardiovascular system to deliver oxygen to the working muscles (aerobic metabolism, as in running a marathon), while other activities depend on strength and short-term speed (anaerobic metabolism, as in running 100 to 400 m). Anaerobic work (as does aerobic work) not only uses the high-energy phosphagen—adenosine triphosphate (ATP)—to produce muscular contraction but also requires the muscle to produce ATP at much higher rates than is normally seen in aerobic metabolism alone. The sources of ATP during anaerobic work are (1) storage in the muscle, (2) rephosphorylation of adenosine diphosphate (ADP) by phosphocreatine (CP), and (3) anaerobic glycolysis. In short-term activities (1 to 20 sec), stored ATP and CP can probably supply the energy needed for work, while in longer events (21 to 120 sec), anaerobic glycolysis is primarily responsible for ATP production.

Preadolescent children demonstrate lower anaerobic work tolerance and lower blood lactate levels than do adults following maximal work. This is not surprising, since children exhibit low muscular levels (40% of the value for adults) of the enzyme phosphofructokinase (PFK), which limits the rate of glycolysis. Why children have this limitation is unknown. A much-cited study by Eriksson (1972) has shown that anaerobic training can increase muscular levels of CP and PFK in 11- to 13-year-old boys. This increase in CP and PFK resulted in an improved anaerobic work tolerance and higher blood lactate levels when compared with pretraining values.

In summary, little is known about the factors involved in the increase of PFK concentrations that takes place during postpubertal growth. However, the increase may not be due to biological maturation alone; physical training also may play a role. As in many areas of pediatric work physiology, more research is needed to clarify the mechanism or mechanisms involved in the increase in PFK in skeletal muscle in children.

WORK CAPACITY IN CHILDREN

Muscular Strength

Physiological Considerations

Muscular strength is dependent on numerous factors and can be considered the integrated expression of the neuromuscular system. The actual force that a given muscle is able to exert depends on the number of motor units activated and the frequency of contraction. Thus, the highest possible tension in human muscle fibers can be obtained when all motor units in a particular muscle are recruited and when their fusion frequency is optimal (probably 50 to 125 stimuli/sec) (Asmussen 1973). The question is whether an individual can recruit all the muscle fibers in a given muscle and fire all the motor units at the optimal frequency. Based on present information, the answer is no. Therefore, since under normal conditions it is not possible to produce the highest tension that the muscle is theoretically capable of producing, there must be a reserve of force in the muscle that might be called on under unusual conditions (Asmussen 1973).

For example, numerous cases are reported of individuals exhibiting superhuman strength in emergency situations, but the factor or factors that normally limit muscular force are not known. In the nervous system, numerous locations exist where inhibition may result from negative feedback from peripheral receptors. Inhibition may also be persistent from the cerebral cortex or reticular formation. A decline in nervous system inhibition, which may result from either maturation or perhaps training, can influence strength or power independently of muscular growth (Asmussen 1973).

Muscle Fiber Types

Another factor that influences the amount of force that a muscle can exert is the predominant contractile properties of the muscle fiber itself. Human skeletal muscle is composed of two primary populations of fiber types[2] with distinct physiological, biochemical, and morphological differences. Type 1 fibers (slow-twitch fibers) depend predominantly on oxidative metabolism, contract slowly, and produce low tension when stimulated, while Type II fibers (fast-twitch fibers) rely predominantly on anaerobic metabolism, contract rapidly, and can produce high muscular tension on shortening (Edington and Edgerton 1976). Both fiber types probably coexist in all of the human muscles, but the proportion of the two fiber types within a given muscle varies among individuals. The proportion of slow fibers varies from 10% to 95%. Top athletes in endurance events have a high percentage of slow-twitch fibers (Astrand and Rodahl 1977). The actual fiber composition of a muscle is genetically determined. For example, identical twins have a similar ratio of the two fiber types in specific muscles, whereas nonidentical twins may exhibit great differences in muscle fiber composition. The differentiation into fast- and slow-twitch fibers takes place before or soon after birth (Edington and Edgerton 1976). Muscle groups that contain a high percentage of fast-twitch fibers are more likely to produce greater tension on contraction than if the same muscle groups were to contain a large ratio of slow-twitch fibers.

To summarize the physiological determinants of muscular force, strength is not simply a question of muscles, but rather is a complex interaction of neuromuscular function. The amount of tension produced depends on the number and types of muscle fibers and their frequency of contraction.

Effects of Age, Sex, and Size on Muscular Force

In assessing the effects of age, sex, and size on muscular strength, a preliminary assumption is that maximum isometric muscle force is proportional to the cross-sectional area of the muscle. Asmussen (1973) and Astrand and Rodahl (1977) have suggested that children after the age of seven have somatotypes that are geometrically similar. Thus, the changes taking place in muscle growth might be predicted if one body dimension is known. For example, if we compare the linear dimensions (L) (i.e., height) of two boys, one 100 cm tall and the other 150 cm tall, the L of the bodies of the two boys may then be expressed as the ratio 1:1.5. The surface area or cross section of the two boys' muscles can then be estimated as L^2. When this line of reasoning is applied, the ratio of the cross-sectional area of a muscle is 1:2.25 between the two boys. Theoretically, the larger boy should be able to exert 2.25 times greater isometric force than the smaller boy. However, in

2. Many investigators conclude that man has at least three different types of muscle fibers. For reasons of simplicity in this discussion, we will consider only two.

performing work such as pull-ups, a large body mass is definitely a disadvantage. This type of athletic achievement is proportional to the force of the muscles and their levers but inversely proportional to body weight and the length of the levers (arm length) performing the work (Astrand and Rodahl 1977). A larger and stronger body may be handicapped by greater body mass in the performance of pull-ups. This may help to explain the common observation that the class pull-up champion is often a small individual with a relatively low body mass.

As discussed previously, muscle strength depends on many factors. In tests of muscular strength, the day to day variation is approximately 10% to 20% (Astrand and Rodahl 1977). Also, the correlation between the strength of different muscle groups in the same child can be low, moderate, or high, depending on the muscle groups used for comparison. The point has already been made that in isolated muscles, the maximal isometric strength is directly related to the cross-sectional area of the muscle. However, in vivo, many factors make the standard deviations relatively large (15% to 20%), and even with a correction for age, sex, and size, large individual differences in muscle strength are observed (Asmussen 1973, Astrand and Rodahl 1977). One of the reasons for strength differences within an age group, especially before the age of 18, is that children mature at different rates (Lamb 1978). For example, two 12-year-old boys may differ as much as 5 years when biological ages are determined by X-ray measurements of bones (Lamb 1978). The 12-year-old who is more mature probably has larger muscles, a more highly developed nervous system, and a higher plasma level of testosterone. All of these factors tend to make the more mature child stronger than his less developed counterpart.

In general, little difference exists in male and female leg strength until puberty (Lamb 1978). Figure 2.6 shows that the greatest change in strength in males occurs after the ages of 13 to 14 years, which is due to increases in the male sex hormone testosterone. Testosterone exerts a strong anabolic effect on muscle tissue, and thus causes an increase in muscular hypertrophy. Strength continues to increase in both sexes into the 20s, and may continue even after physical growth has stopped. This further increase in strength across time is possibly due to a maturation of the nervous system. Thus, strength may increase independent of muscular growth. This argument may be further advanced by the observation that between 6 and 20 years of age, only one-third of maximum height is attained; however, four-fifths of the development of strength takes place (Asmussen 1973).

In Figure 2.7, note that the peak isometric torque of the knee extensors increases linearly with age for boys from 13 to 17 years but remains relatively constant for girls over 14 years. Note that boys are consistently stronger than girls at each age group. When comparing strength in adult men and women, the strength of any muscle group in women is lower than that for men by about one-third. However, when strength in women is corrected for body size, the difference in strength between the sexes is greatly reduced, especially for leg strength. Strength relative to muscle size (expressed as a cross-sectional area of the muscle) is the same for males and females (Ikai and Fukanaga 1968). Therefore, the quality of muscle fiber (i.e., the ability to exert force) is independent of sex. Thus, the absolute biological variance in strength between the sexes results largely from differences in body size.

Jumping

Performance in the broad jump or long jump depends, in part, on the maximal muscular force that can be developed and the distance that muscle can shorten before the body leaves the ground

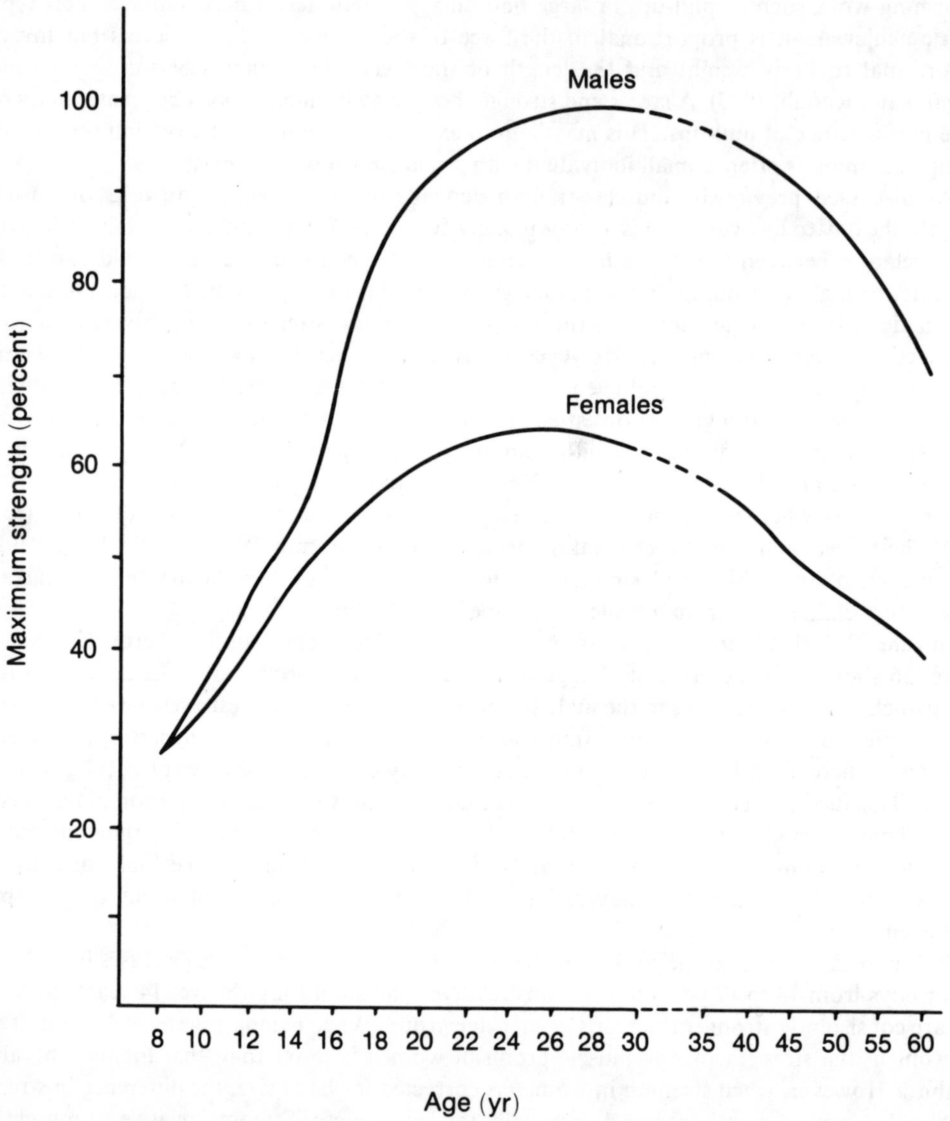

Figure 2.6. Average strength of large muscle groups as a function of age and sex. (Based on data from Hettinger 1961.)

(Astrand and Rodahl 1977). Therefore, all other things being equal, the child with the greatest cross-sectional area of muscle (i.e., leg extensors) should produce the best jump. However, in the high jump, the aim is to lift the body as high as possible. Since taller children have a higher center of gravity, they consequently have an advantage over shorter individuals. This hypothesis can be supported empirically, since the outstanding high jumper is usually a tall individual. Further, this

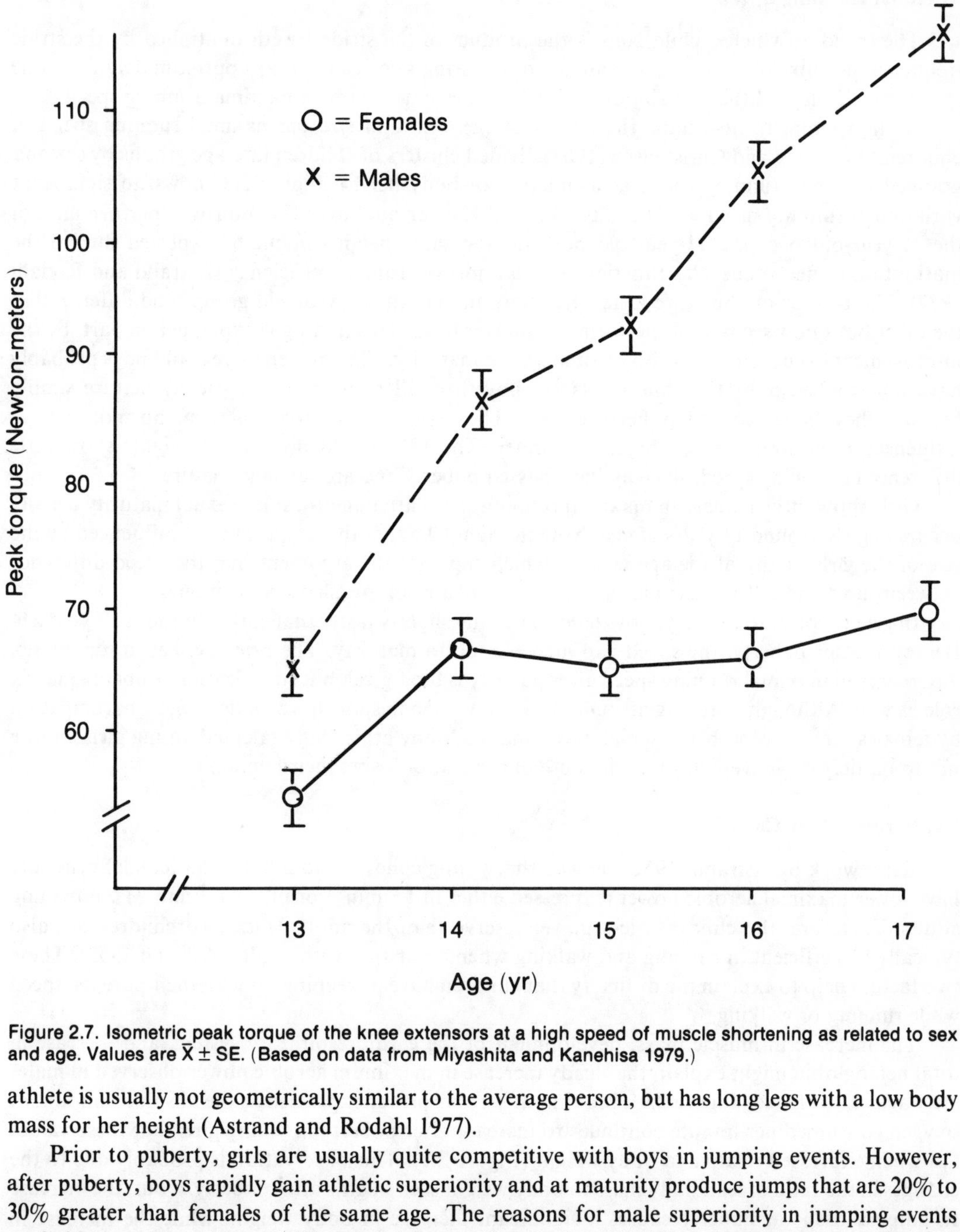

Figure 2.7. Isometric peak torque of the knee extensors at a high speed of muscle shortening as related to sex and age. Values are $\bar{X} \pm$ SE. (Based on data from Miyashita and Kanehisa 1979.)

athlete is usually not geometrically similar to the average person, but has long legs with a low body mass for her height (Astrand and Rodahl 1977).

Prior to puberty, girls are usually quite competitive with boys in jumping events. However, after puberty, boys rapidly gain athletic superiority and at maturity produce jumps that are 20% to 30% greater than females of the same age. The reasons for male superiority in jumping events probably center on the sex differences in strength, speed, and body composition that exist after puberty.

Maximal Running Speed

The speed at which a child runs is the product of the stride length multiplied by the stride frequency per unit of time. Many animals of differing sizes can run at approximately the same speed, which suggests that the size of the animal does not determine maximal running speed.

In an attempt to determine the effects of age, sex, and size on maximal running speed in children, Asmussen and Christensen (1967) divided clusters of children into age groups by sex and graphed maximal running speed as a function of body height. Figure 2.8 shows no significant variation in running speed with height in 11- and 12-year-old boys. The improved performance of the 12-year-old over the 11-year-old boys (at the same height) might be expected due to the maturation of neuromuscular function, which improves running efficiency (Astrand and Rodahl 1977). The 14-year-old boys are faster than both the 11- and 12-year-old groups and differ in that the taller boys now seem to outperform the shorter boys. This finding is explained, in part, by the improvement in coordination with age and sexual maturity. The smaller 14-year-old boys probably have not reached puberty, while the larger boys are taller and more physically mature simply because they have reached puberty earlier. The result is that the male sex hormones have influenced their strength in a positive manner. The 18-year-old boys at all heights show little difference in running speed, since all have passed puberty and are sexually mature.

Girls show little increase in maximal running speed after age 14, since sexual maturity usually occurs in girls around 11 years of age. Note in Figure 2.8 that the results are not influenced by the size of the girls in any of the age groups, which supports the argument that the speed difference between short and tall 14-year-old boys is primarily a result of male sex hormones.

In general prior to puberty, boys tend to be only slightly faster than girls running a 50-yd dash. However, after puberty, the speed gap increases up to maturity. The primary reason for the sex differences in maximal running speed after puberty is biological, but socialization probably plays a role as well. Although changing attitudes toward women in sport have made athletic participation by females more acceptable, a social bias remains. Many athletically talented young girls choose not to participate actively in sports because of the fear of losing their femininity.

Cardiorespiratory Capacity

Early work by Astrand (1952) showed that young children (both male and female) generally have lower maximal aerobic power (expressed either in $l \cdot min^{-1}$ or $ml \cdot kg^{-1}\ min^{-1}$) than young adults. Therefore, the child has less power reserve than the adult. Untrained children are also typically less efficient in running and walking when compared with adults (Astrand 1952). These two factors help to explain the difficulty that children have in keeping up with their parents' speed while running or walking.

The increase in muscle mass, development of the cardiorespiratory system, and increase in total hemoglobin might explain the steady increase in maximum aerobic power observed in males after ages 12 to 13 (see Figure 2.9). Maximum aerobic power expressed as the absolute amount of oxygen consumed per minute continues to increase after puberty in young girls, but these values fall when expressed relative to body weight (Figure 2.9). This observation is probably due to the changes in the ratio of lean body mass to body weight seen in girls after puberty. Thus, the increase in adipose tissue at puberty causes a significant increase in body weight, while the increase in maximum oxygen consumption (liters min^{-1}) is relatively small. Therefore, $\dot{V}O_2$ max ($ml \cdot kg^{-1} \cdot min^{-1}$) continues to fall in young girls from about age 11 until maturity.

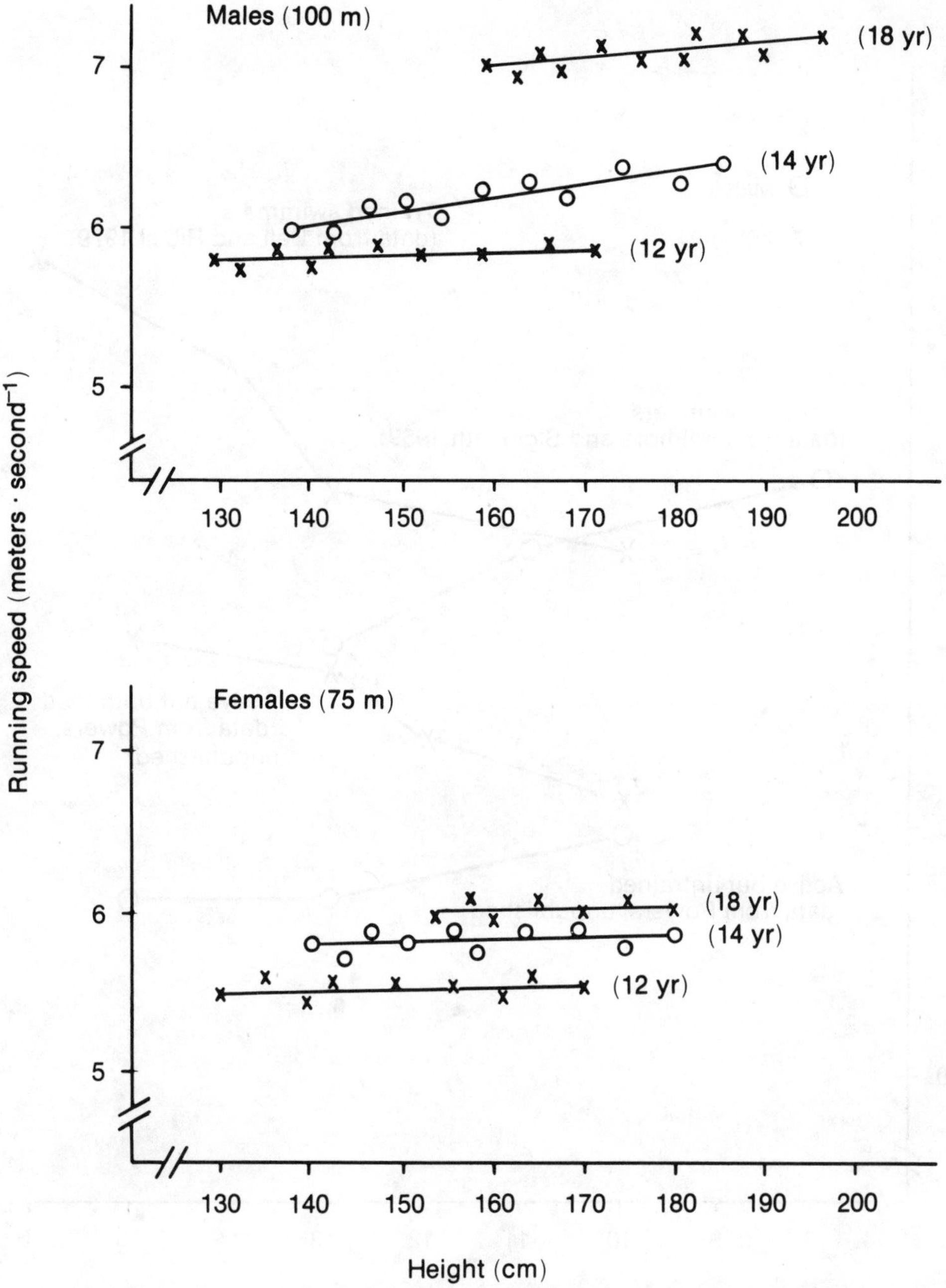

Figure 2.8. Maximal running speed in relation to body height for boys and girls of different ages. (Modified from Asmussen and Christensen 1967.)

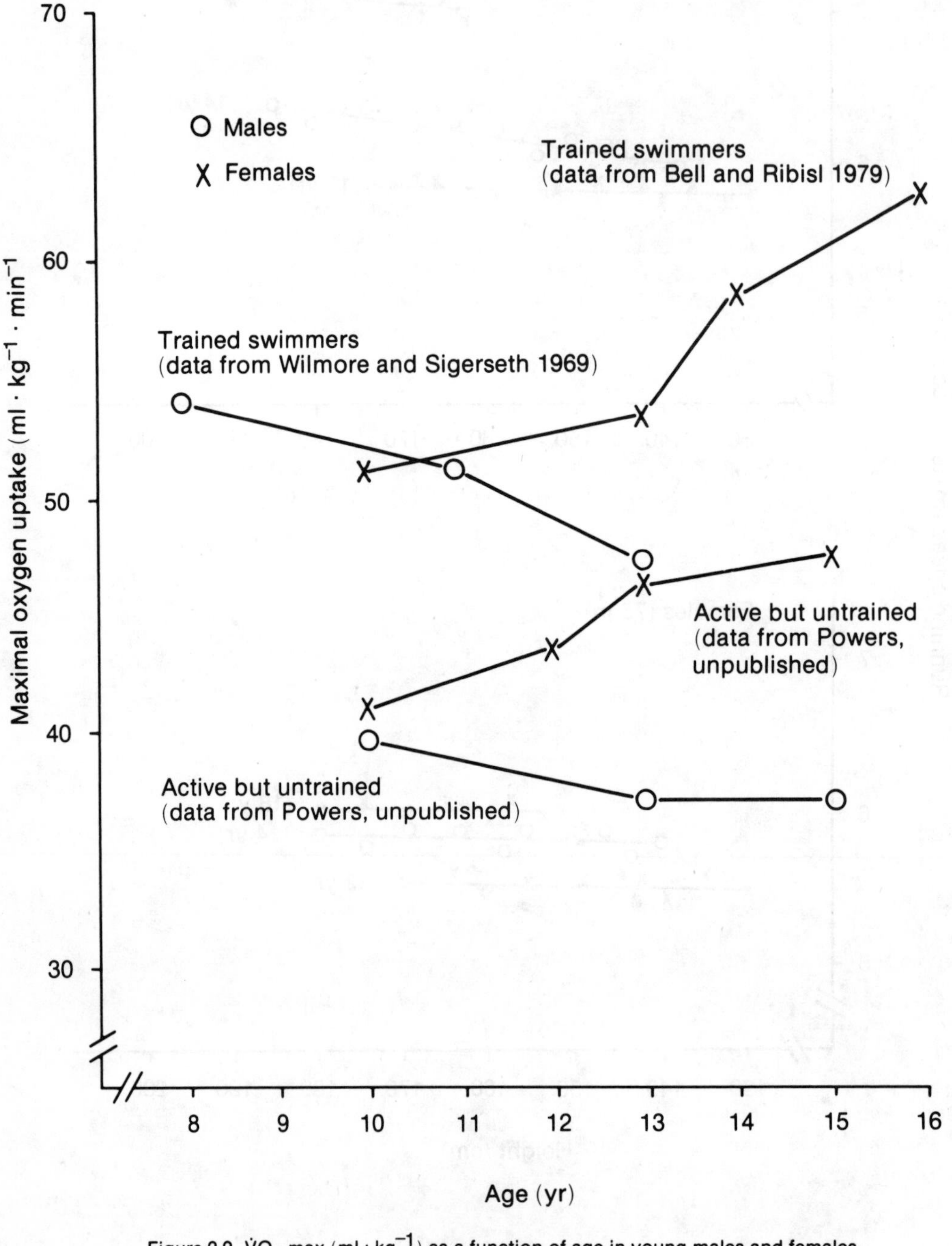

Figure 2.9. $\dot{V}O_2$ max (ml · kg^{-1}) as a function of age in young males and females.

Approximately 80% of an individual's $\dot{V}O_2$ max is determined by genetics (Fox and Mathews 1981). The inherited characteristics of muscle fiber types (the ratio of fast- to slow-twitch fibers in the muscle) and circulatory parameters (maximal cardiac output) are probably the variables that account for a child having a high or low $\dot{V}O_2$ max. As seen earlier, recent training studies involving children report a 10% to 20% change in $\dot{V}O_2$ max when compared with control groups. This finding suggests that only those children with high aerobic power initially are likely to become endurance champions after training. For example, two children with different genetic makeups (in terms of muscle fiber types) join the junior high school track team and begin training to become distance runners. Child A has an initial $\dot{V}O_2$ max of 40 ml · kg^{-1} · min^{-1}, while child B has a $\dot{V}O_2$ max of 55 ml · kg^{-1} · min^{-1}. After 16 weeks of training, each child's $\dot{V}O_2$ max has reached a plateau and is 20% above starting values. Thus, child A now has a $\dot{V}O_2$ max of 48 ml · kg^{-1} · min^{-1} and B has a $\dot{V}O_2$ max of 66 ml · kg^{-1} · min^{-1}. This example clearly shows that although all individuals can improve their cardiorespiratory capacity by training, only those individuals with high working capacities before training have the potential to become highly successful endurance athletes as a result of conditioning.

FITNESS TESTING IN CHILDREN

Cardiorespiratory Fitness

In recent years, physical education programs have reflected a renewed interest in the development of cardiorespiratory fitness. This concern is directly linked to the growing body of scientific knowledge that not only relates endurance fitness to health but also cites the possibility that regular endurance exercise may reduce the risk of coronary artery disease.

Paralleling this interest in fitness has been the refinement of measurement procedures to evaluate cardiorespiratory fitness in school children. Exercise physiologists generally agree that the measurement of an individual's maximal aerobic power (expressed ml · kg^{-1} · min^{-1}) is perhaps the best single measure of cardiorespiratory function. Although sensitive, direct measurement of maximal aerobic power is possible in the laboratory, these techniques require a great deal of time and necessitate expensive equipment. Since this type of testing is not practical for the public schools, to alleviate this problem, several researchers have developed field tests to estimate maximal aerobic power in children from distance runs. As a result, a variety of walk-run tests to estimate maximal aerobic power are currently in use in the public schools. The distances of these tests vary from 600 yd to 1.5 mi and differ in time from 3 to 12 min. Research has shown that the shorter runs (i.e., 3 to 6 min or 600 yd) are poor predictors of $\dot{V}O_2$ max, while runs of 9 to 12 min appear to provide valid estimates of $\dot{V}O_2$ max in both males and females of elementary age (Vodak and Wilmore 1975, Jackson and Coleman 1976). An important consideration in the administration of walk-run tests for fitness is that the validity of the test is improved if the children have had experience in pacing themselves prior to the actual administration of the test. Thus, several practice days should be allowed prior to the final testing session.

The estimated error of walk-run tests of maximal aerobic power is approximately 10%. Although this value may seem large, it appears quite reasonable when considering that even with direct measurement of $\dot{V}O_2$ max in the lab, the values obtained may represent an absolute error of 6% to 8% due to biological variation and experimental error (Katch et al. 1982).

Evaluating Muscular Strength and Endurance

Two often-tested components of physical fitness are muscular strength and muscular endurance. Strength and endurance, although different components of fitness, are related in many activities and have been used as a measure of physical fitness for years. Muscular strength is defined as the maximal resistance that a muscle or muscle group can overcome in one contraction (i.e., one maximal repetition). Muscular endurance, on the other hand, is the ability of a muscle group to perform repeated contractions against some specified resistance (e.g., lifting one's body weight in pull-ups). Thus, the emphasis in muscular endurance is on the number of repetitions and not the absolute amount of work being performed.

One of the most common methods of evaluating muscular strength is with the use of a hand-held dynamometer. This instrument measures the strength of the hand and forearm flexors. The disadvantage of this measurement is that grip strength does not always correlate well with the absolute strength of other muscle groups. Another concern is that few elementary school physical education programs are designed to increase strength in the forearm flexors. Whether teachers should evaluate a fitness parameter that is not being modified as a result of training in physical education is questionable (see Chapter 9 for a more detailed discussion).

Elementary school physical educators have used muscular endurance tests extensively for years because they provide reasonable estimates of muscle endurance. Each test has been selected to measure muscle groups used primarily in moving the weight of the body (e.g., push-ups, sit-ups, pull-ups). Other criteria that have influenced test selection are the ease with which the above activities may be scored and administered and the reliable measurements that can be obtained. Endurance tests that use the body's weight as the resistance factor result in individuals performing different amounts of work (e.g., pull-ups). However, these tests allow the physical education teacher to monitor each child's progress and thus may determine if a specific teaching unit was successful in increasing muscular endurance. Norms are available for many endurance measures.

Flexibility Testing

Flexibility can be defined as the range of motion of a particular joint. The loss of the ability to bend, twist, and stretch may result from muscle disuse or through shortened muscles and tendons. Since flexibility is considered a desirable trait for health, activities that increase flexibility should be promoted in physical education classes, with progress evaluated across time. Simple tests of flexibility, such as trunk flexion and extension, are useful measures of the range of motion in the trunk and back. Norms are available for flexibility measures.

SUMMARY

Muscular strength in children depends on numerous factors but can be considered the integrated expression of the neuromuscular system. In general, there is little difference in muscular strength between boys and girls prior to puberty. At puberty, however, boys begin to show rapid gains in strength and quickly become stronger than girls.

Maximal running speed improves in both sexes during maturation; boys show the greatest gains after puberty, while girls show little improvement past age 14. As a general rule, when matched for age, boys are faster than girls.

Prepubescent children generally have lower aerobic capacities (expressed either in $1 \cdot min^{-1}$ or $ml \cdot kg^{-1} \cdot min^{-1}$) than do young adults. Males show a steady increase in maximum aerobic power after age 12 until maturity; however, females tend to show a fall in $\dot{V}O_2$ max ($ml \cdot kg^{-1} \cdot min^{-1}$) after puberty owing to the gains in body weight resulting from increased adipose tissue.

Finally, $\dot{V}O_2$ max in children can be estimated accurately from distance runs of either 9 or 12 min. Prior to testing, time should be allowed for practice runs to allow the student to gain experience in running pace.

REFERENCES

Asmussen, E. Growth in muscular strength and power. In G. L. Rarick (Ed.), *Physical activity: Human growth and development*. New York: Academic Press, 1973.

Asmussen, E. & Christensen, E. H. Kompendium i legemsö velsernes specieele teori. Köbenhavns Universitets Fond til Tilvejebringelse of Läremidler Köbenhavn, 1967.

Astrand, P. O. *Experimental studies of physical working capacity in relationship to sex and age.* Copenhagen: Ejnal Munksgaard, 1952.

Astrand, P. O. & Rodahl, K. *Textbook of work physiology*. New York: McGraw-Hill, 1977.

Bar-Or, O. & Zwiren, L. D. Physiological effects of increased frequency of physical education classes and endurance conditioning on 9 to 10 year old girls and boys. In Bar-Or, O. (Ed.) *Pediatric work physiology: Proceedings of the fourth international symposium*. Tel-Aviv: Technodaf, 1972.

Bell, G. H. & Ribisl, P. M. Maximal oxygen uptake during swimming of young competitive swimmers 9 to 17 years of age. *Research Quarterly*, 1979, **50**, 574-582.

Berg, K. & Eriksson, B. (Eds.) *Children and exercise IX: Proceedings of the ninth international symposium.* Baltimore: University Park Press, 1980.

Borms, J. & Hebbelinick, M. (Eds.) *Pediatric work physiology*. Basel, Switzerland: S. Karger, 1978.

Brown, C. H., Harrower, J. R. & Deeter, M. F. The effects of cross country running on pre-adolescent girls. *Medicine and Science in Sports*, 1972, **4**, 1-5.

Clarke, D. H. & Vaccaro, P. The effect of swimming training on muscular performance and body composition in children. *Research Quarterly*, 1979, **50**, 9-17.

Daniels, J. & Oldridge, N. Changes in oxygen consumption of young boys during growth and running training. *Medicine and Science in Sports*, 1971, **3**, 161-165.

Edington, D. W. & Edgerton, V. R. *The biology of physical activity*. Boston: Houghton Mifflin, 1976.

Ekblom, B. Effect of physical training in adolescent boys. *Journal of Applied Physiology*, 1967, **27**, 350-355.

Eriksson, B. O. Physical training, oxygen supply and muscle metabolism in 11-13 year old boys. *Acta Physiologica Scandinavica*, Suppl. 384, 1972, 2-48.

Eriksson, B. O. & Koch, G. Cardiac output and intra-arterial blood pressure at rest and during submaximal and maximal exercise in 11-13 year old boys before and after physical training. *Pediatric work physiology*. Tel Aviv: Technodaf, 1973.

Fox, E. L., Bartels, R. L., Billings, C. E., O'Brien, R., Bason R. & Mathews, D. K. Frequency and duration of interval training programs and changes in aerobic power. *Journal of Applied Physiology*, 1975, **38**, 481-484.

Fox, E. L. & Mathews, D. K. *The physiological basis of physical education and athletics.* (3rd ed.) Philadelphia: Saunders, 1981.

Gatch, W. & Byrd, R. Endurance training and cardiovascular function in 9 and 10 year old boys. *Archives of Physical Medicine and Rehabilitation*, 1979, **60**, 574-577.

Gutin, B., Trinidad, A., Norton, C., Giles, E., Giles, A. & Steward, K. Morphological and physiological factors related to endurance performance of 11 to 12 year old girls. *Research Quarterly*, 1978, **49**, 44-52.

Holmgen, A. F. & Astrand, P. O. DL and dimensions and functional capacities of the 0_2 transport system in humans. *Journal of Applied Physiology*, 1966, **21**, 1463-1470.

Ikai, M. & Fukunaga, T. Calculation of muscle strength per unit cross-sectional area of muscle by means of ultrasonic measurements. *Int. Z. Angew Physiol.*, 1968, **26**, 26-32.

Jackson, A. S. & Coleman, A. E. Validation of distance run tests for elementary school children. *Research Quarterly*, 1976, **47**, 86-94.
Katch, V. L., Sady, S. S., & Freedson, P. Biological variability in maximum aerobic power. *Medicine and Science in Sports and Exercise*, 1982, **14**, 21-25.
Lamb, D. R. *Physiology of exercise: Responses and adaptations*. New York: Macmillan, 1978.
Magel, J. R. & Anderson, K. L. Pulmonary diffusing capacity and cardiac output in young, trained Norwegian swimmers and untrained subjects. *Medicine and Science in Sports*, 1969, **1**, 131-139.
McArdle, W. D., Katch, F. I. & Katch, V. L. *Exercise physiology: Energy, nutrition and human performance*. Philadelphia: Lea & Febiger, 1981.
Miyashita, M. & Kanehisa, H. Dynamic peak torque related to age, sex and performance. *Research Quarterly*, 1979, **49**, 249-255.
Parizkova, J. *Body fat and physical fitness*. Hague: Martinus Nijhoff, 1977.
Ribisl, P. M. Effects of training upon the maximal oxygen uptake of middle-aged men. *Int. Z Angew Physiol.*, 1963, **27**, 154-160.
Sady, S., Katch, V., Freedson, P. & Weltman A. Changes in metabolic acidosis: Evidence for an intensity threshold. *Journal of Sports Medicine and Physical Fitness*, 1980, **20**, 41-46.
Shaver, L. G. *Essentials of exercise physiology*. Minneapolis: Burgess, 1981.
Shephard, R. J. *Frontiers of fitness*. Springfield, Illinois: Charles C Thomas, 1971.
Spryranova, S. Development of the relationship between aerobic capacity and the circulatory and respiratory reaction to moderate activity in boys 11-13 years old. *Physiol. Bohenoslov*, 1966, **15**, 253-264.
Vaccaro, P. & Clarke, D. H. Cardiorespiratory alterations in 9 to 11 year old children following a season of competitive swimming. *Medicine and Science in Sports*, 1978, **10**, 204-207.
Vodak, P. A. & Wilmore J. H. Validity of the six-minute jog-walk and the 600-yard run-walk in estimating endurance capacity in boys 9-12 years of age. *Research Quarterly*, 1975, **46**, 230-234.
Wasserman, K., Whipp, B. J., Koyal, S. N. & Beaver, W. L. Anaerobic threshold and respiratory gas exchange during exercise. *Journal of Applied Physiology*, 1973, **35**, 236-243.
Wilmore, J. H. & Sigerseth, P. O. Physical work capacity of young girls, 7-13 years of age. *Journal of Applied Physiology*, 1967, **22**, 923.

SUGGESTED READINGS

Undergraduate Students

Bar-Or, O. (Ed.) *Pediatric work physiology: Proceedings of the fourth international symposium*. Tel-Aviv: Technodaf, 1972.
Berg, K. & Eriksson, B. (Eds.) *Children and exercise IX: Proceedings of the ninth international symposium*. Baltimore: University Park Press, 1980.
Clarke, D. H. & Vaccaro, P. The effect of swimming training on muscular performance and body composition in children. *Research Quarterly*, 1979, **50**, 9-17.
Fox, E. L. & Mathews, D. K. *The physiological basis of physical education and athletics*. (3rd ed.) Philadelphia: Saunders, 1981.
McArdle, W. D., Katch, F. I. & Katch, V. L. *Exercise physiology: Energy, nutrition and human performance*. Philadelphia: Lea & Febiger, 1981.
Rarick, G. L. *Physical activity: Human growth and development*. New York: Academic Press, 1973.

Graduate Students

Astrand, P. O. *Experimental studies of physical working capacity in relationship to sex and age*. Copenhagen: Ejnal Munksgaard, 1952.
Astrand, P. O. & Rodahl, K. *Textbook of work physiology*. New York: McGraw-Hill, 1977.
Bar-Or, O. (Ed.) *Pediatric work physiology: Proceedings of the fourth international symposium*. Tel-Aviv: Technodaf, 1972.
Berg, K. & Eriksson, B. (Eds.) *Children and exercise IX: Proceedings of the ninth international symposium*. Baltimore: University Park Press, 1980.

Borms, J. & Hebbelinick, M. (Eds.) *Pediatric work physiology*. Basel, Switzerland: S. Karger, 1978.
Clarke, D. H. & Vaccaro, P. The effect of swimming training on muscular performance and body composition in children. *Research Quarterly*, 1979, **50**, 9-17.
Eriksson, B. O. Physical training, oxygen supply and muscle metabolism in 11-13 year old boys. *Acta Physiologica Scandinavica*, Suppl. 384, 1972, 2-48.
Miyashita, M. & Kanehisa, H. Dynamic peak torque related to age, sex and performance. *Research Quarterly*, 1979, **49**, 249-255.
Parizkova, J. *Body fat and physical fitness*. Hague: Martinus Nijhoff, 1977.
Rarick, G. L. *Physical activity: Human growth and development*. New York: Academic Press, 1973.
Vaccaro, P. & Clarke, D. H. Cardiovascular alterations in 9 to 11 year old children following a season of competitive swimming. *Medicine and Science in Sports*, 1978, **10**, 204-207.

Laboratory 2 from Chapter 14 should be used at the completion of this chapter.

3

Changing Motor Patterns During Childhood

Mary Ann Roberton

The orderliness of motor development over time is fascinating, and the degree and causes of this orderliness are a source of scientific speculation. The regularity of motor development has allowed researchers to chart sequential changes in a number of motor skills. As children have the opportunity to practice these skills, they seem to move through developmental sequences in much the same order. Their rates of progress clearly differ, however, as do the end points they achieve by the conclusion of their elementary school years.

This chapter summarizes what is known about developmental sequences for a few motor skills within the categories of locomotion, object projection, and object receipt. Bibliographies at the end of the chapter direct the reader to more detailed information about the specific courses of development for these and other motor skills.

PRIMITIVE MOTOR PATTERNS IN INFANCY

The observable course of motor development begins about 7½ weeks after conception when, for example, the fetus flexes its head laterally away from stimulation in the lip region (Hooker 1952). By 8½ weeks after conception, this isolated avoidance response has radiated into a pattern of movements organized in space and time. Lip stimulation now elicits (1) contralateral (to the opposite side) flexion of the neck and trunk, (2) extension (backward movement) of the arms at the shoulders, with no elbow, wrist, or finger participation, and (3) rotation of the pelvis away from the side of stimulation (Hooker 1952).

By the time the child is born seven months later, these early patterns have evolved into an amazing repertoire of motor acts. The child can suck, swallow, cry, sneeze, and turn her head to free her nose for breathing or to seek the nipple for nourishment. Newborns can support their own weight hanging from a rod for several seconds while using a fingers-only or digital grasp (Figure 3.1A). They can swim, using flexion extension, pedaling movements of the legs, and sometimes the

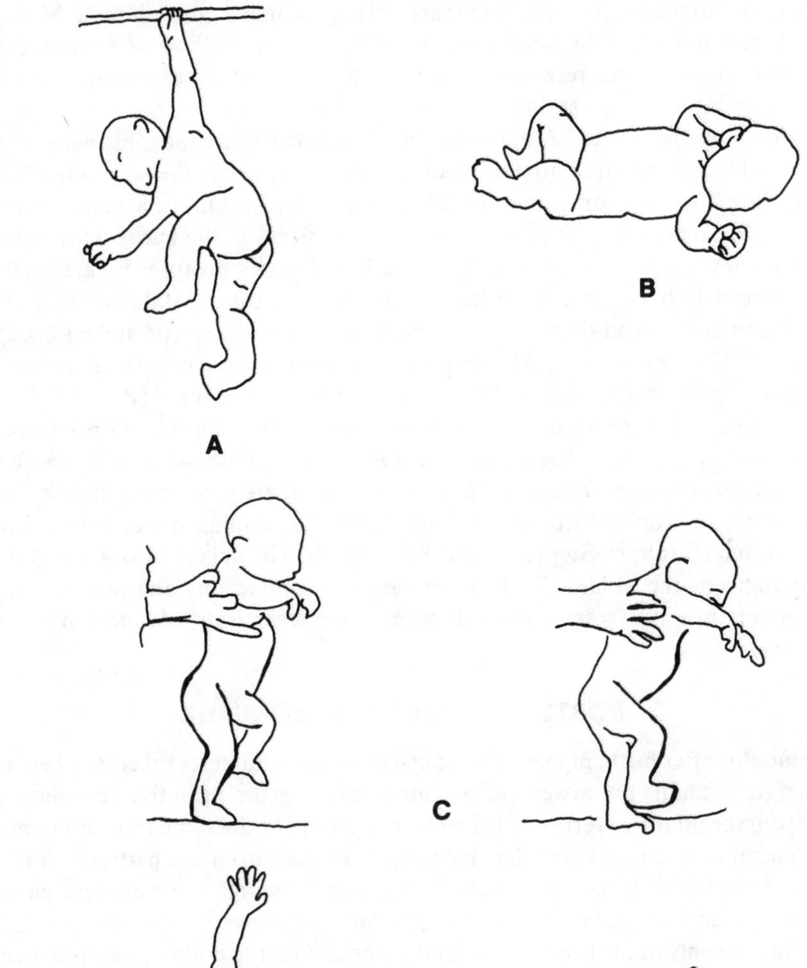

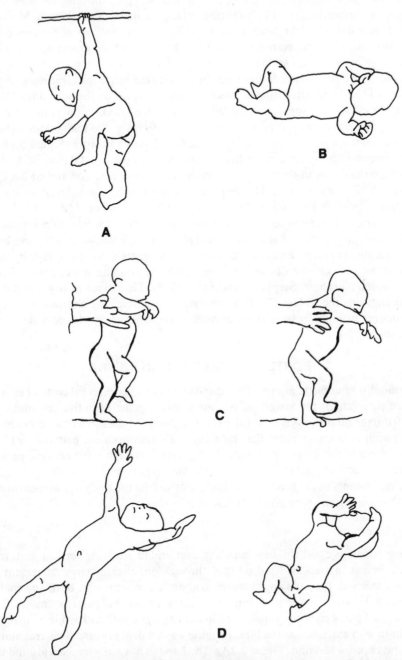

Figure 3.1. Primitive reflexes. **A**: Digital grasp. **B**: Asymmetrical tonic neck. **C**: Stepping. **D**: Moro. (A, C, D drawn from Myrtle McGraw research films, motor development and child study laboratory, Department of Physical Education and Dance, University of Wisconsin–Madison. B redrawn from M. Blankenstein, U. Walbergen, & J. H. deHaas. *The development of the infant*. London: Heinemann, 1975.)

arms (McGraw 1963). The newborn can make alternate stepping movements when held erect with feet touching a surface (Peiper 1963) (Figure 3.1C). Neonates also show a Moro response to vestibular stimulation when the head is displaced forward or backward. Sneezes and downward dropping frequently elicit this response, which consists of (1) spinal extension and horizontal arm abduction followed by (2) arm adduction (Figure 3.1D).

Two other movement patterns in the newborn's repertoire are the tonic neck responses. If the newborn's head is rotated, stretching the neck muscles, the arm on the nose side of the head tends to extend at the elbow (and sometimes the leg extends at the knee). The arm to the back side of the head tends to flex at the elbow (and sometimes the leg flexes at the knee). This response is called the asymmetrical tonic neck response (Peiper 1963) or fencer's posture (Figure 3.1B). If the neck muscles are stretched by ventroflexion (tucking the head in the sagittal plane), newborns tend to flex their elbows and extend their knees. If the head is dorsiflexed (or arched back), the elbows tend to extend while the knees flex. This response is known as the symmetrical tonic neck response. However, this response is less frequently observed in normal newborns (Peiper 1963).

Neural centers in the spinal cord or lower brain stem control the infant's primitive responses or reflexes. Milani-Comparetti (1981) and Gesell (1946) have hypothesized that these behaviors help the fetus to get along in its prebirth environment and, ultimately, to orient itself in the birth canal. The use of ultrasound can now document more clearly the jumping and orienting behaviors of the fetus in the womb (Birnholz, Stephens, and Faria 1978). The degree of organized motor activity recorded strengthens the Milani-Gesell hypothesis as an interesting alternative to the traditional belief that infants' primitive responses are atavisms, phylogenetically old movements of little use to the human species.

POSTURAL REACTIONS IN INFANCY

In the months after birth, higher brain stem centers and the cerebral cortex begin functioning. As they do, they inhibit the lower brain centers, causing the primitive responses gradually to disappear from the infant's overt repertoire (Peiper 1963). At the same time, other motor patterns known as postural reactions enter that repertoire. These movement patterns, controlled by the higher brain centers, can be grouped under three categories: righting reactions, parachute (propping or placing) reactions, and tilting reactions (Milani-Comparetti and Gidoni 1967). The patterns coordinate movements of the head, trunk, and limbs so that the body can automatically adjust its posture with changing environmental conditions.

Righting Reactions

Righting reactions assist children in rolling over and in attaining vertical postures. When the prone infant begins to arch his head upward through dorsiflexion, this movement is called the head-righting reaction. It occurs anywhere up to about 1½ months after birth and enables the child to lift the head. When the spine joins into the arching action via spinal extension, the reaction is known as sagittal trunk righting. Finally, the infant can right her trunk while lying prone and have her legs join in with extension at the hips, forming a swan dive posture. This reaction is called the Landau or pivot prone reaction (Figure 3.2A). The Landau normally appears around three months of age.

Derotative righting refers to a postural reaction that appears about the fourth month. If the infant's head is rotated to the side, the shoulders and then the pelvis follow in sequence. Similarly,

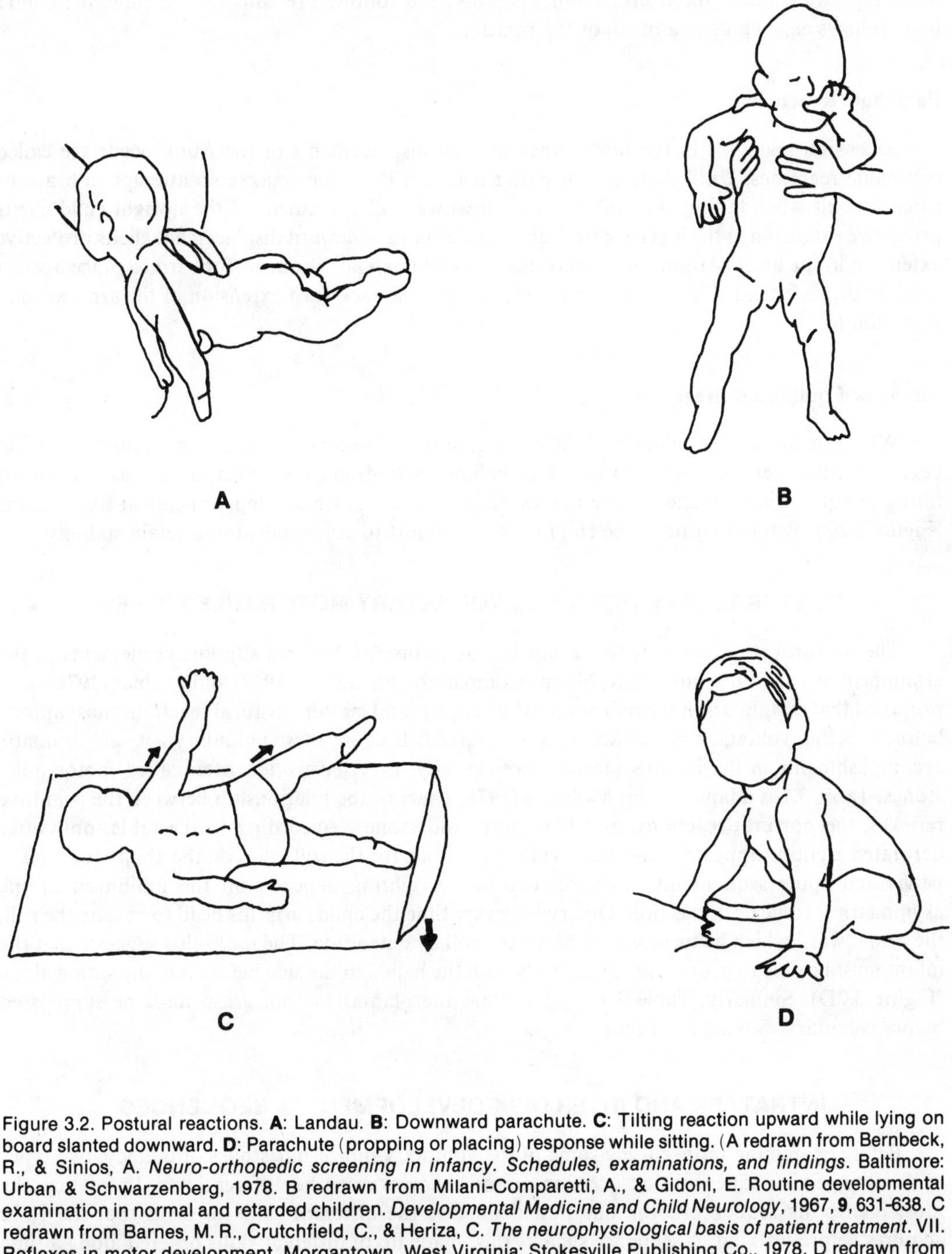

Figure 3.2. Postural reactions. **A**: Landau. **B**: Downward parachute. **C**: Tilting reaction upward while lying on board slanted downward. **D**: Parachute (propping or placing) response while sitting. (A redrawn from Bernbeck, R., & Sinios, A. *Neuro-orthopedic screening in infancy. Schedules, examinations, and findings*. Baltimore: Urban & Schwarzenberg, 1978. B redrawn from Milani-Comparetti, A., & Gidoni, E. Routine developmental examination in normal and retarded children. *Developmental Medicine and Child Neurology*, 1967, **9**, 631-638. C redrawn from Barnes, M. R., Crutchfield, C., & Heriza, C. *The neurophysiological basis of patient treatment*. VII. Reflexes in motor development. Morgantown, West Virginia: Stokesville Publishing Co., 1978. D redrawn from Blankenstein, M. et al. *The development of the infant*. London: Heinemann, 1975.)

if the hips are rotated, the trunk, shoulders, and head follow. Previous to that time, the child's body follows as a whole in a block or log rotation.

Parachute Reactions

Extension reactions in the limbs when sudden displacements of the trunk occur are called parachute reactions. Until these motor patterns occur, the infant makes no attempt to brace or catch himself when falling. At four months, downward displacement of the upright child elicits protective extension in the legs (Figure 3.2B). At 6 months, sideward displacement elicits protective extension in the arms. Around seven months, the child extends the arms forward to brace against forward displacement. Finally, a push backward elicits a backward extension of the arms around nine months.

Tilting or Equilibrium Reactions

When the surface on which a child is lying, sitting, kneeling, or standing is tilted, the child begins to curve her spine upward to retain balance. Children's responses in this case are called tilting or equilibrium reactions. The earliest tilting response, while lying, appears at five months (Figure 3.2C). Before that time, the child makes no effort to adjust posture to retain stability.

POSTURAL REACTIONS AND VOLUNTARY MOTOR MILESTONES

The postural reactions that the infant begins to display become supportive elements in the attainment of voluntary movement. Milani-Comparetti and Gidoni (1967) and Molnar (1978) have proposed that certain primitive reflexes must disappear and certain postural reactions must appear before specific, voluntary motor acts can be attained. Because these voluntary acts are dramatic accomplishments in the infant's mastery over gravity, they have often been called motor milestones. Table 3.1 is adapted from Molnar's (1978) chart of the relationship between the primitive reflexes, the postural reactions, and five motor milestones. According to the table, only after derotative righting appears is voluntary rolling possible, for the roll relies on the ability to turn the pelvis and spine sequentially. In turn, derotative righting depends on the inhibition of the asymmetrical tonic neck reaction. Otherwise, every time the child turns his head to initiate the roll, the arm toward which he turns would block the roll by extending. The table also suggests that the infant must be able to prop or brace his body with the hands to the side before initially sitting alone (Figure 3.2D). Similarly, Table 3.1 suggests that the plantar or foot grasp must be suppressed before voluntary walking can occur.

INTRATASK AND INTERTASK DEVELOPMENTAL SEQUENCES

Before examining more closely some of the voluntary motor milestones of infancy, two types of developmental sequences that occur in motor behavior must be differentiated. In infancy, the most interesting sequence is the one that delineates the different skills or tasks that the child acquires before walking. A sequence such as this, made up of different skills ordered along a time span, is called an intertask (or skill) sequence. When a sequence focuses on the changes that occur

Table 3.1. Relationship Between Primative Reflexes, Postural Reaction, and Infant Motor Milestones

	Motor Milestones				
Reflexes and Reactions	**Rolling Over**	**Sitting**	**Creeping**	**Standing**	**Walking**
Primitive reflexes					
Moro	−	−	−	−	−
Asymmetrical tonic neck	−	−	−	−	−
Palmar grasp	±	−	−	−	−
Plantar grasp	+	+	+	±	−
Postural reactions					
Righting					
Head in space	+	+	+	+	+
Body derotative	+	+	+	+	+
Propping					
Lateral	−	+	+	+	+
Anterior	−	−	+	+	+
Posterior	−	−	−	+	+
Tilting					
Prone	+	+	+	+	+
Supine	−	+	+	+	+
Sitting	−	±	+	+	+
On hands and knees	−	−	±	±	+
Standing	−	−	−	−	±

+ = present and well developed
± = beginning to disappear or emerge
− = absent

Modified from Molnar, G. Analysis of motor disorder in retarded infants and young children. *American Journal of Mental Deficiency,* 1978, **83**, 213–222, who adapted from Milani-Comparetti, A., & Gidoni, E. Routine developmental examination in normal retarded children. *Developmental Medicine and Child Neurology,* 1967, **9**, 631–638.

within a given task until that task is mastered, the sequence is called an intratask sequence. More will be said about intratask sequences later.

INTERTASK MILESTONES IN THE VOLUNTARY MOVEMENTS OF INFANCY

The intertask sequence (which leads to what is commonly referred to as the motor milestones of infancy) is exciting for parents to observe (Figure 3.3). An intertask sequence represents the child's gradual mastery over gravity. Paralleling this mastery is the change from the dominance of the neonatal posture of flexion to the dominance of extension in the toddler.

At seven months, as the child is developing head control, upper back extension, and sideward parachute responses, the milestone of sitting alone occurs. Meanwhile, in the prone position, as the infant develops skills in sagittal trunk righting and in weight bearing by the forearms, and then by the hands, one hand becomes free for exploration. The free hand pushes against the surface on which the child is lying, finally resulting in the milestone of locomotion. The actual locomotor form varies among children. Usually crawling—a dragging motion along a surface—begins, and then hand-knee or hand-foot creeping. An important predictor of hand-knee creeping is rocking

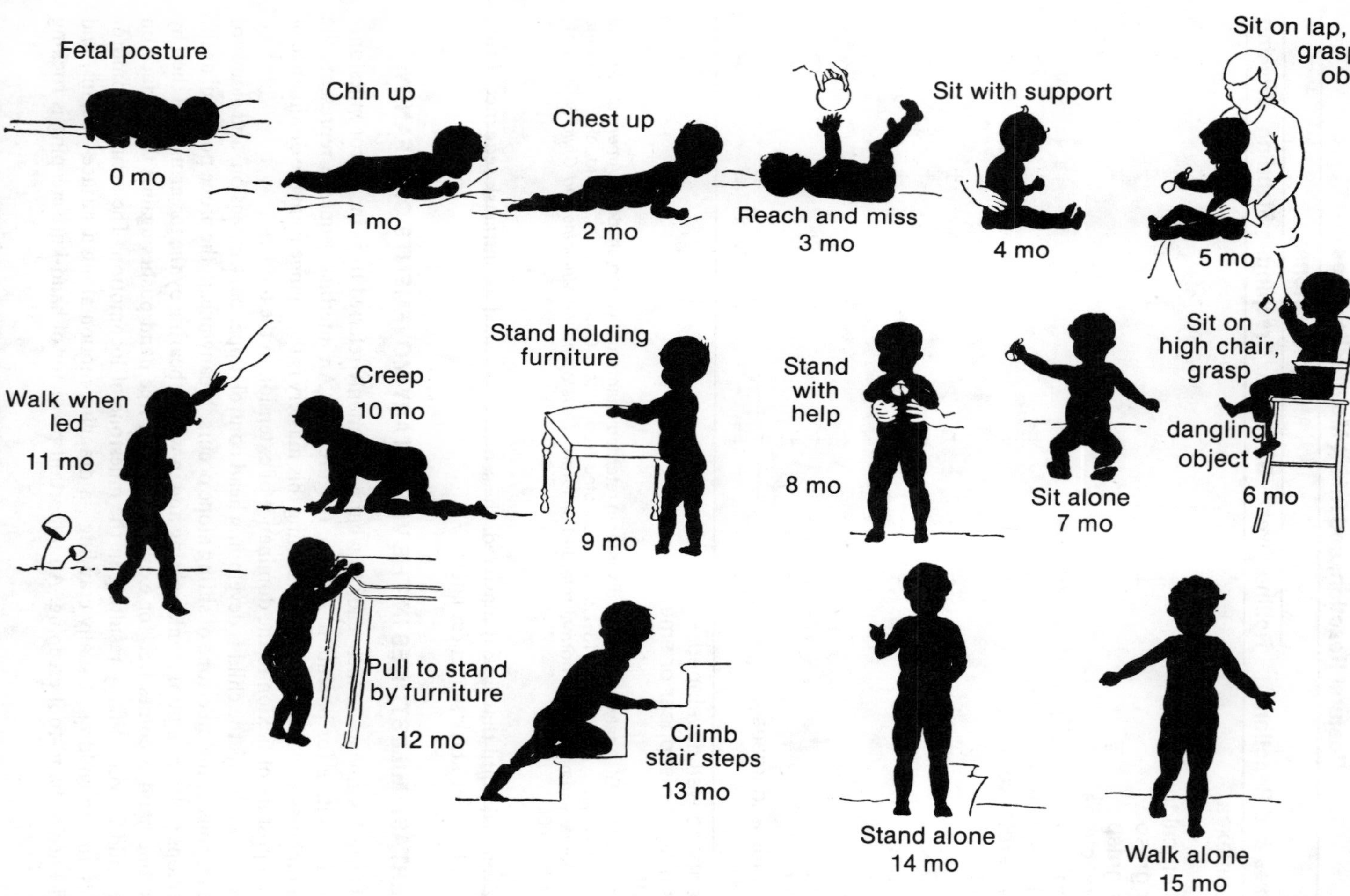

Figure 3.3. The motor milestones of infancy. Note milestone ages in this figure tend to be slightly older than ages quoted in the text. (From *The first two years*. Vol. II. Intellectual development. M. Shirley, University of Minnesota Press, Minneapolis. Copyright 1933 by the University of Minnesota Press. Reprinted by permission.)

behavior when the infant is in the all-fours position. By 10 months, many children are pulling themselves to a standing position and are beginning to take steps while holding on to the sides of their playpen or furniture. Finally, about one year after birth, the average child has taken his first independent steps.

WALKING—AN INTRATASK SEQUENCE

The toddler's first steps are unlike the steps she takes when an adult. Changes in walking continue to occur through childhood. Muscle action becomes adultlike by about seven years of age (Okamoto 1973), although Bernstein (1967) reported continuing changes in the generated force curves through adolescence.

Changes in the walk during childhood are hypothesized to occur as listed in Table 3.2. No validation of these particular sequences exists.

Complexity and Walking

Even during the elementary school years, temporary regressions occur in children's walking movements when they encounter a more complex environment. Particularly noticeable is the effect that stair climbing has on the alternate stepping action of the legs. Two-year-olds can climb stairs by themselves, but they use a marking time approach: one leg steps, then the other catches up. Even when children can alternate feet on the way up the stairs, they will still mark time on the way down. This reversion to a more stable walking pattern occurs through the elementary school years whenever the child encounters a tricky climbing situation. Coming down remains more difficult than going up, resulting in the common sight of a preschooler or primary school youngster stuck at the top of a jungle gym.

UNDERSTANDING AN INTRATASK SEQUENCE

Since walking is the first set of intratask sequences presented, the organization of such sequences needs consideration. The first factor is the level of analysis used to study the sequence.

Description of sequential change in motor skills has traditionally been of several types, each of which represents a different level of analysis. Sometimes the end result of the movement is studied, such as the distance a child walked before falling or the velocity with which a ball was thrown. These performance scores are charted over time, yielding a developmental curve. At other times, verbal descriptions of the changes in the spatial-temporal organization of the movement are listed in an ordinal sequence as provided in the walking sequence just described. Still on other occasions, the displacement, velocity, or acceleration of body parts have been measured and plotted over time.

All of these approaches to describing sequential change are legitimate, depending on the researcher's intent. Each level of analysis reflects yet another picture of motor development. The more parts of the mosaic that can be assembled, the better the view of the phenomena being described.

The two levels of analysis chosen to describe motor development for this chapter are (1) changes in performance scores and (2) verbal descriptions of the changes in spatial-temporal motor organization. Emphasis is on the verbal descriptions, since they help the reader to visualize development. At this level of analysis, recent research (Roberton 1977, 1978; Roberton and

Table 3.2. Developmental Sequences for Walking[a]

	Leg Action Component
Level 1	Toddler's primitive leg movements are characterized by short, wide steps, with excessive leg lift due to flexion of thigh at hip. Little ankle action occurs, and steps are flat footed. Knee is partially flexed when foot strikes ground, then locks into extension during support phase. Latter movement is known as single-knee–lock walk (Figure 3.4).
Level 2	Flexion of thigh at hip decreases while hip extension at end of stance increases, producing longer strides. Base of support narrows.
Level 3	Heel strikes first as foot contacts, then body weight rides over rest of foot. As heel strikes, knee locks into extension. It flexes as weight rides onto foot, then extends (locks) again at midstance. This adultlike action is called *double-knee–lock* walk (Figure 3.5C).
	Trunk Action Component
Level 1	Toddler's walk contains no pelvic rotation (Figure 3.4).
Level 2	Pelvis rotates forward with leg that is swinging and rotates backward with supporting leg.
	Arm Action Component
Level 1	Arms do not participate in walking movements. Hands are held about shoulder high. Sometimes laterally rotated arms are abducted at shoulder with elbows flexed, causing hands to ride even higher. This position, called the high guard position, appears as protective, ready-to-parachute position (Milani-Comparetti and Gidoni 1967) or as balancing position (Figure 3.4).
Level 2	Lateral rotation decreases, allowing hands to be held about waist high at middle guard position. Hands remain motionless, except in reaction to shifts in equilibrium (Figure 3.5A).
Level 3	Elbows are extended so that hands hang down at sides or slightly ahead of body (low guard position). Arms still do not swing except in reaction to equilibrium shifts (Figure 3.5B).
Level 4	Flexion at elbow occurs in response to forward movement of the leg opposite arm. Extension occurs when leg on same side steps forward. Excursion of hands forward may be unequal (Wickstrom 1977) and irregular. Sometimes both hands may be in front of body simultaneously.
Level 5	During vigorous walking, each arm swings forward from shoulders and elbows in time with forward step of leg opposite side of body. Arm swings back as leg on same side steps forward. Relaxed arms swinging forward and backward pass each other at coronal midline; thus, both arms are never in front or behind body at same time. Arm swing seems to be due to counter-rotation of shoulders in reaction to pelvic rotation (Figure 3.5C).

[a]These sequences have not been validated.

and Langendorfer 1980) suggests that systematic development lies at a partial pattern (Hooker 1952) or body component level. That is, the notion of a developmental sequence within skills is most valid for parts of the body rather than for the body as a whole. In the walk, for instance, separate sequences were noted for leg, trunk, and arm action. To a surprising extent, these sequences are somewhat independent. For instance, the level to which a child's arm action has

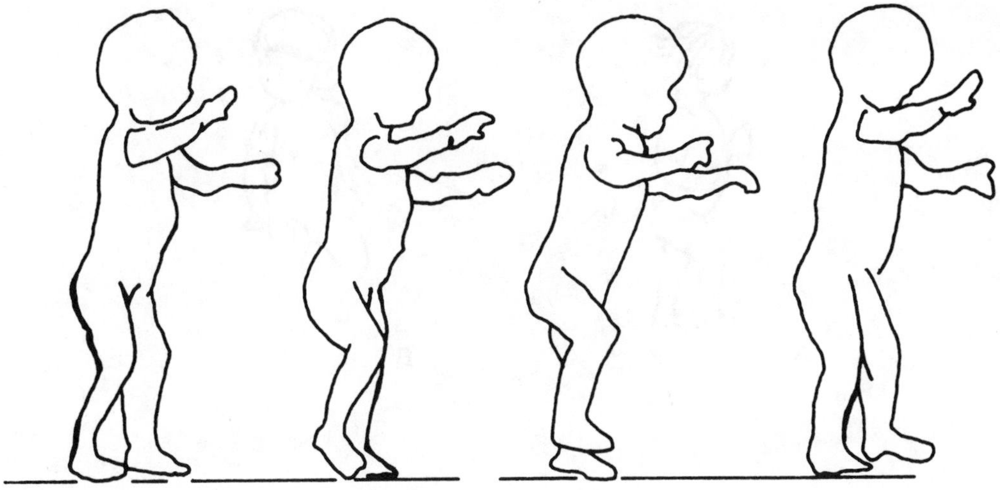

Figure 3.4. Toddler's walk. Leg action—Level 1. Position 2 shows single-knee lock in left leg. Position 4 shows knee flexion and flat-footed contact of right foot. Trunk action—Level 1. Arm action—Level 1. High guard. (Drawn from Myrtle McGraw research films, motor development and child study laboratory. Department of Physical Education and Dance, University of Wisconsin–Madison.)

progressed is not directly predictable from knowledge of that child's level of development in leg action. The early toddler probably is at the most primitive levels (Level 1 in Table 3.2) in all components. Similarly, when a person masters a task such as walking and becomes skilled at it, he has achieved the most advanced levels in all components. How he travels from primitive to advanced levels—which component develops when and how far in relation to other components—seems somewhat peculiar to the individual. Thus, the total movement of two children passing through the component sequences may look quite different, depending on the combination or profile of developmental levels they exhibit at any one time.

This understanding of development at the component level is new. Ongoing research, for instance, is just beginning to address the degree to which component development is independent (Roberton and Langendorfer 1980) and the relationship of development across tasks having similar components (Breihan 1982, Langendorfer 1982).

One nice feature of the component model is that it corresponds with the human observer's ability to see movement. Even with the aid of slow-motion photography, the observer cannot see all phases of a complex skill at once (Barrett 1979). Thus, to assess motor development, the teacher or clinician needs to study one facet of that movement at a time. For instance, as the toddler "toddles" by, the observer first studies the leg action and categorizes the movement developmentally. Then she looks for the presence of pelvic rotation. Last to be categorized is the action of the child's arms. This three-step assessment process not only helps the observer to visualize motor development but also parallels the way that development seems to occur.

A second factor in understanding intratask developmental sequences is to understand their organization into ordinal categories. Sometimes students think that ordinal categories imply that

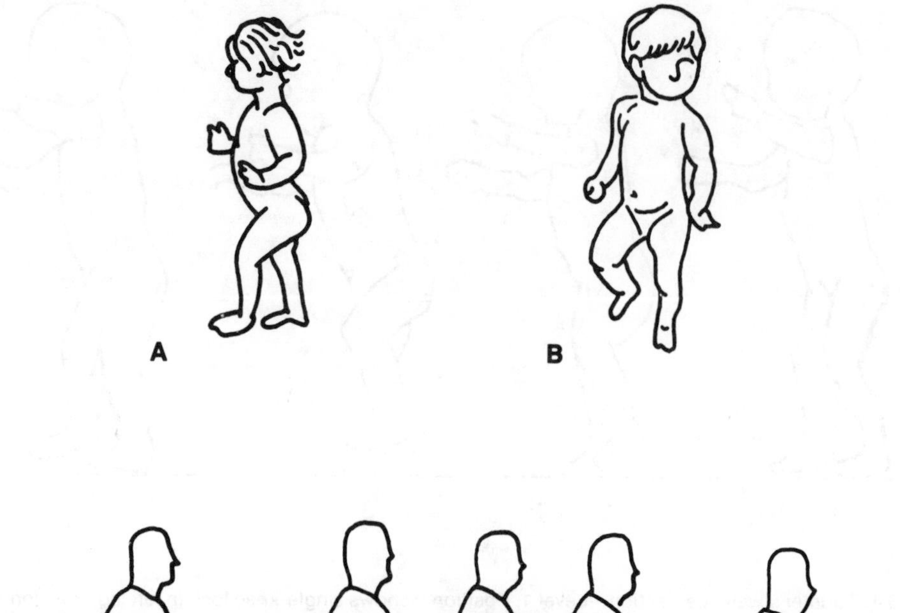

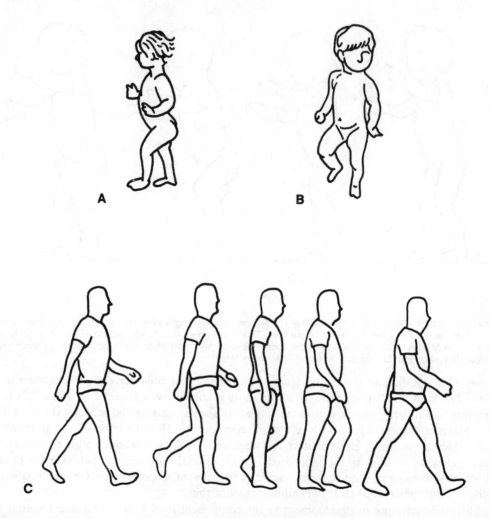

Figure 3.5. Key changes in arm action in walking. **A**: Level 2, middle guard. **B**: Level 3, low guard. **C**: Level 5, opposition. Note, too, the Level 3 leg action. (A and B redrawn from Blankenstein, M. et al. *The development of the infant.* London: Heinemann, 1975. C from longitudinal film collection, motor development and child study Laboratory, Department of Physical Education and Dance, University of Wisconsin–Madison.)

development is discontinuous and that it jumps from one category to the next with no transitional behavior. Simple observation of motor development confirms that this interpretation is not true. Each of the categories phases in and out, overlapping with its neighbors (McGraw 1943, 1963). The child gradually acquires pelvic rotation in the walk, for instance, and once acquired, the degree of rotation gradually increases.

Finally, a third point about intratask sequences is their relationship to age. Because children differ in the degree of practice they give to their motor skills, developmental sequences are not age determined. Age represents time, along which all development is charted; therefore, all sequences are age-related. What has happened to a child during the time represented by age is the critical factor in determining when that child will reach the different levels of a sequence (Roberton and Halverson 1977).

INTERTASK SEQUENCE FOR LOCOMOTION ON THE FEET

The advent of walking is a harbinger of further exciting events in locomotion. The developmental order of the remaining seven of the often-cited eight basic locomotor forms has not been studied empirically. It seems that early forms of running, jumping in place, jumping down, leaping, and galloping appear in the child's repertoire between two and three years of age (Roberton and Halverson 1977). All of these skills are dramatic because they involve a moment of flight, a time when neither foot is on the ground. The incipient forms of these skills are nowhere near what they are by the end of childhood. By definition, however, when the child's fast walk achieves enough propulsion to yield a small flight phase, running appears. When an obstacle is placed in the path of that run, the child leaps (Cooper, Adrian, and Glassow 1982). Similarly, when a child's step down from a height contains a brief moment of flight, the jump down is said to have appeared, even though a simultaneous two-foot takeoff has yet to occur (Figure 3.6).

After running, jumping, leaping, and galloping is the hop, first on the dominant and then on the nondominant foot. When at least a primitive hop can be performed on each foot, the child can learn to skip. Sideward galloping (or sliding) usually is differentiated from forward galloping about this same time.

The most interesting aspect of the intertask sequence for locomotion on the feet is that children frequently substitute earlier locomotor forms for those they cannot do. When they cannot jump down, they step down. When they cannot hop, they jump. When they cannot skip, they gallop. When they cannot jump for distance, they leap. Watching for substitutions tells the observer much about a child's location within the intertask locomotor sequence.

Intratask Sequences for Foot Locomotion

Few of the developmental sequences for childhood motor skills, including the walking sequence described earlier, have been validated by longitudinal studies having sufficient numbers of subjects; work in this direction is only now under way in motor development laboratories. References have been provided in the bibliography for readers interested in the techniques of validation.

The information provided here is therefore intended to be heuristic: it is a simplification and consolidation of many studies, each contributing incomplete parts to the picture of development. The reader is encouraged to use observation skills and study of the literature to add to, refute, or rearrange the information provided here. The bibliography is intended as a stimulus toward this goal.

Locomotor Terminology

Locomotor movements involving leg alternation can be described in terms of the action of the support leg (the leg receiving and projecting the child's weight) and the swing leg (the leg moving forward to become the support leg). Takeoff relates to the moment in all locomotor movements when the support or projecting leg or when both legs leave the ground. Flight is the period when no body part is in contact with the ground. Landing refers to the point when weight is received by the support leg or legs.

Figure 3.6. A moment of flight develops in the primitive jump. **A** and **B**: Child steps off an elevation at 17 months of age. **C**: Momentary flight (third figure) occurs in child's jump at 18 months. **D**: Beginning of upward projection when child is 21 months old. (Reprinted with permission from Hellebrandt et al. 1961, copyright by Williams & Wilkins Co.)

Running: Intratask Development

Performance Data

Around age two, children may exhibit a momentary flight phase in their fast walk. At this time the run begins its developmental course. Figure 3.7 is an estimate of that course in terms of velocity achieved over the childhood years. Espenschade (1960) composed the graph by compiling data from several cross-sectional and longitudinal studies. Because it is a compilation based primarily on cross-sectional data, the exact shape of the curve is probably not developmentally accurate (Damon 1965). It does, however, give a picture of what is currently known about velocity differences in fast running across ages.

One question not answered by the graph is how children increase their velocity as they grow older. Smith (1977) shed considerable light on this question by studying longitudinal data on five children as they performed a run for speed. Her results are presented in Figure 3.8. Covering the time between approximately ages 3 and 14, the graph indicates that these children substantially increased their stride length while maintaining essentially the same stride rate or, in some cases, slowing the rate slightly. Thus, speed with age does not seem to come by moving the legs more

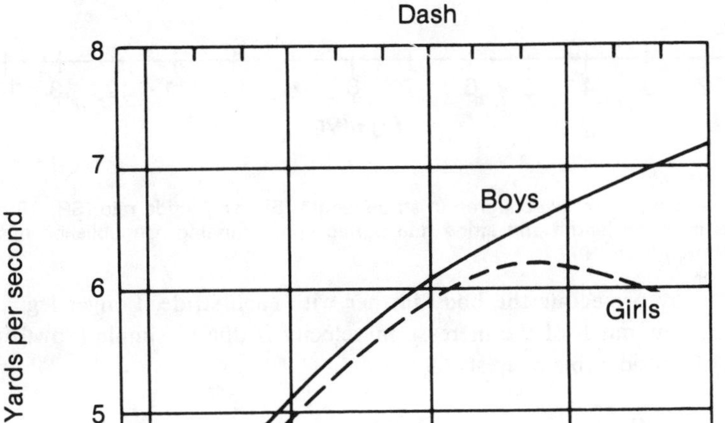

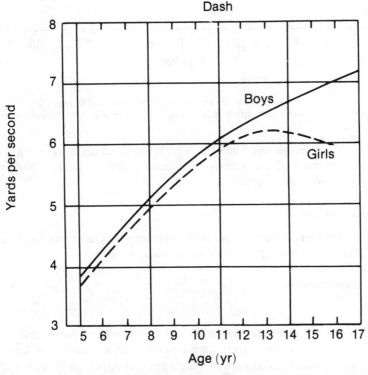

Figure 3.7. Age differences in running velocity. (From "Motor development" by Anna Espenschade & Helen Eckert in *Science and medicine of exercise and sport*, Second Edition, edited by Warren R. Johnson and E. R. Buskirk. Harper's Series in School and Public Health Education, Physical Education, and Recreation, edited by Delbert Oberteuffer. Copyright 1974 by Warren R. Johnson and Elsworth R. Buskirk. By permission of Harper & Row, Publishers, Inc.)

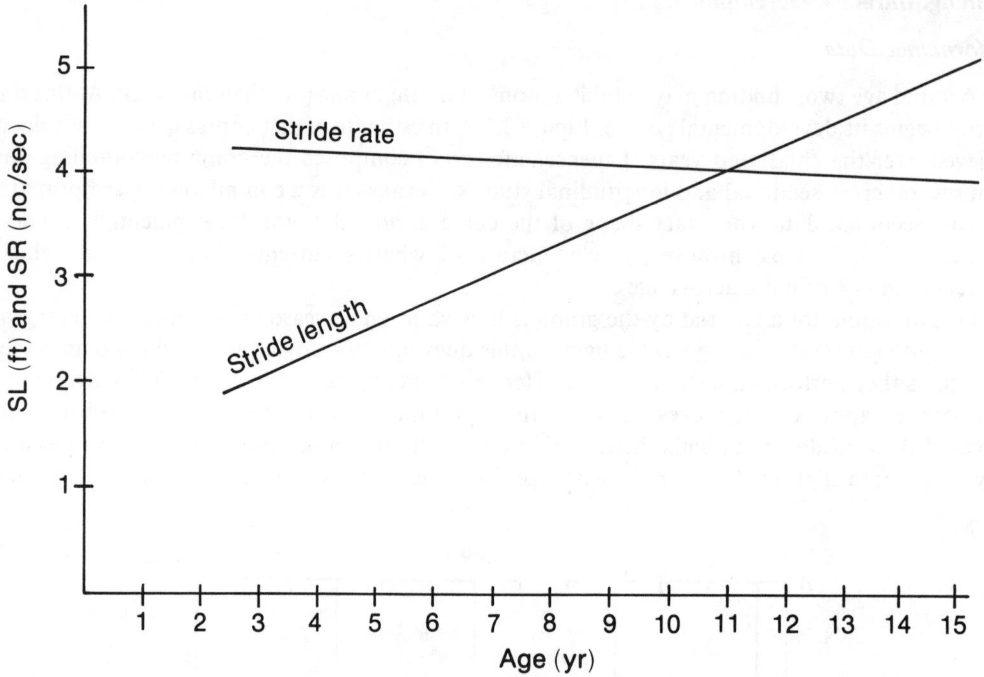

Figure 3.8. Longitudinal changes in five children in stride length (SL) and stride rate (SR). (From Smith, S. Longitudinal changes in stride length and stride rate during sprint running. Unpublished master's thesis, University of Wisconsin–Madison, 1977.)

frequently but rather by projecting the body farther with each stride. Longer legs clearly take longer strides. Thus, how much of the increase in velocity is due to simple growth remains an unstudied question of considerable interest.

Developmental Sequence Data

Listed in Table 3.3 are developmental sequences for running that have been hypothesized from available literature. No validation of these particular sequences exists.

Jumping: Intratask Development

Performance Data

Considerable data have been amassed on the horizontal and vertical distances that children of different ages can jump. Again, some of these data are cross sectional and some longitudinal. In 1960, Espenschade summarized existing data in the graphs that appear as Figures 3.10 and 3.11. More recently, DeOreo and Keogh (1980) summarized several of Keogh's studies in a graph which appeared remarkably similar to Espenschade's.

The long jump data (Figure 3.10) show through the elementary years a steady increase of three to five in. per year in distance jumped (DeOreo and Keogh 1980). Vertical jump data (Figure

Table 3.3. Developmental Sequences for Running[a]

	Leg Action Component
Level 1	Run is flat footed, with minimal flight. Swing leg is slightly abducted as it comes forward. When seen from overhead, path of swing leg curves out to side during movement forward (Wickstrom 1977). Foot eversion gives toeing-out appearance to swinging leg (Wickstrom 1977). Angle of knee of swing leg is greater than 90 degrees during forward motion.
Level 2	Swing thigh moves forward with greater acceleration, causing 90 degrees of maximal flexion in knee (Figure 3.9). Viewed from rear, foot is no longer toed out nor is thigh abducted. Sideward swing of thigh continues, however, causing foot to cross body midline when viewed from rear (Wickstrom 1977). Flight time increases. After contact, which may still be flat footed, support knee flexes more as child's weight rides over his foot (Seefeldt, Reuschlein, and Vogel 1972).
Level 3	Foot contact is with heel or ball of foot. Forward movement of swing leg is primarily in sagittal plane. Flexion of thigh at hip carries knee higher at end of forward swing. Support leg moves from flexion to complete extension by takeoff.
	Arm Action Component
Level 1	Arms are held in high to middle guard position, as described in development of walking (Seefeldt, Reuschlein, and Vogel 1972).
Level 2	Spinal rotation swings arms bilaterally to counterbalance rotation of pelvis and swing leg. Frequently oblique plane of motion plus continual balancing adjustments give flailing appearance to arm action.
Level 3	Spinal rotation continues to be prime mover of arms. Now elbow of arm swinging forward begins to flex, then extend, during backward swing. Combination of rotation and elbow flexion causes arm rotating forward to cross body midline and arm rotating back to abduct, swinging obliquely outward from body (Figure 3.9).
Level 4	Humerus (upper arm) begins to drive forward and back in sagittal plane, independent of spinal rotation. Movement is in opposition to other arm and to leg on same side. Elbow flexion is maintained, oscillating through approximately 90-degree angle during forward and backward arm swings.

[a]These sequences have not been validated.

3.11) are similar, with yearly increases of around 2 in. for boys and 1.6 in. for girls from ages 5 to 10 (DeOreo and Keogh 1980).

Developmental Sequence Data

Hellebrandt et al. (1961) published a classic study on the development of long-jump behavior. Figures 3.6 and 3.12 to 3.14 have been reproduced from that study, which produced two important findings: (1) the earliest jump is characterized by a one-foot takeoff, which persists in some children well into their elementary school years (Figure 3.12), and (2) the arm action of primitive jumpers moves backward as the jumper takes off and then assumes a winging action during flight (Figure 3.13). These movements are in contrast to the more advanced jumping actions illustrated in Figure 3.14.

Figure 3.9. Early run. Position 3 is takeoff, position 4 landing. Leg action Level 2. Arm action, Level 3. (Traced from longitudinal film collection, motor development and child study laboratory, Department of Physical Education and Dance, University of Wisconsin–Madison.)

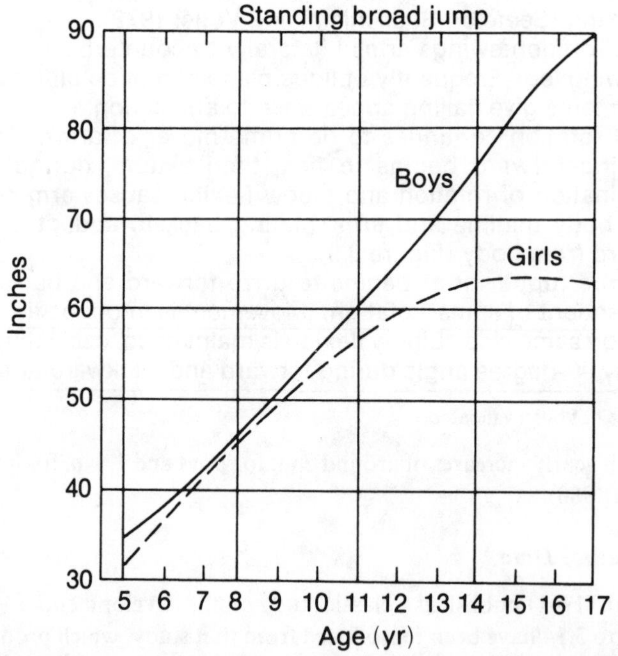

Figure 3.10. Age differences in horizontal distance jumped. (From "Motor development" by Anna Espenschade & Helen Eckert in *Science and medicine of exercise and sport*, Second Edition, edited by Warren R. Johnson and E. R. Buskirk. Harper's Series in School and Public Health Education, Physical Education, and Recreation, edited by Delbert Oberteuffer. Copyright 1974 by Warren R. Johnson and Elsworth R. Buskirk. By permission of Harper & Row, Publishers, Inc.)

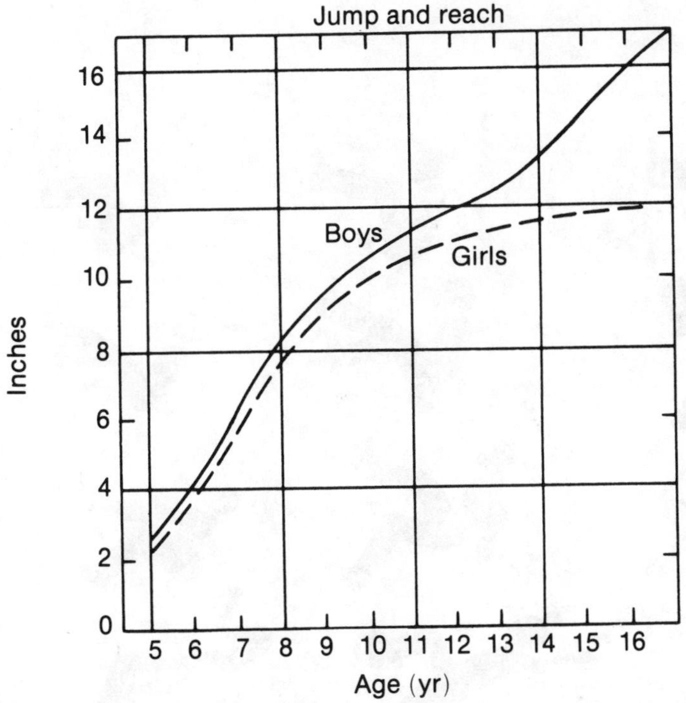

Figure 3.11. Age differences in vertical distance jumped. (From "Motor development" by Anna Espenschade & Helen Eckert in *Science and medicine of exercise and sport*, Second Edition, edited by Warren R. Johnson and E. R. Buskirk. Harper's Series in School and Public Health Education, Physical Education, and Recreation, edited by Delbert Oberteuffer. Copyright 1974 by Warren R. Johnson and Elsworth R. Buskirk. By permission of Harper & Row, Publishers, Inc.)

VanSant[1] has reanalyzed the film data originally used by Hellebrandt et al. (1961). The developmental sequences for the long jump in Table 3.4 have been hypothesized from her observations. They have not been validated on additional subjects.

Hopping: Intratask Development

Performance Data

Keogh (1965) studied children's ability to hop 50 ft without stopping or exchanging hopping legs. In comparing his findings with those of Jenkins (1930), he found that 31% to 38% of five-year-old boys could not complete the distance; 18% to 19% of five-year-old girls could not. By age seven, 2% to 23% of the boys still could not accomplish the task, while 2% to 7% of the girls could not. By age nine, a few girls and boys still were unable to hop 50 ft. In general, however, girls were approximately a year ahead of boys in performance.

1. VanSant, A. Development of the standing long jump. Motor development and child study laboratory, Department of Physical Education and Dance, University of Wisconsin–Madison. Study in progress, 1983.

Figure 3.12. Persistent, asymmetrical leg action in an elementary school boy during the primary grade years. **A**, first grade: leg action at takeoff and during flight and landing (assumed to be second to last figure)—Level 1, arm action at takeoff—Level 1, arm action during flight and landing—Level 2. **B**, second grade: leg action at takeoff—Level 1, leg action during flight and landing—Level 2, arm action at takeoff and during flight and landing—Level 3. **C**, fourth grade: leg action at takeoff—Level 2, leg action during flight and landing—Level 2, arm action at takeoff and during flight and landing—Level 3. Across all three years, the trunk action at takeoff remained at Level 2 and during flight and landing at Level 1. (Reprinted with permission from Hellebrandt et al. 1961, copyright by Williams & Wilkins Co.)

Figure 3.13. Winging arms during jump. Arms move backward to takeoff and retain this winging position in flight. **A**, 37 months: leg action at takeoff (third figure from left)—Level 2, leg action during flight and landing—Level 1, trunk action at takeoff—Level 3, trunk action during flight and landing—Level 2, arm action at takeoff—Level 2. **B**, 41 months: leg action at takeoff—Level 2, leg action during flight and landing—Level 3, trunk action at takeoff—Level 4, trunk action during flight action and landing—Level 2, arm action at takeoff and during flight and landing—Level 2. (Reprinted with permission from Hellebrandt et al. 1961, copyright by Williams & Wilkins Co.)

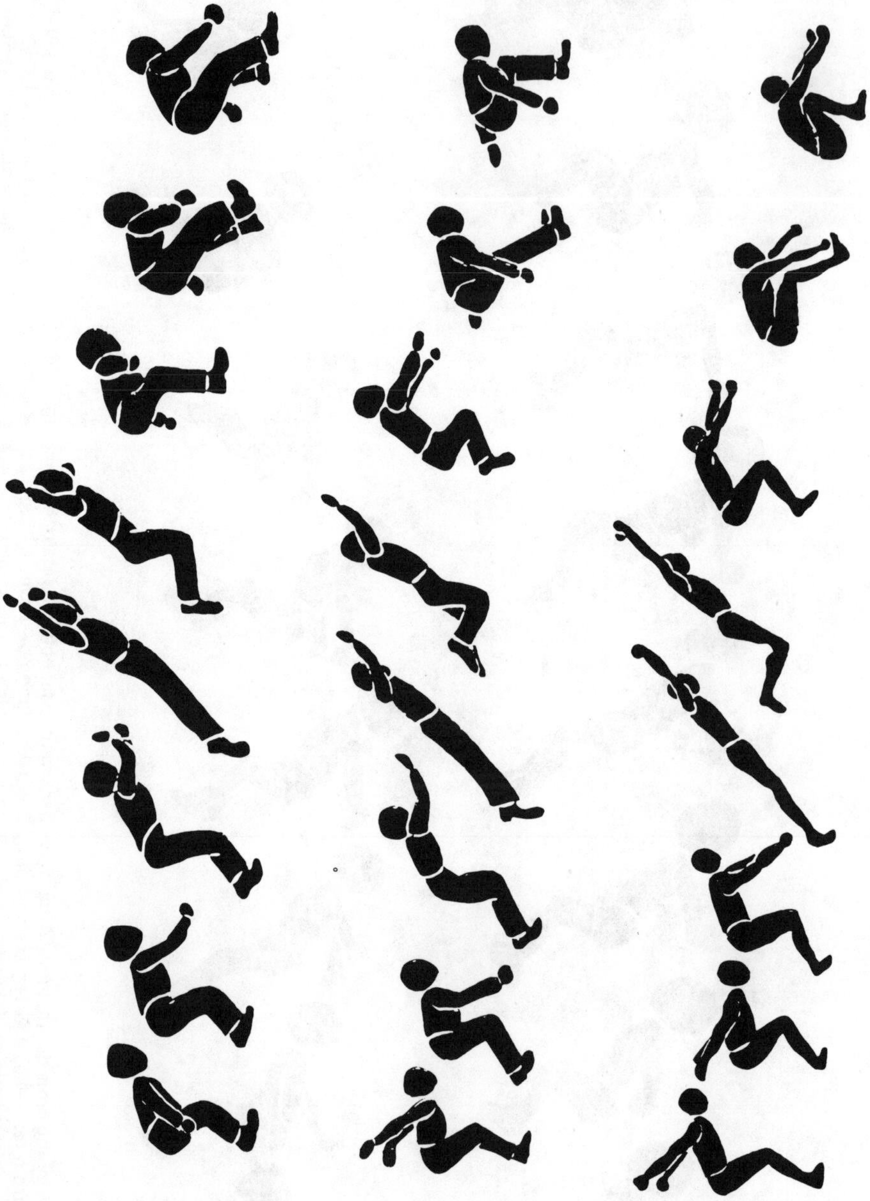

Figure 3.14. Two-footed takeoffs in the jump (Level 3). **A**, first grade: arm action at takeoff (fourth figure from left) and during flight and landing—Level 3. **B**, fourth grade: arm action at takeoff (fourth figure from left)—Level 4, arm action during flight and landing—Level 3. **C**, adult: arm action at takeoff—Level 5, arm action during flight and landing—Level 4. Trunk action at takeoff is Level 2 in A, Level 4 elsewhere. Trunk action during flight and landing is Level 1 in A, Level 2 in B, Level 3 in C. (Reprinted with permission from Hellebrandt et al. 1961, copyright by Williams & Wilkins Co.)

Table 3.4. Developmental Sequences for the Standing Long Jump[a]

Takeoff: Leg Action Component	
Level 1	One foot leads in asymmetrical takeoff.
Level 2	Both feet leave ground symmetrically, but hips or knees or both do not reach full extension by takeoff.
Level 3	Takeoff is symmetrical, with hips and knees fully extended.
Takeoff: Trunk Action Component	
Level 1	Trunk is inclined forward less than 30 degrees from vertical. Neck is hyperextended.
Level 2	Trunk leans forward less than 30 degrees, with neck flexed or aligned with trunk at takeoff.
Level 3	Trunk is inclined forward 30 degrees or more at takeoff, with neck flexed.
Level 4	Trunk is inclined forward 30 degrees or more. Neck is aligned with trunk, or slightly extended.
Takeoff: Arm Action Component	
Level 1	Arms move in opposition to legs or are held at side, with elbows flexed.
Level 2	Shoulders retract, arms extend backward in winging posture at takeoff.
Level 3	Arms are abducted about 90 degrees, with elbows frequently flexed, in high or middle guard position.
Level 4	Arms flex forward and upward with minimal abduction, reaching incomplete extension overhead by takeoff.
Level 5	Arms flex forward, reaching full extension overhead by takeoff.
Flight and Landing: Leg Action Component	
Level 1	Legs assume asymmetrical run pattern in flight, with one-footed landing.
Level 2	Legs assume asymmetrical run pattern, but swing to two-footed landing.
Level 3	During flight, hips and knees flex in a synchronous fashion. Knees then extend for two-footed landing.
Level 4	During flight, flexion of both knees precedes hip flexion. As hips flex, knees extend, reaching forward to two-footed landing.
Flight and Landing: Trunk Action Component	
Level 1	Trunk maintains forward inclination of less than 30 degrees in flight, then flexes for landing.
Level 2	Trunk corrects forward lean of 30 degrees or more by hyperextending. It then flexes forward for landing.
Level 3	Trunk maintains forward lean of 30 degrees or more from takeoff to midflight, then flexes forward for landing.
Flight and Landing: Arm Action Component	
Level 1	Arms move in opposition to legs as if child were running in flight and on landing.
Level 2	Shoulders retract and arms extend backward (winging) during flight and move forward (parachuting, page 51) during landing.
Level 3	During flight, arms assume high or middle guard positions and may move backward in windmill fashion. They parachute for landing.
Level 4	Arms lower or extend from flexed position overhead, reaching forward at landing.

[a]Validation of these sequences is in progress (VanSant, note 2).

Keogh (1965, 1968) has also experimented with several tests of hopping in place. Again, girls tended to be as much as a year ahead of boys. Rhythmical patterns emphasizing motor control (e.g., two hops right, two hops left) seemed particularly difficult for boys. At age five, 3% of the boys could pass a rhythmical hop test compared with 23% of the girls. By age nine, 67% of the boys and 87% of the girls passed the test (Keogh 1968). More recently, Denckla (1974) assessed children's ability to perform 50 hops in place. In contrast to Keogh's data, this task did not distinguish between boys and girls. Her data indicated that 85% of five-year-olds could do only 12 hops in place on at least one foot; 85% of six-year-olds, 25 hops; and 90% of seven-year-olds, 50 hops (at least).

Developmental Sequence Data

Roberton and Halverson (1977) presented developmental sequences for the hop for distance that were generated from longitudinal data. Halverson and Williams (1983) have recently modified the arm action component through cross-sectional validation. Table 3.5 lists the hopping sequences.

OBJECT PROJECTION SEQUENCES

Projecting an object forcefully demands that muscle groups be mobilized in a precise pattern of movement, each timed carefully in relation to the other. When object projection has accuracy rather than force as its goal, the movements used may change considerably. In general, force demands recruitment of many moving body parts, while accuracy demands stabilization of body parts.

Throwing, striking, and kicking are three common methods of projecting an object. Throwing and striking appear similar in many ways, although striking adds the further complication of having to hit a moving object. Recent research (Langendorfer 1982) suggests that if the ball for striking is suspended in midair, the developmental sequences of throwing and striking are similar. Only throwing is discussed here, since the throwing sequence has received considerable validation.

Throwing: Intratask Development

Performance Data

Considerable data have been collected over the years on the distances children can throw at various ages. A more valid reflection of force mobilization, however, is the actual velocity imparted to the ball. Figure 3.16 shows longitudinal ball velocity changes from kindergarten through seventh grade for a group of 39 children studied by Halverson, Roberton, and Langendorfer (1982). Girls increased their ball velocities approximately 2 to 4.5 ft/sec/year during elementary school. Boys increased 5 to 8 ft/sec/year. In kindergarten, the girls threw at 29 ft/sec; by seventh grade, they averaged 56 ft/sec. Kindergarten boys threw at 39 ft/sec; by seventh grade, they achieved 78 ft/sec.

Developmental Sequence Data

The developmental sequences for the overarm throw for force are the most extensively studied of any intratask sequence in motor development (Wild 1938; Seefeldt et al. 1972; Roberton 1977,

Table 3.5. Developmental Sequences for Hopping[a]

	Leg Action Component
Level 1	Momentary flight. Support knee and hip quickly flex, pulling (instead of projecting) foot from floor. Flight is momentary. Only one or two hops can be achieved. Swing leg is lifted high and held in inactive position to side or in front of body.
Level 2	Fall and catch, swing leg inactive. Swing leg is inactive and usually held in front of body, although sometimes position varies (Figure 3.15). Body leans forward, allowing still minimal knee and ankle extension to help body fall forward off support foot and then quickly catch itself again. Repeated hops are now possible.
Level 3	Projected takeoff, swing leg assists. Swing leg now pumps up and down to assist in projection. Range of swinging is insufficient to carry swing leg behind support leg as seen from side (Figure 3.15). Support leg now comes closer to full extension at takeoff.
Level 4	Projection delay, swing leg leads. Range of pumping action in swing leg is great enough to carry it behind support leg (seen when viewed from the side, Figure 3.15). Weight of child is now smoothly transferred along foot to ball before ankle and knee extend to takeoff.
	Arm Action Component
Level 1	Bilateral inactive. Arms are held bilaterally, usually high and out to side, although other positions behind or in front of body may occur. No movement of arms occurs.
Level 2	Bilateral reactive. Arms may exhibit some movement. During flight they assume winging or equilibration postures in reaction to precarious balance (Figure 3.15).
Level 3	Bilateral assist. Arms move up and down together, usually in front of body. Each arm may be held at different level during pumping action.
Level 4	Semiopposition. Arm on side opposite swing leg swings forward with that leg and back as leg moves down. Other arm is variable, often staying in front of body or to side (Figure 3.15).
Level 5	Opposing assist. Arm opposite swing leg moves forward and upward and down and back in synchrony with movement of that leg. Other arm moves in direction opposite to action of swing leg (Figure 3.15).

[a]These sequences were hypothesized by Roberton and Halverson (1977). Modification and validation has been reported in Halverson, L. E. & Williams, K. Cross-sectional evidence for developmental sequences in hopping. Motor development and child study laboratory, Department of Physical Education and Dance, University of Wisconsin–Madison. Manuscript in progress, 1983.

1978; Langendorfer 1980; Roberton and Langendorfer 1980; Halverson et al. 1982). Validation has also extended to profoundly and educable mentally retarded children (Roberton and DiRocco 1981). Because throwing for force demands the sequential action of many body parts, a number of critical components have been identified. These appear in Table 3.6.

Kicking: Intratask Development

Performance Data

DeOreo and Keogh (1980) created the graph in Figure 3.18 to summarize unpublished data on place kicking from Williams, Clement, Logsdon, Scott, and Temple, as well as published data

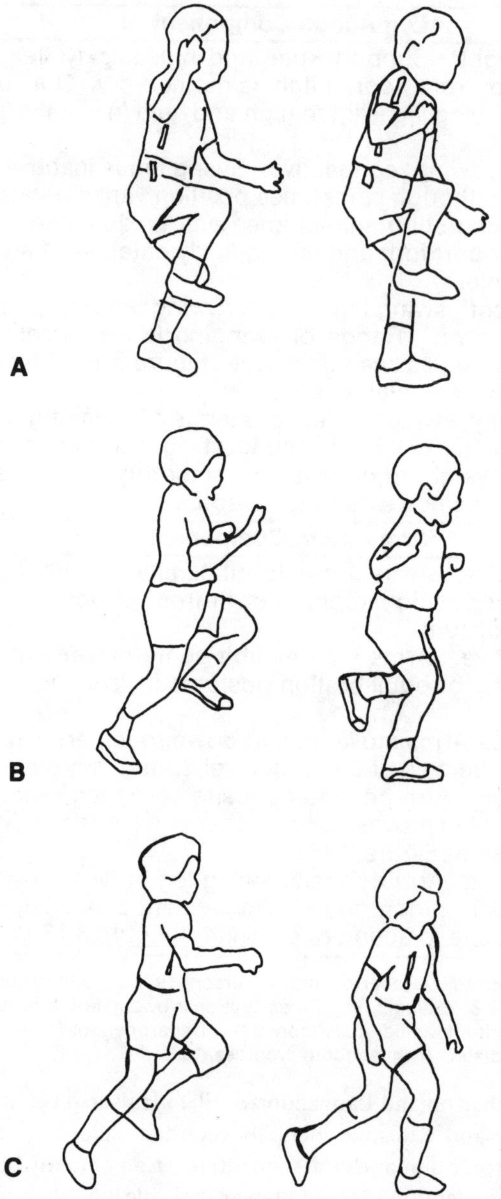

Figure 3.15. Key changes in development of hopping. **A**: Leg action—Level 2, swing leg remains stationary. Arm action—Level 2. **B**: Leg action—Level 3, swing leg begins pumping. Arm action—Level 5, arm opposite swing leg begins pumping. **C**: Leg action—Level 4, swing leg passes behind hopping leg. Arm action—Level 5, both arms move in opposition. (Drawn from longitudinal film collection, motor development and child study laboratory, Department of Physical Education and Dance, University of Wisconsin–Madison.)

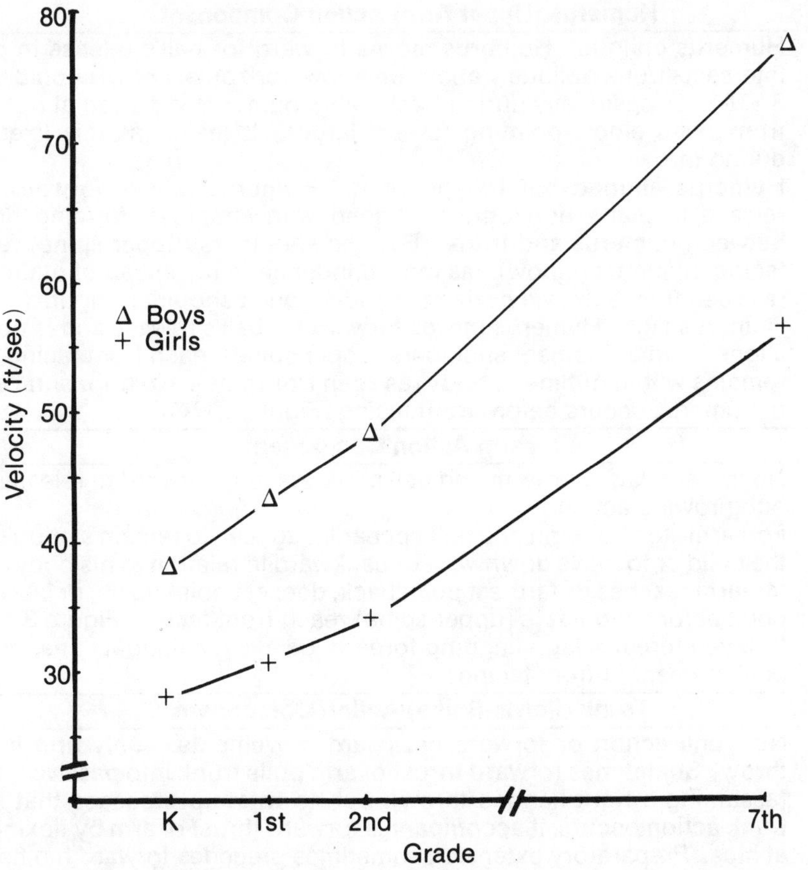

Figure 3.16. Longitudinal changes in ball velocities during overarm throw. (Data from Halverson, L., Roberton, M. A., & Langendorfer, S. Development of the overarm throw: Movement and ball velocity changes by seventh grade. *Research Quarterly for Exercise and Sport*, 1982, **53**, 198-205.)

Table 3.6. Developmental Sequences for the Overarm Throw for Force[a]

Preparatory Arm Backswing Component[b]	
Level 1	No backswing. Ball in hand moves directly forward to release from its position when hand first grasped ball.
Level 2	Elbow and humeral flexion. Ball moves away from intended line of flight to position behind or alongside head by upward flexion of humerus and concomitant elbow flexion.
Level 3	Circular, upward backswing. Ball moves away from intended line of flight to position behind head via circular overhead movement with elbow extended, or oblique swing back, or vertical lift from hip.
Level 4	Circular, downward backswing. Ball moves away from intended line of flight to position behind head via circular, down and back motion that carries hand below waist.

Table 3.6. (continued)

	Humerus (Upper Arm) Action Component
Level 1	Humerus oblique. Humerus moves forward for ball's release in plane that intersects trunk obliquely above or below horizontal line of shoulders (Figure 3.17A). Occasionally during backswing, humerus is placed at right angle to trunk, with elbow pointing toward target. It maintains this fixed position during throw.
Level 2	Humerus aligned but independent. Humerus moves forward for ball's release in plane horizontally aligned with shoulder, forming right angle between humerus and trunk. By time shoulders (upper spine) reach front facing, humerus (elbow) has moved independently ahead of outline of body (as seen from side) via horizontal adduction at shoulder (Figure 3.17B).
Level 3	Humerus lags. Humerus moves forward for ball's release and is horizontally aligned, but at moment shoulders (upper spine) reach front facing, humerus remains within outline of body (as seen from side). No horizontal adduction of humerus occurs before front facing (Figure 3.17C).
	Forearm Action Component
Level 1	No forearm lag. Forearm and ball move steadily forward to release throughout throwing action.
Level 2	Forearm lag. Forearm and ball appear to lag (i.e., to remain stationary behind the child or to move downward or backward in relation to his body). Lagging forearm reaches its farthest point back, deepest point down, or last stationary point *before* shoulders (upper spine) reach front facing (Figure 3.17).
Level 3	Delayed forearm lag. Lagging forearm delays reaching its final point of lag until moment of front facing.
	Trunk (Pelvis-Spine) Action Component
Level 1	No trunk action or forward-backward movements. Only arm is active in throw. Sometimes forward thrust of arm pulls trunk into passive left rotation (assuming a right-handed throw), but no twist-up precedes that action. If trunk action occurs, it accompanies forward thrust of arm by flexing forward at hips. Preparatory extension sometimes precedes forward hip flexion.
Level 2	Upper trunk rotation or total trunk block rotation. Spine and pelvis both rotate away from intended line of flight and then simultaneously begin forward rotation, acting as unit or block. Occasionally, only upper spine twists away and then twists toward direction of force. Pelvis then remains fixed, facing line of flight, or joins rotary movement after forward spinal rotation has begun.
Level 3	Differentiated rotation of trunk. Pelvis precedes upper spine in initiating forward rotation. Child twists away from intended line of ball flight and then begins forward rotation with pelvis while upper spine is still twisting away.
	Foot Action Component[c]
Level 1	No movement. Child throws from whatever position feet happen to be in.
Level 2	Child steps with foot on same side as throwing hand.
Level 3	Child steps with foot on opposite side from throwing hand.
Level 4	Child steps with opposite foot a distance of over half his standing height.

[a]Validation studies (Roberton 1977, 1978; Roberton and Langendorfer 1980; Roberton and DiRocco 1981; Halverson et al. 1982) support these sequences with the exception of notes b and c.

[b]Preparatory arm backswing sequence hypothesized from work of Langendorfer (1980).

[c]Foot action sequence hypothesized from work of Leme and Shambes (1978), Seefeldt et al. (1972), and Wild (1938).

Figure 3.17. Key changes in development of throwing. **A**: humerus action—Level 1, humerus is oblique to horizontal line of shoulders. **B**: humerus action—Level 2, humerus is horizontally aligned with shoulders, but by front facing, has independently adducted so that elbow is outside of outline of body. **C**: left, forearm action—Level 2, ball is at deepest lag before body has rotated to front facing. Right, forearm action—Level 3, ball is at deepest lag at front facing. Humerus action—Level 3, at front facing, humerus remains in line with body. (Drawn from longitudinal film collection, motor development and child study laboratory, Department of Physical Education and Dance, University of Wisconsin–Madison.)

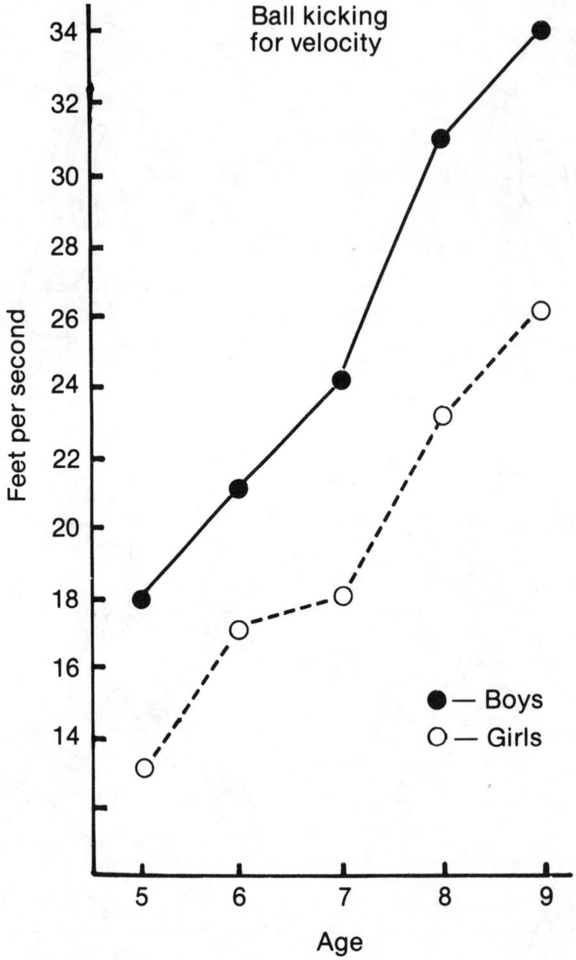

Figure 3.18. Age differences in place kicking ball velocity. (Reprinted with permission from DeOreo, K., & Keogh, J. Performance of fundamental motor tasks. In C. Corbin (Ed.), *A textbook of motor development*. (2nd ed.) Dubuque, Iowa: Brown, 1980, copyright by Wm. C. Brown Company, Publishers.)

from Dohrmann (1964). The graph shows the almost linear increase in velocity of the kicked ball for both boys and girls ages five through nine. Kicking for accuracy (Lathchaw 1954, Johnson 1962) also shows a steady increase across the elementary school years, with boys somewhat more accurate than girls. Punting follows the same trend, although girls may be as much as two grade levels behind boys in the distance they can punt (Hanson 1965).

Developmental Sequence Data

The running place kick evolves out of the walking-running pattern. Planting the support leg in the proper spatial relationship to the ball is the greatest developmental problem for the young kicker. Of even greater difficulty is the punt, in which the child has to drop a ball to coincide with the forward path of her kicking foot.

No developmental sequences have been validated for punting. Table 3.7 contains sequences hypothesized from the longitudinal study by Halverson and Roberton (1966) and Poe (1973), and the cross-sectional work of Wickstrom (1977) and Elliott, Bloomfield, and Davies (1980).

Object Reception

Skills under the classification of object reception include all those tasks in which an oncoming object is slowed and controlled by some part of the body (e.g., trapping in soccer) or by some implement held by a body part or parts (e.g., receiving a pass in hockey or lacrosse). Two general developmental difficulties in such skills are (1) timing the flexion of body parts to give as the object

Table 3.7. Developmental Sequences for Punting[a]

	Ball Release: Arm Component
Level 1	Hands are on sides of ball. Ball is tossed upward from both hands after support foot has landed (if step was taken).
Level 2	Hands are on sides of ball. Ball is dropped from chest height after support foot has landed (if step was taken).
Level 3	Hands are on sides of ball. Ball is lifted upward and forward from waist level and released as, or just prior to, landing of support foot (Figure 3.19).
Level 4	One hand is rotated to side and under ball. Other hand is rotated to side and top of ball. Hands carry ball on forward and upward path during approach. Ball is released at chest level as final approach stride begins (Figure 3.19).
	Ball Contact: Arm Component
Level 1	Arms drop bilaterally after ball is released to position on each side of hips at ball contact (Figure 3.19).
Level 2	Arms abduct bilaterally after ball is released. Arm on side of kicking leg may pull back as that leg swings forward.
Level 3	After ball is released, arms abduct bilaterally during flight. At ball contact, arm opposite kicking leg has swung forward with that leg. Arm on side of kicking leg remains abducted and to rear (Figure 3.19).
	Leg Action Component
Level 1	No step or one short step is taken. Kicking leg swings forward from position parallel or slightly behind support foot. Knee may be totally extended at contact or, more frequently, still flexed 90 degrees with contact above or below knee joint. Thigh is still moving upward at contact. Ankle tends to be flexed (Figure 3.19).
Level 2	Several steps may be taken. Last step onto support leg is long stride. Thigh of kicking leg has slowed or stopped forward motion at contact. Ankle is extended. Knee has 20 to 30 degrees of extension still possible by contact.
Level 3	Child may take several steps but last is actually a leap onto support foot. After contact, momentum of kicking leg pulls child off ground in a hop (Figure 3.19).

[a]These sequences have not been validated.

Figure 3.19. Key changes in development of punting. A: leg action—Level 1, arm action at ball release—Level 3, arm action at ball contact—Level 1. B: leg action—Level 2, arm action at ball release—Level 3, arm action at ball contact—Level 3. C: leg action—Level 3, arm action at ball release—Level 4, arm action at ball contact—Level 3. (Drawn from longitudinal film collection, motor development and child study laboratory, Department of Physical Education and Dance, University of Wisconsin–Madison.)

makes contact and (2) moving the body and body parts into the path of the object to make the reception.

Catching: Intratask Development

Since hand catching has received the most developmental study of the object reception tasks, it is the focus here.

Performance Data

Clear performance data on development in catching is difficult to present because many research studies have mixed levels of analysis when trying to define "success" or "able to catch." That is, most studies of catching have not used two separate variables, one for performance (number of catches or interceptions) and one for description (how the body parts were used in the catch attempt). Rather, they devised scoring systems that confounded the two levels of analysis by giving credit to the way in which the catch was made as well as to the success of the catch. Such studies still contribute knowledge about catching development in a general sense, but their scoring has made unclear precisely what was changing when a score changed.

In general, those studies most clearly using end product data (Seils 1951) report the customary, steady improvement across the elementary school years in the ability to intercept and retain control of an object. Paralleling this is a considerable improvement in children's abilities to estimate where a projected ball will land without having to catch the ball (Williams 1967).

Developmental Sequence Data

As Wickstrom (1977) has pointed out, catching is a difficult skill to describe developmentally because it is so clearly an open skill, one that has to conform to a changing environment. Thus, what the catcher does on any given catch reflects not only the movement options available in his nervous system (i.e., his developmental level) but also the constraints of ball size, distance the ball has traveled, speed of the ball, and other important environmental variables. With these limitations in mind, catching sequences in Table 3.8 have been hypothesized (but not validated) by Harper (1979) from the work of Seefeldt (1972), Hellweg (1972), and Wickstrom (1977).

SEX DIFFERENCES IN INTRATASK DEVELOPMENT

In almost every task considered thus far, clear-cut differences have existed in the mean performances of boys and girls of the same age. A comment is warranted about these differences.

First, sex differences occur between *mean* performances. At each age level, large individual differences within each sex indicate that the performance of many boys is similar to that of many girls. For instance, in the study of the ball velocities achieved by boys and girls in the overarm throw (Halverson et al. 1982), a dramatic difference between mean performances was evident (Figure 3.16). Yet the top female thrower in seventh grade was throwing with a ball velocity only 5 ft/sec less than the ball velocity of the top seventh grade boy (87 ft/sec versus 92 ft/sec).

From a developmental view, therefore, mean data by age are interesting but not particularly useful. The progress of each child must be considered in relation to that child—where she was before and where she is now. The true developmentalist looks at individual progress rather than comparison with a group norm.

Table 3.8. Developmental Sequences for Catching[a]

	Preparation: Arm Component
Level 1	Arms await ball toss, outstretched, with elbows extended (Figure 3.20A).
Level 2	Arms await ball toss, with some shoulder flexion still apparent but flexion now appearing in elbows.
Level 3	Arms await ball in relaxed posture at sides of body or slightly ahead of body. Elbows may be flexed.
	Reception: Arm Component
Level 1	Arms remain outstretched and elbows rigid. Little or no give occurs, so ball bounces off arms (Figure 3.20D).
Level 2	Elbows flex to carry hands upward toward face. Initially, ball contact is primarily with arms, and object is trapped against body (Figure 3.20E).
Level 3	Initial contact is with hands. If unsuccessful in using fingers, child may still trap ball against chest. Hands still move upward toward face.
Level 4	Ball contact is made with hands. Elbows still flex but shoulders extend, bringing ball down and toward body rather than up toward face (Figure 3.20F).
	Hand Component
Level 1	Palms of hands face upward (Figure 3.20A). (Rolling balls elicit palms-down, trapping action.)
Level 2	Palms of hands face each other.
Level 3	Palms of hands are adjusted to flight and size of oncoming object. Thumbs or little fingers are placed close together, depending on height of flight path (Figure 3.20C).
	Body Component
Level 1	No adjustment of body occurs in response to flight path of ball (Figure 3.20A).
Level 2	Arms and trunk begin to move in relation to ball's flight path (Figure 3.20B).
Level 3	Feet, trunk, and arms all move to adjust to path of oncoming ball (Figure 3.20C).

[a]These sequences have not been validated. They were hypothesized by Harper (1979).

To speculate on the reasons for sex differences in mean performance is still interesting. In general, these differences favor boys on force production tasks (jumping, throwing, kicking) and girls on balance and foot locomotion (hopping, skipping). Some of the sex differences may be attributable to differences in body size. For instance, the graphs showing performance score increases (Figures 3.7 to 3.11, 3.16, 3.18) are strikingly similar to each other and to charts of growth increases during childhood. A large portion of individual differences in performance may be related to individual differences in growth. Work by Peterson, Reuschlein, and Seefeldt (1974) suggested that up to 25% of the variance in performances of children in kindergarten through second grade may be related to measures of linearity and weight.

Differences in developmental levels attained may also be attributed, in some cases, to growth differences. For instance, Table 3.9 compares the developmental levels of boys and girls for the forearm action component of the overarm throw. The girls clearly lag behind the boys through the

Figure 3.20. Key changes in the development of catching. Changes in the body component: **A**, Level 1 (also Level 1 in preparation arm action and hand action); **B**, Level 2; **C**, Level 3 (also Level 3 in hand action). Changes in arm component at reception: **D**, Level 1; **E**, Level 2; **F**, Level 4. Arms are moving down. (Drawn from longitudinal film collection, motor development and child study laboratory, Department of Physical Education and Dance, University of Wisconsin–Madison.)

Table 3.9. Percentage of Children Distributed Across Developmental Levels for Forearm Action in the Overarm Throw for Force[a]

			Developmental Level		
Age Group	Sex	*n*	1	2	3
5-year-olds					
	M	13	30.8	69.2	0
	F	19	73.7	26.3	0
6-year-olds					
	M	38	34.2	68.4	5.3
	F	29	72.4	34.5	0
7-year-olds					
	M	39	25.6	66.7	10.3
	F	31	74.2	32.3	0
8-year-olds					
	M	27	18.5	85.2	3.7
	F	15	60.0	40.0	6.7

[a]Row percentage totals exceed 100% in cases in which children exhibited two model levels across trials.

Adapted from Roberton, M. A., & DiRocco, P. Validating a motor skill sequence for mentally retarded children. *American Corrective Therapy Journal,* 1981, **35**, 148–154.

age range listed. Haubenstricker and Sapp (1980) reported that the forearms of boys are 6 mm longer than those of girls by age 5½ and that this difference persists through the elementary school years. The forearm action component of the overarm throw could be affected by the length of the level involved. Thus, growth differences might, in some instances, affect developmental levels attained.

Of more importance, however, to the differences charted in Table 3.9 is the amount of practice that children give to a skill. In retrospective reports on time spent practicing the throw, seventh grade boys remembered considerably more practice over the years than did girls (Halverson et al. 1982). Whether a child places value on practicing a skill may, in turn, reflect cultural, sex-role expectations (Herkowitz 1978).

EFFECTS OF TRAINING ON MOTOR DEVELOPMENT

A discussion of the amount of practice children give to their motor skills leads quite naturally to the further question of the effects of teaching or intervention on children's motor development. Physical education literature is filled with attempts to affect performance scores through teaching. Locke and Nixon (1973) have reviewed this literature and pointed out many methodological flaws. Studies attempting to assess the effects of teaching on a motor development sequence itself are more rare.

Three basic questions can be asked about intervention effects on a developmental sequence: (1) whether the order of the sequence can be changed (i.e., whether children can be helped to skip levels in the sequence or to progress through a different sequence entirely), (2) if the order of the sequence does not change through teaching, whether instructed children can be accelerated through the sequence, and (3) whether certain ages within the life span are more conducive to intervention techniques than others. While the word intervention has been used here in a positive sense, it can also be used in a negative sense. Deprivation is a means of intervention, as is enrichment.

In general, these three questions have not been sufficiently answered, primarily because work on developmental sequences occurred in the early 1920s and 1930s, stopped, and only recently has received renewed interest. Thus, the dependent variable for enrichment or deprivation studies has not been available.

Deprivation Studies

Much of the available intervention research deals with the motor milestones of infancy. Deprivation studies (Dennis 1935, 1938; Spitz 1945; Dennis and Narjarian 1957) suggests that both the lack of opportunity for movement and perceptual stimulation does slow the infant's attainment of intertask milestones and may change the order in which certain milestones are reached. The severity of the retardation is related to the severity of the restriction. Where care is minimal, institutionalized youngsters show definite motor retardation (Provence and Lipton 1962); youngsters who are restricted somewhat but who are still given some chance for gross motor activity and perceptual stimulation seem to develop on schedule (Dennis and Dennis 1940). Little research has been done on following deprived infants into childhood. Consequently, whether deprived infants with infant motor retardation catch up, or whether those who seemed on schedule show later effects of their early deprivation, is not known.

Instruction and Training Studies

Because of the ethical problems in conducting deprivation studies on human children, enrichment is more often used as the experimental variable. Two classic studies on twins compared the intratask effects of motor skills in one twin who was trained with the other who was not trained. Both studies have usually been quoted as supporting the futility of early training. A close reading of the original studies leaves this conclusion in doubt. Gesell and Thompson (1929) selected two twins who were showing signs of readiness for stair climbing and cube building at 46 weeks. For 10 min a day over six weeks, one child (T) was stimulated to climb stairs and to build cube towers. At the end of training, the other twin (C) was given a two-week crash course in the same activities. After the two-week training, the authors were impressed that C seemed to have caught up to T in her motor development. They concluded that T's early training had been of no use, since the second twin had easily matched T's achievements with less practice when she was older. Their data, however, clearly showed that the trained twin was more agile, walked faster, and was less afraid of falling 16 weeks after the experiment. Even 26 weeks later, differences were still noted in favor of the trained child.

In an even more famous study of twins, McGraw (1935, 1975) trained one youngster, Johnny, in a variety of motor activities from the age of 21 days until he was 22 months old. His brother, Jimmy, was kept in a crib in the laboratory during the training sessions. McGraw found that the degree to which the training affected specific sequences in Johnny's motor development depended on a number of factors. The first was the level of the nervous system most in control of the sequence. Behavior controlled subcortically showed little result of training. The second was the degree to which the sequence was fundamental to the child as a biologically normal human being.

These phylogenetic skills, such as walking, could be modified in minor ways only. The third was the degree to which the behavior was idiosyncratic to the child. Activities not fundamental to life (ontogenetic skills), such as roller skating, were most affected by training. The fourth factor was that the degree to which even ontogenetic skills would be affected depended on the plasticity of the behavior pattern at the time the training was introduced. Those times when a skill seemed most affected by the environment were considered critical periods during which intervention was found to be most effective (McGraw 1946).

For some reason, citations of McGraw's (1935, 1975) study have focused on her comments about phylogenetic skills and concluded that her research found that intervention did not affect motor development. Quite to the contrary, McGraw concluded that intervention not only had influenced specific skills but also had had a general influence on the children's total motor behavior. In a follow-up study of Johnny and Jimmy at six years of age (McGraw 1939), Johnny still exhibited "greater motor coordination and daring in physical performances," while Jimmy was "more awkward and timid" in his motor behavior. Films of the two youngsters at age 21[2] still revealed decided differences in favor of the trained twin. McGraw, however, has carefully pointed out that many variables had intervened between the time of her experiment and the entrance of these two men into adulthood. Also, Johnny and Jimmy were fraternal rather than identicial twins.

A more recent intervention study focused on effecting changes in the overarm throwing sequence (Halverson and Roberton 1979). A group of kindergarten children was given a variety of experiences designed to improve their throwing skills. The teacher was unaware of the specific levels that occurred within the throwing sequence, although she was knowledgeable about the advanced throw and about the early developmental work of Wild (1938). Instruction took place for 120 min over a 12-week period. Films of the instructed children were then made for comparison with films of a group of kindergarten children receiving physical education but no throwing practice and with films of a second group of kindergarteners receiving no physical education at all.

The movement components that had been affected by the instruction were action of the forearm, trunk, and foot. The children who had made developmental progress in these components had been accelerated in rate in comparison with the control groups, but they were still going through the sequence in the same order. Humerus action had not been affected by the instruction, nor had ball velocity (Halverson et al. 1977).

McGraw (1946) and Thompson and Grusec (1970) have all reviewed literature dealing with environmental effects on motor development. These reviews, however, have distinguished neither the level of analysis used to access motor development in each research report nor the type of developmental sequence under study, whether intratask or intertask. Until that is done, the best conclusion seems to be that the rate of acquisition of all motor sequences can be affected by severe deprivation. The order of intertask sequences probably can be affected as well. Enrichment, or extra instruction, seems of little use for infants in normal environments, although many claims are to the contrary (Ridenour 1978). Intratask motor sequences of the ontogenetic variety are clearly affected by instruction, with the children's rate of acquisition most susceptible to modification. What is unclear, however, is which of the motor skills of childhood are ontogenetic and which are phylogenetic. In 1969, Espenschade and Eckert saw little evidence that running, jumping, or

2. McGraw, M. *Growth—A study of Johnny and Jimmy*. A 16-mm film sequence assembled for the International Jubilee Congress of Sports Medicine, Moscow, May 1958, motor development and child study laboratory, Department of Physical Education and Dance, University of Wisconsin–Madison.

throwing could be modified; in 1980, they had decided that throwing skills might be affected by instruction. Halverson and Roberton (1979) were able to affect only some throwing components. They were also unable to affect an end product measure—ball velocity.

Sensitive Periods

Finally, all discussion of intervention must be considered in relation to the timing of the intervention. As McGraw (1946) pointed out, at certain times, now called "sensitive periods" (Seefeldt 1975; Oyama 1979), the child may be more able to profit from intervention than at other times. To make the issue more complex, these sensitive periods seem to differ for each skill (McGraw 1946). Thus, training does affect motor developent, but the degree to which it does depends on when the training occurs, the type of skill, the component within the skill, and perhaps, the developmental level of the child.

As more motor development sequences are validated, they can then be used reliably as dependent variables in intervention studies. Until that time, the uncertainty of our knowledge presents an exciting challenge to teachers and researchers alike.

SUMMARY

The orderly way in which motor behavior changes over time has encouraged scientists to chart *intertask* and *intratask motor sequences.* The most well-known intertask sequence, sometimes referred to as the *motor milestones*, leads to the development of walking skills. Underlying these milestones is the development of key *postural reactions.* These *righting, parachute*, and *equilibrium* reactions act as supportive elements in attaining voluntary control. As the postural reactions appear, certain contents of the *neonatal* motor repertoire disappear. These *primitive reflexes* are inhibited by higher brain centers. Thus, motor development is characterized both by the coming-to-be and by the passing-away of various motor behaviors.

As childhood proceeds, the child works at mastering the locomotor, manipulative, and nonlocomotor tasks demanded for success in the play, school, and home environments. This mastery takes most of the childhood years. Some children never achieve advanced levels in all skills. This long childhood period of attainment has drawn scientists' attention to the description of intratask sequences. These verbal descriptions of *changes in the spatial-temporal patterning of body parts* during motor performance typify one *level of analysis* in the study of motor development. Other descriptive levels of analysis are *performance score changes* over time and changes in the *kinematic parameters* of movement.

Intratask sequences have been described for *components* of the body's movement as it accomplishes a task. While all children seem to pass through the levels of the sequences for each component, they do so *at their own rate.* Thus, the profile across components that describes the child's total movement at any one age may be quite different from the profile of another child of the same age. By assessing a child's developmental level in each component of a skill, the teacher can tell which component should be the focus of instruction for any child at any point in time.

Research on whether *deprivation* and *teaching* affect progress through motor sequences has focused on (1) whether the *order* of a sequence can be changed, (2) whether children can be *slowed or accelerated* through the sequence, and (3) whether children have some periods in life that are more *susceptible* to intervention than other periods. Much more research is needed on this question. Available studies suggest that all motor sequences can be affected by severe deprivation.

The effect of teaching, on the other hand, seems dependent on (1) when the teaching occurs, (2) the type of motor sequence involved (intertask or intratask), (3) the type of motor skill (*phylogenetic* or *ontogenetic*), (4) the component within the skill, and perhaps, (5) the current developmental level exhibited within the component. These questions are some of the interesting challenges that future teachers and researchers need to investigate.

REFERENCES

Barrett, K. R. Observation for teaching and coaching. *Journal of Physical Education and Recreation*, 1979, **50** (1), 23-25.

Bernstein, N. *The coordination and regulation of movements*. London: Pergamon Press, 1967.

Birnholz, J., Stephens, J., & Faria, M. Fetal movement patterns: A possible means of defining neurologic developmental milestones in utero. *American Journal of Roentgenology*, 1978, **130**, 537-540.

Breihan, S. Consistency of arm-leg opposition in performing three tasks. *Perceptual and Motor Skills*, 1982, **54**, 203-208.

Cooper, J., Adrian, M., & Glassow, R. *Kinesiology*. (5th ed.) St. Louis: Mosby, 1982.

Damon, A. Discrepancies between findings of longitudinal and cross-sectional studies in adult life: Physique and physiology. *Human Development*, 1965, **8**, 16-22.

Denkla, M. Development of motor coordination in normal children. *Developmental Medicine and Child Neurology*, 1974, **16**, 729-741.

Dennis, W. The effect of restricted practice upon the reaching, sitting, and standing of two infants. *Journal of Genetic Psychology*, 1935, **47**, 17-32.

Dennis, W. Infant development under conditions of restricted practice and of minimum social stimulation: A preliminary report. *Journal of Genetic Psychology*, 1938, **53**, 149-158.

Dennis, W., & Dennis, M. The effect of cradling practices on the age of walking in Hopi children. *Journal of Genetic Psychology*, 1940, **56**, 77-86.

Dennis, W., & Narjarian, P. Infant development under environmental handicap. *Psychological Monographs*, 1957, **71**, No. 7.

DeOreo, K., & Keogh, J. Performance of fundamental motor tasks. In C. B. Corbin (Ed.), *A textbook of motor development*. (2nd ed.) Dubuque, Iowa: Brown, 1980.

Dohrmann, P. Throwing and kicking ability of 8-year-old boys and girls. *Research Quarterly*, 1964, **35**, 464-471.

Elliot, B., Bloomfield, J., & Davies, C. Development of the punt kick: A cinematographic analysis. *Journal of Human Movement Studies*, 1980, **6**, 142-150.

Espenschade, A. Motor development. In W. R. Johnson (Ed.), *Science and Medicine of Exercise and Sport*. New York: Harper & Row, 1960.

Espenschade, A., & Eckert, H. *Motor development*. Columbus, Ohio: Merrill, 1969, 1980.

Gesell, A. The ontogenesis of infant behavior. In L. Carmichael (Ed.), *Manual of child psychology*. New York: Wiley, 1946.

Gesell, A., & Thompson, H. Learning and growth in identical infant twins: An experimental study of the method of co-twin control. *Genetic Psychology Monographs*, 1929, **6**, 1-124.

Halverson, L. E., & Roberton, M. A. A study of motor pattern development in young children. Research report to the National Convention of the American Association for Health, Physical Education, and Recreation, Chicago, 1966.

Halverson, L. E., & Roberton, M. A. The effects of instruction on overhand throwing development in children. In G. Roberts & K. Newell (Eds.), *Psychology of motor behavior and sport—1978*. Champaign, Illinois: Human Kinetics, 1979.

Halverson, L. E., Roberton, M. A., & Langendorfer, S. Development of the overarm throw: Movement and ball velocity changes by seventh grade. *Research Quarterly for Exercise and Sport*, 1982, **53**, 198-205.

Halverson, L. E., & Roberton, M. A., Safrit, M. J., & Roberts, T. Effect of guided practice on overhand-throw ball velocities of kindergarten children. *Research Quarterly*, 1977, **48**, 311-318.

Hanson, M. Motor pattern testing of elementary school age children. Unpublished doctoral dissertation, University of Washington, 1965.

Harper, C. J. Learning to observe children's motor development. Part III. Observing children's motor development in the gymnasium. Paper presented to the National Convention of the American Alliance for Health, Physical Education, and Recreation, New Orleans, 1979.

Haubenstricker, J., & Sapp, M. A longitudinal look at physical growth and motor performance: Implications for elementary and middle school activity programs. Paper presented to the National Convention of the American Alliance for Health, Physical Education, Recreation, and Dance, Detroit, 1980.

Hellebrandt, F., Rarick, G. L., Glassow, R., & Carns, M. Physiological analysis of basic motor skills. I. Growth and development of jumping. *American Journal of Physical Medicine*, 1961, **40**, 14-25.

Hellweg, D. An analysis of perceptual and performance characteristics of the catching skill in 6-7 year old children. Unpublished doctoral dissertation, University of Wisconsin–Madison, 1972.

Herkowitz, J. Sex-role expectations and motor behavior of the young child. In M. Ridenour (Ed.), *Motor development: Issues and applications.* Princeton, New Jersey: Princeton Book Co., 1978.

Hooker, D. *The prenatal origin of behavior.* Lawrence, Kansas: University of Kansas Press, 1952.

Jenkins, L. *A comparative study of motor achievements of children five, six, and seven years of age.* New York: Teachers College, Columbia University, 1930.

Johnson, R. Measurements of achievement in fundamental skills of elementary school children. *Research Quarterly*, 1962, **33**, 94-103.

Keogh, J. *Motor performance of elementary school children.* Technical report for PHSR Grant MHO8319-01 (NIHM) and HD 01059 (NICHHD). Department of Physical Education, University of California, Los Angeles, 1965.

Keogh, J. *Developmental evaluation of limb movement tasks.* Technical report 1-68 (USPHS Grant HD 01059), Department of Physical Education, University of California, Los Angeles, 1968.

Langendorfer, S. Longitudinal evidence for development changes in the preparatory phase of the overarm throw for force. Report to the Research Section, National Convention of the American Alliance for Health, Physical Education, Recreation, and Dance, Detroit, 1980.

Langendorfer, S. Developmental relationships between throwing and striking: A pre-longitudinal test of motor stage theory. Unpublished doctoral dissertation. University of Wisconsin–Madison, 1982.

Latchaw, M. Measuring selected motor skills in fourth, fifth, and sixth grades. *Research Quarterly*, 1954, **25**, 439-449.

Leme, S., & Shambes, G. Immature throwing patterns in normal adult women. *Journal of Human Movement Studies*, 1978, **4**, 85-93.

Locke, L., & Nixon, J. Research on teaching physical education. In R. Travers (Ed.), *Second handbook of research on teaching.* Chicago: Rand McNally, 1973.

McGraw, M. Later development of children specially trained during infancy. *Child Development*, 1939, **10**, 1-19.

McGraw, M. Maturation of behavior. In L. Carmichael (Ed.), *Manual of child psychology.* New York: Wiley, 1946.

McGraw, M. *Neuromuscular maturation of the human infant.* New York: Hafner, 1963. (Originally published: 1943.)

McGraw, M. *Growth: A study of Johnny and Jimmy.* New York: Arno, 1975. (Originally published: 1935.)

Milani-Comparetti, A. The neurophysiologic and clinical implications of studies on fetal motor behavior. *Seminars in Perinatology*, 1981, **5**, 183-189.

Milani-Comparetti, A., & Gidoni, E. Routine developmental examination in normal and retarded children. *Developmental Medicine and Child Neurology*, 1967, **9**, 631-638.

Molnar, G. Analysis of motor disorder in retarded infants and young children. *American Journal of Mental Deficiency*, 1978, **83**, 213-222.

Okamato, T. EMG study of the learning process in walking in 1- and 2-year old infants. *Biomechanics III.* Karger: Basel, 1973.

Oyama, S. The concept of the sensitive period in the developmental studies. *Merrill-Palmer Quarterly*, 1979, **25**, 83-103.

Peiper, A. *Cerebral function in infancy and childhood.* New York: Consultants Bureau, 1963.

Peterson, K., Reuschlein, P., & Seefeldt, V. Factor analyses of motor performance for kindergarten, first, and second grade: A tentative solution. Report presented to the Research Section, National Convention of the American Association for Health, Physical Education, and Recreation, Anaheim, California, 1974.

Poe, A. Developmental changes in the movement characteristics of the punt. A case study. Report presented to the Research Section, National Convention of the American Association for Health, Physical Education, and Recreation, Minneapolis, 1973.

Provence, S., & Lipton, R. C. *Infants in institutions.* New York: International Universities Press, 1962.

Ridenour, M. Programs to optimize infant motor development. In M. Ridenour (Ed.), *Motor development: Issues and applications.* Princeton, New Jersey: Princeton Book Co., 1978.

Roberton, M. A. Stability of stage categorizations across trials: Implications for the "stage theory" of overarm throw development. *Journal of Human Movement Studies*, 1977, **3**, 49-59.

Roberton, M. A. Longitudinal evidence for developmental stages in the forceful overarm throw. *Journal of Human Movement Studies*, 1978, **4**, 161-175.

Roberton, M. A., & DiRocco, P. Validating a motor skill sequence for mentally retarded children. *American Corrective Therapy Journal*, 1981, **35**, 148-154.

Roberton, M. A., & Halverson, L. E. The developing child—His changing movement. In B. Logsdon (Ed.), *Physical education for children: A focus on the teaching process.* Philadelphia: Lea & Febiger, 1977.

Roberton, M. A., & Langendorfer, S. Testing motor development sequences across 9-14 years. In C. Nadeau, W. Halliwell, K. Newell, & G. Roberts (Eds.), *Psychology of motor behavior and sport—1979.* Champaign, Illinois: Human Kinetics, 1980.

Seefeldt, V. Developmental sequence of catching skill. Paper presented to the National Convention of the American Association for Health, Physical Education, and Recreation. Houston, March 1972.

Seefeldt, V. Critical learning periods and programs of early intervention. Paper presented to the National Convention of the American Alliance for Health, Physical Education, and Recreation, Atlantic City, New Jersey, March 1975.

Seefeldt, V., Reuschlein, S., & Vogel, P. Sequencing motor skills within the physical education curriculum. Paper presented to the National Convention of the American Association for Health, Physical Education, and Recreation, Houston, March 1972.

Seils, L. G. The relationship between measures of physical growth and gross motor performance of primary grade school children. *Research Quarterly*, 1951, **22**, 244-260.

Smith, S. A. Longitudinal changes in stride length and stride rate during sprint running. Unpublished master's thesis, University of Wisconsin–Madison, 1977.

Spitz, R. Hospitalism: An inquiry into the genesis of psychiatric conditions in early childhood. *Psychoanalytic Study of the Child*, 1945, **1**, 53-74.

Thompson, W., & Grusec, J. Studies of early experience. In P. Mussen (Ed.), *Carmichael's manual of child psychology.* Vol. 1. New York: Wiley, 1970.

Wickstrom, R. *Fundamental motor patterns.* (2nd ed.) Philadelphia: Lea & Febiger, 1977.

Wild, M. The behavior pattern of throwing and some observations concerning its course of development in children. *Research Quarterly*, 1938, **9**, 20-24.

Williams, H. Perception of moving objects by children. *Research Abstracts* of the 1967 Convention of the American Association for Health, Physical Education, and Recreation, 1967.

SUGGESTED READINGS

Undergraduate Students

Prenatal Development

Nilsson, L., Wirsen, C., & Ingelman-Sundberg, A. *A child is born: The drama of life before birth.* New York: Dell Publishing, 1966.

Infant Motor Development

Milani-Comparetti, A., & Gidoni, E. Routine developmental examination in normal and retarded children. *Developmental Medicine and Child Neurology*, 1967, **9**, 631-638.

Molnar, G. Analysis of motor disorder in retarded infants and young children. *American Journal of Mental Deficiency*, 1978, **83**, 213-222.

Twitchell, T. E. Attitudinal reflexes. *Journal of the American Physical Therapy Association*, 1965, **45**, 411-418.

Skills Development in Childhood

Espenschade, A., & Eckert, H. *Motor development*. Columbus, Ohio: Merrill, 1980.

Halverson, L. Development of motor patterns in young children. *Quest*, 1966, **6**, 44-53.

Roberton, M. A., & Halverson, L. E. *Developing children—Their changing movement: A guide for teachers*. Philadelphia: Lea & Febiger, 1983.

Seefeldt, V., Reuschlein, S., & Vogel, P. Sequencing motor skills within the physical education curriculum. Paper presented to the National Convention of the American Association for Health, Physical Education, and Recreation, 1972.

Wickstrom, R. *Fundamental motor patterns*. Philadelphia: Lea & Febiger, 1977.

Observing and Using Motor Sequences in Teaching

Barrett, K. R. Observation for teaching and coaching. *Journal of Physical Education and Recreation*, 1979. **50** (1), 23-25.

Cohen, D. The young child . . . Observing to learn. In G. Engstrom (Ed.), *The significance of the young child's motor development*. Washington, D.C.: National Association for the Education of Young Children, 1971.

Langendorfer, S., & Roberton, M. A. Observing children's motor development: A component analysis. *Journal of the Wisconsin Association for Health, Physical Education, and Recreation*, 1980, **9**, 14-15.

Roberton, M. A., & Halverson, L. E. *Developing children—Their changing movement: A guide for teachers*. Philadelphia: Lea & Febiger, 1983.

Sex Differences in Motor Development

Herkowitz, J. Sex-role expectations and motor behavior of the young child. In M. Ridenour (Ed.), *Motor development: Issues and applications*. Princeton, New Jersey: Princeton Book Co., 1978.

Lewko, J., & Greendorfer, S. Family influence and sex differences in children's socialization into sport: A review. In D. Landers & R. Christina (Eds.), *Psychology of motor behavior and sport—1977*. Champaign, Illinois: Human Kinetics, 1978.

Effects of Instruction on Motor Development

Halverson, L. E., & Roberton, M. A. The effects of instruction on overhand throwing development in children. In G. Roberts & K. Newell (Eds.), *Psychology of motor behavior and sport—1978*. Champaign, Illinois: Human Kinetics, 1979.

McGraw, M. Maturation of behavior. In L. Carmichael (Ed.), *Manual of child psychology*. New York: Wiley, 1946.

Ridenour, M. Programs to optimize infant motor development. In M. Ridenour (Ed.), *Motor development: Issues and applications*. Princeton, New Jersey: Princeton Book Co., 1978.

Graduate Students

The main readings for any topic should be the references cited in that section of this chapter. A few other suggested readings not previously cited for a specific topic are listed below. Graduate students with minimal background in motor development should begin with the undergraduate readings.

Fetal and Infant Motor Development

Clark, D., Kreutzberg, J., & Chee, F. Vestibular stimulation influence on motor development in infants. *Science*, 1977, **196**, 1228-1229.

Milani-Comparetti, A. The neurophysiologic and clinical implications of studies of fetal motor behavior. *Seminars in Perinatology*, 1981, **5**, 183-189.

Pontius, A. Neuro-ethics of walking in the newborn. *Perceptual and Motor Skills*, 1973, **37**, 235-245.

Zelazo, P., Kolb, S., & Zelazo, N. Newborn walking: A reply to Pontius. *Perceptual and Motor Skills*, 1974, **39**, 423-428.

Zelazo, P., Zelazo, N., & Kolb, S. Walking in newborns. *Science*, 1972, **176**, 314-375.

Motor Sequence Theory

Flavell, J. An analysis of cognitive-developmental sequences. *Genetic Psychology Monographs*, 1972, **86**, 279-350.

Roberton, M. A. Describing 'stages' within and across motor tasks. In J. A. S. Kelso & J. Clark (Eds.), *The development of movement control and coordination*. New York: Wiley, 1982.

Roberton, M. A., Williams, K., & Langendorfer, S. Prelongitudinal screening of motor development sequences. *Research Quarterly for Exercise and Sport*, 1980, **51**, 724-731.

Seefeldt, V., Reuschlein, S., & Vogel, P. Sequencing motor skills within the physical education curriculum. Paper presented to the National Convention of the American Association for Health, Physical Education, and Recreation, Houston, Texas, 1972.

Wohlwill, J. The study of development stages. *The study of behavioral development*. New York: Academic Press, 1973.

Descriptive Studies of Historical Interest

Bayley, N. The development of motor abilities during the first three years: A study of sixty-one infants tested repeatedly. *Monographs of the Society for Research in Child Development*, 1935, **1**, 1-26.

Bayley, N. *Manual for the Bayley scales of infant development*. New York: Psychological Corp., 1969.

Deach, D. Genetic development of motor skills of children two through six years of age. Unpublished doctoral dissertation. University of Michigan, 1958.

Espenschade, A. Motor development. In W. Johnson (Ed.), *Science and medicine of exercise and sports*. New York: Harper & Row, 1960.

Frankenburg, W., & Dodds, J. The Denver developmental screening test. *Journal of Pediatrics*, 1967, **71**, 181-191.

Gutteridge, M. V. A study of motor achievements of young children. *Archives of Psychology*, No. 244, 1939.

Halverson, H. M. An experimental study of prehension in infants by means of systematic cinema records. *Genetic Psychology Monographs*, 1931, **10**, 107-286.

Halverson, L. Development of motor patterns in young children. *Quest*, 1966, **6**, 44-53.

Shirley, M. *The first two years: A study of twenty-five babies*. Vol. 1. Minneapolis: University of Minnesota Press, 1931.

Laboratory 3 from Chapter 14 should be used at the completion of this chapter.

4

Children's Motor Skill Development

Jerry R. Thomas

A number of factors that influence motor skill development have already been reviewed in this book: physical growth (Chapter 1), exercise (Chapter 2), and fundamental motor patterns (Chapter 3). The purpose of this chapter is to discuss how cognitive processes influence skilled performance during the childhood and adolescent years. The chapter particularly focuses on the normal development of cognitive processes that influence performance. In addition, emphasis is placed on how these cognitive processes may be influenced so that the performances of younger children become more similar to those of older children and adults. In pursuing this purpose, I concentrate more on applying research to real examples rather than providing complete coverage of the literature.

The application of research to real settings is sometimes referred to as *ecological validity*. Obtaining ecological validity is difficult, and was described by Bronfenbrenner (1979) as "being caught between a rock and a soft place. The rock is rigor and the soft place relevance." What he meant is that in laboratory research, many controls are used ("rigor" or the "rock"). However, in the real (ecologically valid) setting, people may not respond in the same way ("relevance" or the "soft place"). Thus, researchers frequently sacrifice relevance (application of the findings) to gain control of the setting (rigor). Bronfenbrenner (1979) was also correct about motor development: "Much of contemporary developmental psychology is the science of the strange behavior of children in strange situations with strange adults for the briefest possible periods of time." This issue has been debated in several places, including the physical education literature (Martens 1979, Siedentop 1980, Thomas 1980).

I am identifying the ecological validity issue because I take some license in this chapter in suggesting applications of findings from controlled research settings to real situations. These suggestions and generalizations may not work exactly as indicated here. Nevertheless, I intend to apply the laboratory setting to the real setting because of the benefits to be derived from doing so.

MEMORY MODEL

Before studying the cognitive factors in children's motor skill development, a brief overview of the functioning of the memory system is appropriate.

Figure 4.1 is a common model of information processing (Thomas, Thomas, and Gallagher 1981) listing several control processes in short-term memory store that develop over the childhood years. Much controversy has revolved around what develops in the memory system—the *structure* (Pascual-Leone and Smith 1969) or *function* (Chi 1976; Thomas 1980). However, the majority of American psychologists appear to favor the idea that function is what changes, and that the size of memory does not change. Increased performance across the childhood years appears to be the result of more efficient memory function along with a larger base of experience. If this is so, and if memory is compared to a computer, then the size of the computer does not change; however, the programming becomes better, and more knowledge and programs are available.

Considerable evidence shows that the memory system operates more slowly in children than in adults (Wickens 1974, Chi 1977; Chi and Gallagher 1982). A specific example, Figure 4.2 depicts the changes for males and females in reaction time across the childhood years. These reaction time measurements involve the release of a telegraphic key as rapidly as possible after a visual stimulus. Note the decline of about 40 msec every two years and that male performance is in advance of females by about two years. However, reaction time may only reflect a better learned (or more automatic) response on the part of the adults. Gallagher and Thomas (1980b) pointed this out by manipulating the post-KR interval. Figure 4.3 shows how the responses of adults and seven-year-olds become more similar on a rapid timing task when the children were given more time to use

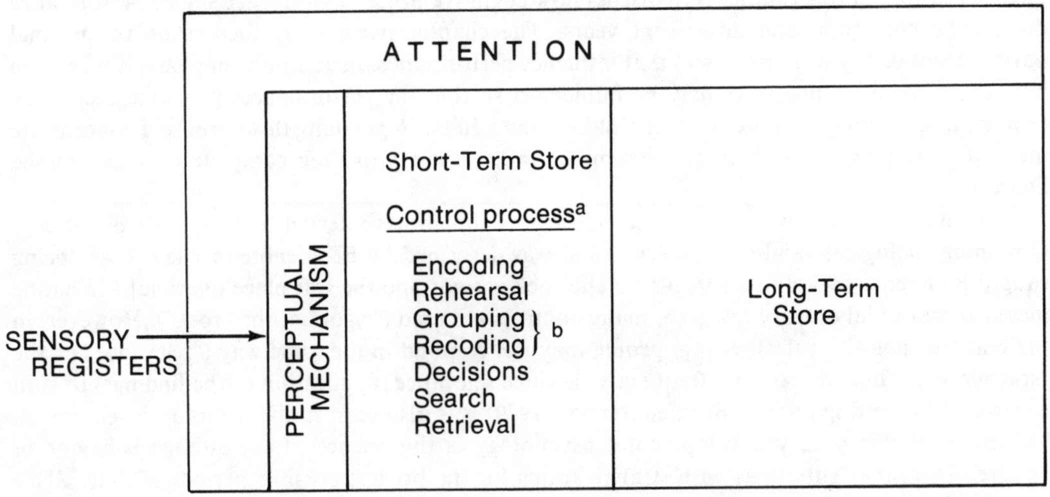

Figure 4.1. Information processing model with developmental implications. (From Thomas, J. R., Thomas, K. T., & Gallagher, J. D. Introduction: Children's processing of information in physical activity and sport. In A. Morris (Ed.), *Motor development: Theory into practice.* New Town, Connecticut: Motor Skills: Theory Into Practice, 1981, 3.)

[a]Control processes develop across childhood.

[b]Grouping and recoding together represent organization in memory.

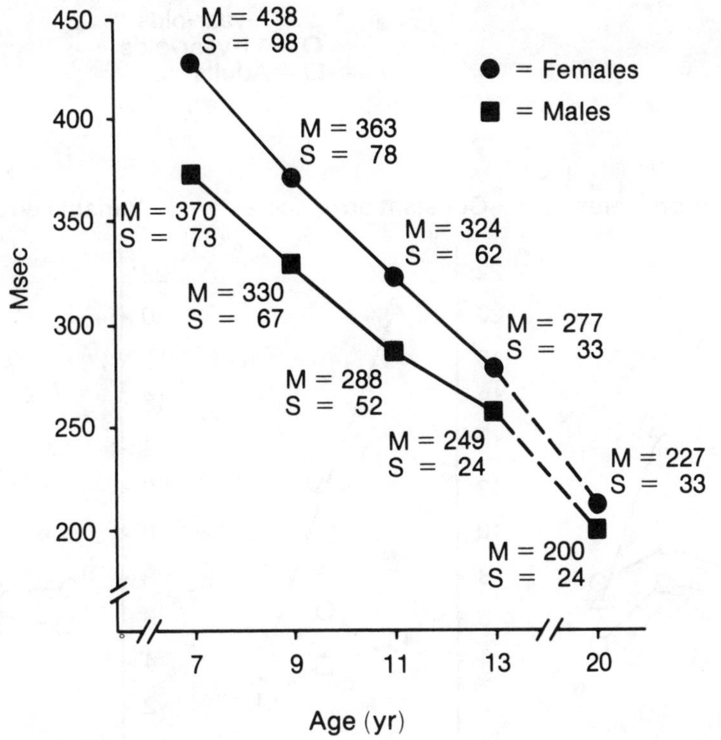

Figure 4.2. Means and standard deviations for reaction time by age and gender. (Reprinted with permission from Thomas, J. R., Gallagher, J. D., & Purvis, G. J. Reaction time and anticipation time: Effects of development. *Research Quarterly for Exercise and Sport*, 1981, **52**, 359-367.)

error information from the previous trial to correct the next movement. The task was to move a handle 40 cm in 400 msec. After the movement, an interval of 15 sec was provided before the next trial. At either 3, 6, or 12 sec before the next trial, the subject was given knowledge of results (KR) about the degree to which the last movement had been too fast or too slow. Thus, the children had either 3, 6, or 12 sec to use the KR to improve performance on the next trial. As more time was given to the seven-year-olds to use the information about their error on the previous trial, they did better on the next trial. If the seven-year-olds had only 3 sec, their performance was much poorer when compared with the adults, but when given 12 sec, the seven-year-olds' performance was equivalent to the adults' performance. This suggests that some of the memory processes are operating more slowly in the younger children. However, given enough time (on a simple task) to process the available information and correct the next movement, the children's and adults' performance were similar.

Sensory Registers

What then develops in the memory system over age that influences children's motor performance? Referring back to Figure 4.1 and considering what might develop, you see that the

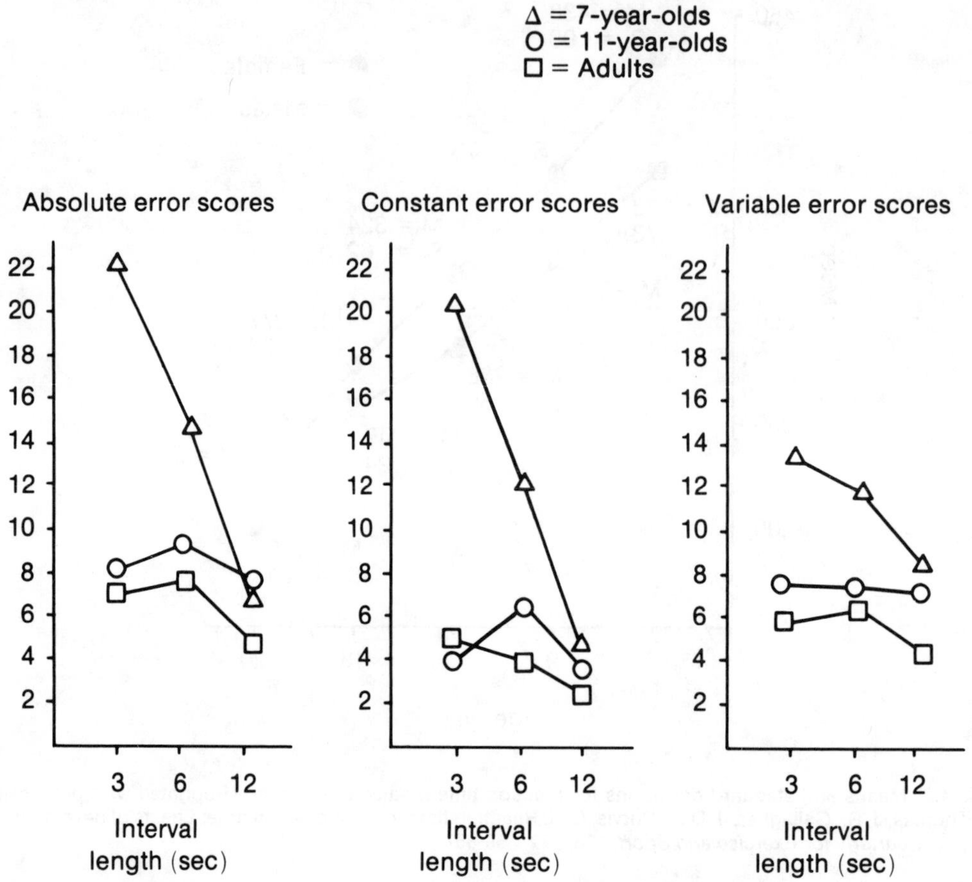

Figure 4.3. Effects of varying processing intervals on performance in a ballistic movement task. (Reprinted with permission from Gallagher, J. D., & Thomas, J. R. Effects of varying post-KR intervals upon children's motor performance. *Journal of Motor Behavior,* 1980, **12**, 41-46, a publication of the Helen Dwight Reid Educational Foundation.)

sensory registers (visual, auditory, kinesthetic) do not change much after five years of age. Thus, the amount of information available about movement does not vary much across the childhood years. The visual sensory register has been estimated to store information for about 250 msec (Crowder 1976), the auditory register for about 10 sec (Eriksen and Johnson 1964), and kinesthetic for 400 to 1600 msec (Gallagher 1980, Gallagher and Thomas 1980a). Thus, while the storage times differ for types of information, neither the amount of information nor the storage times change significantly across the childhood and adolescent years. Said another way, equivalent levels of initial information are available to children and adults. Thus, the functions of the sensory registers are not the source of the increase in motor peformance seen as children grow and develop.

Perceptual Mechanism

The next part of the model is the perceptual mechanism. Marteniuk (1976) indicates that the perceptual mechanism translates physical circumstances into meaningful internal representations, that is, it attaches some meaning to what has been stored temporarily in the sensory registers. This must be done within the storage time limit previously given for a particular sensory register.

A major developmental issue is whether sensitivity to movements differs among children of various ages. Sensitivity thresholds involving visual and auditory acuity, brightness, color, pitch, size, and other elements have been determined to differ among individuals. This threshold is sometimes called just noticeable differences, or difference limens, and represents the keenness of the perceptual mechanism.

In general, the perceptual mechanism becomes more sensitive across the childhood years (Winther and Thomas 1981), although there are large individual differences. In slow positioning movements, adults have been reported to have a difference limen on both a one- and two-dimensional positioning task of about 3 cm (Winther and Thomas 1981a, Parks and Magill in press). Both 5- and 7-year-old children had difference limens greater than 9 cm on a two-dimensional positioning task, while 11-year-old children had a 6 cm difference limen (Winther and Thomas 1981a). Thus, an adult could judge the end point of a movement as different from another position 3 cm away, but a difference of 6 cm was required for an 11-year-old and 9 cm for a 7-year-old.

If these results can be generalized to a ballistic real task, such as batting a pitched ball,[1] then some of the developmental implications can be seen. Thus, an adult could swing the bat three times more accurately than could a seven-year-old when trying to strike a ball. Add to this the fact that the adult's reaction time (approximately 200 msec) is twice as fast as the seven-year-old's (approximately 400 msec) (Thomas, Gallagher, and Purvis 1981), and that the adult is much more accurate and less variable in anticipation timing than the seven-year-old (Thomas et al. 1981), then the difficulties a seven-year-old has in batting a thrown ball can be understood. The practical implications of these findings are already in common practice; to simulate the game of baseball, seven-year-olds usually play T-ball because the typical seven-year-old batter seldom strikes a thrown ball.

The perceptual mechanism (specifically the keenness of perceptual judgments) appears to increase in sensitivity to movement location as age increases. Since difference limen studies involve tasks that have been learned well (usually many trials are given) and a minimum level of cognitive involvement, more efficient use of the memory system is unlikely to overcome these developmental differences. In other words, children's motor control systems have more variability than do adults'. Little apparently can be done about this motor control problem except to allow maturation to proceed. This does not mean children's performances cannot be drastically improved with quality practice and the use of good cognitive strategies (to be discussed next), but more variability does seem to appear in children's motor output systems when compared with those of adults. While this increased variability has been established only for end location in a movement, in all likelihood children's control over limb movements involving accuracy is probably more variable than for adults.

1. A ballistic, rapid-timing task (e.g., batting) would probably result in larger, rather than smaller, difference limens.

SHORT-TERM STORE (STS)

Short-term store (STS) is roughly described as the equivalent of working memory or the location where thinking occurs. The capacity of STS is limited; people can only think about so many things at once. The control process in Figure 4.1 shows ways in which humans think. For instance, encoding may involve labeling incoming information so that the label enhances recall of the information. Thus, teachers often use verbal labels (or mnemonics) to cue children about their movements. In baseball, young children are aided in placing their gloves for fielding by these labels: "ball on the ground, fingers down; when the ball is a fly, fingers to the sky."

Cueing

Younger children frequently do not label a movement, making recall more difficult. One study (Winther and Thomas 1981b) found that when movements from a central point outward (resembling a clock face) were used, kindergarten children did nothing specific to remember the end locations of the movements. When asked what they did to remember, a typical comment was, "I used my brain." Most fifth graders used a visual image to recall the movement pattern, as in, "I saw a peace sign." However, the adults used a clock face label to remember. Under these conditions, the adult performances were best, followed by those of the fifth graders, with the kindergarten children performing most poorly. When cued to use a clock face as an encoding label and then as a means of recall, the fifth graders were as accurate as the adults, and the kindergarten children were as accurate as the fifth graders who had used a visual image. Thus, children's performance was enhanced considerably by forcing the use of adultlike encoding strategies.

Poor encoding affects at least two memory features: (1) the search and retrieval of long-term store is made more difficult if the information is not encoded under an effective label, and (2) a poor labeling strategy may result in a poorer movement response. If the child encoded a series of two linear movements as a peace sign, this would describe the shape but not the location of the movements. If the movements are encoded as moving from the center of the clock to 2 o'clock and then 4 o'clock, both the shape and location are easy to recall. In addition, Weiss (1981) has pointed out the value of a verbal label in combination with a model for aiding young children in skill acquisition.

Rehearsal and Rehearsal Strategies

Another important control process is rehearsal. At least three developmental questions about the features of rehearsal bear examination: (1) whether a rehearsal strategy can be used, (2) whether rehearsal is used spontaneously, and (3) whether rehearsal positively influences performance. These features in question are roughly equivalent to what Flavell (1970) has called the "production-mediation" hypothesis. The first level of rehearsal is typical of about four- to six-year-old children. Children at this age can use a strategy but usually do not unless cued to do so. Around seven to eight years of age, children begin to rehearse spontaneously. They know they need to do something to remember. Rehearsal strategies become increasingly effective at mediating performance over the childhood years. Several studies have noted (Gallagher 1980, Gallagher and Thomas 1984, Thomas 1981, Thomas et al. 1983) that when children are forced to use adultlike rehearsal strategies, the average accuracy of the movements is increased but variability remains higher than for adults. This reflects the fact that the adults are probably using both a more sophisticated version of the strategy and applying the strategy more consistently. The higher variability in the children's performances may also reflect the differences in perceptual sensitivity discussed previously.

Rehearsal is used to signify many things. Sometimes it refers to the general control process. At other times rehearsal may refer to a specific mnemonic, such as using counting to estimate time. In the more general sense, when a series of movements are to be remembered, practicing previously presented positions enhances recall (Gallagher 1980, Gallagher and Thomas 1980b). Subjects at four age levels (children at 5, 7, and 11 years of age and adults) were divided into three groups and presented with eight movements. The groups were then given three rehearsal strategies. *Childlike* responses consisted of rehearsing the end point of the presented movement. *Adultlike* responses constituted rehearsing the end point of the current movement and then previously presented movements. *Subjective* responses were those in which the type of rehearsal was up to the subject. Forcing the younger subjects to use adultlike strategies improved both their degree of accuracy and amount of recall, while the childlike strategy somewhat depressed the older children's performances. Also of interest was the fact that the two younger age groups in the subjective strategy group (choosing their own ways to rehearse) spontaneously used the childlike strategy—they stayed at the end point of the movement presented. The two older groups (11-year-olds and adults), however, practiced previously presented positions during their rehearsal time. This further substantiates findings that the quality of rehearsal influences performance, and that rehearsal quality improves over the childhood years.

A specific mnemonic strategy, such as step counting to remember the distance jogged, develops spontaneously across the childhood years but also can be enhanced in younger children by practice (Thomas et al. 1983) or by cueing (Thomas 1981). In these experiments, children at 7 and 11 years of age and adults were divided into two groups at each age level. Both groups had to jog down a line on the playground and then reproduce the distance jogged on another line at a right angle to the first. One group in each experiment either practiced a step-counting strategy (Thomas et al. 1983) or was cued to use the step-counting strategy (Thomas 1981), while the control groups in both experiments were only told they would have to reproduce the distance jogged. Figures 4.4a and 4.4b show the error estimates for accuracy (Figure 4.4a) and variability (Figure 4.4b) from the Thomas (1981)[2] study.

When children at each age in the no-strategy groups (reflecting the spontaneous development of the counting mnemonic) were questioned about how they remembered the distance jogged, none of the 7-year-olds (out of 20) gave a strategic response. A typical answer was, "I thought about it." However, 30% (6 of 20) of the 11-year-olds and 100% (20 of 20) of the adults used a step-counting strategy to remember the distance jogged. The use of this strategy is reflected by the linear increase in accuracy (Figure 4.4a) of the control group and the fact that the three groups (strategy) cued to use step counting were not different from each other (or from the adult group without strategy). Note, however, that variability (Figure 4.4b) is not so sharply reduced by the use of strategy. The 7-year-olds made two types of errors that contributed to variability: counting and inconsistent step size. The 11-year-olds made no counting errors but did have some variability in step size. The adults were quite consistent, making neither type of error. This probably reflects better strategy application, but may also reflect the poorer motor control of the younger children.

2. The interaction from the Thomas et al. (1983) study is nearly identical.

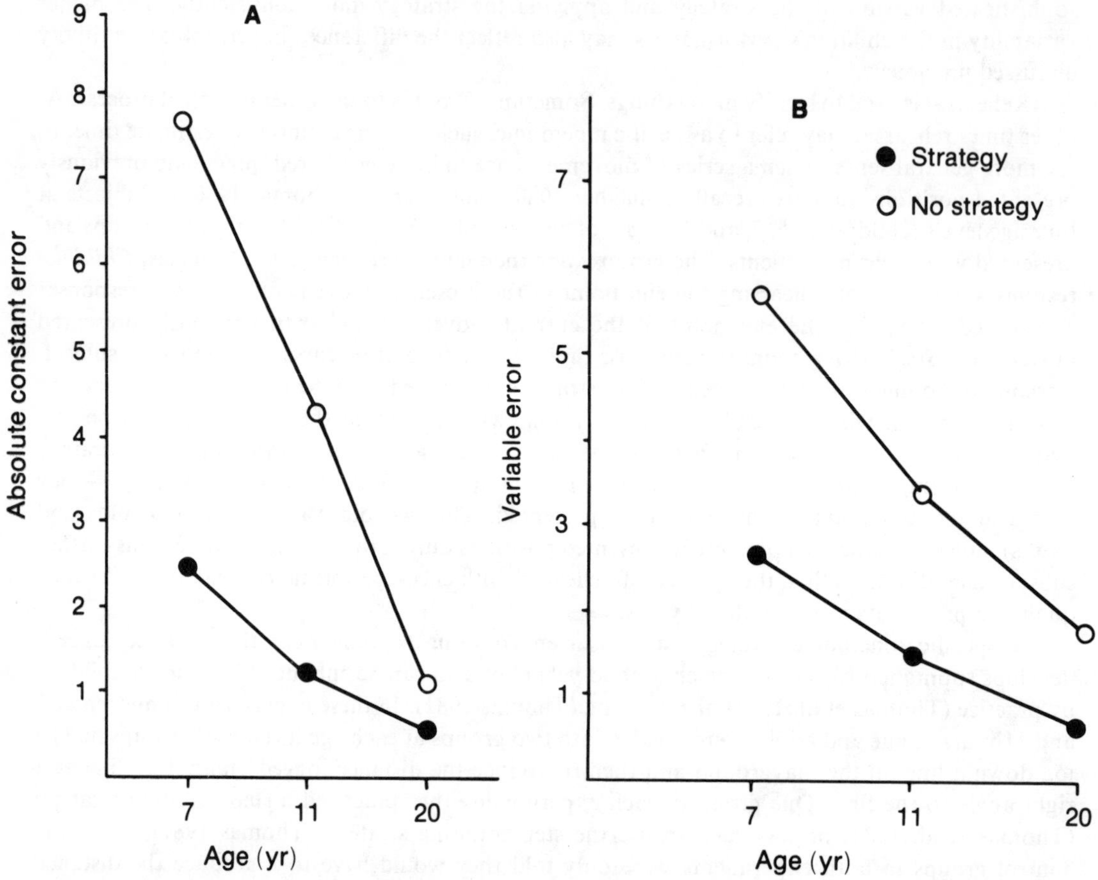

Figure 4.4. Age-related effects of strategy use on accuracy (**A**) and variability (**B**) in recalling the distance jogged. (Reprinted with permission from Thomas, K. T. Age differences in memory for movement: Effects of strategy and preselection when ecological validity is varied. Unpublished doctoral dissertation, Louisiana State University, 1981.)

The two studies just discussed also provide a more ecologically valid test of the control process of rehearsal. Reproducing a practiced distance moved is frequently important in sport. This is made more difficult in some sports when location is an unreliable cue. For instance, in football a pass receiver must have some way to know how to run a 12-yd square out. The yardage lines (locations) are unreliable because the play may begin anywhere on the field. To adults, counting steps seems obvious, but it is not necessarily obvious to a nine-year-old. In swimming the 50-m back stroke in a 25-m pool, counting arm strokes is a good way to know when to make a flip turn.

Grouping and Recoding

Organization of memory involves both STS and long-term store (LTS). Two processes (Figure 4.1) are included under organization: grouping and recoding. Both of these control processes reduce the demands on memory, especially STS. Grouping means putting incoming information together for storage in LTS. For example, given a series of new movements to remember, adults typically group the movements on some characteristic (e.g., length of movement or speed of movement). Children, however, try to remember each individual movement. As an easy example, think how a person remembers a series of numbers; adults usually group the numbers in sets of three, but young children rehearse each individual number.

Recoding involves the combining of two individual pieces of information stored separately in LTS. For instance, a five-year-old child may have a motor pattern in LTS for both a hop and a step. However, until the two patterns are combined (recoded) into one movement, the skip does not appear in the movement behavior of the child. Thus, both processes involve combining separate units of knowledge; grouping involves new, incoming information, while recoding involves information that already exists in LTS.

Generally, research on memory organization has shown that young children may attempt to organize information but that they usually employ the perceptual attributes (e.g., color, size) of the information; adults are likely to use a semantic dimension (e.g., the meaning of the information) (Paris 1978). Several studies have indicated that the cognitive performances of children as young as 8 or 9 years of age benefit from adult-imposed memory organization, but an organizational strategy does not begin to transfer across situations until 12 or 13 years of age (Bjorklund, Ornstein, and Haig 1977). A recent study (Gallagher 1980, Gallagher and Thomas 1980a) found that forcing memory organizational techniques enhanced the performances of younger children. By 11 years of age, children were trying to organize information about movements, but the organization did not transfer to mediate performance in new situations. Thus, teaching organizational techniques about movement information enhances performances, but children need a lot of experience (usually corresponding to increased age) for this general control process to transfer among various movement tasks.

Rehearsal Quality

From these studies and numerous others, shaping young children's motor performance by cueing or teaching them adultlike strategies and organizational techniques appears advantageous. Clearly the quality of the rehearsal is also an important feature. In serial tasks, to include previously presented movements in that particular rehearsal is important to quality recall. By stretching a point, this suggests that movements should be practiced under conditions similar to that in which they are to be used. To practice just the individual movements is not productive when the movements are to be used in combinations. Task-specific strategies are useful in enhancing performance, but as in more general control processes, they need to be taught and used with younger children.

In summary, to paraphrase a statement by Chi (1976), the memory task for children is to select and assemble the correct rehearsal process, learn when to use the process, and then to execute it correctly. Thus, rehearsal is cognitively demanding, particularly for children. Teachers and coaches must understand what these memory deficits are in children, and find a way to structure the learning environment to overcome children's memory problems. By doing so, motor skill acquisition can be made both easier and more rapid, thus improving performance. However, good strategy use cannot overcome all the deficits among younger children, older children, and adults. In tasks when physical size, strength, or mechanics offer advantage, cognitive strategies cannot compensate. Also, some motor control limitations appear to be associated with maturation (e.g., perceptual sensitivity and possibly reaction time, among others). In addition, Chapter 5 covers some body size factors that appear quite significant. Yet all these qualifications do not negate the value of understanding the memory deficits associated with children's performances and the value that the teacher or coach can obtain by using knowledge about the child's memory system to improve acquisition and performance of motor skills.

LONG-TERM STORE (LTS)

Long-term store involves the lasting and rather limitless retention of facts, concepts, and strategies by humans. Humans search and retrieve information from LTS to STS for use in thinking, action, or both. Movement plans are assumed to be in LTS where they can be retrieved and used for controlling skilled movements. The exact mechanics of this process are in considerable doubt. Some researchers believe that the stored plans (sometimes called schemas) include (or can be programmed to include) all the parameters of movement (e.g., force, velocity), while others believe that a general plan exists, but that the fine tuning of the movement occurs at lower levels (e.g., the spinal column or muscles) in a system that constrains the degrees of freedom of action. Regardless of the exact answer, the movement experiences in LTS are surely a major source of the performance improvement noted across the childhood years. That this difference is associated with experience rather than age is important, although age and experience tend to covary. Recently, Chi (1978) and Ornstein (in press) have provided interesting examples showing that the LTS differences are due to experience and not to age. Chi compared children who were experts at chess with similar children and adults who were not experts, using two tasks—recalling frequently used chessboard configurations and recalling configurations that would not normally occur. In the frequently occurring configurations, the expert children were better than the novice adults, who were noted to be better than the novice children. However, in configurations that did not normally occur, the adults were better at recall than both groups of children, who did not differ in recall skills. This example clearly points out the role of experiences in LTS on recall.

In all likelihood, the fact that a general strategy fails to transfer to a similar task in younger children reflects a lack of experience with the strategy (Ornstein, in press). Thus, the child is unable to recognize the similarity of the situation and generalize the strategy that is in LTS. This is similar to a production deficit (Flavell 1970) in which the strategy is not spontaneously used; however, in this case, the strategy does not transfer, probably because of a lack of experience, and thus is a LTS rather than an STS problem. Current terminology classes this as a metamemory problem. To oversimplify, younger children do not understand how they know or how they plan to acquire knowledge. Until they gain this insight (in essence, "What do I do to remember this knowledge or skill?"), cognitive functions such as organization of memory and transfer of strategies are not particularly effective. Thus, teachers and coaches of motor skill development should *structure learning environments to promote this metamemory function.* Examples include pointing out similarities of current strategies with those previously used, having kids explain their approaches to problem solving, cueing the need to rehearse and organize skill sequences, providing and discussing categories for organizing movement knowledge, and using other similar approaches.

ATTENTION

Attention with regard to children's memory is most frequently defined in three ways. Children are often said to have a short attention span, usually meaning they are easily distracted from the task. Sometimes attention is used to refer to a scanning of what is in the visual field: that is, selecting a certain feature from what is seen (called selective attention).

In Figure 4.1, however, attention is used as the pervasive controller of memory. In this view, attention is depicted as overriding the memory system. The amount of attention is finite but can be directed anywhere memory is operating. When the total amount of attention is used, then additional requirements result in decreased performance, as doing several activities at once overloads the memory system. For example, a young child dribbling a soccer ball down the field is concentrating on controlling the ball. Having to consider another player (defensive) when planning and controlling the ball may be more than the child can handle (attention capacity is exceeded). An older child may have learned the dribbling skill well (the skill has become less demanding on attention or more automatic) and can consider the defensive player in planning appropriate movements. However, a coach yelling "Cut to your left and pass the ball to Susie!" frequently results in a loss of ball control. In this case, attending to the coach results in more than the child can do while simultaneously controlling the ball and planning movements. Again, the attentional capacity of the system is exceeded.

SUMMARY

The memory system plays an important role and accounts for many of the motor performance differences observed across the childhood and adolescent years, as well as for many of the differences between children and adults. To understand how children perform and develop motor skills, the teacher or coach must understand physical growth, physiological development, mechanics of movement, body dimensions, and memory development in children, and then must use this knowledge effectively.

The major areas of development in memory across the childhood years are in perceptual mechanisms, STS, LST, and speed of processing. Differences in the perceptual mechanisms are basically found in movement sensitivity. These differences are hard to overcome and probably reflect a maturational increase in kinesthetic keenness.

The control processes and mnemonics used in STS are open to manipulation by knowledgeable teachers and coaches. In particular, considerable evidence exists that encoding, rehearsal, and organization are all memory functions that younger children use less effectively than do older children. The latter, in turn, use these processes less efficiently than do adults. These processes have at least three levels—presence or absence, spontaneous use, and quality of use—which roughly correspond to age but which more likely reflect experience.

Experience is in large part the knowledge base in LTS. In general, children have less knowledge than do adults, but research has shown that when children have a larger knowledge base than do adults, the children's performance is better. Thus, enriching the knowledge base through varied movement experiences should be a major objective of teachers and coaches. Remember that the base of knowledge about movement not only includes the movement patterns themselves but also how, why, and when to use these movements. Thus, cognition is a vital and important part of the effective acquisition and performance of motor skills.

Finally, the speed with which children process information is a reflection of all the other memory deficits. I suspect the memory system functions more slowly not because of a structural limitation but because children (1) lack perceptual keenness, (2) encode more poorly, resulting in slower search and retrieval, (3) use inefficient rehearsal, (4) have poorer organizational techniques, and (5) have less experience in LTS on which to base decisions and actions. These factors, both individually and interactively, produce slower processing rates in children.

In conclusion, consider an example of the application of this type of knowledge. A nine-year-old boy hitting golf balls on a practice range probably lines up 15 balls in a row. He then hits the first ball; without a look at where it is going, he steps up and hits the second ball, and so on, until all 15 balls have been struck as rapidly as possible. The boy is failing to use a major source of information in learning to strike the ball effectively—the connection between how the swing felt and where the ball went.

This failure to use error information has also been demonstrated in the literature. A controlled experiment by Newell and Kennedy (1978) showed that eight- to nine-year-old children chose to make the next movement as soon as they received knowledge about the previous movement. Thus, the children had no time to use error information to increase knowledge about the previous movement to correct the next one. Yet we (Gallagher and Thomas 1980) showed that on a simple task, if the child was forced to take the time to use the knowledge about the previous movement, performance was drastically improved. In the example, forcing the nine-year-old boy to watch the flight of the first ball may induce him to correct the next swing or to recall and try to reproduce a previously effective swing. While this example may appear to reflect a relatively minor point, performance is clearly improved by proper use of this knowledge.

REFERENCES

Bjorklund, D. F., Ornstein, P. A. & Haig, J. R. Developmental differences in organization and recall: Training in the use of organizational techniques. *Developmental Psychology,* 1977, **13**, 175-183.

Bronfenbrenner, U. *The ecology of human development.* Cambridge, Massachusetts: Harvard University Press, 1979.

Chi, M. Age differences in the speed of processing: A critique. *Developmental Psychology,* 1977, **13**, 543-544.

Chi, M. Short-term memory limitations in children: Capacity or processing deficits? *Memory & Cognition,* 1976, **4**, 559-572.

Chi, M. T. H. Knowledge structure and memory development. In Siegler (Ed.), *Children's thinking: What develops?* Hillsdale, New Jersey: Erlbaum, 1978.

Chi, M. T. H. & Gallagher, J. D. Speed of processing: A developmental source of limitation. *Topics in Learning and Learning Disabilities,* 1982, **2**, 23-32.

Crowder, R. G. *Principles of learning and memory.* Hillsdale, New Jersey: Erlbaum, 1976.

Eriksen, C. W. & Johnson, H. J. Investigating of the effect of a riming stimulus on backward masking. *Psychonomic Science*, 1964, **1**, 249-250.

Flavell, J. H. Developmental studies of mediated memory. In H. W. Reese & L. P. Lipsitt (Eds.)., *Advances in child development and behavior.* Vol. 5. New York: Academic Press, 1970.

Gallagher, J. D. Adult-child motor performance differences: A developmental perspective of control processing deficits. Doctoral dissertation, Louisiana State University, 1980.

Gallagher, J. D. & Thomas, J. R. Adult-child differences in movement reproduction: Effects of kinesthetic sensory store and organization of memory. Presented at Research Consortium, AAHPERD, Detroit, April 1980.

Gallagher, J. D. & Thomas, J. R. Rehearsal strategy effects on developmental differences for recall of a movement series. *Research Quarterly for Exercise and Sport*, 1984, in press.

Gallagher, J. D. & Thomas, J. R. Effects of varying post-KR intervals upon children's motor performance. *Journal of Motor Behavior,* 1980, **12**, 42-46.

Magill, R. A. & Parks, P. F. The psychophysics of kinesthesis for positioning responses: The physical stimulus-psychological response relationship. *Research Quarterly for Exercise and Sport*, in press.

Marteniuk, R. G. *Information processing in motor skills.* New York: Holt, Rinehart and Winston, 1976.

Martens, R. About smocks and jocks. *Journal of Sport Psychology,* 1979, **1**, 94-99.

Newell, K. & Kennedy, J. Knowledge of results and children's motor learning. *Developmental Psychology,* 1978, **14**, 531-536.

Ornstein, P. A. & Naus, M. J. Effects of knowledge base on children's memory processing. In J. B. Sidowski (Ed.), *Conditioning, cognition, and methodology: Contemporary issues in experimental psychology.* Hillsdale, New Jersey: Erlbaum, in press.

Paris, S. G. Memory organization during children's repeated recall. *Developmental Psychology,* 1978, **14**, 99-106.

Pascual-Leone, J. & Smith, J. The encoding and decoding of symbols by children: A new paradigm and neo-Piagetian model. *Journal of Experimental Child Psychology,* 1969, **8**, 328-353.

Siedentop, D. Two cheers for Rainer. *Journal of Sport Psychology,* 1979, **1**, 94-99.

Thomas, J. R. Acquisition of motor skills: Information processing differences between children and adults. *Research Quarterly for Exercise and Sport,* 1980, **51**, 158-173.

Thomas, J. R. Half a cheer for Rainer and Daryl. *Journal of Sport Psychology,* 1980, **2**, 266-267.

Thomas, J. R., Gallagher, J. D. & Purvis, G. J. Reaction time and anticipation time: Effects of development. *Research Quarterly for Exercise and Sport,* 1981, **52**, 359-367.

Thomas, J. R., Thomas, K. T. & Gallagher, J. D. Introduction: Children's processing of information in physical activity and sport. In A. Morris (Ed.), *Motor Development: Theory Into Practice.* New Town, Connecticut: Motor Skills: Theory Into Practice, 1981, 3.

Thomas, J. R., Thomas, K. T., Lee, A. M., Testerman, E. & Ashy, M. Age differences in use of strategy for recall of movement in a large scale environment. *Research Quarterly for Exercise and Sport,* in press.

Thomas, K. T. Age differences in memory for movement: Effects of strategy and preselection when ecological validity is varied. Unpublished doctoral dissertation, Louisiana State University, 1981.

Weiss, M. The effects on age, modeling, and verbal self-instruction on children's performance of a sequential motor task. Unpublished doctoral dissertation, Michigan State University, 1981.

Wickens, C. D. Temporal limits of human information processing: A developmental study. *Psychological Bulletin,* 1974, **81**, 739-755.

Winther, K. T. & Thomas, J. R. Developmental differences in children's labeling of movement. *Journal of Motor Behavior,* 1981, **13**, 77-90.

Winther, K. T. & Thomas, J. R. Development of hierarchial processes in motor performance. Paper presented at North American Society for Psychology of Sport and Physical Activity, Asilmar, California, May 1981.

SUGGESTED READINGS

Undergraduate Students

Clark, J. E. Memory processes in the early acquisition of motor skills. In M. V. Ridenour (Ed.), *Motor development: Issues and applications,* Princeton, New Jersey: Princeton Book Co., 1978.

Gallagher, J. D. The effects of developmental memory differences on learning motor skills. *Journal of Physical Education, Recreation & Dance,* 1982, **53** (5), 36-37, 40.

Thomas, J. R., Thomas, K. T. & Gallagher, J. D. Introduction: Children's processing of information in physical activity and sport. In A. Morris (Ed.), *Motor Development: Theory Into Practice,* New Town: Connecticut: Motor Skills: Theory Into Practice, 1981, 3.

Graduate Students

Chi, M. Short-term memory limitations in children: Capacity or processing deficits? *Memory & Cognition,* 1976, **4**, 559-572.

Chi, M. T. H. & Gallagher, J. D. Speed of processing: A developmental source of limitation. *Topics in Learning and Learning Disabilities,* 1982, **2**, 23-32.

Lange, G. Organization-related processes in children's recall. In P. A. Ornstein (Ed.), *Memory development in children.* Hillsdale, New Jersey: Erlbaum, 1978.

Newell, K. M. & Barclay, C. R. Developing knowledge about action. In J. A. S. Kelso & J. Clark (Eds.), *The development of control and coordination in movement.* New York: Wiley, 1982.

Ornstein, P. A. & Naus, M. J. Effects of knowledge base on children's memory processing. In J. B. Sidowski (Ed.), *Conditioning, cognition and methodology: Contemporary issues in experimental psychology.* Hillsdale, New Jersey: Erlbaum, in press.

Ornstein, P. A. & Naus, M. J. Rehearsal processes in children's memory. In P. A. Ornstein (Ed.), *Memory development in children.* Hillsdale, New Jersey: Erlbaum, 1978.

Thomas, J. R. Acquisition of motor skills: Information processing differences between children and adults. *Research Quarterly for Exercise and Sport,* 1980, **51**, 158-173.

Thomas, J. R. et al. Age differences in use of strategy for recall of movement in a large scale environment. *Research Quarterly for Exercise and Sport,* 1983, in press.

Thomas, J. R., Gallagher, J. D. & Purvis, G. J. Reaction time and anticipation time: Effects of development. *Research Quarterly for Exercise and Sport,* 1981, **52**, 359-367.

Winther, K. T. & Thomas, J. R. Developmental differences in children's labeling of movement. *Journal of Motor Behavior,* 1981, **13**, 77-90.

Laboratory 4 from Chapter 14 should be used at the completion of this chapter.

5

Physical Constraints to Development of Motor Skills[1]

Karl M. Newell

Motor skill development is a complex phenomenon that has stimulated theorizing, analysis, and commentary from a variety of disciplinary and professional fields of study. One consequence of this situation is that attempts to integrate the different levels of analysis (e.g., biochemical, anatomical, physiological, behavioral) into a unified theory of motor skill development are rare. The lack of general integration is, however, less troubling than it might seem at first, because such an approach to science often leads to eclecticism and the merging of incompatible lines of theorizing.

A more significant problem arising from diverse orientations to understanding a phenomenon is that description and explanation at one level of analysis are oftentimes not constrained by extant theorizing at another level of analysis. Such constraint should not necessarily be viewed in a causal sense (although it could be), but rather as the natural relationship that must exist between attempts to describe the same phenomenon, albeit from different levels of analysis. Understanding the constraints imposed on one level of movement analysis by another level is probably more viable when the levels of analysis are close to each other on the holism-reductionism disciplinary scale from sociology to physics (see Rose 1976, Chapter 1, for an introduction to the levels of analysis problem).

The study of the development of motor skill is undertaken predominantly from a behavioral orientation, which is natural given that skilled performances in physical activity are usually observed and measured at that level. Skill is usefully viewed in Guthrie's (1935) terms as the ability to bring about a predetermined outcome with maximum certainty, and with a minimum outlay of time and energy. Thus, the theory and methods of psychology have been principally used in attempts to understand motor skill acquisition in developing organisms (see Newell and Barclay

1. This work was supported in part by the National Science Foundation, Award No. DAR80-16287.

1982; Thomas, Chapter 4, this volume, for current orientations to this approach). Reference to other levels of analysis has been made in the psychological approach to skill development, but this has been motivated primarily through appeals to maturation as an explanatory construct (after Gesell 1929) and its implicit link to the control of development through genetics. The maturation-learning debate has become a rather tired issue in analysis and synthesis of development. This is reflected in the current loss of clarity of the maturation constuct, to the extent that invariably it is employed synonymously with the term *growth* and even with *development.*

Physical growth is another broad field, in part because it too can be approached from a variety of levels of analysis, including whole body, organ, cellular, and molecular levels. The most directly relevant level of growth analysis to skill development is the study of the growth or change in size of the whole body (Chapter 1). These changes are particularly dynamic, and hence evident, during the time span from conception to maturity. They also exist, however, even if at a slower rate, throughout the life span. Despite the sizable amount of literature on the growth of body size, the significance of these changes on the development of motor skills is rarely addressed *directly*, particularly in theoretical orientations to skill development.

In a similar vein, physiological and neurological orientations to development have provided an array of empirical findings with respect to the process of development, but the significance of these constraints to skilled performance in physical activities over the life span is less established. This situation is due in part to the fact that the neurological evidence for development is invariably gleaned either from species or from preparations rather than from normal, healthy humans. Furthermore, the neurophysiological recordings that are made are rarely taken during natural physical activity. Thus, the neurophysiological data from animals and from human pathological cases may be less relevant than previously thought. Fortunately, the development of noninvasive or acceptably invasive techniques suggests that the barriers to a neurophysiology of natural activities may soon be breached (e.g., John 1977; Nilsson et al. 1977).

This chapter outlines the impact of some physical constraints on the development of motor skills. A particular focus is a sketch of how and in what way our understanding of anatomy, morphology, and neurophysiology *constrains* our psychological theorizing with respect to skill development. A claim often made is that there is no prevailing reason why physiology should constrain psychological theorizing (e.g., Mandler 1975), although this philosophy might change as our understanding of these lower levels of analysis increases. One outgrowth of the psychological approach to movement science is that constructs are often created on an undisciplined basis, and thus are divorced from the physical realities of the organism and environment interaction. This chapter is sympathetic to the view that a firmer understanding of the physical constraints on action may lead to a more principled basis on which to theorize about action. Furthermore, these physical constraints raise problems that developmental accounts of action must accommodate because of the various physical changes that naturally occur with growth (Kugler, Kelso, and Turvey 1980, 1982).

MECHANICAL CONSTRAINTS

The coordination and control of the body and limbs in skilled action reflects an optimal interplay of forces from both nonmuscular and muscular sources, including: (1) the environment, (2) the activity of the organism, and (3) the reactive forces that emerge from interaction between the organism and the environment. Psychological approaches to skill learning have not recognized the significance of this confluence of forces, and have also generally failed to acknowledge that mechanical constraints are features of the coordination problem. This section outlines both some of the mechanical constraints that arise during action and the significance of physical growth on those constraints in the development of motor skills.

The impact of environmental constraints on movement control is considerable, just as the range of surfaces and mediums on and in which physical activities are conducted is considerable. The role of these constraints on action is often forgotten or underplayed, presumably because it seems so obvious. More significant is that most theoretical notions of skill development focus on the developing organism without consideration of the environment in general (Kugler et al. 1982).

Animals have evolved to survive in earth's gravitational field. The human form would most certainly take on different proportions without this environmental constraint, or if a different gravitational field existed. Gravity is a prevailing, although variable, force on land and underwater. Human actions must accommodate gravitational forces and, where possible, use the force supplied by gravity to advantage. Although observation of neonatal or even childhood activity has yet to take place in the weightless environment of space, the swimming skills of children have been investigated (McGraw 1939; Tokuyama, Okamoto, and Kumamoto 1976). In swimming, the fluid environment in which the activity takes place provides the additional force of buoyancy, which counteracts to varying degrees the gravitational force.

In this regard, McGraw's (1939) observation that the reflexive swimming exhibited during the first nine months or so of a baby's life reflects a better organization than newborn crawling or stepping movements. This activity, like reflex stepping on land, is presumed to reflect the control of subcortical nuclei. The relatively gravity-free environment of water may well allow neuromuscular organization to occur unbridled by the mechanical constraints that are apparent during activity on land and that are too great for the undeveloped neuromuscular system of the neonate to overcome.

The atmosphere and surface with which the organism interacts can also produce different environmental forces that need to be integrated with those derived from muscular output. These physical constraints are probably of little significance to the development of children's physical activities, usually because they remain fairly constant. However, slippery surfaces, for example, have less friction and may impede the neonate's locomotion on the shiny kitchen floor but not on the heavy rug in the dining room. With experience, the baby learns to accommodate reduced surface friction as do adults, who learn to shorten their stride lengths and keep their feet flat on icy pavements.

The greater proportion of mechanical variation in the development of motor skills is due to the growth of the organism in terms of its height, weight, individual limb length and mass, and so on. The changes in body form and muscular strength that accompany development have to be taken into account in any theorizing about the coordination and control of body and limbs in support of action. Surprisingly, such a significant developmental factor as growth has been conspicuously absent from developmental accounts of skill learning (cf. Connolly 1970, Wade 1976).

Consideration of Figure 5.1, the often-reproduced schematic of Robbins et al. (1928, Figure 63), drives home the magnitude of the problem of physical growth on mechanical constraints. The figure shows the changes in human form and proportions through the fetal and infant stages up to adulthood. Growth causes the head and upper parts of the body to become proportionately smaller, while the lower parts become correspondingly larger. The length of a newborn's head is

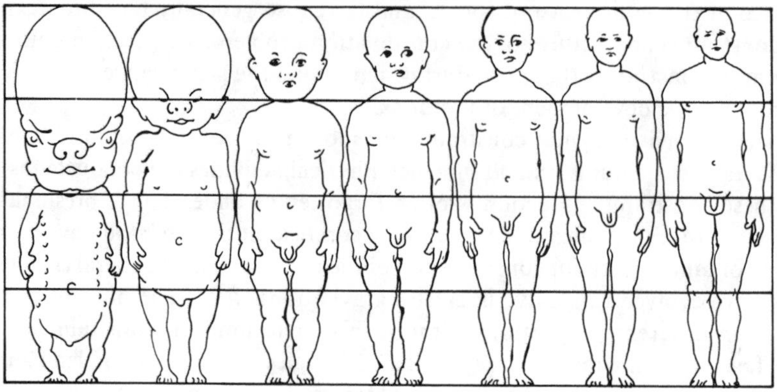

Figure 5.1. Changes in form and proportion of human body during fetal and postnatal life. (From Robins et al. 1928.)

about one quarter of body height, whereas it is about one eighth the height in the adult. Thus, not only does the absolute height and weight of the individual change during development but also the proportional size of given limbs or body features to the total body changes. Furthermore, the *rate* at which these changes occur also varies. For example, height and weight undergo transitory periods of fast and slow increases (Shuttleworth 1939; Chapter 1, this volume). The study of the dimensions of organisms and the effects of size on their proportions is called allometry (Gould 1966).

One major impact of the change in the absolute and relative sizes of body parts is on the moment of inertia of each body part. The moment of inertia of each body part can be viewed as an index of its resistance to acceleration. The changing moment of inertia of body parts during growth is an important problem for theories of action to accommodate.

Surprisingly, a recent study by Jensen (1981) claims (apparently justifiably) to be the only examination of the effects of growth on the moment of inertia of children's body parts, given that in vivo methods of calculating segmental moment of inertia have been available for some time (Herron et al. 1974, Brooks and Jacobs 1975). Repeated observations of children's growth parameters and skills in physical activities have been documented, but the direct measurement of moment of inertia has not been made in either case. Jensen selected 12 Caucasian boys so that one endomorph, one mesomorph, and one ectomorph (Tanner 1962) were examined at the ages of 4, 6, 9, and 12 years. The children were somatotyped, and the principal whole body moment of inertia calculated, using standard biomechanical procedures at the beginning and end of 12 months.

The results of Jensen's (1981) analysis showed that as a consequence of growth, the moment of inertia of the centroidal transverse axis reflected individual increases from 12% to 57% (mean 30.8%), while the increments for the longitudinal centroidal axis ranged from 8% to 92% (mean 33.5%). For most of the children, these percentage changes in moment of inertia far exceeded the percentage changes in age, height (mean 4.7%), and mass (mean 15.8%). Jensen proposed that the best indicator of the constraints on rotational movements imposed by growth was the product of the mass multiplied by the square of the standing height. This showed an average subject increase of 27.7% over the 12-month time span. Given the increased rate of growth during puberty, it was anticipated that the 12-year-old children would produce the most substantial changes in the principal moments of inertia, but surprisingly, the greatest changes were found in the ectomorph between the sixth and seventh year, and in the endomorph between the fourth and fifth year. Thus, Jensen found no relationship between body type and the amount of change in the moment of inertia, but further systematic study of this important problem is required.

Jensen's study clearly reveals that if motor performance is to be maintained or improved with growth, then an increased force compensation also has to accommodate the increments in the moment of inertia of the body. This force compensation must be proportionately greater than the increments of either body mass or height. The various changes in body form and moment of inertia presumably reflect a continuous rate of change over time, but these growth-instilled changes can still degrade performance. A prime example is the decline in skill level that elite gymnasts often demonstrate when they pass through puberty. This decline is due to the failure to keep strength increments consistent with changes in body length, mass, and the resulting moment of inertia.

These changes in moment of inertia also suggest that growth may dictate a different set of kinematics for the same activity when the task criteria allow such changes. Kinematic parameters are derived from the dimensions of length and time. Common kinematic parameters include displacement, velocity, and acceleration values of body segments. A child could compensate by a proportional increment in strength, but these mechanical changes often warrant compensation in the kinematics or movement pattern of the body links. Wickstrom (1975) has provided many age-related differences in fundamental motor skills, and these should be considered in the determination of the optimal kinematics of body links in skilled performance.

Shirley (1931) and Bayley and Davis (1935) showed a more direct example of the potential impact of body form on children's development of fundamental skills in their detailed observations of the chronological milestones. They found that children with proportionately longer legs who were not overweight tended to walk earlier than did children with proportionately shorter legs. Norval (1947) observed a similar relationship with newborns of the same weight in that an increase in body length of 1 in. led (on average) to an earlier onset (by 22 days) of voluntary walking. Proportionately longer legs in the development of upright locomotion may have some mechanical advantage, but this has not been systematically investigated. In fact, the general impact of mechanical considerations in the development of fundamental movement patterns is rarely considered (Chapter 3).

Changes in body form are often accompanied by changes in muscular strength. Strength increments can compensate for gains in body mass through growth, but this compensation is invariably nonproportional. The principles of simple geometry are worth remembering in considering the allometry of human form. Area increases as the square of the linear dimensions, while volume increases as a cube function. Thus, strength gains generally have to be proportionately greater than length and mass gains to maintain parity in performance during physical growth.

The above examples should be sufficient to demonstrate the notion that mechanical constraints on human movement arise from both the organism and from the environment. Changes in body form and strength during growth can accommodate or significantly alter the impact of these constraints. The changes in moment of inertia, while most dramatic during the period from birth to maturity, also take place throughout adult life. Thus, mechanical considerations in movement control are a developmental factor in what is a lifelong process.

Skilled action reflects the optimal confluence of organismic and environmental forces for the specified activity. An identifying feature of skilled performers is that they use to advantage the forces in the environment along with those forces that result from the body's interaction with it. The problem for developmental theories of skilled motor behavior is how to accommodate the ever-changing flux of mechanical constraints, particularly those that arise from the growth of the individual, into principles of coordination and control.

The majority of theoretical notions in motor control and skill acquisition, including those that discuss development, have accommodated the problem by omission. The early leaders in developmental psychology either tacitly assumed that their notions of maturation (e.g., Gesell 1929) and learning accommodated changes in constraints with growth, or they simply failed to consider the problem. Similar criticisms might be leveled at the motor program (Pew 1974, Schmidt 1975) or feedback (Adams 1971) theories of motor learning. These, although not explicitly directed toward the issue of growth through development, have to accommodate the related problem of temporary body dimension changes resulting from the use of implements in physical activity. The only theoretical orientation on the coordination and control of movement that meets directly the problems of growth is that of Kugler et al. (1982).

The Kugler et al. (1982) perspective is based on principles drawn from a wide range of disciplines. A distinguishing theoretical thrust is the wedding of principles of the ecological perspective of perception and action with those from physical biology, particularly nonequilibrium thermodynamics. This view proposes a basis for conceptualizing information on movement coordination and control during development while taking into account changing body dimensions and scales. I recommend reading the original source for an appreciation of this wide-ranging approach to the problems of body scaling for movement control.

PHYSIOLOGICAL CONSTRAINTS

The preceding analysis of human form and its impact on motor performance suggests that the developing child is not simply a scaled-down adult. A consideration of physiological development, which is the level of analysis we turn to now, reinforces this view.

Physiological development of the growing child is considered from the time of conception rather than from the moment of birth, which is the predominant marker for the behavioral level of analysis. Thus, it is useful in several issues in development to distinguish between the biological and chronological ages of an individual. Indicators of biological age include skeletal maturation and the assessment of secondary sex characteristics (Chapter 1).

To take the view that anatomy constrains behavioral function is intuitively appealing, yet as stated in the introduction, the evidence in support of this statement regarding the physiology of motor systems is not as strong as it might appear. Much of the evidence comes from comparative studies with inert animal preparations or human pathological cases. These approaches might provide us with an understanding of the functioning limits of the system at hand, but not with a veridical picture of the natural organization of the human motor system.

To facilitate discussion of physiological constraints, this section is split into considerations of both structural and functional issues. Structure at any level should not be viewed as an entity impervious to change but rather as an element that undergoes a much slower rate of change than is typically associated with functional processes. Thus, the structure-function distinction is not as qualitative as it appears at first and might be more useful if viewed as an organizing principle for discussions of related issues (Newell 1972).

Structure

The developing brain appears to mature according to the need for certain structures to exist for the performance of vital functions. The priorities differ according to species and to the demand of the specific econiches to which the organism has adapted phylogenetically (Anokin 1964). Thus, separating environmental and physiological components of development is difficult, and the continuation of this practice is largely based on heuristic grounds.

Figure 5.2 shows the growth in weight of the human body and various organs during prenatal and postnatal life. These graphs are based on the weight of the organs in fetuses and children who died from causes other than dissipating maladies (Scammon 1930). Prenatal growth rates are all essentially similar, but once newborns encounter the outside environment, growth patterns vary with the organ up to maturity. The different environments encountered in the embryonic, fetal, and neonatal states may well require the evolution of specific morphological, biochemical, physiological, and behavioral mechanisms (Gould 1977). This view highlights the fallacy of the view that the fetus is an immature adult; undoubtedly, the fetus is mature for the environment with which it is in contact.

Thus, growth at the organ and whole body levels reflects a complex variety of individual rates. Against this background of structural development, functions emerge, including the development of movement. There are many more neuromuscular developments than can be discussed here, particularly if a thorough understanding of their functional significance is to be advanced. However, only some of the most significant neuromuscular developments will be highlighted, linking these physical constraints to behavioral function. A richer physiological account may be found in developmental, medical, or physiological texts (Falkner 1966; Hooker 1969; Ounsted and Ounsted 1973; Timiras 1973) and review articles (Wyke 1975). The foregoing outline also assumes some working knowledge of basic anatomy and physiology.

Table 5.1, reproduced from Wyke (1975), charts some of the major developmental neuromuscular milestones. Several general points emerge from a perusal of the contents of this table. First, the in utero period is a phase of significant neuromuscular development as the individual passes from the embryonic to fetal stage. Second, the distinction between biological and chronological age is clearly reflected, in that, for example, the biological age for voluntary locomotion is on the order of 100 weeks, whereas chronological age estimates for the onset of this activity are on the order of 50 to 60 weeks. Third, the onset of functional activities in utero is closely tied to the development of the relevant neuromuscular architecture, particularly in brain mechanisms of the nervous sytem. The central nervous sytem includes the brain, spinal cord, and peripheral nerves that contribute to the innervation of muscle. Finally, to put the neuromuscular developments in the context of the mechanical constraints outlined in the preceding section, on leaving the embryonic stage at 8 weeks, the average individual is 4 cm long; at 20 weeks, 21 cm; and at birth, about 50 cm (Nilsson et al. 1977).

Generally, all of the muscle fibers are present at birth, although they increase in length and breadth with development. Table 5.1 indicates that by the fifth to sixth week of the embryonic stage, sufficient muscular differentiation has occurred to respond to direct stimulation. This differentiation precedes innervation from related alpha motoneurons and is prevalent initially in relation to the head and neck musculature. Subsequently, segmentally related afferent neurons also differentiate to form central-peripheral connections. This development reflects a polysynaptic

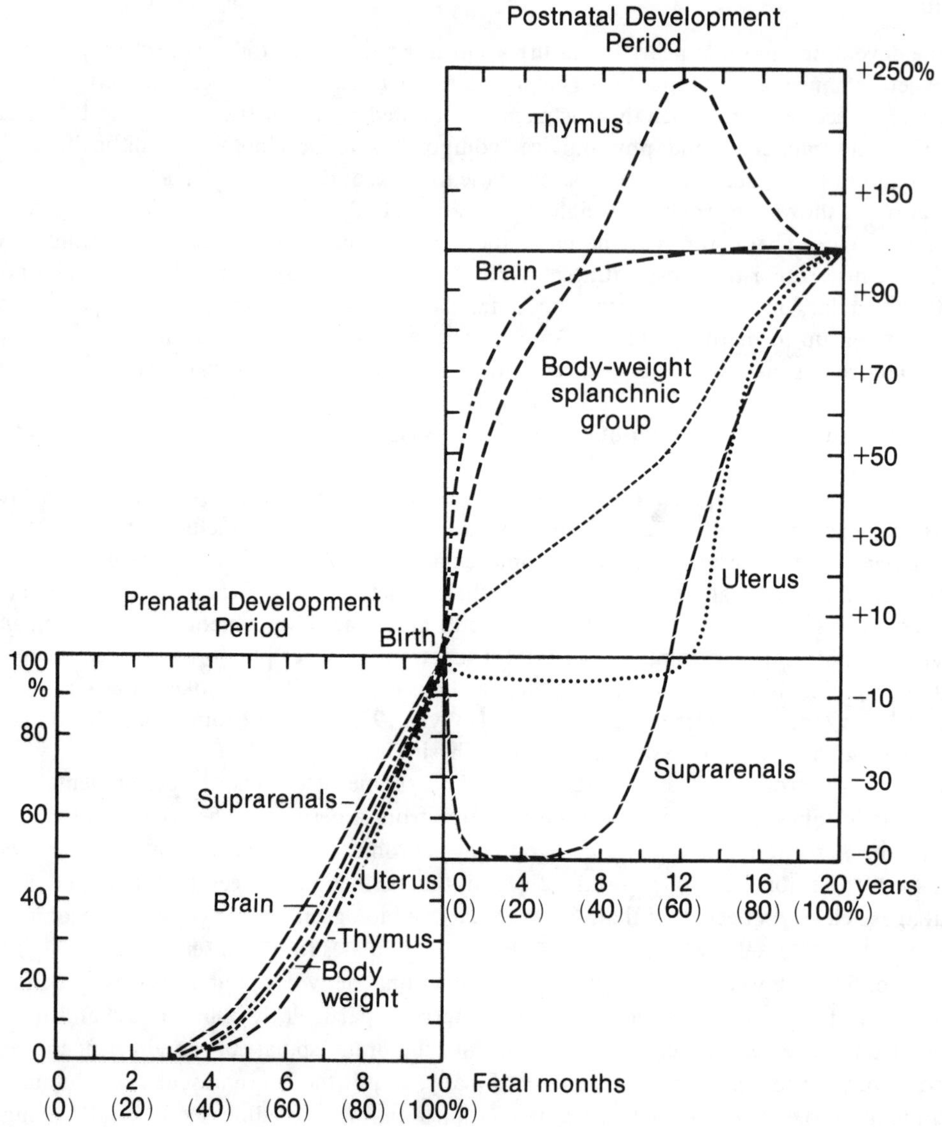

Figure 5.2. Diagram showing growth in weight of human body and organs during prenatal and postnatal life. Abcissa indicates age, and ordinate size attained in percentage of final weight (taken at 100%) reached at birth or at 20 years. (Modified from Scammon 1930 with permission from Timiras 1973.)

reflex arc that during weeks 8 through 14 activates stimulation of general responses of the head and arms, and thereafter a more sensory-specific response.

Thus, the musculature of a given body part develops before the communicating channels to the central nervous system do. This neuromuscular development, and subsequent reflexive activity, generally also follows the cephalocaudal and proximodistal principles (Gesell 1929) in that head

Table 5.1. Developmental Emergence of Neuromuscular Behavior

Developmental Period	Weeks of Age From Conception	Neuromuscular Developmental Phenomena
Embryonic	5-6	Excitable muscle fiber differentiation. Innervation from alpha motoneurons.
	6-7	Motoneuron activation of motor units (through fine unmyelinated axons).
	7-8	Afferent neurons establish fine unmyelinated peripheral and central connections (trigeminal system first).
	8	Orofacial cutaneous mass reflexes elicitable. Ampullary cristae active.
Fetal	9-10	Mass "spontaneous" movements of whole musculature. Moro reflex elicitable (from vestibular receptors).
	12	Muscle spindles differentiate. Movements of eyeballs. Generalized cervical reflexes. Palmar and plantar reflexes elicitable.
	14	Spinal gray nuclei differentiate. Fusimotor neurons active. Localized movements of lips, tongue (swallowing), head, trunk, limbs.
	16	Respiratory muscle movements (intercostals before diaphragm). First myelin lamellae in CNS (in cervical intersegmental tracts and vestibular nerves).
	24	Myelin lamellae in spinal dorsal columns and medial longitudinal bundle. Commencing myelinization of cranial motor nerves, followed by afferents (vestibular first); and of reticulospinal, tectospinal, and vestibulospinal tracts. Myelin lamellae in spinal nerves (motor before afferent).
	28	Facial mimetic muscle reflexes. Cervical reflexes regionally coordinated (Magnus and de Kleyn reflexes). Myelin lamellae in spinocerebellar and spinothalamic tracts.
	32	Vestibular reflex effects on eyes and limb muscles.
	36	Myelin lamellae in cortical projection tracts, and in optic nerves.
Birth	36-37	
Neonatal	38	Reflex walking, crawling, and swimming movements elicitable.
	40	Ocular pursuit movements present. Voluntary control begins.
Infancy	42	Reflex head extension in prone position.
	50	Visuomotor reflex effects on neck, trunk, and limb muscles. Positive supporting reflexes in arms.
	60	Head held up in supported sitting position.
	64	Sits unsupported. Exploratory creeping.
	68	Stands with support. Cerebral dominance emerging.
	70	Exploratory crawling. Positive supporting reflexes in legs.
	80	Walks with support.
	100	Stands and walks unaided.

Reprinted with permission from Wyke 1975.

and neck activities precede movement of the lower body and limbs. During weeks 12 to 14, specific activity in the facial features, such as the eyeballs, lips, and tongue, occurs. Voluntary muscular contractions are observable by weeks 13 to 16, while vestibular reflex activity cannot be elicited until about the 32nd week.

As Figure 5.1 suggests, the brain is proportionately more representative of its adult size than many other body organs. Indeed, by the fifth year, the weight of the brain is about 90% of its adult weight. Despite this change in size, the estimated 10 billion brain cells are present at birth, although they grow and form more interconnections with development. The increase in the number of dendrites emerging from each cell facilitates cellular interconnections. The dendrites are the messenger arms of each cell in that they allow the conduction of impulses to other cells. This general increase in connecting fibers with and between brain mechanisms is associated with gains in the functioning capacity of the developing child. By the same token, the development of interconnecting fibers appears to be related to the behavioral experience of the developing organism, so that, for example, animals raised in an enriched environment develop a more complex network of cellular connections than do their counterparts raised in an impoverished environment.

The phylogenetic development of the human brain has resulted in different mechanisms and hence functioning capabilities. The brain may be categorized into the major sections of (1) cerebral cortex, (2) midbrain, (3) cerebellum, (4) brain stem, and (5) spinal cord. Phylogenetically, the midbrain is one of the oldest brain sections. One reflection of this is that it is the area most fully developed at birth. The midbrain controls the automatic primitive reflexes of the infant, which are subsequently brought under increasing voluntary control with development of the phylogenetically newer brain area of the cerebral cortex. The development of interconnections in these cortical areas does not proceed at a uniform rate and is consistent with the behavioral development of the specific functional activities associated with each brain area. The cortex has identifiable areas associated with a variety of functions, including motor, sensory, language, and other symbolic activities.

One physiological change that tends to correlate with brain growth and general functioning of the individual is myelination of cerebral neuronal axons. Myelination effectively insulates the nerve fibers from extraneous molecules. The process occurs in a definite order with respect to the pathways involved in the developmental sequence of fundamental activities outlined in Table 5.1. Myelination occurs up to at least adolescence, but many efferent and afferent pathways involved in movement control remain unmyelinated. The efferent and afferent pathways transmit neuronal impulses to and from peripheral musculature, respectively, so that the efferent pathway is sometimes labeled motor outflow and the afferent pathway the sensory return. Myelination increases the diameter of the nerve fiber systems and hence their conduction velocity. Chase (1976) has estimated that myelin accounts for approximately 25% of the weight of the adult brain.

The increase in conduction velocity that follows myelination of nerve fibers has sometimes been advocated as the basis for the faster reaction time observed through the passage of childhood (Hodgkins 1963). This growth period, however, is associated with exponential increments in body size, thus lengthening the communication distance between the cortex and the muscular apparatus. Wyke (1975) claims that these gains in body size are accommodated by myelination, so that reflex times remain relatively constant during childhood, even though voluntary reaction times decrease. Conduction velocity remains a modest constraint, however, with respect to temporal aspects of movement control, with motor outflow time from cortex to hand musculature being on the order of 10 msec for adults.

The detailed mapping of microanatomical structural changes in the developing human is not complete. Conel (1939-1960) has published one of the most detailed studies of the maturing cerebral cortex through the first four years of life, but since the information is based on children who have died, this structural mapping cannot be directly linked to function. Generally assumed, however, is that brain maturation throughout the life span contributes to normal variations in behavioral development. Most emphasis has been given to brain changes during the primary growth period, but indications show that this dynamic process continues to some degree throughout adult life (Raisman 1978). The ever-increasing size of the senior citizen pool in this country's population has helped stimulate interest in aging and the impact of physical constraints on this aspect of the developmental process.

Function

By the time the individual is ready to leave the uterus, a number of vital functions can be performed. These activities include sleeping and waking, breathing, sucking, swallowing, and crying. The control of these vital functions is not due to simple monosynaptic reflexes but rather to a developing, complex system, which Figure 5.1 and Table 5.1 show is still not adultlike.

A traditional claim, which has been echoed even recently (Wyke 1975), is that the individual is essentially a reflex machine even up to the third month of extrauterine life. That is, the movements of the infant up to 12 weeks after birth are not due to cortical control but rather to the expression of brain stem, cerebellar, and intersegmental spinal reflex mechanisms. Thus, behavior in the first three months of extrauterine life is under the control of the phylogenetically older subnuclei parts of the brain rather than under the more recently acquired cerebral cortex. Discussion of some experimental findings that argue against this claim follows.

The reflex, which has strong traditions in physiological accounts of motor control (Sherrington 1906), has also been accommodated into most accounts of child development, particularly with respect to motor development. The orderly reflex sequence of appearance and disappearance noted in the fetal period continues through the initial year of life (Capute et al. 1978). The so-called primitive reflexes, such as the grasp and Moro reflexes, disappear during the first six months of chronological age. Indeed, their persistence beyond this time is taken as an indicator of central nervous system dysfunction. On the other hand, the postural, labyrinthine, tonic, and righting reflexes become more apparent in the first six months of life, and thus support the acquisition of fundamental movement patterns. These postural reflexes seem to disappear after infancy, although they become readily observable in certain circumstances with adults.

Fine-grained analysis of movement control suggests that postural reflexes support adult physical activities. For example, they are apparent in a range of sporting activities (Fukuda 1961) and can facilitate muscular endurance or strength activities (e.g., Hellebrandt, Schode, and Carns 1962). A long-standing developmental issue is the role that these postural reflexes play in voluntary instrumental activities. Part of the problem is definition, in that the reflex is sometimes defined from a physiological perspective regarding the question of innateness and monosynaptic (or spinal) connections and other times is defined behaviorally with respect to its latency and invariant response characteristics.

Before considering the debate on the role of postural reflexes in voluntary instrumental activities, noting ways in which reflex activities have been modified is worthwhile, as well as looking at examples in which exercising the reflex speeds up the onset of voluntary control of that activity. Consider the study of Bruner and Bruner (1968) on the modification of the sucking reflex. They showed that infants as young as 4 weeks could modify their regular, reflexive sucking of milk from a bottle to bring an image of a videotape picture on a screen into focus. Thus, through the presentation of an attractive stimulus that was linked to the recording of sucking rates, young infants demonstrated that they could modulate a reflex. If the required sucking strategy for picture clarity was too complex, the infants would return to their normal reflexive sucking routine. Similar observations have been made by Kaye (1967).

Zelazzo, Zelazzo, and Kolb (1972) have shown that exercising the stepping reflex during the first and second months of life can accelerate the onset of voluntary walking in infants. Lagenspetz, Nygard, and Strandwick (1971) made corresponding findings for crawling. Similarly, Bower (1974) has demonstrated the role of experience in facilitating the onset of reaching and grasping skills. These findings suggest that specific experiences—in this case, exercising the reflex that forms the substrate for the voluntary activity—can facilitate the onset of fundamental skills. Mere activity or training does not always speed up the voluntary control of a given activity (Gesell and Thompson 1929), which indicates that the appropriate antecedent behavior is an important determinant of the effects of experience on the development of motor skills. On the other hand, the exercise of the reflex may be just that, in the sense that it realizes all the traditional benefits of exercise, particularly increasing muscular strength and endurance.

The central theoretical problem has been how to incorporate the postural reflexes into a developmental account of the acquisition of fundamental motor skills. Bruner (1969) has proposed that voluntary activities become effective only when the appropriate reflexes for the given activity are inhibited. In this view, reflexes are an unwanted constraint for the executive function of the motor system to accommodate, and a poor basis for explanatory accounts of the voluntary control of physical activities. In contrast, Zelazzo (1976), extrapolating from his work on locomotion, argues that reflexes are superimposed by cognition in a hierarchical arrangement of movement control. Thus, the capacity to control reflexes by some higher order construct is essential to this viewpoint, despite the fact that locomotion remains intact in decerebrate animals (Grillner 1975).

Reflexes are not seen as an unwanted constraint for Easton (1972); rather, these wired-in synergies or functional groupings of muscles are viewed as features of which the motor system should take advantage. Thus, Easton proposes that reflexes are, in effect, coordinative structures and are the basis of all voluntary activities in that they offer a natural way in which to harness the multiple degrees of freedom requiring constraint by humans engaged in action. Thus, in Easton's view, reflexes represent preorganized acts that may be activated by the higher levels of the central nervous system as all or part of a movement. Furthermore, reflexes may prime the relevant motoneurons for some postures or movements. For example, the tonic neck reflex may prepare movement in the direction of the gaze and facilitate the speed of response. Conversely, reflexes may have inhibitory effects on response production, particularly if incompatibility exists between the reflexive postural set and the movement sequence.

An alternative view of the biological basis of motor development is that centrally generated motor patterns form the substrate for a variety of skilled actions. Thelen (1979) conducted a naturalistic, longitudinal study of 20 normal infants during their first year, identifying a range of rhythmical and highly stereotyped behaviors. Forty-seven specific movement patterns were described that involved the legs, feet, head, arms, fingers, and entire torso in various postures. These stereotypic behaviors followed developmental regularities in terms of both their onset and movement form. For example, the behaviors often exhibited the simple patterns of repetitive, identical alternation of flexion and extension, or of limb rotation around an axis. The onset of particular stereotypic behaviors was found to closely correlate with other traditional measures of fundamental motor patterns, and the degree of stereotypic behavior was inversely related to the amount of vestibular stimulation that the infant experienced (Thelen 1980). In summary, rhythmic stereotypes are viewed as manifestations of incomplete cortical control of endogenous patterning in maturing neuromuscular pathways, and vestibular stimulation may well play an important role in this maturation process (Clark, Kreutzberg, and Chee 1977).

Thelen (1979) has suggested that the link between the stereotypic behaviors and adult movement patterns is not obvious. Furthermore, the relationship between reflexes and stereotypic behaviors in the formulation of fundamental movement patterns has not been addressed. These basic responses are reflective of the biological substrate of action, and their development provides both inhibitory and facilitative constraints to the organization of voluntary movement.

Functional lateralization is another behavioral constraint and is a manifestation of hemispheric specialization of the cerebral cortex. Whether hemispheric specialization is structurally determined at birth or emerges through wide-ranging reorganization during ontogeny is still a hotly debated issue (Kinsbourne 1975; Corballis and Morgan 1978). Nevertheless, preference for the use of one hand or the other generally becomes stronger during the early years, with an average of about 93% of the adult population favoring the right hand. Foot and eye dominance is not biased so predominantly to the right side of the body. This functional constraint of asymmetry could be modified by a greater tolerance on the part of modern day society to left-handed individuals. The predominance of right-handedness, however, appears to have a long tradition (Coren and Porac 1977). This functional asymmetry of limb control may bring some constraint to coordination among limbs and their successful engagement in a variety of activities. The potential of long-term practice to overcome this functional asymmetry in limb control is not well understood, nor is the extent to which practice may alleviate other physiological and mechanical constraints.

SUMMARY

The central focus of this chapter is to outline ways in which various physical properties of both the human system and the environment naturally constrain the control and coordination of body and limbs in skilled physical activity. A significant feature of development, particularly as a consequence of physical growth, is that the physical properties of the system are dynamic. Thus, physical constraints are not invariant from moment to moment, no matter which level of analysis is chosen to theorize about the action. In traditional notions of skill development, this fluctuating circumstance of system and environmental variables is accommodated by appeals to cognitive constructs and highly detailed computation by some executive function in a hierarchically controlled motor system (Newell and Barclay 1982). In this view, the control of the large number of degrees of freedom inherent in the interaction of the performer with the environment is realized through cognitive computational notions—a burden that has been argued to be beyond the capabilities of even the most sophisticated machine (Kugler et al. 1980).

The physical constraints of the system naturally reduce the degree of freedom requiring control, as evidenced, for example, in the reflexive and stereotypic muscular organization in infants. Furthermore, analysis of the confluence of forces present in skilled activity suggests that the laws of physics contribute to movement control. Thus, one benefit of an understanding of the physical principles should be a reduction in the functional burden placed on notions of executive function in theorizing about the development of skilled action.

REFERENCES

Adams, J. A. A closed-loop theory of motor learning. *Journal of Motor Behavior,* 1971, **3**, 111-150.

Anokhin, P. K. Systemogenesis as a general regulator of brain development. *Progress in Brain Research,* 1964, **9**, 54-68.

Bayley, N., & Davis, F. C. Growth changes in bodily size and proportions during the first three years: A developmental study of sixty-one children by repeated measurements. *Biometrika,* 1935, **27**, 26-87.

Bower, T. G. R. *Development in infancy.* San Francisco: Freeman, 1975.

Brooks, C. B. & Jacobs, A. M. The gammer mass scanning technique for inertial anthropometric measurement. *Medicine and Science in Sport,* 1975, **7**, 290-294.

Bruner, J. S. Processes of growth in infancy. In A. Ambrose (Ed.), *Stimulation in early infancy.* New York: Academic Press, 1969.

Bruner, J. S. & Bruner, B. M. On voluntary action and the hierarchical structure. *International Journal of Psychology,* 1968, **3**, 239-255.

Capute, A. J., Accardo, P. J., Vinung, E. P. G., Rubenstein, J. E. & Harryman, S. *Primitive reflex profile.* Baltimore: University Park Press, 1978.

Chase, H. P. Undernutrition and growth and development of the human brain. In J. D. Lloyd-Still (Ed.), *Malnutrition and intellectual development.* Littleton, Massachusetts: PSG Pub. Co., 1976.

Clark, D. L., Kreutzberg, J. R. & Chee, F. K. W. Vestibular stimulation influence on motor development in infants. *Science,* 1977, **196**, 1228-1229.

Conel, J. *The postnatal development of the human cerebral cortex.* Vols. I-VI. Cambridge, Massachusetts: Harvard University Press, 1939-60.

Connolly, K. J. Skill development: Problems and plans. In K. J. Connolly (Ed.), *Mechanisms of motor skill development.* London: Academic Press, 1970.

Corballis, M. D. & Morgan, M. J. On the biological basis of human laterality: 1. Evidence for a maturational left-right gradient. *Behavioral and Brain Sciences,* 1978, **1**, 261-269.

Coren, S. & Porac, C. Fifty centuries of right-handedness: The historical record. *Science,* 1977, **198**, 631-632.

Easton, T. A. On the normal use of reflexes. *American Scientist,* 1972, **60**, 591-599.

Falkner, F. (Ed.) *Human development.* Philadelphia: Saunders, 1966.

Fukuda, T. Studies on human dynamic postures from the viewpoint of postural reflexes. *Acta Ota-Laryngologica,* 1961, **161**, 9-52.

Gesell, A. Maturation and infant behavior pattern. *Psychological Review,* 1929, **36**, 307-319.

Gesell, A. & Thompson, H. Learning and growth in identical infant twins: An experimental study by the method of co-twin control. *Genetic Psychology Monograph,* 1929, **6**, 1-124.

Gould, S. J. Allometry and size in ontogeny and phylogeny. *Biological Reviews,* 1966, **41**, 587-640.

Gould, S. J. *Ontogeny and phylogeny.* Cambridge, Massachusetts: Belknap Press, 1977.

Grillner, S. Locomotion in vertebrates: General mechanism and reflex interaction. *Physiological Review,* 1975, **55**, 247-304.

Guthrie, E. R. *The psychology of learning.* New York: Harper, 1935.

Hellebrandt, F. A., Schade, M. & Carns, M. L. Methods of evoking the tonic neck reflexes in human subjects. *American Journal of Physical Medicine,* 1962, **41**, 90-139.

Herron, R. E., Cuzzi, J. R., Goulet, D. V. & Hugg, J. E. *Experimental determination of the mechanical features of adults and children.* U.S. Department of Transportation Report, H5 801 168, Washington, D.C., 1974.

Hodgkins, J. Reaction time and speed of movement in males and females of various ages. *Research Quarterly,* 1963, **34**, 335-343.

Hooker, D. *The prenatal origin of behavior.* New York: Hafner, 1969.

Jensen, R. K. The effect of a 12-month growth period on the body movements of inertia of children. *Medicine and Science in Sports and Exercise,* 1981, **13**, 238-242.

John, E. R. *Functional neuroscience.* Vol. 2. *Neurometrics: Clinical applications of quantitative electrophysiology.* New York: Wiley, 1977.

Kaye, H. Infant sucking behavior and its modification. In L. P. Lipsitt & C. C. Spiker (Eds.), *Advances in child development and behavior.* Vol. 3. London: Academic Press, 1967.

Kinsbourne, M. Lateral interactions of the brain. In M. Kinsbourne & N. L. Smith (Eds.), *Hemispheric disconnections in cerebral function.* Springfield, Illinois: Charles C Thomas, 1975.

Kugler, P. N., Kelso, J. A. S. & Turvey, M. T. On the concept of coordinative structures as dissipative structures: I. Theoretical lines of convergence. In G. E. Stelmach & J. Requin (Eds.), *Tutorials in motor behavior.* Amsterdam: North Holland, 1980.

Kugler, P. N., Kelso, J. A. S. & Turvey, M. T. On the control and coordination of naturally developing systems. In J. A. S. Kelso & J. E. Clark (Eds.), *The development of movement control and coordination.* New York: Wiley, 1982.

Lagerspetz, K., Nygard, M. & Strandwick, C. The effects of training in crawling on the motor and mental development of infants. *Scandinavian Journal of Psychology,* 1971, **12**, 192-197.

Mandler, G. *Mind and emotion.* New York: Wiley, 1975.

McGraw, M. B. Swimming behavior of the human infant. *Journal of Pediatrics,* 1939, **15**, 485-490.

Newell, A. A note on process-structure distinctions in developmental psychology. In S. Farnham-Diggary (Ed.), *Information processing in children.* New York: Academic Press, 1972.

Newell, K. M. & Barclay, C. R. Developing knowledge about action. In J. A. S. Kelso & J. Clark (Eds.), *The development of control and coordination in movement.* New York: Wiley, 1982.

Nilsson, L., Furuhjelm, M., Ingelman-Sundberg, A. & Wirsén, E. *A child is born.* (2nd ed.) New York: Delacorte Press, 1977.

Norval, M. A. Relationship of weight and length of infants at birth to the age at which they begin to walk alone. *Journal of Pediatrics,* 1947, **30**, 676-678.

Ounsted, M. & Ounsted, C. *On fetal growth rate.* Philadelphia: Lippincott, 1973.

Pew, R. W. Human perceptual-motor performance. In B. J. Kantowitz (Ed.), *Human information processing: Tutorials in performance and cognition.* Hillsdale, New Jersey: Erlbaum, 1974.

Raisman, G. What hope for repair of the brain? *Annals of Neurology,* 1978, **3**, 101-106.

Robins, W. J., Brody, S., Hogan, A. G., Jackson, C. M. & Greene, C. W. *Growth.* New Haven, Connecticut: Yale University Press, 1928.

Rose, S. *The conscious brain.* New York: Vintage Books, 1976.

Scammon, R. E. The measurement of the body in childhood. In J. A. Harns, C. M. Jackson, D. G. Paterson & R. E. Scammon (Eds.), *The measurement of man.* Minneapolis: University of Minnesota Press, 1930.

Schmidt, R. A. A schema theory of discrete motor skill learning. *Psychological Review,* 1975, **82**, 225-260.

Sherrington, C. S. *The integrative action of the nervous system.* New Haven, Connecticut: Yale University Press, 1906.

Shirley, M. M. *The first two years: A study of twenty-five babies.* Vol. 1. *Postural and locomotor development.* Minneapolis: University of Minnesota Press, 1931.

Shuttleworth, F. The physical and mental growth of girls and boys age six to nineteen in relation to age at maximum growth. *Monographs of the Society for Research in Child Development,* 1939, **4**, (3).

Tanner, J. *Growth at adolescence.* (2nd ed.) Oxford: Blackwell, 1962.

Thelen, E. Rhythmical stereotypes in normal human infants. *Animal Behavior,* 1979, **27**, 699-715.

Thelen, E. Determinants of amounts of stereotyped behavior in normal human infants. *Ethology and Sociobiology,* 1980, **1**, 141-150.

Timiras, P. S. *Developmental physiology and aging.* New York: Macmillan, 1973.

Tokuyama, H., Okamoto, T. & Kumamoto, M. Electromyographic study of swimming in infants and children. In P. V. Komi (Ed.), *Biomechanics V-B.* Baltimore: University Park Press, 1976.

Wade, M. G. Developmental motor learning. In J. Keogh & R. S. Hutton (Eds.), *Exercise and sports science reviews.* Vol. IV. Santa Barbara, California: Journal Publishing Affiliates, 1976.

Wickstrom, R. L. Developmental kinesiology: Maturation of basic motor patterns. In J. H. Wilmore & J. F. Keogh (Eds.), *Exercise and sport science reviews.* Vol. 3. New York: Academic Press, 1975.
Wyke, B. The neurological basis of movement—A developmental review. In K. S. Holt (Ed.), *Movement and child development.* London: SIMP/Heinemann Medical; Philadelphia: Lippincott, 1975.
Zelazo, P. R. From reflexive to instrumental behavior. In L. P. Lipsitt (Ed.), *Developmental psychobiology.* Hillsdale, New Jersey: Erlbaum, 1976.
Zelazo, P., Zelazo, N. & Kolb, S. "Walking" in the newborn. *Science,* 1972, **177**, 1058-1059.

SUGGESTED READINGS

Undergraduate Students

Connolly, K. J. (Ed.) *Mechanisms of motor skill development.* New York: Academic Press, 1970.
Rose, S. *The conscious brain.* New York: Vintage, 1976.
Wyke, B. The neurological basis of movement—A developmental review. In K. S. Holt (Ed.), *Movement and child development.* Philadelphia: Lippincott, 1975.

Graduate Students

Connolly, K. J. & Prechtl, H. J. (Eds.) *Maturation and development: Biological and psychological perspectives.* Philadelphia: Lippincott, 1981.
Easton, T. A. On the normal use of reflexes. *American Scientist,* 1972, **60**, 591-599.
Kugler, P. N., Kelso, J. A. S., & Turvey, M. T. On the control and coordination of naturally developing systems. In J. A. S. Kelso & J. E. Clark (Eds.), *The development of movement control and coordination.* New York: Wiley, 1982.

PART II

Applications of Knowledge of Motor Development to Children's Movement

The four chapters in this section suggest ways that the information from Part I may be applied to enhance children's motor development. Chapter 6 demonstrates the steps involved in using a motor development data base to plan an elementary physical education program. The chapter suggests that the curriculum should be based on scientific literature about motor development. It provides a conceptual model and specific examples of how a teacher may use theoretical and empirical knowledge to teach children.

Another important area in which to use the motor development data base is presented in Chapter 7. The reader is given specific examples of how to plan the physical environment to develop and maintain motor skills and physical fitness in children. The chapter outlines how equipment and facilities accommodate physical growth, anticipation timing, catching, posture, safety, and other factors.

Chapter 8 discusses how memory functions and motor performance differ between retarded and nonretarded children. In particular, the chapter notes the implications of these differences for planning physical activity programs for retarded children.

The last chapter in this part is included, because while the purposes of assessment of children's motor development are quite important, they are often poorly understood. The chapter discusses how to understand what is to be measured, why a feature is measured, and when the measurement should be taken. The chapter is condensed because specific tests are not discussed. However, it presents rationales for determining the important characteristics and behaviors to be measured, based on the intent of the program.

This part serves to complement knowledge of motor development with professional aspects of planning physical education programs for children.

Knowledge for its own sake is important, but certainly of greater value if teachers and coaches understand how to apply their knowledge of motor development to the everyday world as they teach children ages 4 to 15.

6

Making Sense of Motor Development: Interfacing Research With Lesson Planning[1]

Jere Dee Gallagher

Teaching motor skills to children of varying ages is a complex process. When planning lessons, the teacher must plan for children who vary physiologically, biomechanically, and cognitively. A major concern of teaching is how to develop children's skills and how to keep the children on the task. This chapter applies the research on adult-child differences presented in Chapters 1 through 5 to planning and teaching developmentally appropriate lessons.

DEMANDS OF THE TEACHER AND LEARNER DURING THE LESSON

An analysis of the demands placed on the learner and teacher is in order before discussing the mechanics of planning. For the child, the first step in learning a skill is to know the goal of the desired behavior. If the goal is to learn a standing triple jump, a sequential hop-step-jump is required. A further breakdown of the goal of the skill might be taking off on one foot, landing on the same foot, pushing off on that foot, and landing on the other foot, followed by pushing off on two feet and landing on two feet, all for distance. Assuming the child understands the goal or objective, she must then *selectively attend to* and *encode* the task appropriate cues into the performance (Figure 6.1). For the triple jump, the child took off on one foot, landed on the other foot, pushed off on that foot, landed on the other foot, pushed off on two feet, and landed on two feet while the arms were at the side for each phase.

Memory is therefore involved in the process, in that the learner must remember his performance and then match the desired goal to the performance. From the discrepancy in this match, the learner identifies errors in the performance. Returning to the example, the triple jump does not

1. The author would like to express appreciation to Michael Sherman for brainstorming on the relationship between motor development and research done on the ways teachers think about and approach motor development, as well as for critical comments on an earlier draft.

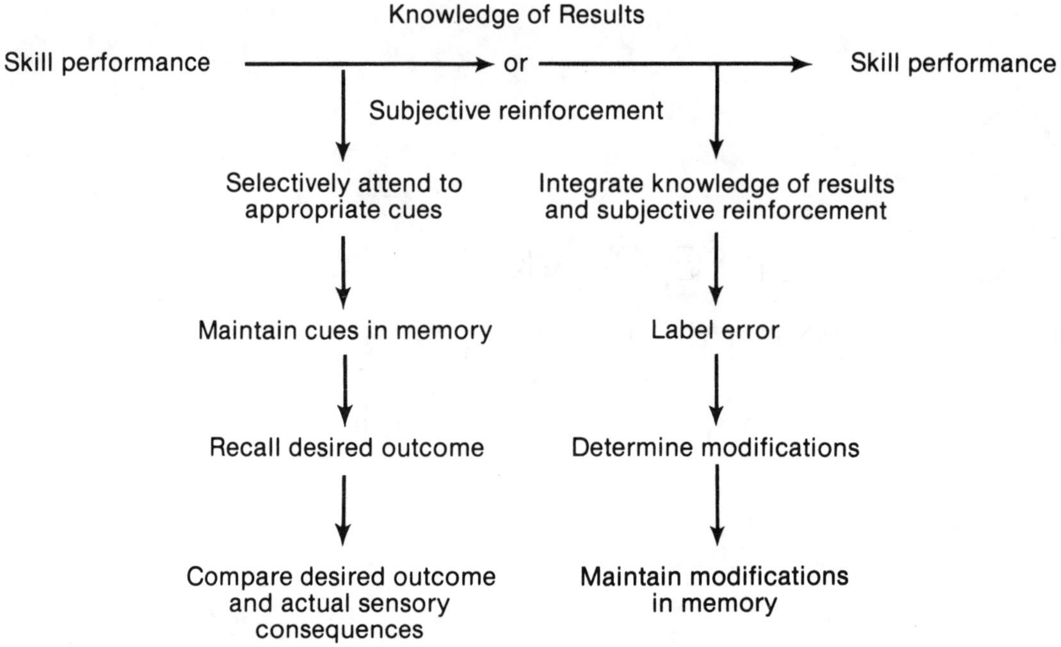

Figure 6.1. Information processing requirements between practice trials.

match the goal; a step-step-jump was performed instead of a hop-step-jump. This information is then incorporated with error information that the teacher gives to the child. The teacher might tell the child that her arms were not used during the jump.

Finally, after integrating error information and past performance to determine error corrections, the learner must *remember* the plan for the next trial. In this case, the child plans to hop-step-jump while giving attention to arm placement.

While the child is attending to her own performance, the teacher must attend to the performances of perhaps 29 other children to give prescriptive feedback. Therefore, the burden of detection and correction of errors is the responsibility of the students, and therefore rapid development of a mechanism for error detection and correction is imperative. If this corrective procedure is done after every trial, and if, as is usually the case, time is limited between trials, the demands on the learner and teacher are significant. Therefore, the teacher needs to be concerned with the time constraints involved (the speed with which the information can be processed by the learner) and then with developing both the children's and the teacher's ability to detect and correct errors.

Thus, the teaching and learning environment is indeed complex, so attention needs to be directed to planning the lesson to reduce task complexity.

PLANNING

Prior to developing unit and lesson plans, an orderly sequence of skills to be taught across the age ranges must be determined (Figure 6.2). Based on research on developmental sequences, an

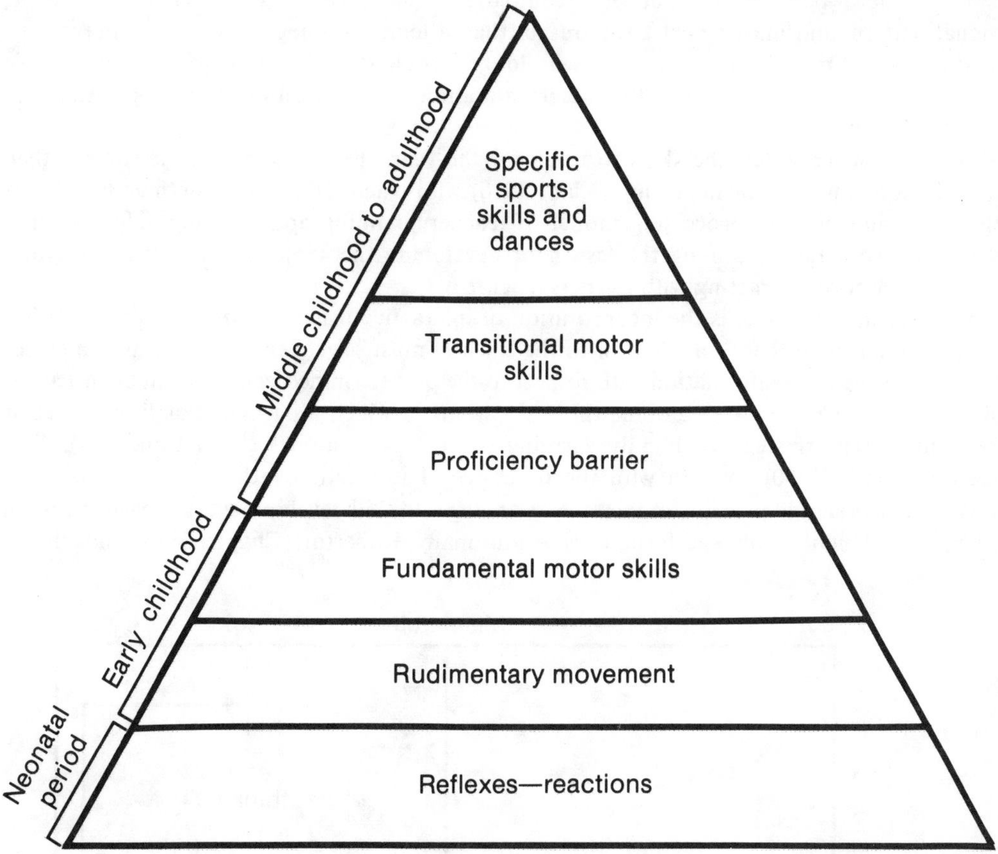

Figure 6.2. Developmental skill acquisition. (Integration of Seefeldt's model [1980, p. 317] and Gallahue's model [1982, p. 2].)

orderly progression has been developed (Gallahue, Werner, and Luedke 1975; Seefeldt 1980; Roberton, Chapter 3).

The initial stage of development is categorized as the reflex-reactive period of development. Roberton (Chapter 3) refers to this stage as primitive motor patterns in infancy. The infant is born with a multitude of reflexes (i.e., Moro, tonic neck, and others) and is prepared for perception (such as depth perception and object constancy). At approximately four months of age, certain reflexes are lost, while others are the foundations for the rudimentary movement stage. During this period, skills such as lifting the head, sitting, rolling over, and grasping are developed. These movements are refined into fundamental motor patterns to include such skills as walking, running, hopping, skipping, and jumping.

Between fundamental motor pattern development and the transition stage, Seefeldt (1980) has noted a proficiency barrier. Those children who have not learned the fundamental motor patterns are unable to combine and modify these patterns to develop more specialized skills. Since the fundamental motor patterns have not been acquired, the child must focus on the mechanics of the individual pattern, and must detect errors rather than attempt to integrate several patterns. The child who has automated the basic skills is no longer required to detect errors from the simple movements, and can then attend to the integration and specialization of the motor patterns to develop sport skills.

Once the teacher selects the skills to teach for the year, the plans for each lesson are then developed. Combining problem solving (Klahr 1980) with teacher thinking, Sherman (1982) has developed an information processing model of teacher planning and thinking. The model is divided into two stages: planning the lesson or developing the script, and implementing and adapting the script or interacting with learners (Figure 6.3).

Important in this model is the incorporation of interactive teaching, which emphasizes that during the lesson the teacher (in addition to the learner) must selectively "perceive and interpret portions of the available information with respect to the predetermined goals . . . and construct a simplified model of reality to determine those situations in which a particular skill or subset of skills is appropriate, instead of blindly carrying out the skills alone" (Shavelson 1981). This parallels Seefeldt's (1980) concern with the processes of instruction rather than with the end product. Teachers should provide for increments or stages in skill development that occur between rudimentary and highly skilled performances. Additionally, Roberton (Chapter 3) expands this to

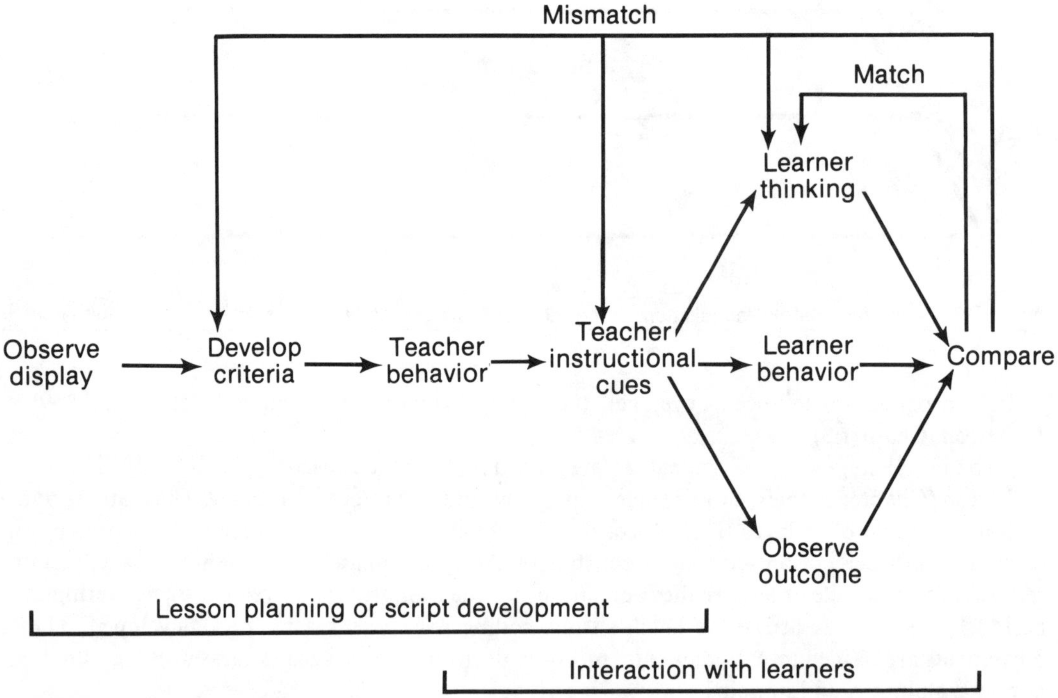

Figure 6.3. Model of teacher thinking. (Reprinted with permission from Sherman, M. A. Teacher thinking model. Personal communication, February 1982.)

suggest that training affects motor development to the degree that training depends on the type of skill, the components within the skill, and perhaps the developmental level of the child.

Although Sherman's model follows a typical information processing model, parallel processing may occur. This is particularly possible during the interactive teaching phase.

SCRIPT DEVELOPMENT

In developing plans, three major concerns (Seefeldt 1980) are selection of appropriate content, analysis of the skills performed by the students, and use of appropriate teaching techniques. This section redefines these concerns into (1) display observation, (2) development of criteria, (3) teacher behavior, and (4) teacher instructional cues.

Observation

Teachers should observe the display and note the conditions under which they will be teaching. Initially, the teacher must focus on three types of cues: contextual, teacher, and learner. Contextual cues are the environmental constraints. The teacher is able to change these, but for a given lesson they are set. Examples of contextual cues are the time allocated for physical education, the area where physical education is taught, available equipment, and other similar factors. To structure a developmentally appropriate environment based on motor development research, see Chapter 6.

Teacher cues include factors inherent to the teacher. The two major factors here are knowledge base and experience. The teacher's knowledge base is developed to analyze the skill and to relay developmentally appropriate messages to the learner (Tobey 1976). During the lesson, the teacher must recognize acceptable and unacceptable response characteristics in the skills and understand how deficiencies in the internal processing operations may contribute to the observed performance (Hoffman 1977). Prescriptive feedback may either relate information concerning the outcome of the movement or focus the child's attention on the task-appropriate cues, which often refer to either the spatial or temporal elements or both of the response (Hoffman 1977, Singer 1977). As mentioned previously, development of a mechanism for error detection and correction is important; thus, error messages should focus on the major discrepancies between the observed and desired response (Welford 1968).

To detect and correct errors, and to give appropriate prescriptive feedback, the teacher must therefore understand the factors that affect children in learning motor skills. The teacher's knowledge base should include four factors: desired behaviors (outcomes), task analysis of the desired behavior, entry level of the children (growth and neurophysiological components), and the developmental memory stages of the children.

Knowledge of the desired behavior allows the teacher to know when the learner has mastered the skill, or how to analyze the performance to detect errors. Structuring the task analysis to determine sequential relationships between task components allows the teacher to introduce the most developmentally appropriate skills to facilitate efficient learning.

Knowledge of the developmental memory level is important. Children of varying ages bring to the learning situation different learning strategies to remember the skills (i.e., labeling, grouping, recoding, rehearsal). By knowing which strategies the child uses spontaneously, others can be forced. This also aids the teacher in structuring appropriate feedback.

Experience comes into play by allowing the teacher to further reduce task demands (selectively encode the task-appropriate cues) and therefore to detect errors more efficiently. Sherman (1979) found that experts planned lessons and forced instructional cues to prevent errors (similar to Seefeldt's learning process and developmental sequences), while novice teachers taught the specific skill and corrected errors (attended to the end product).

Also, a teacher's implicit theory of instruction and her emotional state affects her performance. A teacher's conceptions of a subject matter are expected to influence his judgments, decisions, and behavior (Barr 1975; Harste and Burke 1977; Bawden, Burke, and Duffy 1979; Duffy and Metheny 1979; Metheny 1980; Pearson and Kamil 1978).

Finally, learner cues include the learner's developmental levels (information processing capabilities, growth status, and neurophysiological development). Most important here is to find the emotional, physical, and cognitive maturational levels of the learner (Magill 1976). The student's capabilities and prior experiences are then assessed to determine the child's entry level in the skill.

Knowledge of the child's physical maturity is important in setting expectations for the child. Three examples showing the application of this knowledge are: (1) Using the knowledge of a child's physical maturity aids the teacher in setting distance and force expectations for each age level. For instance, a five-year-old using the same throwing form as a seven-year-old would not be expected to throw the ball as far. (2) Using knowledge of the sequences of gains in height, weight, and strength aid the teacher in understanding temporary awkwardness or regression in distance or force expectations. A child first gains in height; this is generally followed by a weight gain 5 months later and a subsequent strength gain 14 months later. (3) An awareness of developing cardiovascular endurance aids the teacher in determining when to teach skill-related versus health-related fitness.

The learner's cognitive maturational level is important when structuring the lesson. Many motor skills require a rapid response to external factors, in addition to rapid movement, such as anticipating when to swing a bat at an oncoming ball. During these skills, the young child not only performs more slowly but also, if the speed requirements are increased, shows an inverse relationship with age and performance. The child appears to be penalized more than can be accounted for by a slower reaction time.

Moving from the performance to a learning environment, the young child requires more time to learn the same task than does an adult. This is because the young child approaches the learning situation with different strategies (control processes). By understanding how young children spontaneously think and the strategies with which they approach the learning environment, the teacher can structure lessons to force mature memory strategies that promote rapid skill development.

A third learner cue is knowledge base or experience or both. Not only does the teacher need to be concerned about her own knowledge base but also she needs to be concerned about developing the learner's knowledge base. Memory strategy differences have been argued to be due in part to knowledge base differences between children and adults (Lindberg 1980). In experimental situations, when children were able to use a knowledge base that was richer than that of adults', they were superior to the adults in terms of both recall and clustering. Thus, knowledge base variation is a sufficient condition for elevating children's memory performances over those of adults. This finding generally indicates the importance of knowledge base development in young children to help them learn the motor skill more efficiently and to detect and correct errors.

Development of Criteria

Teachers should determine what skills to work on in each day's lesson. Determining the specific skills to be taught and the level of attainment to be reached helps to state goals and objectives (Figure 6.4). Five substages are included in this step: terminal objective, task analysis, instructional analysis, enabling objectives, and enabling activities.

Terminal objectives are extracted from the pyramid (Figure 6.2) to determine whether the students are at a rudimentary, fundamental, transitional, or sport skill developmental stage. The terminal objective is analyzed two ways: breakdown of skills into the component parts (intratask developmental sequence) and determination of developmental sequences (intertask developmental sequences). The component parts and developmental sequences can be gleaned from textbooks on fundamental motor pattern development (Wickstrom 1978). In Chapter 3, Roberton covers component analyses for walking, running, long jumping, hopping, throwing, catching, and punting. An intratask sequence for rope jumping is shown in Figure 6.5.

The intertask developmental sequences enable the teacher to determine appropriately the level of the learner in skill development. For example, Roberton and Halverson (1977) have detected that the prerequisite skills for running are jumping in place, jumping down, leaping, and galloping. An example of an intertask developmental sequence for jumping is shown in Figure 6.6. Moving from simple to complex, the initial skill is the step down, which removes emphasis on strength and balance. The final skill in the sequence is the one-foot hop, which requires an integration of strength and balance.

The component analysis and developmental sequences (intertask and intratask) are combined to develop a learning hierarchy similar to Singer and Dick's (1980) instructional analysis. The learning hierarchy includes all variables involved in the performance of the skill. The analyses should not be confused; the intertask sequence informs the teacher about what skill the child is ready to learn, while the intratask analysis evaluates quality or stage of movement or both. Thus, the instructional analysis aids the teacher in planning sequential lessons.

The next step in developing the criteria is matching the learner's skills and experiences to the instructional analysis to determine entry level. Once the child's entry level is assessed, enabling

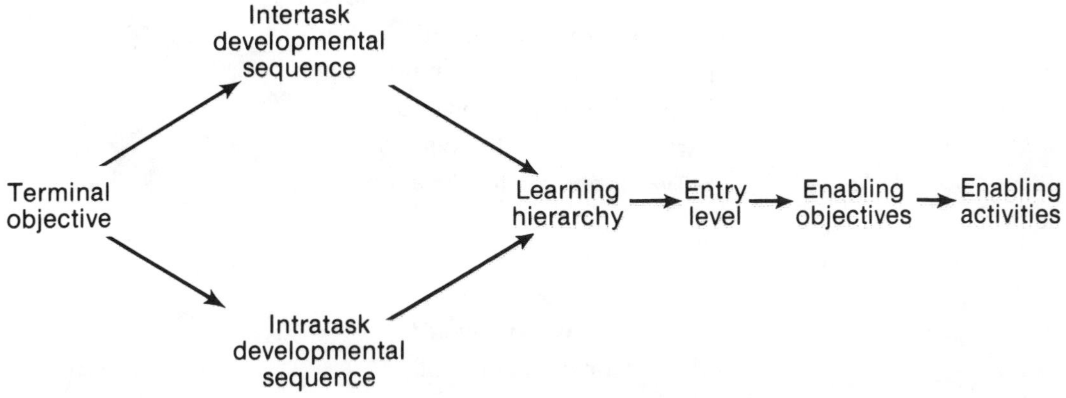

Figure 6.4. Criteria development.

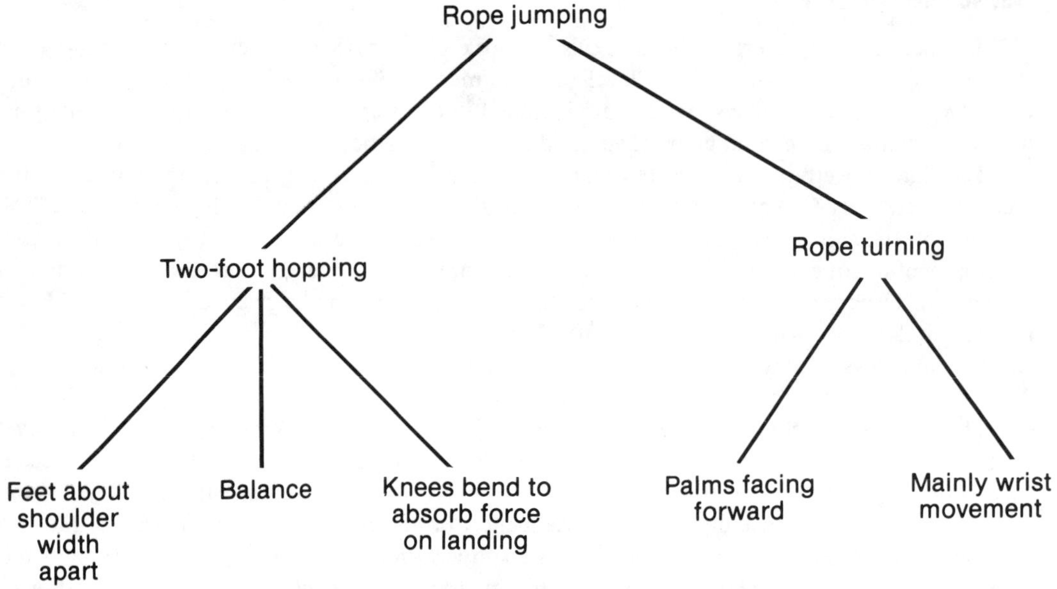

Figure 6.5. Intratask components of rope jumping.

objectives are developed. The terminal objective and enabling objectives are included in the learning hierarchy; the terminal objective is the top of the learning hierarchy, whereas the enabling objectives are the components of the hierarchy. Associated with each enabling objective are several enabling activities (for further explanation, see Singer and Dick 1980) to provide for growth or developmental differences and the adaptability of the movement.

Step down from height with support
Step down from height with no support
Jump down from height with support
Jump down from height with no support
Two-foot jump with support
Two-foot jump with no support
Two-foot jump for distance
Jump over barrier
One-foot takeoff
Two-foot landing
Hop with two feet
Hop with one foot

Figure 6.6. Intertask developmental sequence for jumping. (From Espenschade and Eckert 1967.)

To illustrate development of the criteria, analyze a two-foot rhythmic rope-jumping task. To perform rhythmic rope jumping, the learner must coordinate the two motor skills of rope turning and two-foot hopping. Since a two-foot hop is used in the skill, refer to Figure 6.6 and note that the two-foot hop develops relatively late in a jumping sequence. A good vertical and horizontal jump must be evident before initiating a rhythmic rope-jumping lesson.

An example of interfacing component and developmental sequence analyses to form a learning hierarchy is found in the rhythmic rope-jumping skill (Figure 6.7). The components of a rhythmic rope-jumping skill are rope turning and two-foot hopping. The subcomponents are the rudimentary patterns that combine to form the motor skills. In this case, the subcomponents of rope turning are that the palms face forward and that the child is to use mainly wrist movement. The skill and experience level of the child is matched to the learning hierarchy to determine the level of instruction.

Teacher Behavior

Once the teacher knows what he wants to teach, the next step is to determine a teaching method. Prior to deciding on the method, the teacher needs to analyze the skill on both open and closed and on self- and externally paced dimensions. In an open skill, the performer never does the same thing twice in exactly the same way, since the stimulus demands are never exactly the same. In the closed skill, the environment is relatively constant not only throughout the performance of

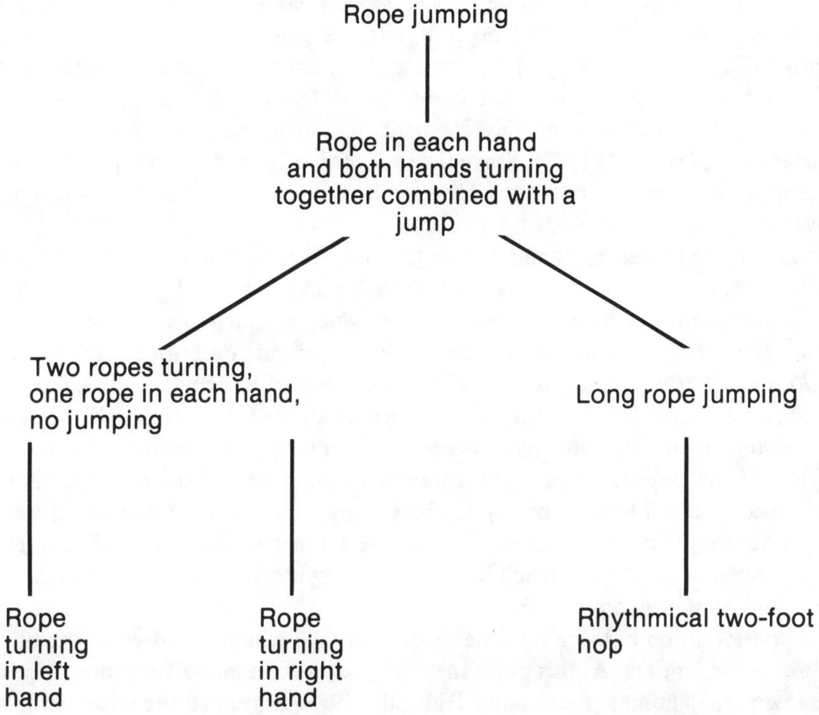

Figure 6.7. Learning hierarchy of rhythmic rope jumping.

the skill but also on different occasions in performing that skill. The performer's task, once the skill is performed correctly, is to attempt to replicate that movement or series of movements time after time. Thus, in an open skill, flexibility and diversification are desirable, whereas a closed skill demands exact replication of a successful movement pattern (Marteniuk 1976).

Self- and externally paced dimensions refer to the initiation of the movement. When performing a self-paced skill, the individual initiates the movement when desired, whereas in an externally paced skill, anticipation timing is involved. The learner is not able to initiate the response when desired, but must respond to a set pace or rhythm.

The parameters of open and closed skills and of self- and externally paced dimensions are not discrete but rather are opposite ends of a continuum. Returning to the rope-jumping lesson skills, determine if rope jumping is open or closed, and self- or externally paced. The components of jumping and rope turning are toward the open skill end. Although the environmental conditions surrounding the skill are relatively fixed, the learner can vary the speed of turning and jumping and the type of jump used. Rope turning is also self-paced unless the learner must turn in rhythm to music or a fixed jumping speed. On the other hand, jumping is externally paced, since the jump must be coordinated with the turning rope.

Now that the skills have been further analyzed as to environmental conditions, the method of teaching can be determined. The method should match the objective. Mosston (1981) has developed a "Spectrum of Teaching Styles" that delineates the roles of both the teacher and the learner. Objectives reached for each style are identified. The style used must match the task demands (Singer 1977). For example, if in a movement education lesson a teacher is working on concept attainment of force production and absorption, either a guided discovery style or the divergent style is appropriate (Schmidt 1977). To promote the learner's ability to repeat the movement, Singer (1977) has suggested the use of the command style (error-free learning) when teaching a self-paced, closed skill. For schema development, a guided discovery (movement education) method appears valid (Schmidt 1977). Since the skill of rhythmic rope jumping is open and hence variability of practice is important, a teaching method should be selected that promotes adaptability (movement education or guided discovery).

Once the method of teaching is matched to the objective, the child's method of learning needs to be considered. Thus, the teacher needs to consider a match between learning styles and teaching styles. Learning styles imply certain conditions under which a student learns best, whereas teaching style describes the behaviors and media used to place demands on both the teacher and learner (*Phi Delta Kappan* 1980). Kolb (1976) classified perception of information on a continuum from concrete to abstract. Additionally, information processing runs the continuum from reflecting and watching to doing. From this two-by-two matrix formed by perceiving and processing, four learning styles are developed. Apparently, teachers fall into one of the four learning styles and consequently tend to teach only in one style (McCarthy 1980). The implication is that when the teacher's style does not match the learner's style, the learner is shortchanged. The general conclusion is that teachers should not teach in merely one style, but should incorporate a variety of styles that depend on the lesson content.

Another consideration in teaching styles is determining whether and when use of a model or demonstration is appropriate. At this point the effectiveness of a model on prompting the learners needs to be reviewed. Thomas, Pierce, and Ridsdale (1977) examined the effects of giving seven- and nine-year-old girls a model either at the beginning of the learning session, after they had already attempted the task, or no model. A model used at the beginning of the performance facilitated learning of both age groups. The model used at the middle of the practice session was equally effective for the nine-year-olds, but hindered the performance of the seven-year-olds. The authors attributed these findings to the greater capabilities of the older children to process information and also to their familiarity with motor skills. Conclusions indicated that nine-year-olds should effectively use modeling cues regardless of when the model was given; the seven-year-olds, however, could use a model's cues to aid performance only when the model was given prior to practice. Thus, the study demonstrated the influential effects of temporal spacing of demonstrations on the developmental levels of the learner.

Supporting Thomas et al. (1977), Weiss (1981) found that the effectiveness of a model depends on differences in cognitive development evident in children of different ages. The major variables in her study were that she used both model and no-model conditions crossed with verbal label and no verbal label groups for five- and seven-year-old children. Results indicated that certain cognitive, developmental factors (attention span, memory capacity, coding capabilities, and physical abilities) were necessary for modeling to occur. Practical implications indicated that verbal or show-and-tell models may be more effective for directing children's attention to task-relevant cues. Not only does a verbal model demonstrate correct performance but also it attaches appropriate verbal labels to components of the skill, thereby facilitating attention to and retention of required movements or both (Winther and Thomas 1981). The powerful influence of verbal models seems especially important for kindergartners and preschoolers, while the seven- to eight-year-old children performed equally well after viewing either silent or verbal models.

Teacher Instructional Cues

Teachers need to consider what to look for in the skill and how their decisions affect learner thinking. Teachers are also limited in their information processing capabilities and therefore must attend to the cues that they think are the most likely to cause errors (Tversky and Kahneman 1974, Nisbett and Ross 1980). These cues are the key points in the movement that forces selective attention of the learner and are used as observational focal points by the teacher. The teacher must reduce the complexities of the original information available to her as antecedents to her judgments (Shavelson 1976; Shavelson and Atwood 1977; Shavelson, Cadwell, and Izu 1977). An example of appropriate cues in teaching a child to jump rope is to instruct him to "jump-bounce, jump-bounce," or in a catching skill to "look-reach-give."

INTERACTIVE TEACHING

Thus far, the teacher's thinking has been done before interaction with students. Planning in the first phase concludes with a script of activities for interaction with the learners. The lesson has been structured to make student behavior in the activity predictable (Shavelson 1981). Therefore, during interactive teaching, the teacher has changed the rather complex environment of having 30 children move within an environment to an environment where few children are making errors.

Student Thinking

Teachers need to consider what the child is thinking. At this point, the student's ability to focus on and maintain the task-relevant cues in memory come into play. The environment needs to be structured so that the cognitive processes not automatic to the child are forced (e.g., labeling, grouping, and recoding).

If the teacher is aware that the younger child has not yet developed an ability to attend selectively to cues that are task appropriate, this allows him to structure both his lesson and the environment to force the development of a selective attention strategy. Stratton (1978) applied basic research on selective attention to a real setting to conclude that teachers should evaluate task requirements, environmental demands, and teacher input. During the performance of most motor skills, a wealth of cues irrelevant to the task are available. For example, when catching a ball, some of the available cues are the color of the ball, the performance of the thrower, the performances of other classmates, verbal information from the teacher, and other classes playing nearby.

Younger children acquire better strategies of selective attention if higher levels of interference are imposed early in the learning situation when the child is also told the cues appropriate to the task. This allows the child to develop a strategy to ignore the irrelevant information. Caution should be used, however, in that the irrelevant information cannot reach a level that prevents learning of the primary task. Implications for the teacher include selecting key words that suggest the important aspects of the skill. In catching a ball, such key words could be "look," "reach," and "give." When performing a headstand, the words appropriate to the task might be "knees on elbows" (force the tripod), "feet on buttocks" (to move the weight over the base of support), and "feet straight" (to maintain a line of gravity).

Combining labeling with selective attention, thus forcing the child to attend selectively to and label certain task-appropriate cues, improves performance. For example, when learning to jump a self-turned rope, a child's performance improves when she is forced to label the movements to develop a rhythm (jump-bounce, jump-bounce).

Note that younger children fail to use other control processes such as rehearsal, grouping, and recoding. Teachers can force these strategies, however, to promote more effective learning. In the triple jump, a child continually thinks and practices in terms of hop-hop-hop-stop, step-step-step-stop, jump-jump-jump. The older child practices hop-step-jump, hop-step-jump, hop-step-jump (combining efficient grouping and rehearsal). Thus, when teaching the triple jump, the child should be forced to integrate practice and be kept from separating the individual components. Another example of rehearsal, grouping, and recoding is in the teaching of a floor exercise routine. First, each individual skill is learned (e.g., handstand, forward roll, front scale, cartwheel, run, roundoff, back handspring). This is followed by grouping of two or three movements and rehearsing the movements together to form a larger unit of information (e.g., handstand, forward roll, front scale, cartwheel; then run, roundoff, back handspring). Subsequent reformation of the units of information forms one run down the mat (thus, handstand, forward roll, front scale, cartwheel, run, roundoff, back handspring).

An example of integrating the information on the developmental use of memory strategies shows how to force the processes of selective attention, labeling, rehearsal, and grouping. When teaching the schottische, the schottische step is learned first by forcing the child to attend selectively to and label the movements step-step-hop. The movements are rehearsed together as a group until the skill becomes automatic. Next, the child practices skipping in a circle by using four step-hops, labeled skip-two-three-four. Finally, the child practices both groups of skills together to recode the movements into one unit while moving to music.

Student Behavior: Observing the Outcome

The teacher needs to observe what the learner is doing, which is related to student thinking. Student thinking, student behavior, and observing the outcome occur simultaneously. As Figure 6.1 shows, several mental operations occur as the child is performing. The child must attend selectively to and encode the cues appropriate to the task. The teacher's instructional cues are the observational guidelines for encoding information for both the teacher and learner. An example given in the instructional cues section was, in learning to catch, to tell the student to "look, reach, give." These are the components important for both the teacher and the learner. For the first cue to look, the child must watch the ball to gather important information (e.g., time and space relationships, anticipation of initiation of movement). For the second cue, to reach, the child must extend his arms to maximize the distance over which the force can be reduced. Finally, in the cue to give, the child must bend her arms to reduce force. If any of these three basic components are missing, the catch is not effective.

Comparing Performances

The teacher must consider whether the skill was performed correctly or incorrectly. This stage refers to the system for error detection and correction. Both learners and teachers compare the performance to the criteria to determine the quantitative and qualitative aspects of the movement. The error is labeled (subjective reinforcement by the learner, knowledge of results by the teacher) and modifications determined. Based on conclusions from literature on memory, young children clearly tend to ignore relevant information and therefore respond immediately without using knowledge of results and without developing subjective reinforcement (Barclay and Newell 1980). Therefore, the child must be forced to make the comparison to develop subjective reinforcement and to integrate knowledge of results.

When a match between desired and actual behavior occurs, the student either stores (remembers) the movement or verifies the correctness of the movement (repeats). If a mismatch exists between the performance and objective, then the information returns to criterion development, teacher instructional cues, and learner thinking. A widespread discrepancy between performance and criteria might indicate that the abilities and experiences of the learners were inappropriately assessed and that the teacher initiated instruction on a level too advanced for the learner's developmental sequence. Therefore, the criteria need revision for a more developmentally appropriate stage in the sequence.

At the same time, the mismatch is used by the thinking teacher and learner. The teacher uses the information to develop prescriptive feedback (knowledge of results) while the learner develops subjective reinforcement. From an integration of knowledge of results and subjective reinforcement, modifications of the movement are determined.

SUMMARY

Development of lesson plans and the interaction between learners and teachers is complex. To plan developmentally appropriate lessons, teachers must understand growth and development differences, effects of exercise on growth, neurophysiological development, fundamental motor pattern development, and developmental skill acquisition.

Since both teachers and learners are processing information, they need to reduce the task demands evident in the lesson. The teacher reduces her task demands by developing a lesson plan. When interacting with the learners, the teacher has a carefully developed script to follow. A good mental plan for interactive teaching minimizes conscious decision making during the interactive stage (MacKay 1977, Joyce 1978-1979, Clark and Yinger 1979). The information processing load of the teacher has thus been reduced by making both timing and sequencing of activities and student behavior predictable during an activity.

The teacher's knowledge and experience with intertask and intratask developmental sequences is important for a clear understanding of both correct and incorrect responses by the learners in action. Knowledge of developmental memory differences allows the teacher to structure appropriate prescriptive feedback for the child. The feedback should include a comparison of the desired versus the actual behavior to develop a mechanism for error detection and correction.

The teacher aids the learner in reducing task demands. This is first considered in determining the level of instruction. If the teacher expects the six-year-old to play three-player dodge ball, the child must be able to catch, throw, and dodge independently.

An additional way the teacher helps the child to reduce task demands is by forcing the use of control processes by the younger child. Integrating selective attention to labeling of the task-appropriate cues aids the child in skill learning, as does forcing grouping, recoding, and rehearsal. Development of the knowledge base of the learner is important for a clear understanding of what constitutes a correct and incorrect response.

In conclusion, the teacher should allow sufficient information processing time for the young child and should structure the lesson to force use of control processes. By contrasting expected performance with the desired goal, the teacher forces the child to *think* while moving instead of merely responding (attending to the process instead of the product).

REFERENCES

Barclay, C. & Newell, K. Children's processing of information in motor skill acquisition. *Journal of Experimental Child Psychology,* 1980, **30**, 98-108.

Barr, R. How children are taught to read: Grouping and pacing. *School Review,* 1975, **83**, 479-498.

Bawden, R., Burke, S. & Duffy, G. *Teacher conceptions of reading and their influence on instruction.* (Research Series No. 47) Institute for Research on Teaching, Michigan State University, 1979.

Clark, C. M. & Yinger, R. J. Teachers' thinking. In P. L. Peterson & H. J. Walberg (Eds.), *Research on teaching*. Berkeley, California: McCutchan, 1979.

Connors, R. D. An analysis of teacher thought processes, beliefs and principles during instruction. Unpublished doctoral dissertation, Department of Elementary Education, University of Alberta, 1978.

Corbin, C. B. *A textbook of motor development.* Dubuque, Iowa: Brown, 1980.

Duffy, G. & Metheny, W. *Measuring teachers' beliefs about reading.* (Research Series No. 41) Institute for Research on Teaching, Michigan State University, 1979.

Espenschade, A. S. & Eckert, H. M. *Motor development,* Columbus, Ohio: Merrill, 1967.

Gallahue, D. *Understanding motor development in children.* New York: Wiley, 1982.

Gallahue, D., Werner, P. & Luedke, G. *A conceptual approach to moving and learning.* New York: Wiley, 1975.

Harste, J. & Burke, C. L. A new hypothesis for reading teacher research: Both the teaching and learning of reading are theoretically based. In P. D. Pearson (Ed.), *Reading: Theory, research and practice.* Twenty-sixth Yearbook of the National Reading Conference, 1977.

Hoffman, S. J. Toward a pedagogical kinesiology. *Quest,* 1977, **28**, 38-48.

Joyce, B. Toward a theory of information processing in teaching. *Educational Research Quarterly,* 1978-79, **3**, 66-67.

Klahr, D. Information processing models of intellectual development. In R. H. Kluwe & H. Spada (Eds.), *Developmental models of thinking.* New York: Academic Press, 1980.

Kolb, D. A. *Learning style inventory technical manual.* Boston: McBer, 1978.

Kriefeldt, J. G. A dynamic model of behavior in a discrete open-loop self-paced motor skill. *IEEE Transactions on Systems, Man, and Cybernetics,* 1972, SCM-2262-273.

Lindberg, M. Is knowledge base development a necessary and sufficient condition for memory development? *Journal of Experimental Child Psychology,* 1980, **30**, 401-410.

McCarthy, B. *The 4 mat system: Teaching to learning styles with right/left mode techniques.* Arlington Heights, Illinois: Mark Anderson, 1981.

MacKay, A. The Alberta studies of teaching: A quinquereme in search of some sailors. *CSSE News,* 1977, **3**, 14-17.

Marteniuk, R. G. *Information processing in motor skills.* New York: Holt, Rinehart and Winston, 1976.

Metheney, W. *The influences of grade and pupil ability levels on teachers' conceptions of reading.* (Research Series No. 69) Institute for Research on Teaching, Michigan State University, 1980.

Mosston, M. *Teaching physical education.* Columbus: Merrill, 1981.

Nisbett, R. & Ross, L. *Human inferences: Strategies and shortcomings of social judgement.* Englewood Cliffs, New Jersey: Prentice-Hall, 1980.

Pearson, P. & Kamil, M. *Basic processes and instructional practices in teaching reading.* (Report No. 7) Center for the Study of Reading, University of Illinois, 1978.

Phi Delta Kappan. On mixing and matching of teaching and learning styles. December 1980, **3**, Bloomington, Indiana.

Roberton, M. A. & Halverson, L. E. The developing child—his changing movement. In B. Lopdon (Ed.), *Physical education for children: A focus on the teaching process.* Philadelphia: Lea & Febiger, 1977.

Seefeldt, V. Developmental motor patterns: Implications for elementary school physical education. In C. H. Nadeau, W. R. Halliwell, K. M. Newell & G. C. Roberts (Eds.), *Psychology of motor behavior and sport—1979.* Champaign, Illinois: Human Kinetics, 1980.

Shavelson, R. J. Research on teachers' pedagogical thoughts, judgements, decisions, and behavior. Unpublished manuscript, University of California, Los Angeles, 1981.

Shavelson, R. J. Teachers' decision making. In N. L. Gage (Ed.), *The psychology of teaching methods.* Yearbook of the National Society for the Study of Education. Chicago: University of Chicago Press, 1976.

Shavelson, R. J. & Atwood, N. Teachers' estimates of student "states of mind." *British Journal of Teacher Education,* 1977, **3**, 131-138.

Shavelson, R. J., Cadwell, J. & Izu, T. Teachers' sensitivity to the reliability of information in making pedagogical decisions. *American Educational Research Journal,* 1977, **14**, 83-97.

Sherman, M. Teacher planning: A study of expert and novice gymnastics teachers. Unpublished manuscript, University of Pittsburgh, 1979.

Singer, R. N. To err or not to err: A question for the instruction of psychomotor skills. *Review of Educational Research,* 1977, **47**, 479-498.

Singer, R. A. & Dick, W. *Teaching physical education: A system approach.* Boston: Houghton Mifflin, 1980.

Stratton, R. Information processing deficits in children's motor performance: Implications for instruction. *Motor Skills: Theory Into Practice,* 1978, **3**, 49-55.

Thomas, J. R., Pierce, C., & Ridsdale, S. Age differences in children's ability to model motor behavior. *Research Quarterly for Exercise and Sport,* 1977, **48**, 592-597.

Thomas, J. T. Acquisition of motor skills: Information processing differences between children and adults. *Research Quarterly for Exercise and Sport,* 1980, **51**, 158-173.

Tobey, C. *A descriptive analysis of the occurrences of augmented feedback in physical education classes.* (Doctoral dissertation, Teachers College, Columbia University). Dissertation Abstracts International, 1974, 3497-A (University Microfilms No. 74-26, 623).

Tversky, A. & Kahneman, D. Judgement under uncertainty, heuristics and biases. *Science,* 1974, **195**, 1124-1131.

Weiss, M. The effects of age, modeling, and verbal self-instruction on children's performance of a sequential motor task. Unpublished doctoral dissertation, Michigan State University, 1981.

Welford, A. T. *Fundamentals of skill.* London: Methuen, 1968.

Wickstrom, R. L. *Fundamental motor patterns.* Philadelphia: Lea & Febiger, 1977.
Winther, K. T. & Thomas, J. R. Developmental differences in children's labeling of movement. *Journal of Motor Behavior,* 1981, **13**, 77-90.

SUGGESTED READINGS

Undergraduate Students

Corbin, C. B. *A textbook of motor development.* Dubuque, Iowa: W. C. Brown, 1980.
Mosston, M. *Teaching physical education.* Columbus, Ohio: Merrill, 1981.
Seefeldt, V. Developmental motor patterns: Implications for elementary school physical education. In C. H. Nadeau, W. R. Halliwell, K. M. Newell & C. G. Roberts (Eds.), *Psychology of motor behavior and sport—1979.* Champaign, Illinois: Human Kinetics, 1980.
Singer, R. A. & Dick, W. *Teaching physical education: A systems approach.* Boston: Houghton Mifflin, 1980.
Stratton, R. Information processing deficits in children's motor performance: Implications for instruction. *Motor Skills: Theory Into Practice,* 1978, **3**, 49-55.

Graduate Students

Hoffman, S. J. Toward a pedagogical kinesiology. *Quest,* 1977, 38-48.
Joyce, B. Toward a theory of information processing in teaching. *Educational Research Quarterly,* 1978-79, **3**, 66-67.
Klahr, D. Information processing models of intellectual development. In R. H. Kluwe & H. Spada (Eds.), *Developmental models of thinking.* New York: Academic Press, 1980.
Kriefeldt, J. G. A dynamic model of behavior in a discrete open-loop self-paced motor skill. *IEEE Transactions on Systems, Man, and Cybernetics,* 1972, SCM-2262-273.
Lindberg, M. Is knowledge base development a necessary and sufficient condition for memory development? *Journal of Experimental Child Psychology,* 1980, **30**, 401-410.
Marteniuk, R. G. *Information processing in motor skills.* New York: Holt, Rinehart and Winston, 1976.
Singer, R. N. To err or not to err: A question for the instruction of psychomotor skills. *Review of Educational Research,* 1977, **47**, 479-498.
Thomas, J. T. Acquisition of motor skills: Information processing differences between children and adults. *Research Quarterly for Exercise and Sport,* 1980, **51**, 158-173.
Tversky, A. & Kahneman, D. Judgement under uncertainty, heuristics and biases. *Science,* 1974, **195**, 1124-1131.
Winther, K. T. & Thomas, J. R. Developmental differences in children's labeling of movement. *Journal of Motor Behavior,* 1981, **13**, 77-90.

7

Developmentally Engineered Equipment and Playgrounds

Jacqueline Herkowitz

The physical environment has an enormous impact both on the development and learning of complex motor skills and on the development and maintenance of physical fitness and normal posture. Abundant evidence indicates that youngsters are highly responsive to the challenge of an appropriate environment (Minerva 1935; McGraw 1935, 1939; Dusenberry 1952; Estes 1959; Leithwood and Fowler 1971), and equally susceptible to the deprivations of an impoverished one (Dennis 1935, 1938). Ripe periods of learning complex motor skills and developing desirable fitness levels (which are largely a consequence of the normal maturation of the nervous system, skeleton, and musculature) occur throughout the preschool and elementary school years. Children who are provided with environmental opportunities to learn complex motor skills and to develop fitness generally do so. On the other hand, when environmental opportunities are limited or unavailable, complex motor skills are often poorly learned and fitness levels generally remain low.

The major part of a child's motor skill acquisition is derived from informal play experiences in home and school environments. Such play experiences are largely made up of the child's interactions with whatever equipment and apparatus the environment contains. Commercially available motor education equipment and playgrounds, however, are rarely engineered to acknowledge and facilitate motor skill acquisition and physical fitness. More often than not, balls that are too large and heavy to be grasped and thrown properly by children are provided. Climbing equipment frequently demands performances that only children having the longest limbs and bravest impulses can accomplish. Implements are often too narrow, too long, or too heavy to enable successful striking performances. Children are often impeded in learning catching skills by balls that are inappropriately small, heavy, or fast. Finally, targets rarely provide information that children can use to adjust their future performances.

The equipment and play areas designed for preschool and elementary school children should provide them with opportunities to build a rich repertoire of complex motor skills and to become physically fit. Therefore, educators and parents directly responsible for the design of these environments need to know how to select properly from commercial equipment and apparatus and, when necessary, to supplement equipment and apparatus inventories with homemade items. Toward that end, this chapter suggests principles of design, design and purchasing strategies, and other information that may help in the selection and construction of developmentally appropriate equipment and playgrounds.

DEVELOPMENTALLY ENGINEERED EQUIPMENT

For equipment and apparatus to be developmentally appropriate for preschool and elementary school children, it must be sensitively engineered to (1) acknowledge the nature of children's physical growth, (2) provide children with information regarding the acceptability and correctness of their motor performances, (3) encourage children's demonstrations of mechanically efficient movement, (4) acknowledge children's visual and perceptual information processing capabilities, (5) encourage the development of normal posture and desirable levels of physical fitness, and (6) provide for children's safety.

Accommodating Growth Characteristics of Young Children

Young children differ widely in growth status and growth rates with regard to body weight, body height, proportional growth of various body segments, skeletal ossification, distribution of fat and muscle tissue, postural characteristics, and somatotype (Sinclair 1973; Malina 1975; Lowrey 1978; Tanner 1978; Malina, Chapter 1). Each child's potential for mastering complex motor skills is limited and shaped to a significant extent by his unique configuration of growth characteristics (McGraw 1939; Tanner 1979; Newell, Chapter 5). One child's center of gravity may be relatively high, making balancing more difficult and possibly limiting potential success in running, jumping, kicking, and climbing activities. On the other hand, another child's body proportions may enhance potential success in activities requiring balance. Thus, since no two children are alike, play areas need to be designed to accommodate all children.

Research has suggested that children's acquisition of sports skills may be facilitated by use of lighter weight (Wright 1967) or scaled-down (Ward and Groppel 1980) equipment. The *Proposed Safety Standard for Public Playground Equipment*, prepared by the National Recreation and Parks Association (1976) for the Consumer Product Safety Commission, suggests that playground apparatus be designed by manufacturers for specific age groups and be labeled as such before being marketed, based on appropriate anthropometric data (e.g., maximum heights, gripping contact surface, clearance, and step height). In addition, three equipment design strategies appear particularly successful in acknowledging the characteristically wide ranges of growth rate and status that are normally encountered when dealing with preschool and elementary school children.

The first equipment design strategy is to provide children with several pieces of equipment that are the same shape but that differ in size. Examples of this principle applied to climbing apparatus include: three vertical ladders, each with rungs of differing distances apart; five staircases, each with differing stair heights (Figure 7.1); and three horizontal bars, each of a differing distance from the ground. Examples appropriate to throwing include: three yarn balls of similar weights but of different sizes; three suspended hoop targets of different diameters; and four 8½-in. diameter balls of different weights. Examples appropriate to catching include: several beach balls of differing diameters; bleach containers of differing sizes with the bottom removed, or funnels of differing size; and four differently sized sponge balls suspended from inverted hangman's nooses. Examples

Figure 7.1. Staircases.

appropriate to striking include: several plastic bats of different lengths but of similar weight and width of striking surface area, and several racquets of similar length and weight but with differing sizes of striking surface area. Examples appropriate to running include three inclines of different steepness and three different running length distances. Examples appropriate to jumping include: twelve rubber balls, each suspended at different heights from differently colored pieces of sash cord, in graduated order, and wands supported by blocks of different heights (Figure 7.2).

A second equipment design strategy is to provide equipment that each child may change to accommodate his own unique growth status. Examples of this principle applied to climbing apparatus include: an inclined sliding board that children can raise or lower on trestle bars; a balance beam that children may change so either a 2-, 4-, or 6-in. wide balance surface may be used for balancing activities (Figure 7.3); and a ladder that has removable rungs (Figure 7.4). Examples appropriate to throwing include: a metal hoop target, adjustable in height; "neat feet" made with a small piece of black rubber floor matting with two yellow footprints painted on it that children may move toward or away from a target (illustrated throughout chapter); and a moving target suspended on the end of a flexible plastic rod that children may choose to move as a pendulum at rapid or slow speeds. Examples appropriate to kicking include: a goal of adjustable width made of traffic cones that children may choose to place close together or farther apart, and plastic pins, or Indian clubs, serving as targets that children may space at varied distances from one another. An example appropriate to catching is a large, adjustable, inclined muslin sheet off of which children

Figure 7.2. Wands and blocks.

Figure 7.3. Adjustable width and height balance beam.

Figure 7.4. Ladder with removable rungs.

catch rolling balls (Figure 7.5). Examples appropriate to jumping and leaping activities are a pair of standards and a crossbar that children may raise or lower (Figure 7.6) and different sizes and colors of rubber floor mat squares on which to jump that children may separate or place closer together. Examples appropriate to striking include a ball that may be adjusted in elevation by means of an inverted hangman's noose from which it is suspended (Figure 7.7) and an adjustable batting T with a funnel top (Figure 7.8). An example appropriate to a fine motor manipulative task is a lockboard with several sizes of key and lock combinations. Examples appropriate for body image activities involve eight incrementally sized squares, circles, and triangles set in bases, and "twiggy sticks," ⅜-in. and ½-in. yard-long dowel rods set in wooden bases, which children can construct for themselves, using heavy-duty rubber bands (Figure 7.9). An example appropriate to climbing is a graduated Swedish box. Children may use one, two, or three sections, depending on the levels they select.

A third equipment design strategy is to provide children with pieces of equipment that incorporate gradual gradations in size. An example of this principle applied to climbing is a walking board that is wide at one end and increasingly narrower toward the opposite end (Figure 7.10). Examples appropriate to leaping and jumping are a long elastic cord fastened to the ground at one end and 5 ft from the ground on a standard at the other end (Figure 7.11) and a "jump-the-stream mat" of graduated widths (Figure 7.12).

Figure 7.5. Catching ramp and foam balls.

Figure 7.6. Hurdle standards and wand.

Figure 7.7. Ball of adjustable height supported from inverted hangman's noose, hanging from long length of steel cable.

Equipment That Provides Knowledge of Results

Information about the acceptability and correctness of a motor skill performance is critical to learning and future performance (Chapter 4). This knowledge of results (KR) may be defined as a score presented verbally or mechanically to a performer as information about the outcome of the movement (Brown 1949, Miller 1953, Holding 1965, Bilodeau 1966). Authorities agree (Ammons 1956, Bilodeau 1966, Adams 1971, Newell 1976) that KR largely serves information, motivation, and reinforcement functions. KR has been shown to increase interest in practicing, develop more accurate concepts about ability to perform, facilitate the monitoring of progress over time, and enhance communication between the learner and others regarding status and progress.

A number of equipment design strategies that are sensitive to the major functions of KR seem particularly capable of facilitating the learning and performance of motor tasks by preschool and elementary school children. For instance, color may be manipulated to serve KR functions. Examples of this include: rope and vertical ladders with rungs that are each differently colored; lines of different color placed at graduated distances from throwing targets; sections of a long elastic cord inclined from the floor to a 4-ft elevation, with elevations marked by differently colored whiffle balls (Figure 7.11); and a rubber floor mat for long jumping that is divided into

Figure 7.8. Adjustable height batting T, sheet metal target, neat feet, and large plastic bat.

Figure 7.9. Twiggy sticks.

Figure 7.10. Narrowing walking board.

Figure 7.11. Inclined elastic cord.

Figure 7.12. Jump-the-stream mat.

equal sections, each section colored differently (Figure 7.13). Numbers, letters, and words (depending on the reading skills of the child) may also be used to serve KR functions. Examples of this include: a jump-and-reach task in which the child must touch a piece of chalk to a progressively numbered piece of vinyl affixed to a wall and a rubber floor mat for long jumping that is divided into equal sections, each section labeled with single letters of the alphabet or a numerical scale (Figure 7.13).

Timing devices may be used to provide KR. An example of a timing device that is appropriate for running is a graduated hourglass device made from large plastic containers that have been filled with birdseed (Figure 7.14).

Sound may also serve KR functions. Examples of this include: a sheet metal target (Figure 7.8), a bicycle horn at the top of a vertical ladder, a series of aluminum pipes suspended from a wooden dowel rod by string that serve as a kicking target (Figure 7.15), a homemade stabilometer that buzzes when the balance platform is parallel to the ground, and a Snoopy kicking target that rings when struck because of bells sewn to it (Figure 7.16).

Light may also be manipulated to serve KR functions. An example is a throwing target incorporating four different-sized circular targets that when struck by a thrown yarn ball, depress microswitches that cause light bulbs of a similar color to the targets to light up and stay on for adjustable amounts of time (Figure 7.17).

The movement of different pieces of apparatus may be used to serve KR functions. Examples of this include: a Cookie Monster windowshade target that is mounted on a wooden board and hung from a wall and that pops up when struck by a ball (Figure 7.18); a Sylvester and Tweety Bird target that is made of two thicknesses of cardboard, thus allowing the Tweety Bird figure to fall on the floor out of Sylvester's arms when struck by a ball sent with sufficient force (Figure 7.19); and Bugs Bunny target that is constructed so the character's teeth fall forward on a hinge if they are struck with sufficient force (Figure 7.20).

Figure 7.13. Long-jump mat and neat feet.

Figure 7.14. Birdseed timer.

Figure 7.15. Sound curtain target and coiled rope ball support.

Encapsulation is another means of providing for KR functions. Children often are motivated effectively to persevere in kicking, striking, and throwing activities when the balls that they are sending toward targets disappear into the target. Yarn balls thrown into the opening of a large boxlike flower target disappear and later reemerge via an internal ramp that sends them back in the direction of the thrower (Figure 7.21). Mouth targets are muslin sheets with large holes in them that are suspended from lengths of sash cord sewn into a top hem and decorated to resemble a mouth or cave. These can be presented singly or in a series to capture balls sent toward them in striking, kicking, and throwing activities (Figure 7.22).

Facilitating the Acquisition of Ballistic Skills

Throwing, striking, and kicking stationary balls at stationary targets, long jumping for distance, and vertical jumping for height to a stationary target are all motor skills that are primarily ballistic in nature. A key to the successful design of apparatus for such activities is acknowledging the unique mechanical demands placed on children as they learn these skills Wickstrom 1977; McClenaghan and Gallahue 1978; Roberton, Chapter 3). The feature that is central to efficient performance of all ballistic skills is effective force production. Consequently, ways of encouraging force production need to be incorporated into successful apparatus design.

The distance and size characteristics of the targets influence effective force production. Targets need to be placed at distances that are challenging to encourage children to produce forceful movements. They also need to be large enough so that children do not attend to the need to be

Figure 7.16. Snoopy kicking target and coiled rope ball supports.

accurate at the expense of producing forceful executions. Targets that are too small and too close to the performer seriously interfere with the ballistic character of throwing, striking, and kicking performances. For example, when a child is directed to throw a ball at a small target located only a few feet in front of her, she will likely toss the ball rather than demonstrate the forceful ballistic performance commonly needed in most sport activities. Such nonballistic practice opportunities provide little transfer potential to situations in which ballistic movements are required. Examples of targets that illustrate these distance and size characteristics include the Snoopy kicking target (Figure 7.16), the Cookie Monster target (Figure 7.18), the Sylvester and Tweety Bird target (Figure 7.19), the flower target (Figure 7.21), the mouth target (Figure 7.22), and the three-tiered kicking target (Figure 7.23). Low rope and traffic cone barriers (Figures 7.17, 7.19, and 7.20), neat feet (Figures 7.8, 7.13, 7.18, 7.21, 7.22, and 7.24), and coiled rope ball supports (Figures 7.15 and 7.23), are effective devices for defining desirable distance requirements.

Additionally, employing targets that provide positive feedback only when desirable amounts of force and accuracy are produced facilitates the learning of ballistic skills. Windowshades (Figure 7.18) that pop up only when struck with sufficient force and that can be adjusted by loosening or tightening the central core are an example of such feedback targets. Another example is the Bugs Bunny target (Figure 7.20) in which the figure's teeth fall forward on a hinged support only when

Figure 7.17. Pink dragon and rope barrier.

Figure 7.18. Cookie Monster windowshade target and neat feet.

Figure 7.19. Sylvester and Tweety Bird target and cone barrier.

struck with sufficient force and accuracy. Still another is the Snoopy kicking target, which makes louder noises when struck with increasingly forceful kicks (Figure 7.16). The sound curtain target, which is made from lengths of aluminum pipe suspended from a long dowel rod and which makes noise when struck by a kicked ball (Figure 7.15), and the three-tiered kicking target made from muslin (Figure 7.23) are still other examples.

Devices that encourage weight shifts during striking, kicking, and throwing activities significantly contribute to performance efficiency. Neat feet, the yellow footprints painted on black floor runner material, serve to remind children of the need for weight shifting (Figures 7.8, 7.18, 7.22, and 7.24). Similarly, when a pressure mat connected to a light bulb is used in conjunction with neat feet, it serves to encourage a desirable weight shift (Figure 7.21).

Three additional devices encourage the pelvic-spinal rotation, opposition, and sequential movement of body parts that are a part of efficient striking, kicking, and throwing performances required in sport activities (Chapter 3). An inclined plastic rope affixed to a basketball hoop and floor plate (Figure 7.25) provides a useful example related to throwing. When children attempt to sling a 1-ft long, 2-in. diameter plastic pipe up the rope toward a cymbal and colored tape markers,

Figure 7.20. Bugs Bunny target and cone barrier.

efficient force production is facilitated. A plastic ball inside a mesh bag that hangs from a piece of sash cord that is parallel to the ground and slightly above head level encourages efficient force production when the task is to strike the ball over the supporting sash cord as many times as possible (Figure 7.24). A ball suspended from an inverted hangman's noose and supported by a shower curtain hook hanging from a long length of steel cable can be struck to travel as far along the cable as possible. Because of the inclination of the cable, the ball returns on its own to the striker (Figure 7.7).

Adjustable supports and other devices that do not interfere with the natural trajectory characteristics of struck or kicked balls also encourage desirable force production and accuracy. Examples of this include: an adjustable batting T (Figure 7.8); a detachable whiffle ball supported by an inverted hangman's noose that is fastened with Velcro; the striking machine, which employs an air jet to support foam balls (Figure 7.22); and a coiled rope support for balls that are to be kicked (Figures 7.15 and 7.23).

The length, surface area, weight, and grip characteristics of striking implements also influence the efficiency of force production. Racquets and bats are most effectively grouped by similar weight but graduated lengths, and by similar length but graduated size of striking surface. In

Figure 7.21. Flower target, pressure-sensitive mat connected to light bulb, and neat feet.

striking activities, shorter, lighter, and larger surface area implements are easier to use than longer, heavier, and smaller surface area implements. Examples of striking apparatus that demonstrate these concepts include oversized plastic bats (Figures 7.8 and 7.24), Ping-Pong paddles, junior-sized tennis racquets, badminton racquets, and racquetball racquets. Care also must be taken to see that children can grip racquets and bats comfortably. Grips that are too large do not permit children to swing effectively, and cause a loss in force production and accuracy.

The size, weight, and rebound characteristics of balls used in ballistic activities also should be considered carefully. Children should be encouraged to progress from larger to smaller balls and from fairly lightweight to heavier balls in striking and kicking activities. Children should progress from lightweight, easily held balls to larger, heavier balls in throwing activities. Balls that do not rebound or that have limited rebound characteristics are far more desirable than balls that do rebound. Balls that rebound distract the young child.

Jumping activities are also ballistic in nature. Consequently, force production is essential to efficient performance of all jumping skills. Apparatus should therefore encourage the production of force in jumping activities. In one such example, the child jumps toward a tin can target of adjustable height that is suspended from sash cord located at a 45-degree angle from the floor in

Figure 7.22. Mouth target, striking machine, and neat feet.

front of the child. As the child jumps and touches the can during flight, it makes noise. In this activity, the landing surface must be absorbent to insure a safe landing.

Facilitating Acquisition of Receipt Skills

Motor skills involving the receipt of projectiles include all catching, kicking, and striking skills in which a performer is required to respond to a moving object. A key to the successful design of developmentally appropriate apparatus for activities involving these skills lies in sensitive acknowledgment of the unique visual and perceptual information-processing demands placed on children as they learn these skills. Compared with older and more skilled children, young, unskilled children appear less capable of (1) processing as much visual information, (2) processing visual information as rapidly, or (3) discriminating task relevant visual information in receipt skill performances (Hagen 1967; Gallahue 1968; Vurpillot 1968; Druker and Hagen 1969; Connolly 1970; Herkowitz 1973; Williams 1968, 1973; Ridenour 1974, 1977; Thomas Chapter 4). Consequently, ways of modulating the amount of visual information to be processed and the speed with which visual information is processed need to be incorporated into successful receipt apparatus design. Addi-

Figure 7.23. Three-tiered kicking target and coiled rope ball support.

tionally, techniques aiding children to discriminate key visual features of receipt task performance more effectively need to be considered.

Several methods to control the amount of visual information that must be processed in receipt activities are available. One is to order sequentially the information content inherent in projectile trajectories to which children are exposed. Children should be asked to respond successively to stationary balls, balloons dropped through the air, balls rolled along the ground, balls rolled down ramps, balls traveling in arcs when supported from above by a length of sash cord, balls bounced along the ground, and balls traveling horizontally through the air. The amount of visual information that must be processed increases as the number of speed change characteristics increases. The stationary ball is the easiest visual information to process, since it does not move. A balloon dropped through the air travels slowly and at a consistent speed due to air resistance. A ball rolled along the ground travels at progressively slower speeds due to friction. A ball rolled down a ramp travels at increasingly faster speeds due to gravity. Balls supported from above by sash cord increase speed as they travel toward the bottom of their arc and decrease speed as they travel toward the top of their arc. A ball bounced along the ground increases speed as it leaves a bounce, slows at the top of a bounce, and speeds once again as it drops from the top of a bounce. Balls traveling horizontally through the air present the most difficult situations in processing information owing to spin, wind resistance, and speed.

Several relevant methods to control the speed with which visual information must be processed in receipt activities are available. For example, large wooden, cloth, or net ramps (Figure 7.5) may be adjusted for length, inclination, and elevation from the ground. These then allow for a good deal of additional control over the amount of time and speed that balls of varying weights

Figure 7.24. Plastic ball inside mesh bag, large plastic bat, and neat feet.

and sizes take to travel down the ramp prior to a receipt response. As children become more skilled, demands on visual information processing may be modified or intensified by increasing the inclination of the ramp, decreasing the length of the ramp, decreasing the size of the ball, or increasing the weight of the ball. Progressively increasing the weight of a balloon that is dropped through the air for striking or catching activities by adding increasing amounts of masking tape to the balloon provides modification of the equipment design. Still another modification involves increasing the traveling disance of a ramped ball, a ball traveling along the ground, or a ball bouncing along the ground. Increasing the ball's traveling distance gives a child more decision time in which to make needed spatial adjustments.

Several design strategies that acknowledge children's limited visual and perceptual discrimination capabilities may be used. Initially, high contrast should be used between the color of the projectile and the color of the background against which it moves (Ridenour 1979). A yellow ball traveling against a grey background is more desirable than a white ball traveling against a white background. Additionally, the complexity of the background against which the projectile moves must be minimized (Herkowitz 1973). A solid-color ball traveling through the air against a solid-color wall is more desirable than a yellow ball traveling through the air against a wall on which are painted many primary-color geometric shapes. As children become more skilled, the contrast and background complexity requirements of the tasks may be made more challenging. Target movement characteristics should also be considered. Initially, targets should move from side to side in

Figure 7.25. Inclined plastic rope.

front of the performer. Children who become more skilled should be given opportunities to respond to targets that move toward them and away from them.

Encouraging Normal Posture and Physical Fitness

The posture of preschool and primary school children is characterized by protruding abdomen, exaggerated lumbar curve, and prominent scapulae. By the end of the intermediate grades, however, these postural characteristics may no longer be considered normal. They, along with rounded shoulders, pronated feet, and forward head, are a testimonial to the lack of formal instructional opportunities or playgrounds or both throughout the preschool and elementary school years. These environments would have nurtured the development of the muscular strength required to cause these postural characteristics to disappear. The development of normal posture does not occur unless the abdominal, shoulder girdle, and arm and leg muscles increase in strength with growth. They only increase in strength when repeatedly stressed in climbing, hanging, and swinging activities provided over long periods on playgrounds and in other physically demanding, instructional settings. For this reason, providing challenging and demanding hanging, climbing, and swinging opportunities on playgrounds is a necessity.

The physical environment of the school can do a good deal to establish and maintain each of the several components of physical fitness: cardiorespiratory fitness, muscular strength and endurance fitness, flexibility fitness, and body weight fitness (Chapter 2). Fitness trails should be provided that have activity stations at the beginning and end designed to increase flexibility fitness and stations in the middle designed to increase muscular strength and endurance. The trails should also demand that users jog or run their full length. These serve not only the needs of schoolchildren but also those of the adult community. Challenge courses, or obstacle courses, serve a similar function, through their contribution to the development of cardiorespiratory fitness is generally negligible. Quarter-mile tracks and cycling or jogging trails strongly encourage cardiorespiratory fitness, as do swimming pools, which also encourage development of strength.

Providing for Children's Safety

Three major types of hazards are related to equipment and playground apparatus: those associated with defects in construction and design, those associated with improper equipment installation and maintenance, and those resulting from human error. At the present time, no mandatory safety standard regulates the construction, design, installation, or maintenance of private or public playground apparatus, sports equipment, or handmade apparatus normally found on playgrounds. Efforts in that direction have been initiated, however. The National Recreation and Parks Association (1976), commissioned by the Consumer Product Safety Commission, produced a draft entitled *Proposed Safety Standard for Public Playground Equipment.* This proposed standard addressed heavy-duty institutional equipment, its installation, and the surfaces on which apparatus is installed. To date, the standard has not been implemented. When the Consumer Product Safety Commission and the Bureau of Engineering Sciences subjected the standard to careful examination, they found many serious errors in research. Additionally, a good deal of controversy arose over whether the standard could be enforced. Furthermore, many thought that extensive public information and education programs could be used to reduce injuries sufficiently. At the present time, the details of the proposed standard, particularly numbers and dimensions, are tentative, and cannot be interpreted as absolute, acceptable standards for all instances. Nevertheless, even with these reservations, the proposed standard does give an idea of what to look for in terms of safety hazards, and anyone who contemplates the construction of a playground should become familiar with its content.

In general, the following recommendations may be considered reflective of the standard's content. Some additional commentary has been included here to cover the topic of small equipment safety that the proposed standard did not address:

1. Equipment should be designed for a specific developmental range, and should be used by the group for which it is developed. Three- to 5-year-old children may be exposed to unnecessary hazards (maximum height, gripping surface of ladders, step heights) on equipment designed for 9- to 12-year-olds. This standard may be accommodated by employing the recommendations made earlier in this chapter with regard to physical growth, and by constructing separate play areas for different age groups. Elementary schools may provide one play area for the kindergarten through second-grade children, and another for the third- through sixth-grade children. This arrangement not only provides for the involvement of larger numbers of children in a given time period, but also the duplication of certain types of equipment at different scales cuts down on equipment wear.

2. Equipment used on playgrounds must be durable. Materials should have a demonstrated record of durability or should be tested. Increasingly, manufacturers are subjecting their apparatus to load tests after it is fully assembled. This is necessary for determining whether linked parts collectively and individually will withstand the loads to which they will be subjected under normal use. Equipment needs to be installed in a manner that prevents tipping and sliding while in use. For heavy equipment, this usually implies fixing the equipment in concrete, or attaching equipment to anchor bolts set in concrete footings. Locking devices should be provided for all bolts so they do not work loose and so that they may not be removed by hand. Hooks and rings should be manufactured from high-carbon steel to ensure their durability. All exposed bolts must be covered with a permanent covering that cannot be removed by hand, or they must be countersunk or recessed.

Definite policies should be established for repairing, marking, and maintaining large and small equipment. When a piece of equipment falls into disrepair, a teacher needs to make a decision on whether the item should be withdrawn for repair, used in its present state, or discarded. Often items requiring repair need attention outside of class hours. Occasionally equipment in disrepair is best used in a state of disrepair until it can no longer be salvaged. This is especially true in the case of rubber utility balls that leak air slowly and basketball goal nets that are slowly unraveling. Sometimes equipment in disrepair is unsafe and should be withdrawn from use immediately.

- Rubber balls can, in some cases, be repaired by means of a vulcanizing patch. For others, a hard-setting rubber preparation is useful.
- Broken wooden bats need to be discarded. Taping around the break does not make them safe.
- Balls need to be inflated to the recommended pressure marked on the ball, using an accurate gauge. Ball pressure should be checked periodically. The needle used to inflate the ball should be moistened before it is inserted into a valve.
- Children need to learn not to sit on balls or kick balls not specifically made for kicking.
- When not in use, balls should be slightly deflated.
- Leather balls should be cleaned with an approved ball conditioner.
- Mats should be stacked or hung. Plastic or plastic-covered mats should be cleaned periodically with soap and water, as should other plastic equipment.
- Equipment that is likely to warp should be laid in a flat position.
- Bats should be taped to prevent slippage.
- Wire baskets are often good containers for small equipment and can be placed on shelves for easy viewing and accessibility.
- Wooden equipment should be inspected periodically for rough edges. Sanding, repainting, or varnishing should be done when necessary.
- All equipment should be marked. Marking can be done with indelible pencils, paint, stencil ink, or a marking set available at sporting goods establishments. Unfortunately, few marking systems are permanent, so remarking at regular intervals may be necessary. Electric burning pencils and stamps are also useful on some equipment.
- If equipment is issued to classrooms, a color system could be used to keep track of each classroom's equipment more easily.

3. The potential impact of swinging elements must be within certain safety limits. Swing seats can be purchased that are made of rubber, wood, plastic, or metal; however, only the belt-type rubber seats are acceptable, as the others frequently are responsible for injuries. Clearance between moving elements and between moving elements and fixed structures should be sufficient to prevent collisions under normal use. Swings that travel in a straight line require less space on each side than do horizontal tire swings, which move in a 360-degree range.
4. The velocity of rotating equipment should be limited. This refers to the speed of the outer edge of the equipment. The outer edge should be of a smooth, circular design, and the base should have no openings accessible to any part of the body. This standard is directed at equipment such as merry-go-rounds. Speed controllers and improvements in design have led to a new look for this particular piece of equipment.
5. Slides should be designed in such a manner that speed of descent and landing are within a safe range. Landing speed from a slide is influenced by the type and condition of the sliding surface, the incline and length of the slide, and the speed of the child on entry. In addition, the distance from the exit end of the slide to the ground and the type of landing surface are relevant safety considerations. A sandpile provides a cushion. Guide rails help to ensure that the child does not fall off the side of the slide. Tall, narrow slides connected directly to a ladder are being replaced with lower, broader structures today.
6. Height of walkways, landings, and decks should be limited according to the group of users. In general, play structures should be no higher than is required to enable children using them to walk underneath without danger of collision with the understructure. Play surfaces on climbing equipment should be enclosed by railings, except for entrance and exit areas. In general, ladders leading to platforms should be installed nearly 90 degrees from horizontal, and stairways should have a gradual incline of 25 to 35 degrees. A protective surface should be installed and maintained under and around all climbing and moving equipment. Sand 8 to 10 in. thick is sufficient for most purposes. The sand should extend across zones where children may fall, and should be contained by a border. Regular maintenance is required to ensure absence of foreign materials such as broken glass. Finally, sand should be replenished or rearranged as needed in heavy-use areas.

PLAYGROUNDS ENGINEERED FOR DEVELOPMENT

Certain fundamental factors should be considered in engineering a playground that enhances development: (1) the manner in which complexity and novelty may be manipulated to encourage high motor activity levels, (2) how provision for all forms of motor play may be made, (3) how amount of space, number of children, and scarcity of play materials interact to influence motor activity, and (4) how to regulate traffic flow on apparatus and in play spaces to encourage broad ranges of movement experience.

Provision of Complex and Novel Settings

A good deal of research indicates that the amount of motor activity evidenced in a play area over time is a dual function of the complexity and novelty of that area. Novelty apparently has the power to elicit responsiveness (Johnson 1935; Cockrell 1935; Mendel 1965; Gilmore 1966a, 1966b;

Wuellner, 1969), and complexity has the power to sustain interest (Cockrell 1935; Johnson 1935; Hutt 1966; Wade and Ellis 1971; Gramza, Corush, and Ellis 1972).

To attract the long-term attention of children, playgrounds in school settings need to change periodically. New pieces of small and large equipment need to be added, while old, unused small and large equipment needs to be removed at regular intervals.

To sustain the long-term interest of playground users, playgrounds in school settings must be complex. When children are exposed to relatively noncomplex play environments that do not change over time, the amount of motor activity evidenced in the play environment decreases while the amount of social activity evidenced in the play environment increases (Scholtz and Ellis 1975a, 1975b; Weilbacher 1980). Such increases in social activity are not necessarily desirable, since fighting and other undesirable social behaviors are often evidenced. Decreases in motor activity are definitely undesirable, since they reflect reduced opportunities for learning motor skills and developing desirable levels of fitness.

To provide for such needed complexity, a number of strategies can be employed. Playgrounds take on high levels of complexity when children are provided with the opportunity to obtain and use readily small, loose equipment, such as balls, ropes, tricycles, bicycles, wagons, ladders, sliding boards, rope ladders, sand equipment, bats, racquets, nets, climbing ropes, targets, horizontal bars, cargo nets, and trestles. The more mobile, small equipment that is provided in accessible storage units located on the playground site, the more complex the playground becomes, and the more it becomes capable of sustaining children's interest over long periods. Many interesting multifunction storage units can be built. Some serve as playhouses and climbing towers as well as storage units.

The incorporation of large, permanently embedded, unchanging pieces of apparatus should be avoided, particularly when they are single-function structures. The functional complexity of a slide, teeter-totter, swing, spring-base animal, merry-go-round, or set of monkey bars is limited. If large, permanently embedded, unchanging pieces of apparatus are to be incorporated on playgrounds and still accommodate what is known about the ability of complexity to sustain children's interest, they should be complex, multifunction structures (Figure 7.26). However, such apparatus is often extremely expensive and takes up a great deal of physical space.

Perhaps the most desirable response to the need for complexity is to install basic skeletal support structures on playgrounds to which many pieces of loose apparatus (taken from a nearby storage unit) could be attached. One example of such a solution is to set four 6 × 6-in. timbers 6 ft high into the ground, one in each of the four corners of a 12-ft-square configuration. This basic skeletal structure (the only elements on the playground when the playground is not in use) can be expanded with: (1) horizontal bars with spring-loaded fittings that can be placed into the posts, (2) staircases, ladders, and sliding boards that rest on the horizontal bars at different inclinations, (3) a cargo net that is attached to a horizontal bar and to permanently installed rings set in the ground various distances from the posts, (4) climbing rope, rope ladders, and a trapeze that are suspended from horizontal bars, and (5) a nylon tent that fits over a horizontal bar and attaches to permanently installed ground rings and that may serve as a playhouse. All the attachable elements may be stored on brackets in a storage house, at levels that make the equipment accessible to children who want to use it.

Another solution to the need for complexity is to build stalls around a central wall on a playground. Targets for kicking, throwing, and striking activities (obtained from storage) can be attached to the wall of one of the stalls, thus eliminating potential safety problems that generally

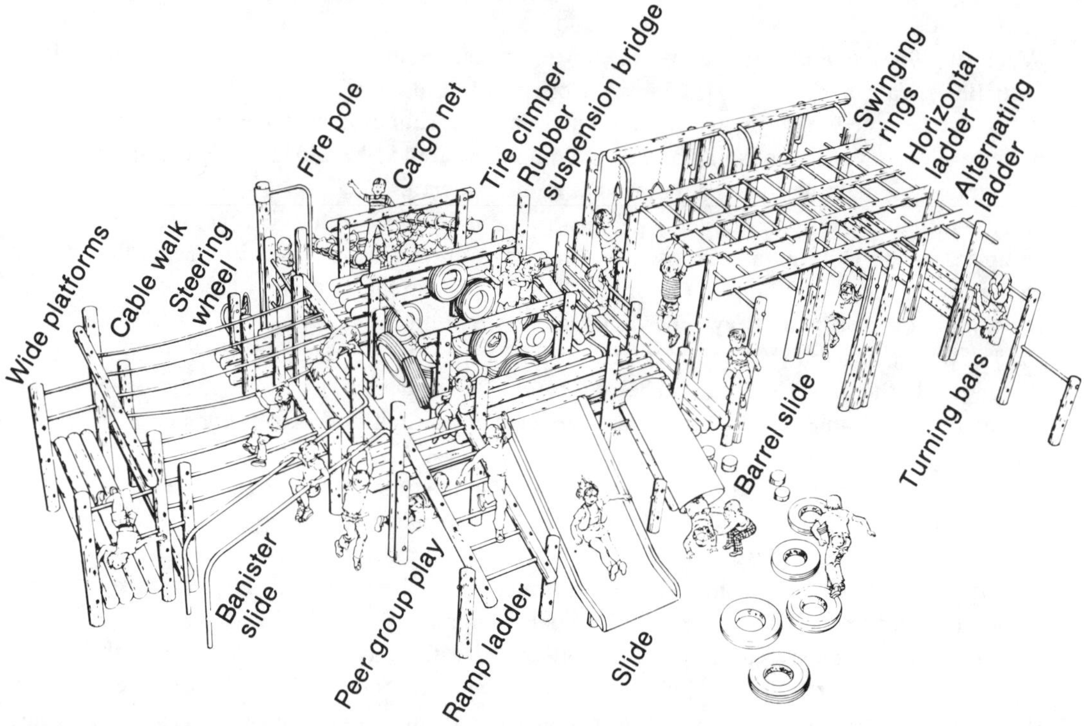

Figure 7.26. Complex multifunction structures appropriate for intermediate school playgrounds. (Reproduced with permission from Northwest Design Products, Schoolyard BigToys, Tacoma, Washington.)

result in the severe restriction of these activities on most playgrounds. Children can also safely engage in racquet games as well as a number of throwing and kicking games in such stall areas.

Making Provisions for All Forms of Motor Play

If many motor skills are to be experienced and learned, normal posture and physical fitness developed and maintained, and game and sport rules and strategies practiced and understood, the playground must be designed effectively to incorporate many forms of motor play (see Table 7.1 for a list of selected equipment manufacturers).

Playgrounds for Preschool Through Second-Grade Children

Preschool and early primary school children need to develop and learn efficient fundamental motor patterns that are prerequisite to the specialized sport performances demanded of intermediate and older children. These fundamental motor patterns include the overarm throw, underarm throw, running, overarm strike, sidearm strike, underarm strike, place kick, punt, catch, vertical jump, broad jump, hurdle jump, jump from a height, stair climb, vertical rope climb, inclined ladder climb, rope ladder climb, vertical pole climb, hop, skip, gallop, slide, and leap. Preschool and primary school children also need to develop normal posture and desirable levels of fitness.

Stalls, as previously discussed, are excellent places for throwing, striking, kicking, catching, and vertical jumping activities. Climbing activities are best provided for with complex, adjustable

Table 7.1. Selected Equipment Manufacturers

Commercially Available Small Equipment

Childcraft Education Corporation
P.O. Box 94
Bayonne, NJ 07002

Cosom Corporation
6030 Wayzata Blvd.
Minneapolis, MN 55416

Creative Playthings
Princeton, NJ 08540

Developmental Learning Materials
7440 Natchez Ave.
Niles, IL 60648

Ed-Nu, Inc.
5115 Rte. 38
Pennsauken, NJ 08109

Educational Activities, Inc.
P.O. Box 392
Freeport, NY 11520

Elementary Gym Closet, Inc.
2511 Leach Rd.
Auburn Heights, MI 48057

Flaghouse, Inc.
18 W. 18th St.
New York, NY 10011

J. E. Gregory, Inc.
P.O. Box 3483
Spokane, WA 99220

GSC Athletic Equipment, Inc.
600 N. Pacific Avenue
San Pedro, CA 90733

Gym-thing
19 W. Pennsylvania Ave.
Towson, MD 21204

J. L. Hammett Company
2393 Vaux Hall Rd.
Union, NJ 07083

Delmer F. Harris Co., Inc.
P.O. Box 288, Dept. J
Concordia, KS 66901

Ideal School Supply Co.
11000 S. Laverne Ave.
Oak Lawn, IL 60453

Jayfro Corporation
P.O. Box 400
Waterford, CT 06385

Lojen Apparatus Inc.
Box 785
Fremont, NE 68025

Passon's Inc.
824 Arch St.
Philadelphia, PA 19107

Physical Education Supply Assoc.
P.O. Box 292
Trumbull, CT 06611

J. A. Preston Corporation
71 Fifth Ave.
New York, NY 10003

Program Aids, Inc.
161 McQueston Pkwy.
Mount Vernon, NY 10550

Shield Manufacturing Company
9 St. Paul St.
Buffalo, NY 14209

Skill Development Equipment Co.
1340 N. Jefferson
Anaheim, CA 92806

Snitz Sports Supply Co.
104 S. Church St.
East Troy, WI 53120

Sport Fun, Inc.
4621 Sperry St.
Los Angeles, CA 90039

Teaching Resources Corporation
100 Boylston St.
Boston, MA 02116

Table 7.1 (continued)

Things From Bell, Inc.
12 S. Main St.
Homer, NY 13077

U. S. Games, Incorporated
1029 Aurora Rd.
Box E G 874
Melbourne, FL 32935

Vantel Corporation
P.O. Box 6590
Orange, CA 92667

W. J. Voit Rubber Corporation
29 Essex St.
Maywood, NJ 07607

Wilson Sporting Goods Co.
2233 West St.
River Grove, IL 60171

Wolverine Sports
745 State Cir.
Ann Arbor, MI 48104

World Publications
P.O. Box 366
Mountain View, CA 94040

Commercially Available Playground Apparatus and Other Large Apparatus

American Athletic Equipment Co.
Box 111
Jefferson, IA 50129

American Gym Company, Inc.
Box 131
Monroeville, PA 15146

Murray Anderson-Olympic
Gymnastic Equipment
128 Dunedin St.
Orillia, Ont.

Atlas Athletic Equipment Co.
2339 Hampton
St. Louis, MO 63139

BigToys
1940 E. D St.
Tacoma, WA 98421

J. E. Burke Company
P.O. Box 549
Fond Du Lac, WI 54935

Centaur Athletics Inc.
P.O. Box 178
Custer, WA 98240

Childcraft
155 E. 23rd St.
New York, NY 10010

Child Life Play Specialities, Inc.
1640 Washington St.
Holliston, MA 01746

Columbia Cascade Timber Co.
1727 N.E. Eleventh Ave.
Portland, OR 97212

Community Playthings
Rifton, NY 12471

Corner Gym
PHAC Company
Physical Fitness Arts and Crafts
914 S. 11th St.
Brainerd, MN 56401

Creative Playgrounds Corporation
1234 E. 99 Dr.
RR 23
Terre Haute, IN 47802

Creative Playthings Inc.
Princeton, NJ 08540

Everglide Playground Co., Inc.
P.O. Box 1068
1133 W. 18th St.
Erie, PA 16512

Exceptional Play, Inc.
P.O. Box 1015
Lawrence, KS 66044

Table 7.1 (continued)

Form Incorporated P.O. Box K South Lyon, MI 48178	Nissen Corporation 930–27th Ave. S.W. Cedar Rapids, IA 52406
Game Time Inc. 903 Anderson Rd. Litchfield, MI 49252	Playground Corporation of America 29–16 40th Ave. Long Island City, NY 11101
GymMaster Co. 3200 S. Zuni Englewood, CO 80110	Playtimber Company P.O. Box 66 Essex Street Station Boston, MA 02112
Gymnastic Supply Co. 247 W. Sixth St. San Pedro, CA 90733	Porter Athletic Equipment Porter-Leavitt Co., MFGR 9555 Irving Park Rd. Schiller Park, IL 60176
Delmer F. Harris Co., Inc. P.O. Box 288, Dept. J Concordia, KS 66901	Recreation Equipment Corporation P.O. Box 2188, Department 578 Anderson, IN 46011
Landscape Structures Inc. Delano, MN 55328	Salsich Recreation, Inc. 2298 Grissom Dr. St. Louis, MO 63141
Lind Climber Company 807 Reba Pl. Evanston, IL 60202	Trojan Playground Equipment Manufacturing Company 11–2nd Ave. N.E. St. Cloud, MN 56301
Mexico Forge Kilgore Corporation P.O. Box 565 Reedsville, PA 17084	R. W. Whittle, Ltd. P.V. Works Monton, Eccles Manchester, England
Miracle Recreation Equipment Company and Jamison, Inc. P.O. Box 275 Grinnell, IA 50112	

Professional Organizations Concerned With Play and Playground Research

American Association for Leisure and Recreation
Association of the American Alliance for Health, Physical Education, Recreation and Dance
1900 Association Dr.
Reston, VA 22091

American Society of Landscape Architects
1900 M St. N.W.
Suite 750
Washington, DC 20036

Table 7.1 (continued)

Alyce T. Cheska, President
The Association for the Anthropological Study of Play
Department of Physical Education
University of Illinois
Urbana, IL 61801

National Association for the Education of Young Children
1834 Connecticut Ave. N.W.
Washington, DC 20036

National Recreation and Park Association
1601 N. Kent St.
Arlington, VA 22209

climbing apparatus set on a deep sand ground cover. The apparatus should be chosen for the varying physical dimensions of the children in the target age group. Hopping and jumping diagrams painted on hard surfaces encourage the development of hopping and long-jumping skills. A jump-the-stream diagram and a graduated long-jump diagram painted on a hard ground surface are appropriate in play areas designed for preschool and primary school children (Figures 7.12 and 7.13). Standards and a bamboo pole, along with a large sandpile that serves as a landing surface, aid in developing hurdle jumping and high-jumping skills.

Running, throwing, and catching activities in relatively uncomplicated games appropriate for the age group require the delineation of rectangles and circles. Play areas designed for preschool and early primary school children should have such boundaries painted on hard surfaces and chalked on turf surfaces in play yards.

Strength and muscular endurance develop during play when children pull wagons loaded with other children, and when they pump the pedals on small vehicles. These activities may be accommodated with a vehicle path or area that incorporates gradual slopes, straightaways, curves, and a variety of surfaces (e.g., rough pebbles set in concrete and smooth concrete).

The greater the variety of surface types included on playgrounds, the greater the potential range of movement opportunities afforded the children who use the play area. Hard, soft, level, inclining, gravel, and sand surfaces each encourage different movement possibilities.

Playgrounds for Third- Through Sixth-Grade Children

Intermediate school children need to apply previously learned, fundamental motor patterns to specialized sports that are popular in our culture. They also need to develop and maintain normal posture and physical fitness.

Further development of climbing skills, along with several components of fitness, may be promoted by providing large, permanently embedded apparatus configurations that have multiple uses and that cover large amounts of physical space on a playground. These areas should be covered with 8 to 10 in. of sand. Such climbing configurations must be enormously complex and designed for the physical dimensions of the children who are to use them.

If children are to learn the rules, strategies, and skills of popular sports, court diagrams for four-square, tetherball, hopscotch variations, basketball, volleyball, tennis, and badminton need to be painted on concrete or asphalt surfaces. Standards and other necessary, permanently embedded equipment should be installed. Turf field spaces need to be chalked for soccer, softball, football, and speedball. Goal areas and backstops need to be installed where necessary. Stalled areas need to be provided on hard level surfaces for racquetball.

Fitness trails, cycling or jogging trails, and quarter-mile tracks encourage improved, well-maintained fitness and aid in teaching lifetime sports skills. For that reason, they are desirable inclusions.

Large, vandal-proof storage units for keeping nets, racquets, bats, bases, balls, ropes, and other small equipment need to be located so that materials can be easily checked out and returned during play sessions. Often such a storage area is located within the school but near an exit that is close to the play area. Students can supervise such an equipment storage area.

Influences on Motor Activity

No simple rule of thumb exists for determining the optimum space that should be allocated for a playground. The amount of space, the number of children using the area and the scarcity and nature of play materials all influence motor activity.

Amount of Space

As the space allocated to play decreases, changes occur in gross motor behaviors. Non-locomotor and climbing behaviors tend to increase, while running and other locomotor behaviors decrease (McGrew 1970, Smith 1974). McGrew (1970) and Rohe and Patterson (1974) have noted that as children are placed in closer proximity with other children and materials, a higher level of social contact and play results. However, increased aggression, destructiveness, disruptive behaviors, irrelevant play, and wandering may accompany these contacts (Hutt and Vaizey 1966, Loo 1972, Shapiro 1975). Additionally, as space levels are reduced (Loo 1972), children may retreat into solitary play to establish psychological distance when physical distance is difficult to establish.

Number of Children Using the Play Area

McGrew (1970) suggests that perceptions of crowding may occur not only when the amount of space is decreased but also when the number of people occupying the space is increased. She observed different types of responses, depending on the cause of crowding. The most important changes occurred when group sizes increased. When group size was small, children's responses tended to be less negative than when the group size was large.

Shapiro (1975) reported that group size also affects teacher behavior. In groups of more than 20 children, levels of teacher-child interaction were lower. The addition of a second teacher to lower the teacher/child ratio did not result in increased teacher-child interaction. Perhaps this helps to explain some of the negative behaviors associated with play in large groups in play areas.

Wade (1970) examined the play behaviors of 16 kindergarten children (8 boys, 8 girls) who visited an experimental playroom. The children were allowed to play freely under minimal supervision. While playing, the children's heart rates were continuously monitored, with each child wearing a miniature heart telemeter that allowed the data to be collected but that did not interfere with the child's activity. In addition, children were observed through a one-way mirror and rated on a four-point activity scale. The children played in three same-sex play groups (alone, dyad, and quadrad) in a playroom configuration with both a minimum of play apparatus and a maximum of play apparatus. During a play session, continuous electrocardiographic recordings and activity scale ratings (on the four-point activity scale) were made for each child. Results indicated that children were more active as they increased their play group size.

Scarcity of Play Materials

Smith (1974) and Gump (1975) have suggested that many reported instances of negative social behaviors demonstrated in play areas may be due to scarcity of play materials and equipment rather than to limited space or large numbers of children. Johnson (1935) concluded that as the amount of playground equipment decreases, the amount of aggressive behavior in particular and the amount of social interaction in general increases. Rohe and Patterson (1974) found that not only did decreases in resources alone result in higher levels of negative behaviors, but also decreases in space alone resulted in high levels of aggression, destructiveness, and irrelevant play. When space was limited, higher quantities of resources resulted in more cooperative play than did lower quantities. Both the low-space, low-resource conditions and the low-space, high-resource conditions resulted in more social play. The quality of this play, however, was less than in the high-space, high-resource condition.

Regulating Traffic Flow on Playgrounds

Playground space should be arranged to invite movement within play zones, between different play zones, and between various points of entry and exit. Play zones should be defined by boundaries that set them apart functionally and visually yet that integrate them spatially with adjacent zones. These boundaries may take many forms. A concrete wall that bounds a large sandpile filled with equipment for climbing, hanging, swinging, and sliding can set that area off from other play zones. If one portion of the wall is up to 8 ft high, the side of the wall opposite the sandpile can also serve as the back wall of a stall area in which striking, throwing, and kicking activities take place. The wall sets the two play zones apart functionally and visually, yet integrates them spatially.

Asphalt or concrete pathways can direct children from one play zone to another. Hedges, trees, and fence barriers can also direct the movement of children through a playground. The flow of traffic on large, complex climbing structures with multiple uses should also be conceptualized carefully. Avenues of entrance and exit on the climbing structures should take into account the physical skills and risk-taking characteristics of the children using the equipment. Many different ways to enter or exit a climbing structure should be created. Entrances and exits on playgrounds should be placed for unobstructed access from school buildings, from the street, and where service will be needed (e.g., the sandpile).

REFERENCES

Adams, J. A. A closed-loop theory of motor learning. *Journal of Motor Behavior,* 1971, **4**, 111-150.

Ammons, R. B. Effects of knowledge of performance: A survey and tentative theoretical formulation. *Journal of General Psychology,* 1956, **54**, 279-299.

Bilodeau, I. M. Information feedback. In E. A. Bilodeau (Ed.), *Acquisition of skill.* London: Academic Press, 1966.

Brown, J. S. *A proposed program of research on psychological feedback (knowledge of results) in the performance of psychomotor tasks.* Research Planning Conference, Perceptual and Motor Skills AFHRRC Conference, Report 49-2, 81-87, U.S. Air Force, San Antonio, Texas, 1949.

Cockrell, D. L. A study of the play of children of preschool age by an unobserved observer. *Genetic Psychology Monographs,* 1935, **17**, 379-469.

Connolly, K. (Ed.) *Mechanisms of motor skill development.* New York: Academic Press, 1970.

Dennis, W. Infant development under conditions of restricted practice and minimal social stimulation: A preliminary report. *Journal of Genetic Psychology,* 1938, **53**, 149-158.

Dennis, W. The effect of restricted practice upon the reaching, sitting and standing of two infants. *Journal of Genetic Psychology,* 1935, **47**, 17-32.

Druker, J. F., & Hagen, J. W. Developmental trends in the processing of task-relevant and task-irrelevant information. *Child Development,* 1969, **40**, 371-382.

Dusenberry, I. A study of the effects of training in ball throwing by children ages three to seven. *Research Quarterly,* 1952, **23**, 9-14.

Estes, M. The role of creative play equipment in developing muscular fitness. Unpublished doctoral dissertation, State University of Iowa, 1959.

Gallahue, D. L. The relationship between perceptual and motor abilities. *Research Quarterly,* 1968, **39**, 948-952.

Gilmore, J. B. Play: A special behavior. In R. N. Haber (Ed.), *Current research in motivation.* New York: Holt, Rinehart and Winston, 1966a.

Gilmore, J. B. The role of anxiety and cognitive factors in children's play behavior. *Child Development,* 1966b, **37**, 397-416.

Gramza, A. F., Corush, J., & Ellis, M. J. Children's play on trestles differing in complexity: A study of play equipment design. *Journal of Leisure Research,* 1972, **4**, 303-311.

Gump, P. V. Ecological psychology in children. In E. M. Hetherington (Ed.), *Review of child development research.* Vol. 5. Chicago: University of Chicago Press, 1975.

Hagen, J. W. The effect of distraction on selective attention. *Child Development,* 1967, **38**, 685-694.

Herkowitz, J. The moving embedded figures test. *Research Quarterly,* 1973, **43**, 479-488.

Holding, D. H. *Principles of training.* London: Pergamon, 1965.

Hutt, C. Exploration and play in children. *Symposium of the Zoological Society of London,* 1966, **18**, 61-81.

Hutt, C., & Vaizey, A. Differential effects of group density on social behavior. *Nature,* 1966, **209**, 1371-1372.

Johnson, M. W. The effect on behavior of variations in the amount of play equipment. *Child Development,* 1935, **6**, 56-68.

Leithwood, K. A., & Fowler, W. Complex motor learning in four-year-olds. *Child Development,* 1971, **42**, 781-792.

Loo, C. M. The effects of spatial density on the social behavior of children. *Journal of Applied Social Psychology,* 1972, **2** (4), 372-381.

Lowrey, G. H. *Growth and development of children.* Chicago: Year Book Medical Publishers, 1978.

Malina, R. M. *Growth and development—The first twenty years in man.* Minneapolis: Burgess, 1975.

McClenaghan, B. A., & Gallahue, D. L. *Fundamental movement: A developmental and remedial approach.* Philadelphia: Saunders, 1978.

McGraw, M. B. *Growth: A study of Johnny and Jimmy.* New York: Appleton-Century, 1935.

McGraw, M. B. Later development of children specially trained during infancy: Johnny and Jimmy at school age. *Child Development,* 1939, **10**, 1-19.

McGrew, P. L. Social and spatial density effects on spacing behavior in preschool children. *Journal of Applied Social Psychology,* 1970, **11**, 197-205.

Mendel, G. Children's preferences for differing degrees of novelty. *Child Development,* 1965, **36**, 453-465.

Miller, R. B. *Handbook on training and training equipment design.* Wright Air Development Center, Technical Report No. 53-136, 1953.

Minerva, A. N. Psychomotor education and the general development of preschool children: Experiments with twin controls. *Journal of Genetic Psychology,* 1935, **46**, 433-454.

National Recreation and Parks Association. Proposed safety standard for public playground equipment. Developed for the Consumer Product Safety Commission. Arlington, Virginia: National Recreation and Parks Association, 1976.

Newell, K. M. Knowledge of results and motor learning. In J. Keogh & R. S. Sutton (Eds.), *Exercise and sport sciences reviews.* Vol. 4. Santa Barbara, California: Journal Publishing Affiliates, 1976.

Ridenour, M. V. Influence of object size, speed, and direction on the perception of moving objects. *Research Quarterly,* 1974, **45**, 293-301.

Ridenour, M. V. Influence of object size, speed, direction, height, and distance on the interception of a moving object. *Research Quarterly,* 1977, **45**, 138-143.

Ridenour, M. V. The influence of ball and background patterns on the perception of visual direction of a moving object. *Perceptual and Motor Skills,* 1979, **49**, 343-346.

Rohe, W., & Patterson, A. H. *The effects of varied levels of resources and density on behavior in a day care center.* Paper presented at the Midwestern Psychological Association, Chicago, May 1974.

Scholtz, G. J., & Ellis, M. J. *Novelty, complexity and play.* Paper presented at the International Seminar on Play in Physical Education and Sport, Wingate Institute, Israel, April 1975a.

Scholtz, G. J., & Ellis, M. J. Repeated exposure to objects and peers in a play setting. *Journal of Experimental Child Psychology,* 1975b, **19**, 448-455.

Shapiro, S. Some classroom ABC's. *Elementary School Journal,* 1975, **75**, 436-441.

Sinclair, D. *Human growth after birth.* London: Oxford University Press, 1973.

Smith, P. Aspects of the playgroup environment. In D. Cantor & T. Lee (Eds.), *Proceedings of the conference: Psychology and the built environment.* London: Architectural Press, 1974.

Tanner, J. M. *Fetus into man: From conception to maturity.* Cambridge, Massachusetts: Harvard University Press, 1978.

Tanner, J. M. *Education and physical growth.* New York: International Universities Press, 1979.

Vurpillot, E. The development of scanning strategies and their relation to visual differentiation. *Journal of Experimental Child Psychology,* 1968, **6**, 632-650.

Wade, M. G. Biorhythms in children during free play. Unpublished doctoral dissertation, University of Illinois, 1970.

Wade, M. B., & Ellis, M. J. Measurement of free range activity in children as modified by social and environmental complexity. *The American Journal of Clinical Nutrition,* 1971, **24**, 1457-1460.

Ward, T. & Groppel, J. L. Sport implement selection: Can it be based upon anthropometric indicators? *Motor Skills: Theory Into Practice*, 1980, **4**, 103-110.

Weilbacher, R. M. A comparison of kindergarten girls' social and motor behaviors in a static play environment and in a dynamic play environment. Unpublished doctoral dissertation, Ohio State University, 1980.

Wickstrom, R. *Fundamental motor patterns.* Philadelphia: Lea & Febiger, 1977.

Williams, H. G. Perceptual-motor development as a function of information processing. In M. G. Wade & R. Martens (Eds.), *Psychology of motor behavior and sport.* Proceedings of the North American Society for the Psychology of Sport and Physical Activity, 1973.

Williams, H. G. The effects of systematic variation of speed and direction of object flight and of skill and age classifications upon visuo-perceptual judgments of moving objects in three-dimensional space. Unpublished doctoral dissertation, University of Wisconsin at Madison, 1968.

Wright, E. J. Effects of light and heavy equipment on acquisition of sports type skills by young children. *Research Quarterly,* 1967, **38**, 705-714.

Wuellner, L. H. A method to investigate the movement patterns of children. Unpublished master's thesis, University of Illinois, 1969.

SUGGESTED READINGS

Undergraduate Students

Homemade Small Equipment

Christian, Q. A. *The bean bag curriculum: A homemade approach to physical activity for children.* Wolfe City, Texas: University Press, 1973.

Corbin, C. B. *Inexpensive equipment for games, play and physical activity.* Dubuque, Iowa: Brown, 1972.

Gallahue, D. L. *Developmental play equipment for home and school.* New York: Wiley, 1975.
Werner, P., & Rini, L. *Perceptual motor development equipment.* New York: Wiley, 1976.
Werner, P., & Simmons, R. *Inexpensive physical education equipment for children.* Minneapolis: Burgess, 1976.

Playground Design and Construction

Allen, Lady of Hurtwood. *Adventure playgrounds for handicapped children.* London: James Galt, Ltd., 1975.
Allen, M. A. *Planning for play.* London: Thames and Hudson, 1968.
Bengtsson, A. *Environmental planning for children's play.* New York: Praeger, 1970.
Dattner, R. *Designs for play.* New York: Van Nostrand Reinhold, 1969.
E'Eugenio, T. *Building with tires.* Cambridge, Massachusetts: Early Childhood Education, 1971.
Friedberg, P. *Handicrafted playgrounds: Designs you can build yourself.* New York: Vintage, 1975.
Friedberg, M. P. *Play and interplay: A manifesto for new design in urban recreational environment.* New York: Macmillan, 1970.
Frost, J. L., & Klein, B. L. *Children's play and playgrounds.* Boston: Allyn and Bacon, 1979.
Helick, R. M., & Watkins, M. T. *Elements of preschool playyards.* Swissvale, Pennsylvania: Regent Graphic Services, 1973.
Hewes, J. J. *Build your own playground.* Boston: Houghton Mifflin, 1975.
Hogan, P. *Playgrounds for free: The utilization of used and surplus materials in playground construction.* Cambridge, Massachusetts: MIT Press, 1974.
Kritchevsky, S., Prescott, E., & Walling, L. *Planning environments for young children—Physical space.* Washington, D.C.: National Association for the Education of Young Children, 1969.
Ledermann, A., & Trachsel, A. *Creative playgrounds and recreation centers.* New York: Praeger, 1959.
National Recreation and Parks Association. Proposed safety standard for public playground equipment. Developed for the Consumer Product Safety Commission. Arlington, Virginia: National Recreation and Parks Association, 1976.
Nicholson, S. The theory of loose parts. *Landscape Architecture,* October 1971.
Seymour, W. N. *Small urban spaces: The philosophy of vestpocket parks.* New York: New York University Press, 1969.

Graduate Students

Play Theory

Ellis, M. J. *Why people play?* Englewood Cliffs, New Jersey: Prentice-Hall, 1973.

Playground Research

Bowers, L. An analysis of the status of research on play apparatus for handicapped children. *Physical Education and Recreation for Impaired, Disabled and Handicapped Individuals—Past, Present, and Future.* Washington, D.C.: American Alliance for Health, Physical Education and Recreation, 1976.
Ellis, M. J., & Scholtz, G. J. L. *Activity and play of children.* Englewood Cliffs, New Jersey: Prentice-Hall, 1978.

8

Applying Knowledge of Motor Development to Mentally Retarded Children

Katherine T. Thomas

This chapter covers skill acquisition, learning, and memory of movement in the mentally retarded and learning disabled. These two groups are presented here both because of their high representation in schools and because the most immediate and permanent changes can be made with these children. Selecting a group that can be remediable is pleasing and more practical than selecting a group with an unalterable handicap. This is not to belittle or ignore smaller percentages of the population placed in other categories, but rather to limit the scope of this chapter and to recognize the high incidence of learning and intellectual deficits in the school populations.

Approximately 8% of the school-aged population is handicapped (Dearman and Plisko 1980). Of those, over half are labeled as learning disabled (LD) or mentally retarded (MR). When the large number of speech-only children (who show no motor or intellectual deficits) are removed from the tabulation, the remaining proportion of MR and LD children is approximately 77%, with the remaining 23% comprised of emotionally disturbed (ED), other health-impaired (OHI), multi-handicapped, orthopedically handicapped (OH), deaf (D), hard of hearing (HH), visually handicapped (VH), and deaf and blind. In the 1978-79 school year, 916,073 MR and 1,154,491 LD children between 5 and 17 years of age were served under Public Laws 94-142 and 89-313.

These statistics identify the most common handicaps found in education and indicate the need for remediation of children with learning difficulties or intellectual deficits or both. Many of these children qualify for special physical education. All of them must have either regular or adapted physical education. Therefore, the problems that they present in a movement setting are of concern and interest, whether those problems are strictly cognitive or involve underlying motor components. MR children and their teachers must learn to deal with both intellectual and motor deficits. In motor skills, 7 of the 11 categories (e.g., OH, OHI, or D, but not ED) might be viewed as conditions to which to adapt, since the handicapping condition remains constant. For example, a blind child can participate in many activities with sighted children when the activity is modified. The modifications are necessary as long as the blindness remains. Programming can be viewed as an accommodation to the handicap. Clearly, this programming must be planned with both the "least restrictive environment" portion of the law and the child's safety in mind.

How does cognitive development in MR individuals relate to motor performance? As Thomas (Chapter 4) has pointed out, the same system controls all learning and memory, whether cognitive, motor, or affective. A problem in the memory system may affect motor skill acquisition in infinite ways, including less understanding of task variables or verbal instructions, poor motor planning, slower processing, and inadequate socialization, among others. Clearly, cognitive development in MR and LD children has the same relationship to motor development as is found with normal children. Cognitive development in these children must be understood so that appropriate activities for this special population can be designed.

Knowledge gained about MR and LD children also helps us to understand normal development better. Generally, a deficit in overall motor performance is associated with MR and LD children. However, these children may be highly skilled in one activity owing to excessive practice in those skills. The issue of training relates closely to the major controversy involving research in mental retardation, a theoretical argument with structural versus functional explanations for depressed intellectual performance.

DELAY VERSUS DEFICIT

Historically, two theories of mental retardation have been debated. The first is the *structural difference*, or *deficit, theory*, which purports a physical, structural, permanent explanation for intellectual impairment (Lewin 1935, Ellis 1963, Spitz 1963, Belmont and Butterfield 1969, Campione and Brown 1977). The second is the *developmental delay*, or *lag, theory*, which ascribes performance decrements to slow, late, or nonexistent strategies and control processes necessary for successful performance of the tasks (Belmont and Butterfield 1969, Ziegler 1969, Campione and Brown 1977, Hagen and Stanovich 1977). The structural difference or deficit theory leaves little if any hope for improvement. Thus, the delay theory is often more attractive to teachers and others interested in MR children.

The delay theory seeks to improve the teaching-learning situation, and offers immediate facilitation of some common learning and memory problems. It may also help to explain why the teaching situation improves performance even when children do not transfer or generalize behaviors. Many examples exist of the performance by MR and LD children being facilitated, especially within the information-processing framework. The implication is that, in most cases, empirical evidence supports the delay theory, whereas only the theorists support the difference theory. Another advantage of working within the delay theory is that the whole body of knowledge from cognitive development, motor development, and the resulting programs then becomes available for use with MR and LD children.

Three etiological categories of mental retardation are commonly used: (1) undiagnosed, (2) cultural-familial, and (3) organic or biological. The latter may refer to cerebral palsy, Down's syndrome, and other biological conditions associated with mental retardation. These individuals often have other impairments relating to but extending beyond intellectual impairment. Most MR children are undiagnosed, and most research deals with cultural-familial and undiagnosed subjects to avoid confounding with other factors such as neurological impairment and growth deviations.

INFORMATION PROCESSING

Information processing, as outlined by Atkinson and Shiffrin (1968), places many mental operations outside of conscious control. More recent versions of information-processing models (Shiffrin and Schnieder 1977) and the framework of levels of processing (Craik and Lockhardt 1972) stress the role of the individual in consciously controlling the memory. The research indicates that young children and MR individuals have little understanding of their role in the memory process (Brown 1975, Campione and Brown 1977). Typically, children do nothing special to remember—they make no plan, execute no strategy, and do little active retrieval. The parallels between chronological age and mental age are consistent, that is, as age increases or intelligence increases, performance improves. Age and intelligence are clearly related developmentally because mental age is a better predictor of performance than chronological age. Thus, the same factors that facilitate performance developmentally also positively influence performance for MR and LD students.

The *production* and *mediation deficiency hypotheses* explain how forced intervention of a strategy or control process affects performance. The mediation deficiency describes a situation in which use of a control process fails to improve performance (Reese 1962). Reese was referring to verbal mediation, but this can probably be generalized to all control processes and strategic behavior. The production deficiency hypothesis applies when the strategy is available but is not used to facilitate performance (Flavell et al. 1966). Therefore, in one case, forcing the use of the strategy does not help performance, while in the other, the forced strategy improves performance. In most cases, the strategy is not produced spontaneously. MR and LD children may produce a strategy that does not work (i.e., facilitate performance), so they can be said to have a mediation deficiency. A production deficiency is almost always evident in MR children.

ATTENTION

Attention can be directed to material in the sensory array (perception), to short-term store (STS), or to long-term store (LTS). Age-related changes in attention refer to changes in intensity, effectiveness, and focus. The first developmental stage is overexclusive attention, and refers to a restricted visual scan (until about age 6), low incidental learning, and focus on one aspect of the stimuli (Ross 1976). This is the stage in which LD children typically remain. Overinclusive attention normally occurs between the ages of 6 to 12 years, when children focus on many aspects of the stimulus array. Incidental learning includes peaks during which children may appear distracted. Older MR individuals tend to stop development at this stage, although in more severe retardation, remaining in the overexclusive stage is common (Burgio, Whitman, and Johnson 1980). Adolescents and adults selectively attend, which means they can choose critical cues and focus with vigilance on selected cues.

Children who are overexclusive need to be aware of the critical cues for successful task performance and direct attention to these cues. For example, to facilitate catching, teachers should vary only one aspect at a time, such as speed, plane, or direction. They should then point out only that aspect and repeat it with many varying trials. This is why rolling a ball works well to teach anticipation of impact for catching. The rolled ball has both plane and direction constants, with speed being varied as appropriate. The overinclusive child is probably attending to many extraneous variables, such as the car driving by, the color of the ball, or a butterfly. Again, cues critical to task success can be given and isolated. When the child cannot selectively attend to the cues, the teacher must compensate by varying the task demands.

Six factors have been identified as helping to develop selective attention to normal and LD children. By varying (1) novelty, (2) complexity, (3) uncertainty, (4) the element of surprise, (5) conflict, and (6) change, interest or vigilance can be maintained. MR children can benefit from this, but tend to be satisfied with repeating the same task over many more trials than do normal and LD children.

SENSORY STORE, PERCEPTUAL MECHANISM, AND ENCODING

The short-term sensory storage system has a large capacity and a short duration, and apparently functions similarly in retarded and nonretarded populations (Berkson 1960, Pennington and Luszcz 1975). Differences in performance may occur when the stimulus is alphanumeric, as the retarded subjects are less familiar with the stimuli than are the normal subjects (Stanovich 1978). Of particular interest is Berkson's (1960) study on storage of location information. Subjects had to recognize the location of a dot placed at one of four locations inside a circle. No differences were obtained between intelligence levels on this visual storage task. The sparsity of research on sensory storage in MR subjects makes definitive statements tenuous. However, in both cultural-familial and undiagnosed MR cases, apparently information in sensory store does not differ with age or IQ. Organically or biologically MR students may have diagnosed neurological impairments that affect one or more of the sensory registers. For these students, providing task-related sensory information and choosing or altering tasks to decrease sensory demands may be necessary.

Perceptual encoding by MR subjects of nonverbal (i.e., not alphanumeric) stimuli from sensory storage has been reviewed and argued for the past decade (Stanovich 1978). In early investigations, IQ and age-related performance decrements were noted. Ryan and Jones (1975) suggest that these are artifacts of typical MR behavior rather than failure or slowness in perceptual encoding. Ryan and Jones pointed out inconsistent trial-to-trial performance, inconsistent or no perceptual strategies, and incorrect verbal responses. Stereotypic response patterns were indicated in both these early studies and our (Chapter 4) developmental work with a motor task. The problem in our research consisted of young children responding with only one answer even when they recognized that at times that answer was incorrect. By designing an experiment that eluded previous criticisms, Ryan and Jones found no IQ-related differences in perceptual sensitivity. In an early study using alphanumeric stimuli and with subjects representing two IQ levels, accuracy and rates of perceptual encoding were poorer for retarded than for nonretarded subjects (Welsandt and Meyer 1974).

Throughout the literature, the use of alphanumeric stimuli has discriminated against MR participants, presumably because of the differing experience levels with this material. This leads to two conclusions. First, when activities are to include MR children with normal children, nonverbal stimuli should be used to equate difficulty of the task. For example, in relays or games that traditionally use the alphabet, numbers, or words as cues, teachers may replace these alphanumeric cues with symbols, shapes, figures, or pictures. Second, retarded children need more experience with alphanumeric stimuli. In situations in which this does not put MR children at a disadvantage, these stimuli can and should be used. As task complexity increases, the distinction between normal and MR individuals increases on performance measures. The short-term memory system either loses information or further processes the information. Processing goes on by keeping data in LTS or continuing to deal actively with or expand on this data in STS.

To sum up, the encoding process begins by taking information from the sensory registers to the perceptual mechanism and finally into STS and LTS. As the information is acted on, three changes occur: (1) the encoding demands more attention, (2) the encoding becomes consciously controlled, and (3) the material becomes less physical and more symbolic (Hagen and Stanovich 1977). As the transition is made from physical to symbolic characteristics, the age- and IQ-related differences become obvious (Hagen and Stanovich 1977, Kail and Siegel 1977).

As the process becomes more consciously controlled and the need for higher encoding levels becomes necessary, teachers can cue appropriate encoding strategies. For example, in a backward roll, a teacher may tell the child to keep his knees near his nose by giving that as a verbal label to the spatial relationship. Eventually the verbal label is associated in long-term memory (LTM) with the backward roll, and thus the two become retrieval cues for each other. At an advanced skill level, the entire movement plan is cued, and little attention is allocated to any aspect other than selection and initiation of the total plan (which includes all previous experience and information in LTM). Another example is encoding the quality of a movement by varying step size from smaller than the length of a foot to greater than the length of a foot. The verbal label helps to encode the physical characteristic of a step size as one foot not extending beyond the other and thus the symbolic notion of a small step. The notion of large steps is encoded as the physical characteristic of steps with space between one heel and toes of the other foot. This can work into seriation and gradation by including the characteristics of large, medium, and tiny step sizes and the descriptions of each.

REHEARSAL

Rehearsal is a control process that maintains information actively in STS, usually by repetition of the items in ordered sets. Rehearsal increases with age, starting around age seven, in both quality and quantity. Inclusion of more items in the sets, more active rehearsal, and more efficient use of time to rehearse are all qualities improved with increased age. Apparently the use of rehearsal depends on the level of cognitive development; therefore, the IQ-rehearsal relationship closely approximates the age-related patterns.

Three types of experiments all indicate that most MR persons do not spontaneously use rehearsal in appropriate settings (production deficiency). Using serial recall, Ellis (1980) found a recency effect (last items presented were recalled effectively) in both MR individuals and college students, but only college students exhibited a primacy effect (early items presented were recalled effectively). This was interpreted as a lack of spontaneous rehearsal by the MR participants. Giving longer interitem intervals did not facilitate the MR individuals' performance. However, the normal individuals used this time to improve their recall. Belmont and Butterfield (1971) allowed subjects to pace rehearsal so that analysis of both the type and success of rehearsal could be accomplished. The college students used a "cumulative rehearsal, fast finish" (long pauses early, short pauses late), while the MR individuals showed similar brief pauses between all items. A third set of experiments studied rehearsal with a probe technique, which varied the number of categories in which the probe might occur (Brown, Campione, et al. 1973). Subjects were asked to identify the last item of a particular category presented. The MR individuals were slower and less accurate in responding. The normal subjects were both quick to reply and accurate, indicating that the items were available in STS because of rehearsal.

The same results could be expected for motor tasks as for those reported for these cognitive experiments, although two additional factors influence the results. Younger and developmentally delayed children are likely to have more experience in motor tasks, but motor task performance is more variable. Frequently, the research using motor tasks is more sensitive because the measures are continuous and not discrete.

Two experiments using motor tasks have predictable results. The first used severely retarded males who were to learn a sequence of movements as responses to a series of lights (Schroeder 1980). Spontaneous rehearsal did not occur, but when forced to rehearse, the MR subjects improved their performance significantly. However, the MR subjects did not transfer a learned strategy for a motor task. The most remarkable factor in this study was that the subjects were severely mentally retarded. Most other experiments use mildly retarded subjects.

Results from the second study are tenuous at best, since only pilot data are available at this time. In this experiment, MR children recalled location information about a movement as well as did nonretarded children of the same chronological age.[1] The MR children could not recall distance information about a movement as well as could nonretarded children unless they were instructed in the strategy. Clearly, MR individuals can be trained to use strategies, even when they cannot spontaneously select or apply a strategy (production deficiency), to facilitate performance.

Rehearsal Strategies for Teaching MR Students

Three common types of rehearsal are effective when used in teaching mentally handicapped children. In the first, a *model* can be used for passive rehearsal. The student then watches the correct execution of the skill. MR and LD children are proficient at copying a visual model (see the earlier mention of the automatic encoding of spatial information presented visually). Reliance on modeling can be due to the exclusion of other types of information. Modeling may be more effective if the child becomes actively involved. Demonstration, then a replication by the child, feedback, demonstration, and further replication cause the child to interact with the model. Questions such as "What happened to my arm?" or "Where was I looking?" direct attention to the critical cues. The child is mentally rehearsing what she sees and hears, and then develops a movement plan.

The second type of rehearsal is simply *practice*. The adage that "practice makes perfect" is correct only when the practice *is* perfect; practice can be varied, but the elements should be as correct as possible on each trial. The distinction lies in detecting and correcting errors versus sloppy repetitions. Sloppy repetitions produce sloppy performances.

Finally, *verbal rehearsal*, which is the use of labels in ordered sets, can be induced. For example, a child could say "step-hop, step-hop" to practice skipping, or "pull, kick, glide" to learn the sequence for the breaststroke. In each case, verbal rehearsal accompanies repetition, feedback, and probably, modeling.

The appropriate use of each of these general categories of rehearsal facilitates learning. These handicapped children do not spontaneously rehearse, as do normal children of the same chrono-

1. Breitschwerdt, A., & Thomas, J. R. Unpublished research paper, Louisiana State University, Baton Rouge, 1983.

logical age. The teacher must therefore force and encourage the application of appropriate rehearsal through the techniques used and the organization of the class.

TRANSFER, GENERALIZATION, RETENTION, AND LTM

Transfer is the application of a task-specific strategy to a similar new task. *Generalization* is the use of control processes or types of strategies in varied, appropriate situations. Transfer is associated with short-term memory (STM), generalization with LTM. Many studies have investigated both generalization and transfer with the same results. MR individuals do not generalize; they rarely transfer, and then only if tasks are similar and if rehearsal is cued (Belmont and Butterfield 1969; Campione and Brown 1977). No research exists on the relationship between motor tasks and IQ, but the prediction is that correlated differences must exist between motor-cognitive skills and age-IQ factors. MR individuals showed maintenance of rehearsal after a six-month delay (Campione and Brown 1977). When the same subjects were probed for generalization of the rehearsal strategy, no effect was found. Once the MR individuals acquired the strategy of rehearsal for the task, they retained as well as did normal individuals.

Retention has been examined in numerous cognitive tasks for MR individuals. No IQ differences were found in rate of loss from memory when the acquisition phase was controlled. In studies in which all subjects reached the same acquisition criteria, no difference appeared. When the number of trials or time were held constant for IQ levels, the groups with lower IQs were unable to get the same amount of information into memory, and therefore the MR participants appeared to lose information at a faster rate.

Two studies have investigated immediate 5-sec and 60-sec retention intervals (Baumeister and Kellas 1967; Belmont and Butterfield 1969). The task was to replace a dot on paper. The MR individuals' performances were significantly poorer in placement of the dot at all intervals than were nonretarded subjects. The interval by IQ interaction showed 0 sec to 5 sec as the critical comparison. Clearly the nonretarded subjects had superior mnemonic strategies that facilitated recall after an interval. The nonretarded subjects measured distances to acquire the location information accurately. This is an acquisition problem that normal individuals can solve with strategy, whereas MR individuals cannot solve the problem. These studies and many others attempt to investigate retention, but are confounded by acquisition deficits in MR individuals. Looking at the rate of loss (the slope of error from 5 sec to 60 sec) for MR individuals and for normal individuals showed little difference.

Fagan (1968) handled this problem by increasing the material presented to the normal individuals so that their acquisition rate closely resembled that of the MR individuals. For 0-sec and 10-sec filled and unfilled retention interval, Fagan found no interaction. He interpreted this as equal rates of forgetting for both normal and MR subjects.

From these results, three concepts can be applied to teaching: (1) Many more trials are necessary for MR children as compared with normal children for them to acquire the same level of performance; similarly, a poorer performance should be expected when MR individuals are given the same amount of time as are normal individuals. (2) The rate of loss from memory is equal across IQ levels, and therefore the extra time and effort necessary to achieve performance criteria are worthwhile. Acquisition is the level of mastery. If MR and LD children master the skills, then retention equals that of nonretarded children. (3) MR students do not transfer strategies or generalize control processes, so on each occasion, the student must be cued to elicit the appropriate strategy or process. If both the delay theory were correct and an infinite amount of time were available, perhaps this transfer and generalization would eventually occur in MR subjects, since both transfer and generalization are developmental in nature.

MR individuals have fewer strategies and control processes available spontaneously to place information into LTS, and each item demands more time or trials to move to LTS. Therefore, LTS cannot contain equivalent amounts of information at the same chronological ages for normal and for MR and LD individuals. This is a major problem for these latter individuals. The problem is circular—without experience, LTS suffers, but because of LTS deficits, acquisition is more difficult.

RESEARCH PARADIGMS AND PROBLEMS

All of the problems associated with developmental research are likely to be associated with research on handicapped children (Chapter 13). Many are magnified with the special MR and LD population. In trying to evaluate, apply, or conduct research on MR-LD individuals, several issues need to be considered. Sample selection must be made carefully and must allow for the etiological, IQ, age, and socioeconomic classifications, along with other possible factors causing individual differences such as physical impairment or institutionalization.

Task selection is critical to success in answering the research hypothesis. For example, alphanumeric stimuli and verbal responses are among many factors that discriminate against MR and LD subjects and therefore mask treatment results. Nonretarded subjects may reach perfect performance on a task, so the treatment appears to have no effect. Conversely, the MR participants may fail every item and show no treatment effect. This often happens in time series studies in which performance was expected to decay over time but in which MR performance could not get worse. These ceiling and floor effects are especially prevalent in some of the early studies. Tasks with time as a factor also discriminate, because MR participants cannot reach normal criteria in equal trials or amounts of time.

The assumptions that are often made with nonretarded subjects are invalid with MR individuals. A perfect example is the retention studies of Belmont and Butterfield (1969). The assumption was that acquisition was equal across age and IQ. Clearly this was a poor assumption when testing retention. When acquisition was equalized for IQ levels, the retention deficits of MR subjects disappeared. In developmental studies, the assumption is that experience (LTS) is equally distributed within equal chronological age groups. However, with the LTS problems of MR subjects, differences associated with IQ levels within chronological age exist. To make the mental ages (MA) match between groups so that MR individuals are of increased chronological age and equal to the mental age of normal individuals places the MR individuals in perhaps another generation of peer influence—some in puberty—most with larger physical size and other gross differences that may confound IQ-related results.

SUMMARY

Mentally retarded (MR) and learning disabled (LD) children account for more than half of the students being served in special programs for the handicapped. The developmental delay theory has considerable empirical support for the supposition that mental retardation and learning disabilities are processing deficits and not structural problems. The problem is a "production deficiency," not a "mediation deficiency." Predictions for MR and LD children follow the developmental predictions for the same mental age. Performance, both qualitatively and quantitatively, also follows the mental age when matched to nonretarded children.

Training studies and other research have manipulated behavior to produce "normal" performance in MR individuals. That is, MR children can perform qualitatively like their chronological age counterparts when taught or forced to do so. Generalization and transfer are the greatest challenge for remediation. MR individuals can be both cued to attend and forced to rehearse, and exhibit normal retention. With more time (or trials), MR students can reach and maintain mastery. These individuals probably have less experience stored in LTS than do normal individuals, and have increased difficulty in placing information there. They also have little knowledge about memory and ways to facilitate memory. All of these factors are alterable.

The research is optimistic; immediate help is available and future solutions are probable. Teachers can now use knowledge to alter performance, facilitate learning, and thus make their jobs less frustrating. The knowledge gained from research helps in understanding both normal development and remediable MR children. Hagen and Stanovich (1977) summarize nicely that "the picture is optimistic concerning the potential value of remedial programs for children in either of these categories. The developmental course of memory for these children is similar to that found in normal children."

REFERENCES

Atkinson, R. C., & Shiffrin, R. M. Human memory: A proposed system and its control processes. In K. W. Spence & J. W. Spence (Eds.), *The psychology of learning and motivation.* Vol. 2. New York: Academic Press, 1968.

Baumeister, A. A. & Kellas, G. Memory for position in undifferentiated and brain injured retardates and normals. *Journal of Psychology,* 1967, **66**, 3-5.

Belmont, J. M. & Butterfield, E. C. The relations of short-term memory to development and intelligence. In L. P. Lipsett & H. W. Reese (Eds.), *Advances in child development and behavior.* Vol. 4. New York: Academic Press, 1969.

Belmont, J. M. & Butterfield, E. C. Learning strategies as determinants of mental deficiencies. *Cognitive Psychology,* 1971, **2**, 411-420.

Berkson, G. An analysis of reaction time in normal and mentally deficient young men. I. Duration threshold experiment. *Journal of Mental Deficiency,* 1960, **4**, 51-58.

Brown, A. L. The development of memory: Knowing about knowing how to know. In H. W. Reese (Ed.), *Advances in child development and behavior.* Vol. 10. New York: Academic Press, 1975.

Brown, A. L., Campione, J. C., Bray, N. W. & Wilcox, B. L. Keeping track of changing variables: Effects of rehearsal training and rehearsal prevention in normal and retarded adolescents. *Journal of Experimental Psychology,* 1973, **101**, 123-131.

Burgio, L. D., Whitman, T. L., & Johnson, M. R. A self instructional package for increasing attending behavior in educable mentally retarded children. *Journal of Applied Behavior Analysis,* 1980, **13**, 443-459.

Campione, J. C., & Brown, A. L. Memory and metamemory development in educable mentally retarded children. In R. V. Kail & J. W. Hagen (Eds.), *Perspectives on the development of memory and cognition.* Hillsdale, New Jersey: Erlbaum, 1977.

Craik, F. I. M. & Lockhart, R. S. Levels of processing: A framework for memory research. *Journal of Verbal Learning and Verbal Behavior,* 1972, **11**, 671-684.

Dearman, N. B. & Plisko, V. W. The condition of education. 1980 statistical report. Washington, D.C.: U. S. Government Printing Office, 1980.

Ellis, N. R. The stimulus trace and behavior inadequacy. In N. R. Ellis (Ed.), *Handbook of mental deficiency.* New York: McGraw-Hill, 1963.

Ellis, N. R. Memory processes in retardates and normals. In N. R. Ellis (Ed.), *International review of research in mental retardation.* Vol. 4. New York: Academic Press, 1970.

Fagan, J. F. Short-term memory processes in normal and mentally retarded children. *Journal of Experimental Child Psychology,* 1968, **6**, 279-296.

Flavell, J. H. Developmental studies of mediated memory. In H. W. Reese & L. P. Lipsett (Eds.), *Advances in child development and behavior.* Vol. 5. New York: Academic Press, 1970.

Flavell, J. H., Beach, D. R. & Chinsky, J. M. Spontaneous verbal rehearsal in a memory task as a function of age. *Child Development,* 1966, **37**, 283-299.

Goulet, L. R. Verbal learning and memory research with retardates: An attempt to assess developmental trends. In N. R. Ellis (Ed.), *International review of research in mental retardation.* Vol. 3. New York: Academic Press, 1968.

Hagen, J. W. & Stanovich, K. E. Memory: Strategies in acquisition. In R. V. Kail & J. W. Hagen (Eds.), *Perspectives on the development of memory and cognition.* Hillsdale, New Jersey: Erlbaum, 1977.

Kail, R. V. & Siegel, A. W. The development of mnemonic encoding in children: From perception to abstraction. In R. V. Kail & J. W. Hagen (Eds.), *Perspectives on the development of memory and cognition.* Hillsdale, New Jersey: Erlbaum, 1977.

Kelso, J. A. S., Goodman, D., Stamm, C. L. & Hayes, C. Movement coding and memory in retarded children. *American Journal of Mental Deficiency,* 1979, **83**, 601-611.

Kephart, N. C. *The slow learner in the classroom.* Columbus, Ohio: Merrill, 1971.

Lewin, K. A. *A dynamic theory of personality.* New York: McGraw-Hill, 1935.

Pennington, F. M. & Luszcz, M. D. Some functional properties of iconic storage in retarded and non-retarded subjects. *Memory and Cognition,* 1975, **3**, 295-301.

Reese, H. W. Verbal mediation as a function of age level. *Psychology Bulletin,* 1962, **59**, 502-509.

Ross, A. L. *Psychological aspects of learning disabilities and reading disorders.* New York: McGraw-Hill, 1976.

Ryan, M. & Jones, B. Stimulus persistence in retarded and non-retarded children: A signal detection analysis. *American Journal of Mental Deficiency,* 1975, **80**, 298-305.

Schroeder, R. K. The effects of rehearsal on information processing efficiency of severely/profoundly retarded normal individuals. Unpublished doctoral dissertation, Louisiana State University, Baton Rouge, 1981.

Shiffrin, R. M. & Schnieder, W. Controlled and automatic human information processing. II. Perceptual learning, automatic attending and a general theory. *Psychological Review,* 1977, **84**, 127-190.

Spitz, H. H. Field theory in mental retardation. In N. R. Ellis (Ed.), *Handbook of mental deficiency.* New York: McGraw-Hill, 1963.

Stanovich, K. E. Information processing in mentally retarded individuals. In B. N. R. Ellis (Ed.), *International review of research in mental retardation.* Vol. 9. New York: Academic Press, 1978.

Sternberg, R. J. Cognitive-behavioral approaches to the training of intelligence in the retarded. *The Journal of Special Education,* 1981, **15**, 165-183.

Welsandt, R. F. & Meyer, P. A. Visual masking, mental age and retardation. *Journal of Experimental Child Psychology,* 1974, **18**, 512-519.

Winther, K. T. & Thomas, J. R. Children's development of hierarchical processes in motor performance. Paper presented at NASPSPA, Asilomar, California, May 1981.

Ziegler, E. Developmental versus difference theories of mental retardation and the problem of mental retardation. *American Journal of Mental Deficiency,* 1969, **73**, 536-555.

SUGGESTED READINGS

Undergraduate Students

Campione, J. C. & Brown, A. L. Memory and metamemory development in educable mentally retarded children. In R. V. Kail & J. W. Hagen (Eds.), *Perspectives on the development of memory and cognition.* Hillsdale, New Jersey: Erlbaum, 1977.

Graduate Students

Belmont, J. M. & Butterfield, E. C. The relations of short-term memory to development and intelligence. In L. P. Lipsett & H. W. Reese (Eds.), *Advances in child development and behavior.* Vol. 4. New York: Academic Press, 1969.

9

Kids and Numbers: Assessing Children's Motor Development[1]

Jerry R. Thomas
Katherine T. Thomas

The assessment of children's movement performances during the preschool and elementary school years can be described as the *infrequent application of strange tests in unusual circumstances to unimportant behaviors.*[2] While this statement may be harsh, it is also frequently true. Regardless, the statement suggests three important measurement questions that are addressed in this chapter:

1. What are the important behaviors and characteristics to be measured?
2. How should tests be selected to sample the important behaviors and characteristics?
3. How often and under what circumstances should assessments be made?

IMPORTANT BEHAVIORS AND CHARACTERISTICS

Development implies changes that occur over time. Programs designed to improve motor performance in children should evaluate behaviors that are influenced by these programs and monitor certain characteristics that result from growth. Difficulties are frequently encountered because physical educators often confuse variables that need to be monitored with those that are to be influenced and then evaluated for change.

First, *growth* means an increase in size across the childhood years. Growth should be monitored by periodic assessments of height, weight, and if needed, body fatness. However, these dimensions generally fall within acceptable bounds for children. The physical educator's responsibility is to be aware of anything unusual in growth so that appropriate action can be taken.

1. This chapter is revised from Thomas, J. R., & Thomas, K. T. Strange kids and strange numbers: Assessing children's motor development. *Journal of Physical Education, Recreation and Dance*, 1983, in press.

2. With an apology to U. Bronfenbrenner. Toward an experimental ecology of human development. *American Psychologist*, 1977, **32**, 513-531.

Second, behaviors of major importance to physical educators relate to children's *physical fitness*, defined narrowly here as cardiovascular endurance, muscular strength, and muscular endurance. While these three aspects of fitness are important, we doubt that most preschool and elementary programs have any impact on cardiovascular endurance or muscular strength.[3] The gains from year to year are accounted for by growth (i.e., children become bigger and stronger). Few programs appear to have the necessary intensity or frequency or both to influence cardiovascular endurance and strength positively. Thus, periodic testing should monitor normal development and identify special problems. Most physical education programs do increase muscular endurance; as a result, the child is able to perform a submaximal movement repeatedly. A measurement schedule should be developed to determine if a specific program increases the muscular endurance for that movement.

Finally, programs are designed to influence specific *motor skill development* and such associated *motor fitness* factors as agility, flexibility, and balance. Improvement in specific motor skills results from growth, improved muscular endurance, and increased motor control—a combination of learning and maturation.

In summary, physical educators should be concerned about monitoring certain motor development characteristics to be sure that these characteristics are within normal bounds (e.g., height, weight, fatness, cardiovascular endurance, and muscular strength). Other behaviors should be assessed with regard to program influence, including muscular endurance, specific motor skill development, and related motor fitness items.

SELECTING TESTS

The selection of appropriate tests to measure identified behaviors and characteristics involves answering three questions:

1. Does the test adequately sample an important behavior or characteristic?
2. Does the test of this behavior or characteristic yield reliable results?
3. Are the facilities, equipment, and knowledge to administer (and interpret) the test available?

For two of the three growth factors to be monitored (height and weight), the answer to all three questions is yes. A steel tape for height, a good scale for weight, along with reliable procedures (i.e., all measurements are made under the same conditions), are all that is required. These measurements should be made and recorded several times per year, probably early fall and late spring. If the physical educator notes any particular fatness problems in certain children, she may want to use skin calipers and standard procedures[4] to measure and estimate fat percentages for these children. Then a specified program of diet and exercise can be prescribed for children at the extremes of the fatness and leanness continuum.

3. We are not suggesting that cardiovascular endurance and strength cannot, or should not, be modified by intervention programs for children, but just that most programs do not produce the intensity or frequency (or both) of exercise required to change these factors (see AAHPERD, *Lifetime health related physical fitness*. Reston, Va.: AAHPERD, 1980, 36-46). If a program is not designed to influence either muscular strength or cardiovascular endurance or both, then these characteristics should be monitored for normal development. If a program is designed to influence those two factors, then a measurement schedule should be developed to determine change.

4. For procedures and norms, see AAHPERD, *Lifetime health related physical fitness*. Reston, Va.: AAHPERD, 1980, 10-16.

The other important behaviors to be measured are physical fitness and motor skill development (with associated motor fitness items). Of major importance in identifying assessment procedures are the age of the child and the use to be made of the data obtained.

Young children's performance tends to be inconsistent from trial to trial. This inconsistency comes from several sources, both internal and external. Internal factors include poor motor programs in memory, usually resulting from less experience in movement situations. A poor motor program for a movement leads to less control at the muscular level and thus inconsistent and inappropriate movements. Younger children typically attend to the task for shorter time periods and have a tendency to give up or quit difficult or strenuous tasks. An important external factor is the ease with which children are distracted from the task.

Given all of these considerations, inconsistent motor performance from occasion to occasion for young children is to be expected, along with low reliability estimates. The best solution is to shift the responsiblity of reliable measurement from the child's performance to the teacher's observation. The most logical way to accomplish this shift is by using a checklist or rating scale. The teacher can observe a child's form and performance on a particular behavior in various situations on several occasions over a period of weeks. For example, as an estimate of cardiovascular endurance, the teacher may check whether the child tires easily during vigorous activity. A recommended procedure is use of checklists or rating scales or both for younger children (younger than 9 to 10 years of age) for all behaviors to be measured.

Older children perform most motor tasks reliably. The important issue then becomes selecting a valid representation of the characteristic or behavior to be measured. This involves not only selecting a good test but also obtaining a representative sample of the behavior being tested. Frequently teachers retain a test score even when they know the score does not truly reflect the child's level of performance. The purpose of a test is to get a valid sample of behavior. If a teacher is convinced a test trial is not representative of the child's real level of performance, the trial score should be eliminated and the child retested. Teachers should not make judgments on bad data, and should *use common sense when testing.*

CIRCUMSTANCES AND FREQUENCY OF ASSESSMENTS

Circumstances for measuring physical fitness and motor skills (and associated motor fitness) should be as similar as possible to the situation in which the behaviors are used. This advice is easy to follow when using checklists or rating scales with young children because the procedure may simply be applied during the regular class setting. However, when testing situations are constructed for older children, the task is more difficult. Most measurement textbooks offer valuable advice for selecting and administering physical fitness, sport skills, and motor fitness tests. Many of these tests are appropriate for the upper elementary school grades. However, if some of the items appear inappropriate, the teacher should not hesitate to alter or eliminate them. Teachers should remember that if they alter test items, the norms that frequently accompany tests are not applicable to their students. In addition, with older children, typical sports skills tests only offer a means for measuring the outcome of performance. Teachers should also be concerned about recording the process (usually the form or technique) that the child uses.

When should tests be administered? Characteristics to be monitored should be assessed twice annually, probably in early fall and late spring. Teachers should remember that variables included are those that teachers want to monitor but are not significantly changed by instructional programs. Behaviors that are expected to change as a result of instruction should be tested immediately before and after the instruction. For example, in a program of six weeks of soccer instruction, the teacher should first identify the sports skills and motor fitness items that measure the important behaviors taught, and then test these characteristics before and after they are taught and practiced.

WHAT TO DO WITH THE NUMBERS

All of the preceding information revolves around one question—*why teachers measure the important characteristics and behaviors of motor development.* Some answers are: (1) to judge if teaching is effective, (2) to make sure children are developing normally, (3) to help the children understand the development of motor skills and fitnesses, (4) to inform parents about their child's motor development, (5) to compare children from a school to national norms, and (6) to compare children with each other.

All of these answers influence what physical educators do with motor development test data. We think the *least* useful procedure is to collapse all the suggested answers into a grade. Six questions remain that the teacher, child, and parent want answered:

1. Is the child growing normally?
2. How much improvement does the child show as a result of instruction (both in form and outcome of performance)?
3. How does the child compare with other children in his class?
4. How does the child compare with national norms for similar children?
5. Is the child giving her best effort?
6. Is the child's behavior satisfactory?

We suggest that teachers design, administer, and report the testing of children's motor development so that these six questions are answered clearly and precisely. Questions 1, 3, and 4 might be answered twice per year, and questions 2, 5, and 6 four to six times per year. This format is undoubtedly more informative and helpful for everyone interested in a child's motor development.

SUMMARY

Since the assessment of motor development appears valuable, teachers must first decide what behaviors and characteristics are important to measure. Then, the behaviors that are expected to change as a result of program intervention must be separated from the characteristics that are to be monitored for normal development. The physical educator must select appropriate tests of the important behaviors and characteristics and establish a measurement schedule to sample the selected variables adequately. Finally, or perhaps initially, teachers should decide what is to be done with the testing results.

PART III

Sport Programs for Children

To some extent, this section could have been included in areas of Parts I and II. The second chapter on psychosocial development is basic information on motor development (Part I), while the other two chapters are concerned with applications of basic knowledge (Part II). However, these chapters were grouped together because of their extensive information on youth sport.

The majority of children in the United States first encounter organized, systematic motor skill development programs in a nonhome, nonschool competitive setting under the supervision of an untrained coach. Physical educators must be concerned about skills, attitudes about sport, and physical activity encountered in these nonschool settings in which an estimated 18 to 20 million children are involved.

Chapter 10 discusses the objectives of children's sport programs. Also presented are patterns of male and female participation, sport programs in two other countries (the Soviet Union and West Germany), sport programs in the United States, and projections for the future in children's sport.

Chapter 11 summarizes psychosocial research in children's sport programs. The findings have considerable value for elementary school physical education or classroom teachers. The chapter aids in understanding psychosocial development, including the areas of competition, adult leadership, children's motivation in sport, and competitive stress.

Chapter 12 outlines characteristics of a good coach in children's sport. Research in understanding and changing the interaction between players and coaches is presented.

While larger volumes about youth sport are available, this part provides a solid overview and background for the reader. A more complete understanding of the topics can be obtained through the suggested readings at the end of individual chapters.

10

Patterns of Participation in Children's Sport

Vern Seefeldt
Crystal Fountain Branta

Children's participation in competitive sport has become so commonplace in American culture that it has been listed as a *right* of childhood (Martens and Seefeldt 1979). While the official position of educators and physicians seems to be changing from one of open opposition to one of neutrality or even guarded support of competitive sport programs, much concern and anxiety about children's involvement in competitive sport programs still exists. The reasons for this apprehension may be well founded, since the news media frequently testify that misguided adults can abruptly reverse the potential positive contributions of youth sport programs. The perplexing predicament in which administrators of such programs find themselves is the unpredictable nature of the interaction between coaches, officials, and parents of young athletes; frequently this interaction is the source of undesirable outcomes.

Participation of children and youth in sport has been increasing, despite the criticisms and objections that are frequently raised by television documentaries (Meagher 1980), popular journals (Underwood 1975), and former sport figures (Roberts 1975; Tarkenton 1970). This increased participation may be viewed as an affirmation of the belief of parents and guardians that youth sport is inherently desirable until proved otherwise. However, not all of the increased participation in children's sport is attributable to the faith that parents have in its positive contributions. Numerous circumstances have augmented both the image of sport and its availability, thereby increasing children's involvement in them. Perhaps the most influential of these, in terms of increased participation, was the passage of Title IX and the mandates for equal opportunities in sport at all levels for girls and women. Provision of comparable sport programs for girls and boys in middle and high schools resulted in a remarkable increase in participation by girls, although enrollment still has not reached the figures reported for boys (National Federation of State High School Associations Handbook 1982). This filter-down effect is also reflected in agency-sponsored programs, but the gains for girls in the community programs do not appear to be as impressive as those reported in the public schools. Whether female participation in public or private activity programs will increase until it equals that of males is an open question.

Additional explanations for the increased participation of boys and girls in sport are:

1. *Greater accessibility of programs* owing to the gradual movement of the population from rural to urban and suburban residences.
2. The *declining role of public schools* in physical education and interscholastic programs below the high school level. The trend for municipal recreation and community agencies to assume the responsibility for activity programs that the public schools once offered has resulted in opportunities for membership on competitive sport teams in lieu of the less competitive physical education and intramural settings of the public schools. Recreation directors, service clubs, and some national sport governing bodies have enacted an "everyone plays" philosophy, and this has received the wide acceptance of children and parents and thereby increased the demand for programs in which this philosophy is enforced.
3. *Changing life-styles of adults*, to include a greater role for self-directed fitness activities, may be influencing positively the decisions that parents are making about their children's involvement in sport.
4. An *increase in the number of women* in the work force may have led to the enrollment of children in activity programs as a caretaking function or because of the structured environment. Opportunities for children to identify with coaches as role models also may have provided an incentive for single-parent families.
5. The *glorification of sport* through its exposure on television may have induced some parents to seek involvement for their children, with the hope that the early exposure ultimately would provide some of the financial benefits and publicity.

OBJECTIVES OF CHILDREN'S SPORT PROGRAMS

The popularity of sport for children is reflected in the numerous objectives that its proponents have suggestd or alleged can be achieved through athletic competition. The following list of objectives (Martens and Seefeldt 1979) includes many that are common to the physical education, intramural, and interscholastic programs of public schools and the various sport governing bodies, service clubs, and recreation departments that offer athletic competition within local communities. The common theme that pervades these objectives is the learning of lifelong values during childhood through organized physical activities. These objectives of children's sport programs are classified according to three major topics:[1]

1. Social and moral development
   - To teach children how to cooperate
   - To develop a sense of achievement leading to positive self-concepts
   - To develop healthy, strong identities
   - To develop independence through interdependent activities
   - To promote and convey the values of society
   - To contribute to moral development
   - To have fun

1. Modified from Martens, R., and Seefeldt, V. (Eds.), *Guidelines for children's sports.* Reston, Va.: National Association for Sport and Physical Education, 1979.

To develop social competencies
To help bring the family together
To develop leadership skills
To develop self-reliance and emotional stability by learning to make decisions and accept responsibilities
To teach sportsmanship
To teach children how to compete
To help children learn about their capabilities through comparison with others

2. Cognitive development
   To provide opportunities for physical-affective learning, including learning to understand and express emotion, imagination, and appreciation for what the body can do
   To develop initiative
3. Motor and physical development
   To develop motor competencies
   To develop physical fitness
   To develop interest in and a desire to continue participation in sports in later years
   To develop speed, strength, endurance, coordination, flexibility, and agility

A review of where competitive athletics for children began and why they were established is appropriate. Berryman (1975) has provided an extensive chronology of the events that provided the basis for the present structure of sport, both within and beyond the public school setting. The vacillating reception and rejection of youth sport by public schools has influenced their development and growth. Organized sport for children began as an extension of the public school day in New York City at the beginning of the 20th century. Their initial purpose was both therapeutic and prophylactic. They were originated to relieve the tensions and restore the deprivation of activity that a sedentary classroom environment produces; they also were to provide a diversion from the temptations of street life, which for some children were substitutes for wholesome work and play. Although the objectives are stated with greater specificity today, the central themes of *therapy* and *diversion* still provide the major justification for activity programs, whether physical education or sport, in the mind of many educators, school board members, and parents.

The lifelong implications of the objectives claimed by protagonists of sport for children represent a paradox in the mind of critics, who cite the exclusion of certain groups of children and the high dropout rate by age 13 of those who were once involved in competitive situations (Orlick 1973, Orlick 1974, Joint Legislative Study 1976, Sapp and Haubenstricker, 1978) as evidence that the objectives are selectively applied and have a short-term influence. Little more than testimonial evidence exists that the influence over time of participation in youth sport has been beneficial, or conversely, that exclusion from them has been harmful. Evidence shows, however, that children are beginning their sport experiences at an early age and that many of them are also discontinuing their involvement long before it is possible for them to gain mastery of the skills involved in sport (Orlick and Botterill 1975, Joint Legislative Study 1976).[2]

2. Gould, D., Feltz, D., & Horn, T. *Reasons for attrition in competitive youth swimming.* Unpublished manuscript, Michigan State University, 1982.

This departure from sport at early ages is perplexing in that the voluntary exclusion of young athletes is a direct reflection of their undesirable experiences as competitors. Any program that purports to teach lifelong values and skills, but that also has the vast majority of its former participants uninvolved by the time they are adolescents, is subject to criticism. What is not known is the influence that these early experiences will have on future attitudes and activity patterns. If an early departure from youth sport leads to the abandonment of all physical activities in later life, then children's competition is far more devastating than its critics have heretofore suggested. However, the high dropout rate during adolescence is not likely to have a permanent effect on any but the most disgruntled participants. Many who find sports uninteresting as teenagers may review their life-styles as adults and renew their association with physical activity programs in which conditions yield greater individual control. The tremendous interest in adult personal fitness is an encouraging development, but what influence, if any, the earlier exposure to activity programs has had on this phenomenon is unknown. If enjoyable experiences and successful performance of skills lead to continued participation, then youth sport programs may be focusing on too many objectives instead of ensuring that their participants achieve the ones with the greatest possibility for a positive contribution in adulthood.

HISTORICAL COMPARISON OF PARTICIPATION OF MALES AND FEMALES IN RECREATIONAL SPORTS

Differences in sport involvement between the sexes have been demonstrated in five major studies (Crosswell 1898, McGhee 1900, Terman 1926, Sutton-Smith and Rosenberg 1961; Fountain 1978). Each of these investigations yielded rank-order lists and frequency counts of the most popular games or sports that each sex played recreationally. The number of questions ranged from 35 in Fountain's 1978 study to 500 in Crosswell's 1898 report. The four earlier investigations included many types of recreational activities (such as playing cards or playing dolls), while the most recent study was designed for sport participation only. To ascertain the relevance of these historical data to each other, the sports and their respective rankings have been excerpted from each checklist. A percentage of participation for each activity has been computed, and the results are depicted in Table 10.1.

These data have limitations when viewed historically (Sutton-Smith and Rosenberg 1961). Each of these studies was conducted in a separate geographical locale—Massachusetts, South Carolina, California, Ohio, and Michigan. Differences in data collection also may have influenced the final results. In 1898, children listed their activities from memory, while the subjects marked a prepared list in the latter four studies. Finally, the variance in composition of each survey could affect the resultant rank-order lists. However, to review the historical changes in sport participation between the sexes, we omitted those activities from each study that were not sport specific.

These rank-order lists indicate considerable reduction in differences between the sexes during an 80-year time span. Sutton-Smith and Rosenberg (1961) reported rank-order correlation coefficients (rho) between the sexes of −.023 in 1900, .328 in 1926, and .451 in 1960 for all of the lists. Relationships in correlations between the sexes were judged to range from little, to slight, to moderate, respectively. Rho for the modified tabulation of sports only are assumed to be similar to those obtained for the complete lists.

Inspection of the data up to 1980 reveals that females had included a greater variety of activities in their play, whereas the list for the males is more restrictive. Invariably, top-ranked

Table 10.1. Historical Change in Recreational Sport Participation[a]

Male			Female		
Rank	Sport	Percent	Rank	Sport	Percent
		1898—Massachusetts			
1	Ball	68	5	Skating	41
4	Skating	54	27	Bicycling	9
5	Football	46	52	Tennis	3
8	Hockey	31	78	Swimming	2
15	Bicycling	16	120	Hockey	0.8
17	Swimming	12	149	Horseback riding	0.4
39	Tennis	5			
115	Horseback riding	0.7			
155	Golf	0.4			
		1900—South Carolina			
1	Baseball	68	18	Tennis	8
2	Football	56	30	Baseball	5
3	Swimming	24	54	Football	3
22	Tennis	5	63	Basketball	2
26	Basketball	4	71	Swimming	1
37	Wrestling	3	106	Golf	0.6
			129	Wrestling	0.1
		1926—California			
1	Baseball	94	3	Bicycling	84
2	Bicycling	87	4	Baseball	83
9	Football	72	6	Basketball	80
12	Basketball	69	9	Skating	78
14	Skating	64	18	Volleyball	55
16	Volleyball	63	27	Horseback riding	49
17	Horseback riding	62	42	Swimming	33
17	Boxing	62	45	Tennis	32
19	Wrestling	61	49	Handball	29
26	Swimming	53	61	Archery	18
29	Archery	49	64	Football	16
35	Handball	40	70	Wrestling	12
43	Tennis	33	79	Boxing	8
51	Soccer	27	82	Bowling	6
77	Bowling	14	87	Skiing	5
			88	Soccer	4
		1960—Ohio			
1	Football	89	4	Bicycling	88
3	Bicycling	88	7	Roller skating	85
5	Basketball	86	11	Swimming	83
8	Swimming	83	19	Skating	80
9	Baseball	82	29	Horseback riding	71
26	Horseback riding	75	39	Basketball	68
28	Ice skating	73	39	Table tennis	68
31	Wrestling	71	57	Baseball	62
36	Table tennis	70	62	Volleyball	61

Table 10.1. (continued)

Male			Female		
Rank	**Sport**	**Percent**	**Rank**	**Sport**	**Percent**
41	Boxing	68	66	Tennis	59
45	Bowling	65	83	Bowling	52
51	Volleyball	61	98	Archery	43
54	Tennis	58	102	Football	42
93	Soccer	42	122	Handball	30
108	Handball	37	126	Soccer	28
109	Skiing	36	132	Skiing	24
			153	Wrestling	23
				Boxing	14
		1978—Michigan			
1	Bicycling	94	1	Bicycling	95
2	Swimming	89	2	Swimming	90
3	Basketball	82	3	Softball	73
4	Softball	79	3	Roller skating	73
5	Tackle football	74	5	Kickball	72
6	Baseball	73	6	Ice skating	66
7	Touch football	69	6	Basketball	66
7	Kickball	69	8	Gymnastics	61
9	Table tennis	65	9	Volleyball	60
10	Bowling	64	10	Badminton	58
11	Ice skating	62	10	Table tennis	58
12	Roller skating	58	12	Bowling	57
12	Jogging	58	13	Jogging	54
14	Wrestling	55	14	Tennis	48
14	Volleyball	55	15	Baseball	45
16	Badminton	54	16	Horseback riding	44
17	Weight lifting	51	17	Touch football	40
18	Tennis	48	18	Soccer	37
19	Soccer	47	19	Tackle football	32
20	Gymnastics	40	19	Miniature golf	32
21	Miniature golf	39	21	Track and field	30
21	Track and field	39	22	Wrestling	20
23	Floor hockey	38	23	Floor hockey	19
24	Horseback riding	35	24	Water skiing	17
25	Archery	32	25	Synchronized swimming	14
25	Ice hockey	32	25	Weight lifting	14
27	Golf	25	27	Archery	13
28	Snorkling	22	28	Downhill sliing	12
29	Water skiing	21	29	Golf	10
30	Downhill skiing	14	30	Ice hockey	9
31	Synchronized swimming	12	31	Snorkling	8
32	Karate	11	32	Karate	5
33	Judo	7	32	Cross country skiing	5
34	Cross country skiing	6	34	Judo	3
35	Scuba diving	5	35	Scuba diving	2

[a]Adapted from Crosswell 1898, McGhee 1900, Terman 1926, Rosenberg and Sutton-Smith 1960, Fountain 1978.

male activities indicated a high percentage of involvement in football, baseball, and basketball, with some swimming and bicycling. However, for females, the top sports still were ranked below the ones for males, indicating participation in play activities other than sports (e.g., dolls). The lists for females also included more activities than did the males' lists. Skating, bicycling, tennis, swimming, volleyball, basketball, and in 1926, baseball were among the top sports that female participants chose in the earliest studies. However, males ranked more sports in the top 20 play activities than did females. Lehman and Witty (1927) found that females had no true sports in their play activities list, although they enjoyed dancing and performing basic fundamental motor skills. Males in the same study marked eight sports as dominating their recreational life.

In 1978, boys and girls were actively involved in a variety of recreational sports. Participation in two sports (bicycling, swimming) approached or exceeded 90%, while participation in several other sports (e.g., basketball, softball, roller skating) was over 70%. Bicycling ranked as the most popular activity, with involvement of 94% of the males and 95% of the females. Swimming ranked second, with 89% and 90% participating, respectively. In one sport—basketball, for males—participation was greater than 80% of the total respondents.

Within the 20 most popular sports in Michigan for each sex, 18 of them were common to both groups. Wrestling and weight lifting appeared 14th and 17th respectively, in the list for males, while horseback riding and miniature golf appeared 16th and 19th in the column for females. Furthermore, five sports (bicycling, swimming, basketball, softball, kickball) were common to both sexes within the top ten ranked sports.

Individual rather than team sports made up a majority of the positions in the top 20 ranked sports for both boys and girls in 1978. Males and females each marked 12 individual sports in the 20 most popular ones, although the distribution of these activities varied by list. Males chose 4 individual-activity sports in the top 10, and 8 of those ranked 11 to 20. Females selected 6 individual-activity sports in the 1 to 10 ranks and 6 in the 11 to 20 ranks. Girls participated most frequently in individual or dual activities, while boys oriented their greatest involvement toward team games.

A striking occurrence in the 1978 survey was that well over half of the participants indicated involvement in the top ten sports. In fact, boys had a total of 17 sports in which at least 50% participated, and girls had 13 such sports. Within the top 20 sports, over one-third of the sample was represented in almost each activity for both sexes. Although these percentages of participation were still quite high, the levels for females dropped more rapidly than those for males. Males participated in 26 sports at a level of 30% or more, while females participated at a level of 30% in 21 sports. However, the amount of participation in the 20 sports ranked highest on each list was similar for both sexes, especially within the top 10. Within the 35 ranked sports, similarities between males and females were seen in the bottom four rankings. Karate, judo, cross country skiing, and scuba diving were ranked last for both sexes, with never more than a 6% difference between the sexes in the levels of participation for any of these activities.

Females in Michigan were involved extensively in sports typically considered masculine (baseball 45%, touch football 40%, tackle football 32%). Even within the sports ranked lowest in the column for females, 20% of the respondents marked wrestling and 14% marked weight lifting. In addition, 9% of the girls played ice hockey. However, when females ranked the sports in which they participated "often" (versus "sometimes"), none of the typically masculine sports had levels higher than 16%. Baseball (16%), touch football (11%), tackle football (9%), wrestling (7%), ice hockey (2%), and weight lifting (2%) all maintained a position relative to each other and within two rankings of those shown in Table 10.1.

The results from these five studies indicate that both sexes have greatly expanded their participation in sports (Table 10.2) over an 80-year period. In 1898, boys marked only 4 sports with levels of participation greater than 25%, while in 1978 this category contained 27 sports. The number of sports in which more than 25% of the girls were involved increased from 1 to 21 between 1898 and 1978.

HISTORICAL CHANGES IN SPORT INVOLVEMENT OF MALES AND FEMALES

The five studies listed above indicate the changes that have occurred in levels of participation for specific sports since 1898. Some activities had participation curves that were nearly identical for both males and females. Bicycling, swimming, and volleyball were representative of this trend (Figure 10.1). Because bicycling was not reported as a sport in 1900 and volleyball was not listed prior to the 1926 study, no indication of participation appears above those years. Note the rapid increase in percentage of participation for both sexes in bicycling, swimming, and volleyball after 1900. Also during the last three studies, levels of involvement for males and females in bicycling and volleyball were fairly constant. In swimming, this was true for the latter two investigations.

Swimming showed a definite increase in similarity between the sexes. Female participation moved from 10, 23, and 24 percentage points behind the males' in 1898, 1900, and 1926, respectively, to equal that of the males at 83% in 1960, and surpassed males' participation by one percentage point in 1978. Also, while the rank position of swimming for males moved up from 17th in 1898 to 2nd in 1978, a change of 76 ranks from 78th to 2nd occurred for females during that time.

The individual sports of tennis, bowling, and ice skating were also representative of a sharp rise in percentage of participation over the past 80 years (Figure 10.2). Levels for both males and females were similar, and the bars show the same general pattern across time. The levels of participation in these sports were not as constant during the latter studies as were those of the three sports discussed previously. With the exception of bowling for females, levels of participation in 1978 decreased from those of the earlier reports.

Some team sports also showed similarities between the sexes in their degrees of participation across time. Involvement in basketball, soccer, and baseball demonstrated a sharp increase after 1900 (Figure 10.3). For basketball and baseball, highest levels for girls were reported in 1926 with

Table 10.2. Historical Comparisons in Recreational Sport Involvement

Investigator	Year	Locale	Number of Sports With Participation ≥ 25% Male	Female
Crosswell	1898	Massachusetts	4	1
McGhee	1900	South Carolina	3	0
Terman	1926	California	14	9
Sutton-Smith and Rosenberg	1961	Ohio	16	15
Fountain	1978	Michigan	27	21

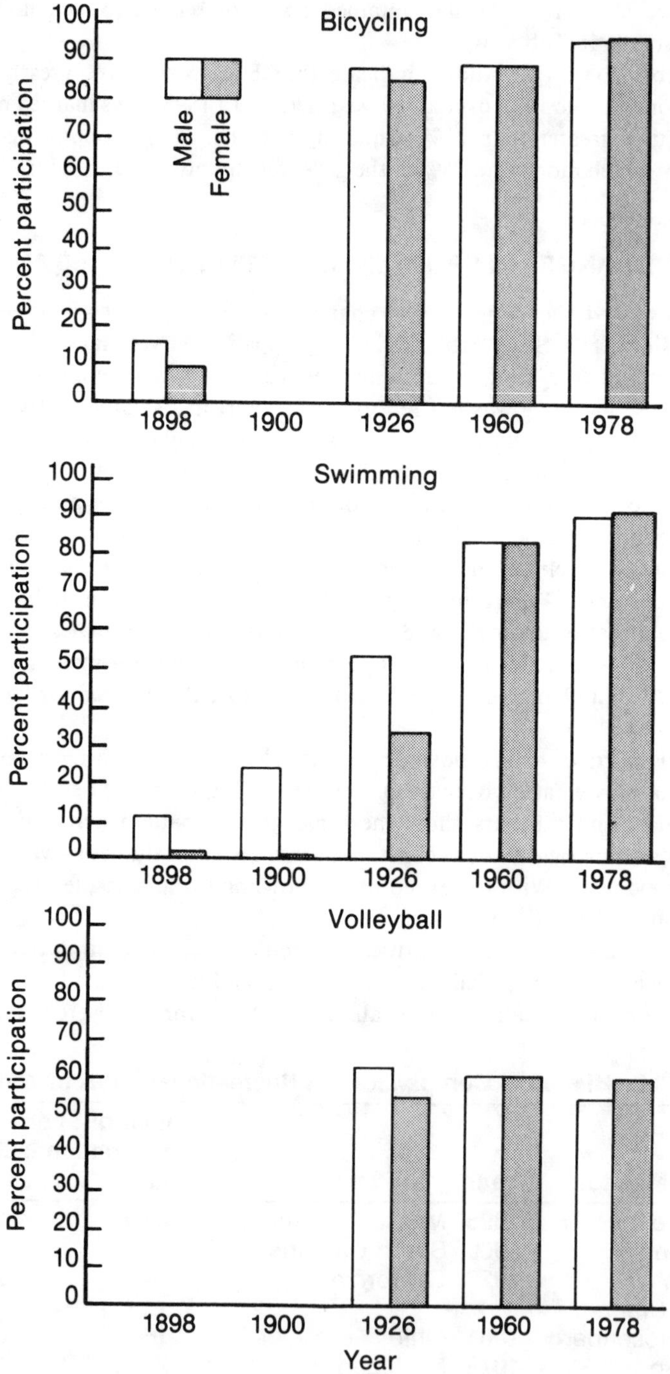

Figure 10.1. Historical comparisons of bicycling, swimming, and volleyball.

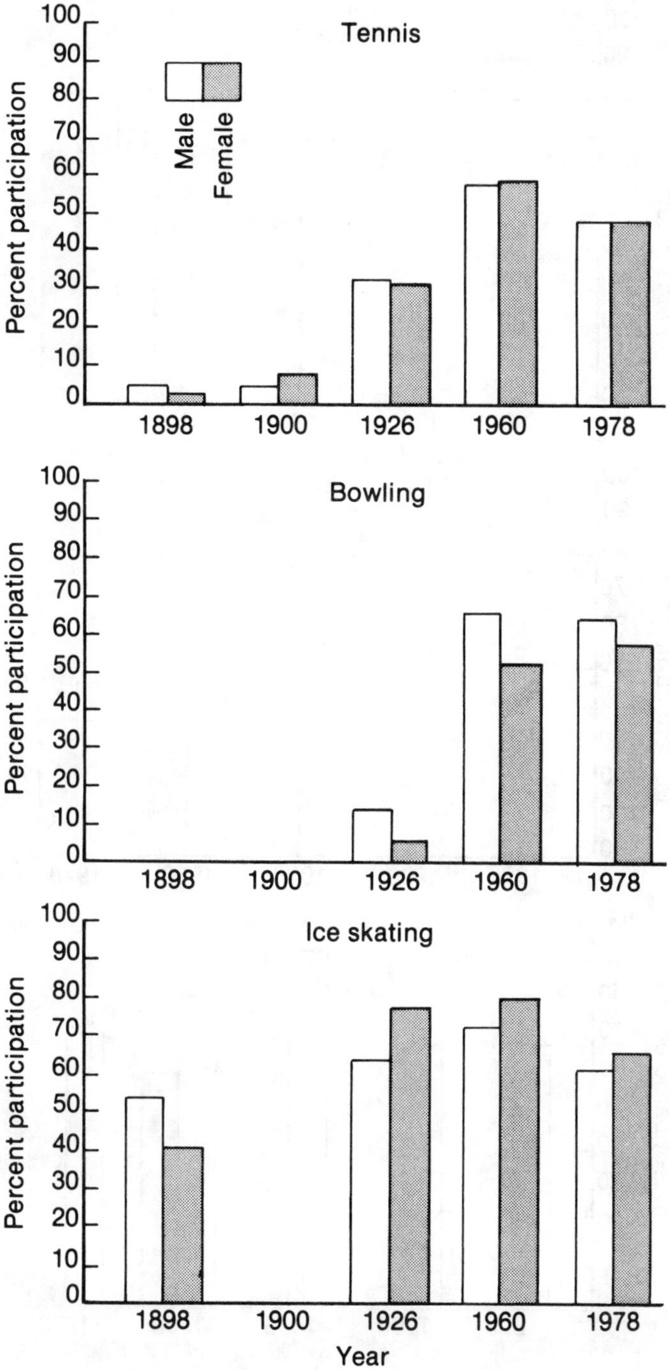

Figure 10.2. Historical comparisons of tennis, bowling, and ice skating.

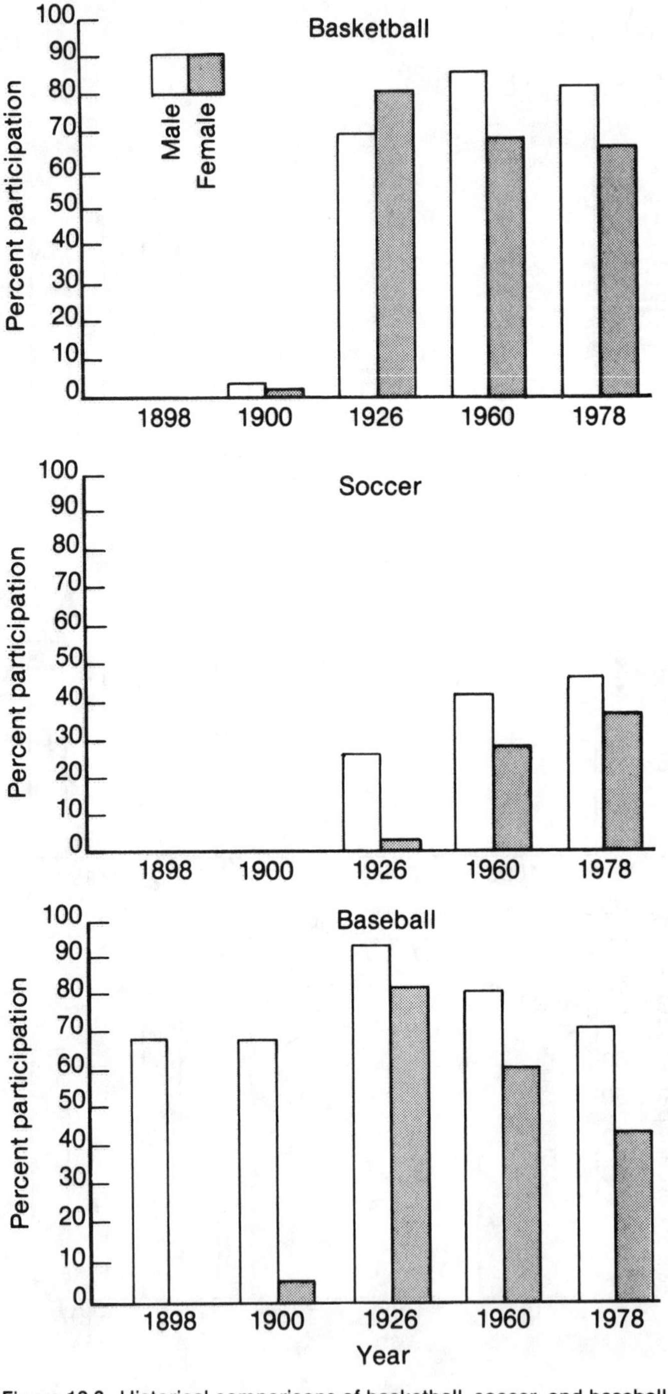

Figure 10.3. Historical comparisons of basketball, soccer, and baseball.

80% and 83%, respectively. Boys' levels were highest for basketball in 1960 with 86%, and for baseball in 1926 with 94%. The levels of participation in soccer increased steadily, especially for girls, since 1926. Male participation increased from 27% to 47%, while female involvement increased almost tenfold during that 52-year span of time.

Sports that are typically considered masculine also showed specific sex patterns of change during these 80 years. In football, difference in the levels of involvement between the sexes was greater than had been evident in previous sports (Figure 10.4). Two bars replace the single bar for each sex in 1978 because the Michigan study sampled both touch and tackle football, whereas the earlier studies made no such distinction. Females displayed moderately high participation after 1926, with 42% in 1960, and with 40% in touch football and 32% in tackle football in 1978. Male participation in tackle football was 89% in 1960 and 74% in 1978, while 69% were involved in touch football.

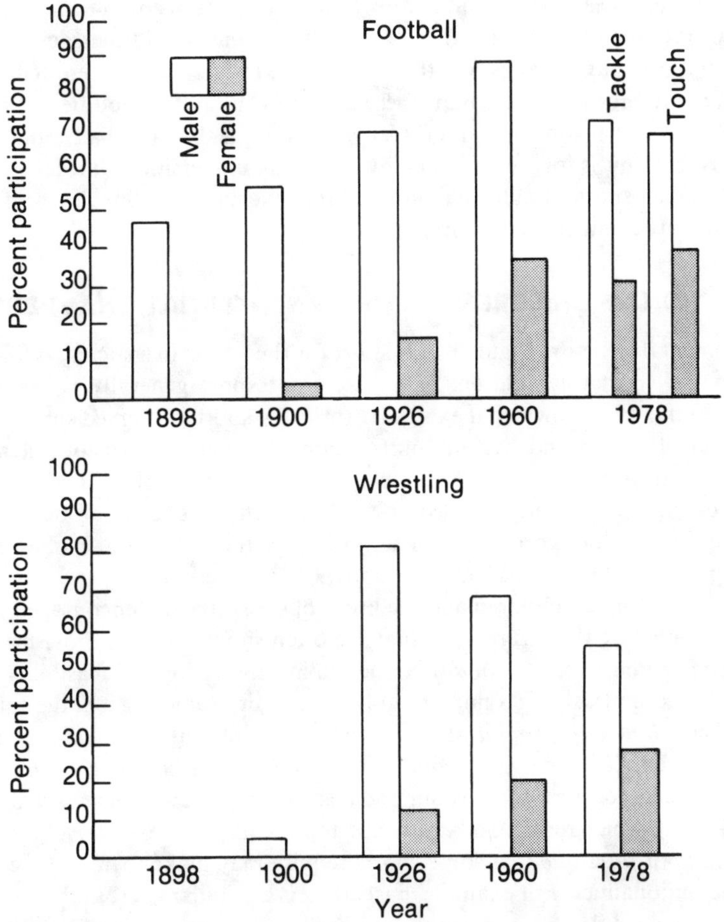

Figure 10.4. Historical comparisons of football and wrestling.

Increased female involvement in contact sports also was depicted in wrestling (Figure 10.4). Even though great differences in participation levels between the sexes appeared in wrestling, females increased their involvement after 1900 to a high of 23% in 1960 and 20% in 1978. A sharp rise in wrestling for males also occurred after 1900, with 61% involved in 1926 and 71% in 1960, but this dropped to 55% in 1978.

Historically, participation of both sexes in recreational sport has expanded greatly. By 1978, well over half of the participants indicated involvement in the top ten sports for boys and girls. The top-ranked activities that males chose were more often team games, whereas the sports that females participated in most frequently were individual in nature. These and other implications for the development of activity programs may be gleaned by reviewing the historical trends in recreational sport participation. Many sports (bicycling, swimming, volleyball, tennis, bowling, and ice skating) ranked high throughout the years, a characteristic for both males and females. High interest remained or has risen in some team sports involving body contact (basketball, soccer, baseball) for both sexes. Softball probably has been substituted frequently for baseball in this category. Like softball, these sports require only a small amount of equipment, but unlike softball, basketball and soccer may provide a higher probability for increased fitness levels of youth.

Another trend over the 80 years was that females steadily became interested in some contact sports usually reserved for males. Perhaps these activities should be modified to satisfy the more aggressive style of play that some females prefer. For example, flag football could be provided for school-aged girls as it now is for women in many American universities. Further study is needed to determine how contact sports should be modified for participation of females, or if females should be encouraged to participate in such sports at all.

ORGANIZATION OF CHILDREN'S SPORT: AN INTERNATIONAL PERSPECTIVE

The governmental structure that controls sport for the adults in a society is likely to influence the organization of sport for children. Likewise, adult sport generally is molded to suit the purposes of the country within which it exists. Historically, sport has served such diverse functions as the promotion of health and hygiene, integration of a nation's patriotism, preparation for defense or war, integration of ethnic or racial classes, enhancement of industrial productivity and prestige, or recognition at international contests. Although the overriding purpose of sport has been for recreation and the worthy use of leisure time, frequently these objectives have been subjugated for preeminent needs that involve survival of a society or nation.

The structure of sport for children and the kinds of sport that are encouraged or permitted to flourish are determined by various reasons that are often subordinate to those mentioned above. *Geographic location* and *climatic conditions* determine the economic feasibility of sponsoring certain sports. For example, skiing is popular in Norway, but promoting it at the equator would be unreasonable. The *ethnic background* of adults in a community is a primary determinant of the sports that its children play. The *socioeconomic status* and *location of residences* determine the feasibility of a sport like soccer, which accommodates large numbers of players in a relatively small space, or one like golf, which requires a large space and accommodates relatively small numbers of players. The *stature* or *physique* that some sports require may make them more compatible with certain races and nationalities. For example, basketball is a popular sport in the United States, but it may never acquire a similar staus in Japan because of the relative lack of success that Japanese teams have experienced in international competition. Conversely, gymnastics, which accommodates a smaller, well-coordinated physique, is relatively more popular in Japan than in the United States. Thus, the primary and secondary reasons for the existence and popularity of sport explain and predict both how children's sporting experiences are organized and the importance they have in the total education of children.

Children's Sport in the USSR

Since the Russian Revolution in 1917, sport in the Soviet Union has been used as a vehicle for social change and for the promotion of physical fitness and health (Riordan 1979). Sport in the Soviet Union has been controlled by the state and oriented as an investment in individuals so that they could give more of themselves to industry and the military complex. Sport and politics are inseparable, as is evident during each olympiad, when sport is used to achieve sociopolitical objectives (Riordan 1980).

Organized sport in the Soviet Union is controlled by 36 sport societies, all but 2 of which trade unions operate. Each society has its own rules and membership. The operation is financed out of trade union dues, which are used to build sport centers, acquire equipment, maintain a staff, and conduct organized competition. These competitions between societies are analogous to the competition within and between leagues or conferences in the United States.

Two structures interlink the sport system in the Soviet Union. The Ready for Labor and Defense (GTO) organization is a mass fitness program, with minimum standards of performance, based on age and sex, beginning at age 10 and extending through age 60. Tests are held throughout the year, the main goal of every club being to acquire as many badges as possible. The GTO's relationship to children's sport is threefold: (1) to involve children at an early age so that physical fitness and sport become part of their life-style, (2) to identify unusual talent at an early age so that special training can be provided, and (3) to use the physical activities as part of military training. The Soviet Sports Ranking System sets an upgraded standard of performance in 80 sports. These standards are upgraded every four years to coincide with the Olympic games. The five levels or ranks are in a hierarchy, and must be achieved in their proper order. Certain awards and monetary inducements are associated with the attainment of the top three ranks. Athletes become eligible for junior rankings at age 15.

Although the Soviet sport system is designed to accommodate the masses, children as young as five to six years of age can get intensive coaching in special schools in specific sports. Six levels of these schools are maintained, each becoming more exclusive as the talent and age of the performers increase. At the apex are the sport boarding schools, which numbered 26 in 1978. Children attend them full time and free of charge, so that they can have access to the best facilities, equipment, and personnel that the Soviet system can provide. At these schools, individual talent is perfected, with a view toward joining one of the nation's top teams or squads. Thus, sport for children is a part of the social structure, with recognition and rewards commensurate with the level of skill displayed (Maclean et al. 1977; Riordan 1979).

Children's Sport in the Federal Republic of Germany (West Germany)

The organization of sport in the Federal Republic of Germany (FRG) is an example of a federal government giving self-governing rights to a social institution, in this instance the sport clubs (Preising 1982). In a recent national survey, 40% of the population indicated that they engaged in sport regularly or at least once a month. Twenty-four percent indicated that their activity occurred in conjunction with a sport club, in which 25% of the population holds membership. Other sources for sport participation are the schools, universities, and commercial sport institutions.

The only compulsory sport experience for FRG citizens occurs in the schools, where students between the ages of 6 and 18 have three hours of "school sport" (in lieu of physical education) each week. School sport involves the acquisition of skills in specific sports and provides a system of competition for the older students. However, the sport clubs, which grew in number from 2300 in 1954 to 5300 in 1982 (Rust and Schofield 1978, Preising 1982) are the basis of the German athletic system.

The growth of sport within the government structure has been delayed since World War II because of the popularity associated with it during the Hitler regime.[3] This was also true of school sport, in which the attention to motor development is just beginning to gain equal acceptance to that of cognitive and social growth. However, sport is exceedingly popular among youth, since 50% of all boys and 33% of all girls between 7 and 18 years are members of a sport club (Preising 1982).

The sport clubs and schools combine resources to offer nationwide sport competitions annually. The Federal Youth Games involve approximately 5 million children throughout the school year in track and field, swimming, gymnastics, skiing, and orienteering. A point system, which equates pupils of different ages, sizes, and schools, controls competition. School teams also compete in events under the title "Youth in Training for Olympia," in which local and state competition leads to final events in Berlin. Competition is held in swimming, gymnastics, volleyball, basketball, handball, cross country skiing, track and field, rowing, soccer, and hockey (Beyer 1978).

Although schools have made recent overtures to become more active in the promotion of sport, the sport clubs provide the basic instruction, build the facilities, provide the technical instruction, and sponsor the competition for the young athletes of West Germany. Attempts are currently under way to make the sport clubs more accessible to handicapped individuals and to those in the lower socioeconomic strata. The concept of "sport for all" has become part of a social criticism directed at what some perceive as elitism surrounding the sport club environment. The greater accessibility of sport clubs to all citizens and an increased emphasis on sport in the public schools are signs of a restored interest in physical activity.

Children's Sport in the United States

The first youth sport programs in the United States were offered on the playgrounds of public schools in New York City at the turn of the century as a means to counteract a sedentary classroom environment (Berryman 1975). These after-school programs were available only to boys and were supervised by teachers who taught in the schools. This humble beginning of sport for children has left its mark on physical education and on intramural, interscholastic, and agency-sponsored sports as we know them today.

Although early competitive sport programs may have resembled intramural rather than interscholastic programs initially, they soon acquired many of the undesirable characteristics that

3. Haag, H. *Sport in the Federal Republic of Germany*. Unpublished manuscript, Institute for Sport and Physical Education, Kiel, Germany, 1982.

have been associated with intensive athletic competition for children. Recruitment of highly skilled athletes, exclusion of those who were less skilled, and suppression of socially acceptable values in lieu of winning were common practices. An astounding proliferation of sport programs in elementary schools paralleled the incorporation of objectionable procedures into competitive situations. By 1930, these had been established throughout the nation, but not without the misgivings of educators and physicians.

The transformation of after-school sports for children—from a recreational orientation to highly competitive experiences in a 30-year period—led to their condemnation by public school educators in the 1930s. This condemnation, while failing to eliminate competitive sports in the elementary schools, had such a profound impact on both school- and agency-sponsored programs that it still influences them today. Two of its most prominent residual effects were the stimulation provided to the growth of agency-sponsored sports and a legacy of antagonism between public schools and the organizations that offered sports for children and youth in the private sector.

The decrease in school-sponsored sports during the 1930s paved the way for programs of physical education and intramural sports. However, the vacillating basis for the existence of sport, physical education, and intramurals suggests an existence based on conflict rather than cooperation. The history of sport in elementary schools provides a clearer perspective of how current programs originated, how they were maintained, and why some are on the verge of elimination.

Withdrawal of public school sponsorship of youth sports prompted a number of family-oriented agencies such as the YMCA, YWCA, and Police Athletic League to offer competitive athletics in private facilities. These offerings became more numerous and diverse as additional agencies were established that were created for the sole purpose of offering sport competition for children. Table 10.3 shows a chronology of events that underscores the emergence of agency-sponsored competitive sport programs in the 1920s; the large enrollments due to nationwide promotions did not occur until after World War II.

Programs of physical education, intramurals, and athletics in elementary schools continued to grow in the 1950s and 1960s as the children born after World War II reached school age. However, new content and methodology were being introduced into the physical education curriculum, thus eventually changing its meaning to children and their parents. No longer was physical education solely responsible for the physical fitness and sport skills, dances, and games of its clients. Its proponents now expanded the content to include perceptual and motor development, movement education, new games, and trust activities. Concurrently, demands from other areas were infringing on the time that was once reserved for physical education. As a result, parents who expected their children to acquire a foundation of sport skills in the schools began to look elsewhere for these experiences. They did not have to search long or far because nearly every urban and suburban community offered a variety of agency-sponsored programs that were more intensive than those provided in the public schools (Joint Legislative Study Committee 1976). By the 1970s, sport offerings at the elementary school level had diminished to the point where they were no longer a troublesome issue for educators. However, as children shifted to agency-sponsored programs for their competitive experiences, the schools also lost much of the support that was previously accorded their physical education programs.

A reduction in the schools' role in physical fitness and motor skill development through the abolition or reduction of programs may have unfortunate consequences on the sport skill development of children. The exigency of budget reductions has led many to the convenient assumption that agency-sponsored and recreational activities can be legitimate substitutions for physical

Table 10.3. Chronology of Events Involving Youth Sport in the United States[a]

1903	First after-school sport programs for boys of elementary school ages offered in New York City
1906	National Collegiate Athletic Association formed in New York City as means to combat injuries and deaths in college football
1906	Beginning of Boys' Clubs of America
1910	Beginning of Boys Scouts of America
1912	Beginning of Girl Scouts of America
1914	United States Soccer Federation became official representative of soccer to Federation of International Football Associations (FIFA)
1916	Over 65,000 females attending YMCA gym classes and 32,000 attending swimming classes
1920	National Federation of State High School Associations established at meeting of five Midwest state representatives in Chicago
1924	Baseball tournaments for boys under age 13 held in Cincinnati
1925	American Legion Baseball established in Milbank, South Dakota
1927	Tackle football for boys under age 12 established in Denver
1928	Junior pentathlon sponsored by Los Angeles *Times*
1929	Pop Warner Football began as four-team league in Philadelphia
1930	Catholic Youth Organization founded junior tennis program, Southern California Tennis Association
1934	Two million Americans played softball under auspices of Amateur Softball Association (ASA)
1936	"Stars of Yesterday" baseball leagues began
1939	Little League Baseball founded in Williamsport, Pennsylvania
1940	Three million Americans played under auspices of ASA
1943	All-American Girls Baseball League founded
1949	Little League Baseball expanded to 300 leagues in 11 states
1952	Babe Ruth Baseball incorporated as nonprofit organization
1952	PONY (Protect Our Nation's Youth) Baseball incorporated as nonprofit organization
1952	One-half million boys played Little League Baseball
1962	American Youth Soccer Association (AYSO) started in Torrance, California, with four teams
1964	Federal charter to Little League Baseball granted by Congress and signed into law by President Johnson
1967	Soccer Association for Youth (SAY) established in Ohio with 400 participants
1972	Over 150 attended golf clinic for girls in Baltimore
1977	350,000 boys participated in Babe Ruth Baseball Program
1977	200,000 children played soccer under AYSO banner
1977	2.26 million boys and girls played Little League Baseball
1978	Pop Warner League reached all-time high of 6,213 football teams
1980	40,600 boys and girls participated in SAY
1982	1.24 million boys and girls involved in YMCA sport programs

[a]Sources for these dates were numerous pamphlets, brochures, and announcements.

education programs. Although the objectives of these various groups may be similar, they differ greatly in the clients they serve and the process through which they achieve their objectives. Physical education programs historically have undertaken the teaching of a broad range of motor skills, while agency sponsorship of programs is usually sport specific. Physical education programs are obligated to serve all children, while agency sport programs have often been selective and exclusive. Physical education programs are, by federal mandate, accessible to all students, while agency-sponsored sports are often available on a first-come basis to those who can afford the time, fees, equipment, and transportation costs. Under traditional procedures, the substitution of agency-sponsored activities for good physical education programs disenfranchises many children.

The forces that initially cast public school programs and agency-sponsored youth sports into adversarial rather than cooperative roles unfortunately have not abated. This is not to depreciate the role of the National Association for Sport and Physical Education (NASPE), an association of the American Alliance for Health, Physical Education, Recreation, and Dance, and other similar organizations that are advocating a closer working relationship between public schools and organizations that offer activity programs for children. Such attempts are likely to show little progress as long as school administrators and teachers believe that agencies are usurping the school's role in activity programs. Agencies, too, must be more sensitive to the criticisms that historically have been associated with their competitive athletic programs.

Public school personnel made a major concession to sport competition for children in the late 1970s as reflected in the NASPE publications *Youth Sports Guide for Coaches and Parents* (Thomas 1977) and *Guidelines for Children's Sports* (Martens and Seefeldt 1979). These documents are significant because they represent a reversal in the attitudes of educators and physicians, who for the previous half century had reflected a general disapproval of sport competition below age 14. The publications signified that sport competition for children can be beneficial and described in detail the conditions under which such programs should be conducted.

Major conflict in children's activity programs revolves around whether sound physical education, intramural, and sport programs in the public schools should be sustained in lieu of support for competitive sports conducted through nonschool agencies. Financial constraints have increased the dependence on nonschool agencies through the reduction or elimination of physical education, intramural, and sport programs once offered in the public schools. Because of their common objectives, schools and agencies could work together for the motor education of children. A redefinition of their respective roles would indicate that both groups have unique, as well as common, contents and clients.

PROJECTIONS FOR THE FUTURE OF CHILDREN'S SPORT

The administration of children's sport is destined to change greatly in the next two decades. These changes are imminent because of the static conditions under which youth sport has been conducted since its rise to popularity in the 1950s. Two conditions have contributed to an unwillingness to change what is essentially a scaled-down version of the games and contests in which adults engage: (1) the lack of a systematic effort to determine if adult sport models were suitable for children and (2) a dependence on unqualified coaches to provide the instruction and, concurrently, to suggest ways in which the experiences could be more meaningful to children. Conversely, changes in these two circumstances will pave the way for modifications in the way sport is conducted.

The scientific community has recently discovered that competitive activities for children pose legitimate research questions. Answers to these questions are likely to suggest ways in which the present conduct of children's sport should be altered to meet their needs. Another significant change in youth sport may result from the present movement to educate volunteer coaches in a variety of topics. The recent development of national education programs for volunteer coaches (Cox 1982) may stimulate the production of pertinent materials in the form of printed matter, films, and videotapes. Accessible coaching information could drastically enhance the competence of youth sport volunteers. The direct beneficiaries of these impending developments will be young athletes, whose skill level and longevity in sports should reflect the improved competence of their coaches.

The inability of public school budgets to keep pace with the rising cost of education has initiated a trend for public schools to reduce their emphasis on physical education, intramural, and interscholastic programs. This shift in responsibility for activity programs from the schools to community agencies is likely to continue as long as school enrollments decline and teachers' ranks diminish through attrition and furloughs. In times of budgetary constraints, physical education and athletics are unlikely to regain their former status in the public school curriculum. Those who are unskilled and socioeconomically deprived are likely to pay the price for this responsibility. Agency-sponsored youth sports are often conducted in an atmosphere in which selection and exclusion rather than inclusion are the modes of operation. Unless the "sports-for-all" theme receives wider acceptance than present procedures imply, many children may be disenfranchised through the reduction or elimination of physical activity programs in the public schools.

The tremendous interest in personal fitness through self-directed sports such as jogging, bicycling, boating, hiking, and cross country skiing is an indication that adults want more from sport than competition and companionship (Jennings 1979, Nelson 1982). This desire to become involved in sports that permit participants to control their own destiny is also evident in children's sport. Some of the current popularity of soccer in the United States may lie in a structure that at times allows all players to become involved simultaneously in the action and yet permits a degree of individual freedom during that involvement. The sports that permit a greater freedom of choice to their youthful participants are likely to grow, while those in which the players are asked to perform on command are likely to decrease in popularity.

Due to a prevailing philosophy that emphasizes personal needs, the number of children's sports programs that are controlled by local agencies is likely to increase. Local ownership of programs may permit greater concentration on personal growth and participation, with less emphasis on the win-at-all-costs philosophy. Goals that may receive higher priority in the future include social development, fun, skill acquisition, and personal fitness. All of these components have historically been part of children's motivation in sport, but they have not always been evident in the playing conditions that adults have imposed on them.

Sport preferences by race and ethnic background are likely to be a determining factor in the rise or decline in popularity of specific sports. An increase in the proportion of Black and Hispanic children and a decreasing proportion of Caucasian children (Ortiz 1979, Ibrahim 1981) during the next two decades suggest that soccer, basketball, and baseball may continue to gain in popularity, while football, ice hockey, gymnastics, and swimming may decrease in popularity. Due to a decrease in the absolute number of children who are eligible for memberships on competitive sport teams, the annual number of competitors may stabilize and then eventually decline as the decreasing birth rate overtakes the ability of sponsoring agencies to provide attractive programs for a greater proportion of the eligible population.

Changing life-styles must also be considered in planning the future in children's sport. Financial constraints have caused municipalities and private agencies to depend more on volunteers to serve as coaches, officials, and administrators. Concurrently, the number of children who are being reared in single-parent homes, most often by the mother, is increasing (Masonick and Bane 1980). Yet with the exception of gymnastics, swimming, and figure skating, most youth sport coaches and officials have been males (Joint Legislative Study Committee 1978). The conflicts between maintaining her own social life, being the primary caretaker, and learning to coach or officiate a sport (in which she most likely did not participate during her high school or college years) present an interesting dilemma to the mother of a single-parent family whose children's eligibility for a team depends on her active involvement.

Despite the numerous qualities that its proponents have attributed to sport, two detracting features cause many parents to prohibit their children's participation: (1) the violence that is associated with certain contact sports (Jennings 1979, Goldstein 1982) and (2) the insidious specter of injury. Neither element has developed into a serious problem in youth athletics, but as parents project their children's experiences beyond adolescence into early adulthood, they are faced with the reality that violence and injuries are directly related to certain sports.

Youth sport directors are genuinely concerned to reduce or eliminate violence and injuries, but until more is known about the circumstances under which these occur, recommending preventive procedures is difficult. In this regard, the national single-sport agencies have not fulfilled their obligations, probably because they do not regard either violence or injuries as a significant problem. However, until youth sports that have a high injury rate among high school and college athletes (such as football, ice hockey, and wrestling) can be administrated in a manner that will prevent these injuries when the sports are conducted at younger ages, these sports are likely to be included with others for which parents hold an aversion. As a result, parents may forbid their children to become involved in them.

The future of children's sport rests in the hands of adults who administer the programs and serve as coaches and officials. Although misguided adults have made errors in judgment, the prevailing sentiment among adults who control children's sport programs is that their every action is intended for the welfare of the young performers. This concern of adults for young athletes allows an optimistic forecast for the future in children's sport. Anticipated information from sport scientists, in conjunction with national education programs for volunteer coaches, could provide the enlightenment that volunteer coaches have eagerly sought for decades. Application of this information should enhance the desirable effects of youth sport programs.

SUMMARY

The inevitable conclusion, after reviewing the history of children's sport, is that its popularity has increased tremendously during its 80-year existence. Most of the growth has been in agency-sponsored rather than in school-sponsored activity programs. Four significant occurrences characterize the development of children's sport in the United States: (1) The increase in female participants, accentuated by the passage of Title IX, has resulted in coeducational or separate-but-equal sport programs in public schools and many agency-sponsored settings. (2) The availability of sport programs is so widespread that virtually every community offers some type of athletic competition for its youth. (3) The variety of sports available to youthful competitors rivals the number available to adults, and in some communities, exceeds them. (4) Finally, the shift from school-sponsored to community-sponsored programs in the United States seems to follow a pattern that countries such as the Soviet Union, West Germany, Finland, Sweden, and Australia established some years ago.

The future of youth sport in the United States can be forecast with optimism. The scientific community has turned its attention to problems that have existed for decades, such as competitive stress in children. The generation of new information, combined with the availability of newly formed national youth sport coaching programs, should expedite the delivery of practical information to volunteer coaches, who are providing much of the instruction in the agency-sponsored programs.

REFERENCES

Berryman, J. From the cradle to the playing field: America's emphasis on highly organized competitive sports for preadolescent boys. *Journal of Sport History,* 1975, **2**, 112-131.

Beyer, E. *Sport science, physical education and sport administration in the Federal Republic of Germany.* Institut fur Sport und Sportwissenschaft: Karlsruhe, Germany, 1978.

Cox, R. (Ed.) *Educating youth sports coaches: Solutions to a national dilemma.* Reston, Va.: American Alliance for Health, Physical Education, Recreation and Dance, 1982.

Crosswell, T. R. Amusements of Worchester school children. *The Pedagogical Seminary,* 1898, **6**, 314-371.

Fountain, C. D. Sex and age differences in the recreational sport participation of children. Unpublished master's thesis, Michigan State University, 1978.

Goldstein, J. Sports violence. *National Forum,* 1982, **62**, 9-12.

Ibrahim, H. Immigrants and leisure. *Journal of Physical Education, Recreation and Dance,* 1981, **52**, 36-37.

Jennings, L. Future fun: Tomorrow's sports and games. *Futurist,* 1979, **13**, 417-432.

Joint Legislative Study Committee. *Joint legislative study of youth sports programs—Phase I.* East Lansing, State of Michigan, 1976.

Joint Legislative Study Committee. *Joint legislative study of youth sports programs—Phase III.* East Lansing, State of Michigan, 1976.

Lehman, H. C., & Witty, P. A. *The psychology of play activities.* New York: Barnes, 1927.

Maclean, N., Wilner, B., & Hoerner, E. *Soviet sports exercise program.* New York: Drake Publishers, 1977.

Masnick, G., & Bane, M. *The nation's families: 1960-1990.* Cambridge: MIT-Harvard Joint Center for Urban Studies, 1980.

Martens, R., & Seefeldt, V. *Guidelines for children's sports.* Washington, D.C.: AAHPERD Publishers, 1979.

McGhee, Z. A study in the play life of some South Carolina children. *The Pedagogical Seminary,* 1900, **7**, 459-478.

Meagher, M. (producer) NBC Magazine (with D. Brinkley). "Youth Sports," October 24, 1980.

National Federation of State High School Associations. *National federation of state high school associations handbook 1981-82.* Kansas City, Missouri: Author, 1981.

Nelson, J. Sport in America: New directions and new potentials. *National Forum,* 1982, **62**, 5-6.

Orlick, T. Children's sports—A revolution is coming. *Journal of the Canadian Association for Health, Physical Education and Recreation,* 1973, **39**, 12-14.

Orlick, T. The athletic dropout: A high price for inefficiency. *Canadian Association for Health, Physical Education and Recreation,* 1974, **41**, 24-27.

Orlick, T., & Botterill, C. *Every kid can win.* Chicago: Nelson-Hall, 1975.

Ortiz, M. *The different 80s: The increasing number of Hispanic Americans.* Whittier, California: Center for Mexican American Affairs, 1979.

Preising, W. *The political function and development of sport in the Federal Republic of West Germany.* Paper presented at the annual convention of the American Alliance for Health, Physical Education, Recreation and Dance, Houston, April 1982.

Riordan, J. *Soviet sport: Background to the Olympics.* New York: New York University Press, 1980.
Riordan, J. *Sport in the USSR.* London: Collet's, 1979.
Roberts, R. Strike out little league. *Newsweek,* July 21, 1975.
Rust, V., & Schofield, T. The West German Sports Club system: A model for lifelong learning. *Phi Delta Kappan,* 1978, **59**, 543-546.
Sapp, M., & Haubenstricker, J. *Motivation for joining and reasons for not continuing in youth sports programs in Michigan.* Paper presented at the national convention of the American Alliance for Health, Physical Education and Recreation, Kansas City, Missouri, 1978.
Sutton-Smith, B., & Rosenberg, B. G. Sixty years of historical change in the game preferences of American children. *Journal of American Folklore,* 1961, **74**, 17-46.
Tarkenton, F. Don't let your son play smallfry football. *Ladies Home Journal,* October 1970.
Terman, L. *Genetic studies of genius.* Vol. I. Palo Alto: Stanford University Press. 1926.
Thomas, J. R. (Ed.) *Youth sports guide for coaches and parents.* Washington, D.C.: AAHPERD, 1977.
Underwood, J. Taking the fun out of games. *Sports Illustrated,* 1975, **43**, 86-98.

SUGGESTED READINGS

Undergraduate Students

Barnes, L. Pre-adolescent training—How young is too young? *The Physician and Sportsmedicine,* 1979, **7**, 114-119.
Berryman, J. W. The rise of highly organized sports for preadolescent boys. In R. A. Magill, M. J. Ash, & F. L. Smoll (Eds.), *Children in sport: A contemporary anthology.* Champaign, Illinois: Human Kinetics, 1978.
Martens, R. *Joy and sadness in children's sports.* Champaign, Illinois: Human Kinetics, 1978.
Martens, R., & Seefeldt, V. *Guidelines for children's sports.* Washington, D.C.: AAHPERD, 1979.
Michener, J. A. Children and sports. *Sports in America.* New York: Random House, 1976.
Rarick, G. L. Competitive sports in childhood and early adolescence. In R. A. Magill, M. J. Ash, & F. L. Smoll (Eds.), *Children in sport: A contemporary anthology.* Champaign, Illinois: Human Kinetics, 1978.
Rarick, G. L. Competitive sports in childhood and early adolescence. In G. L. Rarick (Ed.), *Physical activity: Human growth and development.* New York: Academic Press, 1973.
Seefeldt, V. Current developments in competitive athletics for children. *Osteopathic Annals,* 1977, **5**(10), 507-512.
Seefeldt, V. The changing image of youth sports in the 1980s. In R. A. Magill, M. J. Ash, & F. L. Smoll (Eds.), *Children in sport.* (2nd ed.) Champaign, Illinois: Human Kinetics, 1982.
Spears, B., & Swanson, R. In Elaine J. Smith (Ed.), *History of sport and physical activity in the United States.* Dubuque, Iowa: Brown, 1978.
Thomas, J. R. (Ed.) *Youth sports guide for coaches and parents.* Washington, D.C.: AAHPERD, 1977.

Graduate Students

Beisser, A. *The madness in sports.* New York: Appleton-Century-Crofts, 1967.
Coakley, J. *Sport in society: Issues and controversies.* St. Louis: C. V. Mosby, 1978.
Eitzen, D. *Sport in contemporary society: An anthology.* New York: St. Martin's Press, 1979.
Goldstein, J. *Sports, games and play.* New York: Wiley, 1979.
Lyssyte, R. *Sportsworld: An American dreamland.* New York: Quadrangle (New York Times Book Company), 1975.
Roberts, G. Children in competition: A theoretical perspective and recommendations for practice. *Motor Skills: Theory Into Practice,* 1980, **4**, 37-51.
Roberts, J., & Sutton-Smith, B. Child training and game involvement. *Ethnology,* 1962, **1**, 166-185.
Smoll, F., & Lefebvre, I. Psychology of children in sport. *International Journal of Sports Psychology,* 1979, **10**, 173-177.
Sports in America, *National Forum,* 1982, **62**, 1-50.

11

Psychosocial Development and Children's Sport[1]

Daniel Gould

Athletic competition for children has had a long history in North America, dating back to the late 1920s and early 1930s (Berryman 1978). Children's sport has existed for a number of years, and since its inception, it has been enormously popular. Today, for example, an estimated 17 million children between the ages of 6 and 16 participate in more than 30 nonschool-sponsored sport programs (Martens 1978). Moreover, recent evidence suggests that these programs will continue to flourish. Thus, children's sport involves a large and important segment of American society.

Three factors have contributed to the growth of children's sport during this century (Berryman 1978). First, society in general placed increased emphasis on sport, and this created a demand for children's sport as well. Second, changes in child labor laws created increased amounts of leisure time for children to take part in sport activities. Third, a marked change occurred in Americans' attitudes toward child rearing. Specifically, childhood became recognized as an important stage of life in and of itself. Consequently, greater emphasis was placed on providing wholesome, constructive activities that would foster physical and psychological development during this phase of an individual's life. Many saw sport as one such wholesome, constructive activity.

While children's sport has had a long, successful history, its development has been rooted in controversy. One area of particular concern has been the effects of participation on the psychosocial development of the child. Proponents of children's sport have argued that athletic competition positively affects the psychological development of the child by instilling such attributes as emotional control, increased self-confidence, good sportsmanship, personality development, and increased motivation. On the contrary, critics have suggested that athletic competition is detrimental to children's psychosocial development because it places children under too much emo-

1. The author would like to acknowledge Thelma Horn for her insightful comments on this chapter.

tional stress, encourages the development of undesirable attitudes and values (e.g., cheating), and undermines their natural or inherent motivation to participate. Because such controversy exists, educators, motor development experts, and sport psychologists have all expressed increased interest in examining the relationship between athletic competition and children's psychosocial development.

Traditionally, physical educators, physicians, and parents have had to rely on conjecture, their own experiences, a few isolated research studies, or a combination of these to determine solutions to the many controversies relating to the effects of athletic competition on children's psychosocial development. Recently, however, sport scientists have shown increased interest in the area, and more evidence is becoming available to help interested adults make decisions and develop policies regarding children's participation in sport.

This chapter examines the research literature focusing on psychosocial development and children's sport. Specifically, the effects of athletic participation on the child's psychosocial development are examined in discussion of the process of competition and children's motivation to begin, continue, and discontinue athletic participation. In addition, the relationship between athletic participation and psychological stress is examined, as well as the development of sportsmanship, aggression, and self-confidence in the child athlete. Not only are important research studies in these areas discussed but also practical guidelines are outlined whenever possible.

UNDERSTANDING THE COMPETITIVE PROCESS

To understand the effects of athletic participation on the psychosocial development of the child athlete, one must understand the process of competition. Too often competition is viewed in an emotional context as something that is inherently good or bad for the child. In fact, thinking of the process of competition as being good or bad in and of itself is a grave error. The end product of the competitive process—positive or negative effects—does not result from the process itself, but rather from the social environment in which the child competes.

While competition has been defined in many ways in the past, a definition directed toward social comparison is most widely accepted today. According to this view, competition is defined as those "activities directed more or less consistently toward meeting a standard or achieving a goal in which performance by a person or by his (or her) group is compared and evaluated relative to that of selected other persons or groups" (Sherif 1976). This definition has several important features. First, competition is not defined in terms of its end product—positive or negative consequences. To the contrary, competition is defined as a process that involves a comparison of performance between individuals, between groups, or between an individual and a group. Moreover, these performance standards are not compared to just anyone or everyone but to "selected other persons or groups." Thus, selected others socially determine the importance of competition itself—the standards one uses for comparison and the consequences of the competitive process. In children's sport, parents, coaches, and teammates constitute this social environment.

The influence of the social environment on the learning of competitive behavior in children was best demonstrated in a classic psychosocial field experiment that Sherif and Sherif (1969) conducted. This investigation took place in a summer camp setting with 12-year-old boys as subjects. Specifically, camp counselors manipulated the social environment of two groups of boys so that a highly competitive, win-at-all costs atmosphere was stressed. This resulted in extreme prejudice and hostility between the groups of boys in both sport and nonsport activities. After creating this highly competitive atmosphere, attempts were made to resolve the conflict between the groups. While appeals to moral values had little effect on inducing a change in the competitive atmosphere, the continued use of superordinate goals (goals that both groups highly desired but that were unavailable without cooperation between the groups) reduced the win-at-all-costs, highly competitive atmosphere. In essence, by manipulating the social environment of the camp, Sherif and Sherif demonstrated that both the importance of competition and its consequences could be highly influenced.

A second example of the critical role that the social environment plays in formulating children's orientations toward competition focuses on the process by which standards for judging performance are developed. For example, the goal-setting literature clearly shows that hard, but realistic, attainable goals result in optimal motivation and best performance. A problem arises, however, when coaches and parents acquire unrealistic expectations of the athletic prowess of their children and set unrealistic goals (e.g., "Sally should never miss a ball"). Children typically adopt these inappropriate standards or goals and, in turn, are forced to compare their performances to unrealistic criteria. Inevitably, this results in the perception of constant failure and, over time, can develop a fear of failure in children (Martens et al. 1981). A more productive approach is for coaches and parents to consider a child's developmental level and past sport experiences, and then to set realistic, attainable goals that can be achieved. In this case, children have reasonable standards against which to compare their performance, and instead of developing a fear of failure, over time will develop a mastery or success orientation to use in achievement situations. Thus, the social environment in which child athletes compete greatly influences the standards of comparison that they use to judge athletic success or failure.

Another common misconception about competition is the belief that individuals are inherently competitive. Competition as defined in this chapter has been shown to be a learned social behavior. Nelson and Kagan (1972) reported that marked differences in the competitive and cooperative behaviors of children exist between cultures and segments within cultures. Specifically, American children were found to be more competitive than Mexican children, and urban children were more competitive than rural children. Moreover, these differences were found to be the result of differing socialization practices within these groups or cultures. American mothers were found to base praise and reinforcement on competitive success, while Mexican mothers rewarded both competitive success and failure. Veroff (1969) has also shown that children learn to compete in stages. Children at young ages (four years) exhibit more cooperative behavior than competitive behavior. Competition begins at ages five to six, and by the time children reach seven or eight years of age, they have learned to compare themselves socially to others and to compete fully. Thus, competition is learned social behavior that the social environment influences.

Not only does the social environment influence competition but also cooperative behaviors are learned as well (Orlick, McNally, and O'Hara 1978). In their experiment, a group of kindergarten children's cooperative behaviors were assessed in classroom situations. The children were then assigned to either a cooperative games physical education class, where they spent 30 to 40 min per week for 18 weeks participating in cooperative games, or to a traditional games physical education class, where they engaged in normal games associated with children of this age. Following the termination of the cooperative and traditional games intervention programs, cooperative behaviors were again assessed. The results revealed that the cooperative games group showed a greater evidence of cooperative classroom behavior than did the traditional games group.

Consequently, these findings demonstrate that cooperation, like competition, is learned social behavior that the social environment in which the child is reared influences.

In summary, competition is not an inherent attribute in children. To the contrary, competition and, for that matter, cooperation are learned social behaviors. Furthermore, the value placed on competition, the standards used for comparison when competing, and the consequences of competition depend on the social context in which the child is reared. These findings have important implications for those interested in motor development. First, children learn to compete and cooperate, and thinking that these characteristics are inborn is a misconception. Second, children learn to compete in stages. Thus, to expect a 4- or 5-year-old child to function as would a 12- to 13-year-old in a competitive atmosphere is unrealistic. Third, the social environment in which the child competes has an important influence on his view of the competition process. Finally, a distinction between the process of competition and the outcome (good versus bad effect) must be made. Too often the outcome of competition is blamed on the process (e.g., competition is bad) and not the social environment in which the competition takes place. Similarly, many individuals mistakenly view competition and cooperation in an all-or-none fashion. That is, competition is good and cooperation is bad, or cooperation is good and competition is bad. A more accurate view is to realize that to effectively function in society, children need to learn about both competition and cooperation.

THE IMPORTANCE OF ADULT LEADERSHIP

While any number of factors in the social environment affect the psychosocial development of the young athlete, one of the most important is the adult leader. Evidence from an extensive Michigan study has shown that most children first learn sport skills not in physical education classes but in nonschool-sponsored sport programs (Joint Legislative Study Committee 1976). Hence, the youth sport coach is most often responsible for a child's initial exposure to sport. Young athletes spend a tremendous amount of time with adult leaders who supervise their programs. On the average, nonschool youth sport coaches supervise young athletes for 11 hr per week during an 18-week season (Martens and Gould 1978). Thus, the total contact between child and coach is greater than the time the child spends in physical education class and, in some cases, greater than the time spent interacting directly with parents. Finally, children are not just involved in youth sport, but are *intensely* involved, as sport is one of the most valued activities of adolescents (Coleman 1974, Feltz 1978).

Not only do adult leaders spend a great deal of time in direct contact with children in an activity that is highly valued, but also their actions have been shown to have a tremendous impact on children's development. Martens (1978a) and Alley (1974), for instance, have both indicated that sport participation can have both positive and negative effects on the child, depending on the quality of adult leadership. When competent adult leaders guide young athletes, the potential for positive psychosocial development is greatly enhanced. Few beneficial and, at times, detrimental psychosocial effects result when incompetent adult leaders guide children. Moreover, competent adult leadership requires more than a proper attitude and philosophy. An awareness and knowledge of the effects that leadership has on the psychosocial development of the young athlete is needed, as well as the knowledge and ability to implement coaching strategies that foster positive psychosocial growth. The young athlete's level of motivation, level of anxiety, and development of affective states are three areas in which adult leaders are highly influential.

UNDERSTANDING CHILDREN'S MOTIVATION IN SPORT

As previously discussed, competitive youth sport programs are enormously popular in North America. While these programs are extremely successful in terms of their popularity, recent statistics also show that the attrition rate within athletic programs is substantial. For example, Chapter 10 presented cross-sectional data on a large sample of Michigan athletes that revealed an increase in youth sport participation up to the ages of 11, 12, and 13 and a marked decline after that. Moreover, follow-up surveys on a subsample of these young athletes showed that approximately 35% of those sampled did not plan to continue participation after the season (Sapp and Haubenstricker 1978). This alarmingly high attrition rate has sparked increased concern on the part of a number of adults interested in youth sport. Therefore, increased research attention has been given to understanding children's motives for athletic participation, as well as reasons for discontinued involvement.

Why Children Participate in Sport

A number of investigators have recently examined children's motives for athletic participation (Alderman and Wood 1976; Sapp and Haubenstricker 1978; Gill, Gross, and Huddleston 1981; Gould et al. 1982). Typically, these investigators have surveyed a number of young athletes ranging in age from 6 to 18 years, and asked them to rate in order of importance various reasons for athletic participation. The findings reveal that children have multiple reasons or motives for participation. Specifically, young athletes most often participate in a sport for the following reasons: (1) to have fun, (2) to improve their skills and learn new skills, (3) to be with friends and make new friends, (4) for thrills and excitement, (5) to succeed or win, and (6) to become physically fit. Some age and sex differences have also been found in children's motives for participation, although no readily interpretable patterns of findings exist. Thus, while children have similar motives for participation, individual differences do exist.

Why Children Discontinue Participation

In addition to studying children's motivation for participating, investigators have also begun to examine children's motives for discontinued athletic involvement. Orlick and Botterill (1975) surveyed 60 athletic dropouts ranging in age from 7 to 19 years. Their results revealed that over 65% of the dropouts indicated that they discontinued for reasons pertaining to the emphasis placed on winning in the program. Of these, over 50% indicated that they discontinued because of an overemphasis on winning. Reasons for discontinued involvement were also found to be age related. Specifically, 60% of the high school aged dropouts discontinued participation because of conflicts of interest. To the contrary, 40% of the elementary school children discontinued because they did not play, while the remaining 60% of the elementary school aged athletes indicated that they were not successful.

As part of the Joint Legislative Study on Youth Sports discussed in Chapter 10, Sapp and Haubenstricker (1978) also studied reasons for discontinued involvement in children's sport programs. Specifically, parents of athletes ages 6 to 10 years ($N = 418$) and athletes ages 11 to 18 years ($N = 1183$) were asked to rate in order of importance their reasons for discontinuing athletic involvement. The results revealed that 35% of the athletes and 24% of the parents of the younger athletes indicated that they or their child did not plan to participate again next season. Furthermore, of the older athletes who indicated that they were going to discontinue, 64% indicated involvement in other activities and 44% indicated working as important or very important reasons for discontinuing. When the responses of the parents of younger athletes were examined, over 65% of the respondents indicated that involvement in other activities was the most important reason for discontinuing, while 43% rated other interests as important. Items such as "did not like the coach," "did not play enough," and "did not like the players" were rated as important by less than 15% of the athletes or parents of athletes who planned to discontinue involvement.

While the Orlick and Botterill (1975) and Sapp and Haubenstricker (1978) studies examined reasons for attrition across a variety of sports, two recent studies specifically examined attrition in soccer (Pooley 1981) and swimming (Gould, Feltz, and Horn 1983). Pooley conducted personal interviews with 50 boys (ages 10 to 15 years) who had discontinued competitive soccer involvement. His findings revealed that 54% of the boys discontinued involvement because of conflict of interests, while 33% indicated that the emphasis on competition in the program (e.g., "the coach yelled at me when I made a mistake") was a major reason for discontinuing involvement. The results also revealed that reasons for discontinuing involvement were related to age. Specifically, 25% of the younger boys (ages 10 to 12) as compared with the 12% of the older boys (ages 13 to 15) more often discontinued because of emphasis on competition. Similarly, 54% of the younger boys discontinued because of conflict of interests in contrast to 31% of the older boys.

In the Gould et al. (1982) study, 50 competitive swimming dropouts (ages 10 to 18) were both surveyed and interviewed regarding the importance of various reasons in their decisions to discontinue participation. The results revealed that 42% of the former swimmers rated "other things to do" as an important reason for discontinuing participation, while 28% rated "not enough fun" and "wanted to play another sport" as important. In addition, 24% of the sample indicated that "not being as good as they wanted to be" and 20% "not liking the coach" as important reasons for discontinuing participation. Few sex or experience differences were found, but older dropouts (ages 15 to 18) differed from younger dropouts (ages 10 to 14) in their reasons for discontinuing participation. Specifically, the older dropouts rated "no team spirit," "parents or friends did not want me to participate," "not enough challenge," and "injured" as more important reasons for discontinuing, while the younger swimmers rated "other things to do" as being more important.

Taken together, the studies focusing on reasons for discontinuing involvement reveal that most children dropped out because of conflict of interests or the desire to work and not because of excessive pressure placed on them, dislike for the coach, constant failure, or a combination of these. However, the results also reveal that some children in some situations discontinue involvement because of negative factors associated with the athletic environment. For example, both Orlick and Botterill (1975) and Pooley (1981) found that a substantial number of elementary school aged children discontinue participation because of an overemphasis on winning. Similarly, Gould et al. found that 28% of the former swimmers interviewed indicated that not having enough fun was an important reason for discontinuing participation. Thus, while the available findings clearly indicate that the majority of young athletes drop out for reasons beyond the control of adult leaders (change of interests), a substantial minority do so because of negative reasons that adult leaders can control.

Maintaining and Increasing Motivation in the Child Athlete

If the importance of athletic participation and its effects on the psychological well-being of the child are considered, one of the most important roles of adult leaders working with young athletes is to maintain or increase the child's desire for participation. One effective way to increase motivation in young athletes is to understand the athlete-by-situation model of motivation and its ramifications.

The athlete-by-situation model of motivation suggests that a child's motivation to participate in sport is a result of both personal (e.g., motives, objectives, goals) and environmental factors (the athletic situation). Thus, optimal interest and motivation result when the child's motives for participation are matched with athletic environments that provide experiences that fulfill these motives. Adult leaders must recognize the motives that young athletes have for participation and provide athletic experiences that meet these objectives. For example, if a young athlete's primary objective is to improve her skills but the coach emphasizes fun with only a few experiences designed for skill improvement, motivation decreases. In contrast, if the young athlete's primary objective is to improve her skills and the coach provides activities that foster skill development, motivation is enhanced. Thus, the interaction of the athlete and the athletic environment determines motivation.

The results of the studies reviewed in this section show that children have multiple motives for participation in sport. Primary motives for participation include having fun, improving skills and learning new skills, being with friends and making new friends, experiencing thrills and excitement, and experiencing success. Furthermore, the results of those studies examining reasons for discontinuing athletic participation show that young athletes lose their desire to participate when their objectives change (e.g., develop other interests) or when their objectives are not achieved (e.g., no fun, skills did not improve, was not as good as wanted to be). Thus, the athlete-by-situation model is a useful way to understand children's motivation for participation.

When the young athlete's objectives for participation are discovered, the adult leader must then examine the athletic situation in which the child is participating. In cases in which the child has desirable objectives (e.g., fun, to improve skills), the coaching style should be adapted to ensure that the athletic environment meets these objectives. If, however, the young athlete's objectives for participation are socially undesirable (e.g., the need to intimidate or dominate others), then an effort to change the child's objectives should be made. Adapting coaching style is an especially useful means of structuring the athletic environment to meet the athlete's needs, as the adult leader has direct control over his own behavior but only indirect control over other aspects of the athletic environment. Specifically, adult leaders can adapt their coaching styles to help achieve athletes' objectives in the following ways.

1. *Provide for fun in games and practices.* The most effective way to keep participation in sport fun is to let the children play. One thing young athletes hate is sitting on the bench or standing around in practice. Therefore, the coach should provide as much playing time as possible for all players, keep everyone active in practice by selecting quick and snappy drills to eliminate standing in line for long periods of time, and above all, foster a friendly, positive attitude with the young athletes in both practice and game settings.
2. *Help the children to improve their skills and learn new skills.* Young athletes rate skill improvement as one of their most important motives for participation. Consequently, the role that coaches play as teachers of sport skills is important. Teaching sport skills is not an automatic or easy process, however, and coaches must concentrate on providing effective instruction. A basic knowledge of fundamental sport skills is needed, but this alone is not enough. The effective coach must also know how to convey this information

to young athletes in a clear, concise manner. Planned and organized practices, good demonstrations, effective explanations, and abundant feedback are needed for effective instruction to occur.

3. *Provide time for players to be with their friends and make new friends.* Many times youth sport coaches focus all of their efforts on teaching new plays, organizing practices, and developing effective strategies for competition. While these are worthy objectives, one of the joys of sport is the camaraderie that children share with each other. Providing time for children to be with their friends and to make new friends is an important coaching responsibility. Moreover, providing for the affiliative needs of the young athletes is relatively easy. For example, allowing the players to have a designated but supervised free time period before practice or arranging a midseason social event is popular, and allows the young athletes to learn more about each other in a warm, friendly, social atmosphere.
4. *Allow the children to enjoy the thrills and excitement of sport.* Most children love sport because it is exciting and challenging. Over the course of a season, however, some of this excitement is lost. One of the best ways to offset boredom in practices is to organize quick, exciting drills that involve all of the players simultaneously. Additionally, many practice games can be scheduled, and these games can sometimes be structured as a change-of-pace activity to initiate excitement. Soccer scrimmages in which three complete passes constitute a goal, a basketball dribbling relay race, or baseball games in which each child is allowed to play a new or different position are all examples of effective methods of instilling excitement in practices.
5. *Help the athletes to feel worthy by understanding the meaning of success.* To think that winning is not an important objective of youth sport programs is unrealistic. Striving to win is important to children, especially as they get older. However, to think that winning is the only objective of the participants is a mistake. From the players' perspective, such fundamental elements as playing, having fun, and learning new skills are equally important as or, in many cases, more important than winning. In two studies (Orlick and Botterill 1975, Griffin 1978), more than 90% of the young athletes surveyed indicated that they would rather be on a losing team and play than sit on the bench on a winning team. Thus, one important role of the coach is to keep winning in perspective and to stress multiple objectives of participation. Winning means more than just who is ahead at the end of the game or match. Winning means trying as hard as possible to improve relative to one's own standards or personal goals. After all, if athletes give their best effort in a contest, what more can be asked of them?

   Helping young athletes to define success is important, because children have been taught to equate their athletic achievement with their self-worth—"to win is to be successful, to be competent, to be a worthy person; to lose is to be a failure, to be incompetent, and unworthy" (Martens et al. 1981). When athletes experience a reasonable amount of success, their further pursuit of excellence is reinforced. If they fail to experience success, athletes may blame themselves and may even develop a fear of failure. Because of this, adult leaders must help young athletes to define success relative to personal goals and ensure that realistic goals are set so that all young athletes experience some degree of success and feel worthy.
6. *Using the positive approach.* One of the most important situational factors influencing athletes' motivation is the style of their coach. All coaches are interested in helping their

athletes to perform well, and several coaching styles or approaches accomplish this goal. A positive style is one in which the coach spends a great deal of time encouraging and praising children for the skills they perform correctly, uses tact when conveying technical instruction, and corrects performance errors with constructive criticism. In contrast, a negative style is one in which the coach focuses on performance errors and often neglects to praise and encourage the athletes when they perform well. Moreover, when errors occur, the coach with the negative style reacts in a punitive fashion, chastizing and harshly criticizing the young athletes for their inept play.

While we all have seen coaches who use a predominantly positive or negative coaching style, most coaches use aspects of both approaches, which is consistent with the person-by-situation model of motivation. The personal makeup of individuals determines who reacts better to a positive style of coaching and who reacts better to a negative style.

When working with younger athletes, however, the positive style has been found to be most effective and should be emphasized (Smith, Smoll, and Curtis 1979). Specifically, coaches must remember that in children's sport they are not working with highly skilled adults who have experienced a great deal of success in sport and have established a self-concept. Instead, they are involved with youngsters who are just developing their skills and have a developing self-concept. Constant criticism, sarcasm, and yelling often frustrate young athletes, deteriorate their self-image and self-confidence, and decrease their motivation. When coaching young athletes, a positive, supportive approach is essential if high levels of motivation are to be maintained.

Understanding Intrinsic Motivation

Anyone who has been involved in youth sport programs has noticed that a number of children seem almost naturally attracted to sport, needing only the experience of play itself as a compensation for their efforts. In essence, these children are playing for the sake of playing, or are what psychologists call "intrinsically motivated." Ironically, a number of authors (Thomas 1978, Martens 1978a, Roberts 1980) have suggested that rewarding children with such things as trophies, jackets, medals, and all-star berths for activities for which they are already intrinsically motivated eventually undermines their intrinsic desire to participate. The following story depicts this undermining of intrinsic motivation:

> An old man lived next to an open field that was a perfect location for the neighborhood children's "pick-up" baseball games. Every afternoon the children would come to the field, choose sides and engage in a noisy game. Finally, the noise became too much for the old man, so he decided to put an end to the games. However, being a wise old man who did not want to stir up trouble in the neighborhood, he changed the children's behavior in a subtle way.
>
> The old man told the children that he liked to hear them play, but because of his failing hearing he had trouble doing so. He then told the children that if they would play and create enough noise so he could hear them, he would give each of them a quarter.
>
> The children gladly obliged. After the game, the old man paid the children and asked if they could return the next day. The kids agreed, and once again they created a great deal of noise during the game. However, this time the old man said he was running short of money and could only pay them 20 cents each. This still satisfied the children. However, when he told them that he would be able to pay only five cents on the third day, the

> children became angry and indicated that they would not come back. They felt that it was not worth the effort to make so much noise for only five cents apiece [adapted from Casady 1974 and taken from Gould 1979].

This story suggests that externally rewarding children for already desirable athletic activities erodes their intrinsic motivation. Moreover, when the external rewards are no longer available, the children no longer desire to participate in the activity.

Do external rewards have negative effects on the intrinsic motivation of young athletes? If so, should external rewards be given in children's sport? These are critical questions that those interested in the psychosocial development of young athletes are posing. Unfortunately, research has shown that no simple answer exists regarding this issue (Halliwell 1978). To the contrary, research has shown that providing external rewards for children's athletic participation may increase intrinsic motivation at times and decrease it at others. In essence, we are faced with the tricky business of giving awards!

The good news is that extrinsic rewards have been found to increase intrinsic motivation when the reward conveys positive information about the young athlete's sense of self-competence or self-worth. Thus, if placing first in a race, being on the winning team, or receiving the most-improved-player award causes the young athlete to feel more competent, intrinsic motivation increases. If the reward provides negative information about self-worth or competence, however, intrinsic motivation decreases. For instance, if a child is constantly criticized and receives the bonehead-play-of-the-game award, it does little to improve his feelings of self-worth and, more than likely, deteriorates feelings of competence. In this case, intrinsic motivation decreases.

A second way extrinsic rewards influence intrinsic motivation is changing what psychologists call the child's locus of control. That is, when the child perceives that her major reason for participation is solely to win a medal or receive a trophy, she has an external locus of control. If, however, she participates primarily out of her own self-interest and the reward is seen as an additional benefit, she has an internal locus of control. Thus, extrinsic rewards undermine intrinsic motivation when they cause the young athlete to change her locus of control from internal to external.

One reason why no simple answer exists regarding the issue of giving extrinsic rewards in youth sport programs is because most rewards in children's sport are contingent on performance (e.g., placing first or second, winning or losing the championship) and provide information about self-worth. Therefore, giving contingent rewards in sport should enhance intrinsic motivation. Halliwell (1978) has indicated, however, that "even though the informational aspects of trophies may provide the athlete with a sense of personal competence, the controlling aspects of these rewards may be more salient than the informational dimension if the reward recipient perceives that his sports involvement is controlled by the pursuit of trophies and other tangible rewards." Instead of increasing intrinsic motivation, the rewards may cause the young athlete to have an external locus of control and a corresponding decline in intrinsic motivation.

In summary, the research shows that external rewards can sometimes enhance and sometimes undermine the intrinsic motivation of young athletes. Thus, no general rule about the propriety of giving external rewards can be made. These findings, however, provide us with sufficient information for developing guidelines for using extrinsic rewards in children's sport. Gould (1979) has outlined a number of these guidelines, which are given below:

1. Adult leaders must be very careful about using extrinsic rewards. These rewards should be relatively inexpensive and not used to "control" or coerce children into participating in already desirable activities.
2. Adult leaders play a vital role in influencing how young athletes perceive rewards. Therefore, these individuals must keep winning in perspective and stress the nontangible values of sports participation (fun, skill improvement) as opposed to participation solely for the reward.
3. One way to increase intrinsic motivation is to give athletes more responsibility (more internal control) for decision making and for rule making (Halliwell 1978). This could be done by getting input from the athletes about making team rules, letting them help organize practices, or letting them be involved in making game decisions. Younger players may be selected to lead a drill or favorite warm-up exercise and given some playing time at positions they desire. Older, more experienced players could help conduct practices and make actual game decisions (allowing the quarterback to call some plays without interference by the coach, for example).
4. Adult leaders can also increase intrinsic motivation by ensuring that when external rewards are given, they provide information that increases the young athletes' feelings of self worth and competence. The easiest way to accomplish this is to have realistic expectations of the players. Not all children will have a winning season or place first in the tournament. However, some realistic goals can be set with each athlete (in terms of improved personal skill, playing time, etc.) and the players can be rewarded for achieving their own goals. This could be accomplished through the use of an "Unsung Hero" or "Most Improved Player" award.
5. These "official" rewards are not nearly as important as the simple ones that coaches can give, though. Some of the most powerful rewards are free (pat on the back, friendly nod, or verbal praise). These rewards should be frequently used to acknowledge each athlete's contribution to the team, personal improvement, or achievement of a personal goal. Yelling at young athletes and constantly criticizing them conveys information that decreases their confidence and self-worth.
6. Adult leaders should structure the environment so the children have a reasonable chance of success in the sport. For example, novice eight-year-old baseball players may only make contact with a pitched ball one out of ten times. However, adult leaders could structure the situation to ensure that the children will meet with more success by having them hit off a batting T.

UNDERSTANDING COMPETITIVE STRESS IN CHILDREN'S SPORT

The effect of competitive or emotional stress on the young athlete has become one of the most controversial topics confronting those involved in children's sport. Critics have argued that young athletes are continually placed under too much stress, and that this stess has long-term negative consequences on their health and well-being. To the contrary, proponents have contended that the critics overreact and exaggerate when discussing the amount and effect of competitive stress on young athletes. The concern about competitive stress continues today, as a recent survey of youth sport researchers and practitioners revealed that understanding competitive stress rated as one of the most important psychological issues needing study (Gould 1982). Thus, when the psychosocial effects of children's sport participation are discussed, competitive stress is a topic of utmost importance.

When attempting to understand stress in children's sport, three issues are particularly important: First, adult leaders must determine if too much competitive stress is being placed on the young athlete. Second, factors associated with heightened stress states in young athletes must be identified. Finally, strategies that can be used to help young athletes control competitive stress must be determined and implemented.

Before these issues are discussed, several terms need definition. *Anxiety* and *stress* are familiar terms, but discussing them can create considerable confusion since they are commonly used in several different ways. For example, sport psychologists define *state anxiety* as a current feeling of nervousness, apprehension, tension, or a combination of these, which is accompanied by physiological activation of the player. Measures of state anxiety include self-report scales that ask respondents to indicate how calm, nervous, apprehensive, or worried they are at a particular moment, and physiological measurements such as heart rate, respiration, and digital sweat gland secretion. In contrast to state anxiety, *trait anxiety* is defined as a personality disposition that causes an individual to perceive evaluative situations as more or less threatening and to respond with varying levels of state anxiety. A child with low trait anxiety, for instance, does not typically view evaluative situations such as athletic competition as threatening and therefore does not experience high levels of nervousness and tension (state anxiety). However, a child with high trait anxiety views the same competitive situation as threatening and typically becomes nervous or tense.

Stress differs from state and trait anxieties in that it is defined as a general process "that involves the perception of a substantial imbalance between environmental demand and response capability, under conditions where failure to meet demand is perceived as having important consequences and is responded to with increased levels of state anxiety" (Martens 1977). Moreover, the stress process can be subdivided into four stages (Passer 1982): First, a person is confronted with a situation that places a demand or constraint or her (e.g., a tied baseball game, with bases loaded, two outs, and the child coming to bat). Second, the person perceives whether this situation is psychologically or physically threatening (e.g., "No one will like me if I strike out," "What if I get beaned?"). Third, the person responds to the situation with some kind of emotional reaction (gets nervous, tightens up). Fourth, some type of psychological or behavioral consequence results (e.g., poor performance, inability to concentrate).

In essence, trait anxiety, state anxiety, and stress are defined differently but are by no means independent. A child's level of trait anxiety influences his state anxiety in evaluative situations. Similarly, a child's level of trait anxiety influences the degree to which she perceives situations to be threatening, while state anxiety is often the emotional response made in the stress process.

Are Young Athletes Placed Under Too Much Emotional Stress?

Skubic (1955) was one of the first investigators to assess the emotional stress that young competitive athletes experience. In this study, galvanic skin response (a measure of sweat-gland secretion) was used to assess the state anxiety of boys participating in youth league baseball competition. Specifically, state anxiety was measured in pregame and postgame situations, as well as in required school physical education competition. Skubic's findings revealed that when pregame and postgame state anxiety measures were compared, the boys exhibited greater postgame anxiety. However, when the boys' state anxiety in the competitive baseball game and physical education class were compared, no significant differences existed. Thus, competitive athletics was not found to be any more stressful than physical education class competition.

More recently, Simon and Martens (1979) examined children's state anxiety responses in both sport and nonsport situations. Comparisons of precompetitive state anxiety levels were made between boys ages 9 to 14 participating in a variety of sport and nonsport competitive activities. The boys participated in either nonrequired, nonsport activities (band solos and band group competitions), required school activities (classroom tests and physical education classes), or nonschool sports (baseball, basketball, tackle football, gymnastics, ice hockey, swimming, and wrestling). State anxiety was measured through a self-report scale taken just prior to competition. The results indicated that nonrequired, nonsport activity participants (band members and soloists) demonstrated higher levels of state anxiety than nonschool sport activity participants, who, in turn, demonstrated greater anxiety than required school activity participants. When comparisons were made between sports, the greatest state anxiety levels were found for individual-sport participants as compared with team-sport participants, but no differences existed between the anxiety levels of noncontact and contact participants. However, individual contact sport participants exhibited the highest state anxiety levels, and team contact sport participants exhibited the lowest levels. Thus, the type of sport played was found to be related to precompetitive state anxiety levels in the boys. More important, however, was the author's conclusion that although anxiety levels were generally evaluated prior to athletic competition, these anxiety changes were *not* excessive.

Finally, in two extensive studies of youth soccer players (ages 10 to 12) Scanlan and Passer (1978, 1979) examined precompetitive state anxiety levels. While no comparisons were made to nonsport activities, these investigators examined the relationships between players' levels of trait anxiety, playing ability, team expectancy of success, self-expectancy of success, game importance, self-concept and practice, and pregame and postgame state anxiety levels. Their findings revealed that higher levels of pregame state anxiety were related to higher levels of player trait anxiety, higher levels of practice state anxiety, lower levels of player self-esteem, lower levels of personal performance expectancies, and lower levels of team expectancies. Game outcome influenced postgame state anxiety, with winners exhibiting the lowest levels of anxiety and losers the highest. Players who reported having more fun also exhibited lower levels of postgame state anxiety.

While only a few investigations have been conducted to assess the amounts of psychological stress that young athletes experience, several preliminary conclusions can be reached. First, the data reveal that most young athletes are not being placed under too much emotional stress. In essence, the stress created in sport seems to be equivalent to or, in some cases, less than that created in other childhood activities. However, sport competition is threatening or anxiety producing for some children in some athletic situations. Thus, efforts need to be made to identify these children and the situations that place excessive stress on them.

Factors Influencing Competitive Stress

A number of interpersonal and situational factors have been found to be associated with competitive stress in young athletes. For example, in the Scanlan and Passer (1978, 1979) studies previously discussed, several important interpersonal factors associated with heightened state anxiety were identified. Specifically, "players who were high competitive trait anxious, who had low self-esteem, and who had low performance expectancies experienced greater perceived threat and experienced higher state anxiety when facing a pending competition than did those who were low competitive trait anxious, who had high self-esteem, and who had high performance expectancies" (Scanlan and Passer 1978). In addition, the amount of fun experienced by the child was favorably related to postgame competitive stress, as well as game outcome, which was also found to be an important determinant of postgame state anxiety.

Hanson (1967) and Lowe and McGrath (1971) also examined sources of stress in young athletes. In both studies, state anxiety was measured via physiological indices (heart rate or respiration, or both) in youth league baseball players (ages 9 to 12 years) in various situations (e.g., each time the player was in the dugout, on deck, at bat). The criticality of a particular game within the season was an important determinant of state anxiety (Lowe and McGrath 1971). In addition, the highest state anxiety levels were evident when the boy was at bat. Thus, the importance of the immediate situation within the game was related to the level of state anxiety experienced. In essence, these investigators found that both situation and game criticality were associated with heightened stress states.

In a recent descriptive study, Pierce and Stratton (1981) also examined factors associated with heightened anxiety states in young athletes. Youth sport participants ($N = 543$) ranging in age from 10 to 17 years were asked to rate their biggest worries when participating in competitive sports. More than 62% of the respondents indicatd that they most frequently worried about "not playing well" and "making mistakes." Approximately 25% of the young athletes indicated that they frequently worried about what their coaches or teammates or both would say. Forty-four percent of the respondents said that they were prevented from playing their best because of certain worries. Thus, a substantial number of respondents feared failure, and these fears were reported to interfere with performance.

Finally, Martens (1978) has identified two major sources of stress in children's sports. These include importance placed on the competition and uncertainty concerning game outcome, relationships with others, and capabilities. For example, the greater the importance a young athlete places on a game or event, the greater the state anxiety experienced. Similarly, the more uncertainty the young athlete perceives regarding the outcome of the game or event and about her capability and relationships with others, the more state anxiety she experiences. Martens (1978) not only indicates that these factors are related to the stress responses of young athletes but also suggests that these factors are often influenced, knowingly or unknowingly, by the actions of adult leaders.

Controlling Competitive Stress

Current research shows that the majority of children involved in competitive athletics are not placed under too much emotional stress. However, some children in some situations experience extremely high levels of competitive stress. Typically, these are either high trait-anxious or low self-esteem children or both who are placed in athletic situations that they perceive as being important and in which they perceive a high degree of uncertainty in the outcome of the event, in relationships with others, and in their capabilities. The adult leaders must develop the skills necessary to identify and assist these youngsters in coping with stress.

One way to facilitate the accurate detection or recognition of heightened anxiety in young athletes is to become aware of the characteristic symptoms, such as a young athlete who: (1) consistently performs better in practice than in major competition, (2) has trouble sleeping the night before competition, (3) has trouble getting loose before games or events, (4) demonstrates marked personality changes just before competition, or (5) demonstrates some combination of these symptoms. If subsequent discussion with the youngster verifies that stress is indeed the problem, attempts should be made to reduce the importance placed on this child's performance, since increasing that importance increases stress. Giving this youngster an emotional pep talk or emphasizing the importance of winning may place excessive pressure on him. Moreover, research on the stress and performance relationship shows that there is a fine line between being up for a game or event and exhibiting the best performance, and being uptight and exhibiting poor performance. Consequently, increasing the importance placed on performance and giving pep talks more often psychs the young athlete "out" rather than "up." A more effective approach to use with these youngsters is to say nothing to them about the importance of the upcoming event or to indicate that all you ask is that they give a 100% effort.

Since feelings of uncertainty about relationships with others create stress in young athletes (e.g., "Will my parents, coach, and teammates still like me if I lose?"), the coach should reduce uncertainty by creating a supportive atmosphere. Young athletes should be helped to realize that others do not base their liking of them on their record of success. Coaches should make clear that when others provide constructive criticism, they are criticizing only the child's performance, not the child as a person.

Finally, many young athletes frequently worry about not playing well and making mistakes. This is not surprising, since the importance of winning is constantly stressed in our society. While striving to win is not wrong—indeed, striving to win is a primary objective of sport—problems do arise when excessive emphasis is placed on winning.

To reiterate, a more effective strategy is to define winning as giving maximum effort and as personal improvement. Additionally, coaches, parents, and athletes must develop realistic expectations. For example, all young athletes, regardless of their ability, are going to make mistakes. In the heat of competition, however, the child is sometimes chastised by her coach, parents, teammates, or even herself. This only frustrates the child and further deteriorates performance. A more productive approach is to teach children to view mistakes in a more positive light. Specifically, coaches should teach them that mistakes do occur, and while no one likes to make mistakes, the key is to learn from these mistakes. Coaches should teach children to analyze what went wrong, learn from it, and then put the mistake out of their mind. After all, worrying about what went wrong in the past only interferes with future performances and creates further stress.

PSYCHOSOCIAL DEVELOPMENT THROUGH SPORT

One of the primary justifications made for the existence of children's sport has been its utility as a vehicle for developing positive psychological attributes such as good sportsmanship and improved self-concept in the participants. In fact, parents and coaches of today's young athletes strongly believe that these positive attributes result from participation (Joint Legislative Study Committee 1978a, 1978b). Unfortunately, little research has been conducted to examine this assumption. The few studies that have been conducted in the area are reviewed in this section. Moreover, related literature, as well as the opinions of experts in the field regarding these issues, are examined.

Developing Sportsmanship in the Young Athlete

Although children's participation in sports is commonly thought to develop sportsmanlike attitudes and values in young athletes, little evidence exists to support this notion. McAfee (1955) and Kistler (1957) assessed the attitudes of young athletes regarding various sportsmanship issues and found that as the children became older and more involved in sport, their attitudes about sportsmanship deteriorated. In a series of studies, Smith (1974, 1975, 1978) found that children learned aggressive behaviors from participation in competitive ice hockey programs. Specifically, Smith surveyed ice hockey players ranging in age from 12 to 21 years and had them rate the degree to which they learned and approved of various aggressive behaviors (e.g., fighting if provoked by another player). The results revealed that the more experience a child has had in hockey, the greater the likelihood of learning and approving of aggressive tactics. Moreover, aggression in hockey appears to be socially learned and sanctioned through the modeling of professional players and the reinforcement of significant others (teammates, coaches, parents).

While the results of the McAfee, Kistler, and Smith studies suggest that participation in competitive sports does not develop sportsmanship in young athletes and, in fact, may foster unsportsmanlike and aggressive actions, Martens (1978b) takes a more positive stand. Martens indicates that while these studies show that sport participation can have negative effects on the development of sportsmanship in children, participation also has the potential to foster positive development. As with the previous sections of this chapter, the key to whether positive or negative effects result depends on the social environment in which the children compete. Thus, the question of primary importance is the identification of the behaviors of significant others that have positive or negative effects on the development of sportsmanship.

Children learn moral and immoral attitudes and behaviors through three mechanisms of social learning: modeling, reinforcement, and social comparison. A primary means of learning right from wrong for a child athlete is through the observation of a model. As the young athlete views significant others, she attempts to model her behavior and attitudes. If significant others exhibit appropriate behaviors, the child learns good sportsmanship. If, however, inappropriate behaviors are modeled, the child learns poor sportsmanship. Modeling comprises only part of the social learning process. Children do not learn modeled behaviors unless they are reinforced for exhibiting them. Thus, the frequency with which significant others reinforce appropriate behaviors and penalize inappropriate behaviors is extremely important. Finally, children learn appropriate attitudes, values, and actions by comparing themselves to their peers. If a child is exposed to a peer group that has inappropriate attitudes and behaviors, poor sportsmanship may be learned. Exposure to peers who exhibit appropriate attitudes and behaviors has more positive effects.

Closely associated with the development of sportsmanship in young athletes is the development of moral reasoning. Moral reasoning is the process by which children make judgments about the appropriateness or inappropriateness (rightness or wrongness) of various actions. Thus, moral reasoning is not a right or wrong action per se, but the process by which a child judges an act to be right or wrong. Consequently, the correspondence between a child's level of moral reasoning and moral action is less than perfect, since factors such as values, norms, and expectations must also be considered to predict behavior accurately. However, knowing how a child makes a moral judgment helps to understand his behavior better.

Kohlberg (1969) has found that moral reasoning is a developmentally based phenomenon. Children move through a sequence of moral reasoning stages that are closely associated with

Table 11.1. Stages of Moral Reasoning

Stage	Explanation	Example
Preconventional	This stage is sometimes labeled the *external control* stage, as the child judges right from wrong on the basis of whether her actions are rewarded or penalized.	"Cheating is wrong because I was punished for cheating."
Conventional	The child determines right from wrong by conforming to the expectations of significant others.	"Cheating is wrong because Mom and Dad would be disappointed in me if I cheated."
Postconventional	The child determines right from wrong on the basis of a moral rule or value that he has internalized.	"It is not fair to everyone else if I cheat."

intellectual development. These stages are outlined in Table 11.1 and include (1) the preconventional stage, (2) the conventional or moral stage, and (3) the postconventional or autonomous stage.

Not only have psychologists identified stages of moral development but also they have found that these stages influence children's moral behavior. Specifically, when children reach the postconventional or autonomous stage, they internalize moral values or rules and are more likely to use these values to guide their behavior. Adult leaders can help children progress through the stages of moral reasoning by providing rationales and explanations for why behaviors are correct or incorrect, and by leading children in discussions of why behaviors are morally right or wrong. In the following passage, for example, Martens (1978b) outlines how adult leaders in youth sports can influence the moral development of young athletes.

> Seven-year-old Billy, a goalie with the Buffalo Bombers of the midget hockey league, becomes entangled with teammates and opponents in a skirmish around the net. Billy is hit and dazed, but is uncertain by whom or what. In his anger, Billy retaliates by punching the nearest opponent in the nose with a solid right. The referee throws Billy out of the game and his coach punishes him by sitting him out of the next game. As a result, Billy may hesitate to hit an opponent again in a similar situation to avoid punishment, but he may not understand why he should not. If, on the other hand, the coach explains that it is wrong to hurt people, Billy may also hesitate to hit other people when he is off the ice (Martens 1978).

Thus, adult leaders can facilitate the development of moral reasoning in young athletes.

Based on the social learning and moral development literature, a number of other practical implications for instilling sportsmanship in young athletes can be made (Gould 1981). Several are included below.

1. *Plan for the development of sportsmanship.* The first step in instilling sportsmanlike attitudes in young athletes is to realize that mere participation does not guarantee such benefits. In essence, adult leaders must plan to develop sportsmanlike qualities in their young athletes and must implement specific psychosocial change strategies to do so.

2. *Clearly define sportsmanship.* Too often everyone assumes that children know what good sportsmanship involves. This is not the case with children, or even with other adult leaders. In baseball or softball, for example, many coaches think that teasing or razzing opposing players is appropriate. Yet, in gymnastics, skating, or diving, this behavior is considered unsportsmanlike. Adult leaders must specifically define what sportsmanship is and convey this to young athletes. To help adult leaders do this, the Youth Sports Institute (Michigan State University) has adopted the sportsmanship code in Table 11.2).
3. *Model good sportsmanship.* If young athletes are to learn good sportsmanship, they must be exposed to models who demonstrate this type of behavior. Moreover, as most experienced teachers and coaches have learned, actions speak louder than words. There-

Table 11.2. Youth Sports Sportsmanship Code

Areas of Concern	Sportsmanlike Behaviors	Unsportsmanlike Behaviors
Behavior toward officials	When questioning officials, do so in the appropriate manner (e.g., lodge an official protest, have only designated individuals such as a captain address officials) Treat officials with respect and dignity at all times	Arguing with officials Swearing at officials
Behavior toward opponents	Treat all opponents with respect and dignity at all times	Arguing with opponents Making sarcastic remarks about opponents Making aggressive actions toward opponents Swearing at opponents
Behavior toward teammates	Give only constructive criticism and positive encouragement	Making negative comments or sarcastic remarks Swearing or arguing with teammates
Behavior toward spectators	Make only positive comments to spectators	Arguing with spectators Making negative remarks, swearing at spectators
Rule acceptance and infractions	Obey all league rules	Intentionally violating league rules Taking advantage of loopholes in rules (e.g., every child must play, so coach tells unskilled players to be sick on important game days)
Spectator behavior	Make only positive comments to players, coaches, officials	Making negative comments or sarcastic remarks

fore, the responsibility of adult leaders is to provide appropriate sportsmanship role models for young athletes. Specifically, adult leaders must exhibit good sportsmanship themselves and should make a continuing effort to recognize and identify college and professional athletes who extol these virtues.

4. *Reward good sportsmanship and penalize poor sportsmanship.* If young athletes are to learn good sportsmanship, adult leaders should continuously reward sportsmanlike behavior and penalize that which is unsportsmanlike. Sportsmanship rules must be consistently enforced for all team members in all situations. For example, to penalize the star athlete for displaying unsportsmanlike conduct is just as important as it is to penalize a less skilled child. Similarly, unsportsmanlike conduct should be penalized in the championship game as well as in practice. If this is not done, children learn that sportsmanship counts only for the less skilled athlete or when winning is not at stake.
5. *Provide explanations when teaching sportsmanship.* When rewarding young athletes for sportsmanlike behavior or penalizing them for unsportsmanlike conduct, adult leaders must remember to provide explanations for why these behaviors are desirable or undesirable. If either explanations or discussions are not provided, young athletes are not likely to advance in their stages of moral reasoning.

Developing Self-Confidence in the Young Athlete

Like good sportsmanship, the development of self-confidence, self-competence, and a positive self-concept is a primary goal of youth sport participation.[3] Unfortunately, little research has been conducted to examine the relationships between these variables and children's athletic involvement. Moreover, the results of those studies that have been conducted are conflicting, with some studies finding these relationships to be significant (Brugel 1972; McGowan, Jarman, and Pedersen 1974; Roberts, Kleiber, and Duda 1981) and other studies finding few relationships (Maul and Thomas 1975, Magill and Ash 1979).

A major reason why no clear pattern of findings appears from this research results from the fact that few studies have been designed to examine the relationship between the quality of the young athlete's sport experience and the development of self-confidence or self-concept. To the contrary, only participants and nonparticipants have been compared. Evidence presented in this chapter, however, suggests that mere participation in sport does not automatically produce psychological benefits. The critical component in influencing psychosocial development is the quality of the young athlete's experience.

Harter (1981) has recently reaffirmed the notion that the quality of experience is the critical determinant for development of competence. Specifically, Harter's theory of competence motivation indicates that the child's level of competence, his confidence in having the ability to perform and master a task, guides his attempts at mastery in achievement situations. That is, a child with a strong sense of competence tends to seek out and succeed in achievement settings such as sport, while the child who is low in perceived competence tends to avoid these achievement settings and performs poorly in them. Moreover, Harter's central thesis is that competence motivation is a

3. Note that distinctions are often made between the terms *self-confidence, self-competence,* and *self-concept.* While making distinctions between these terms is often useful, doing so is beyond the scope of this chapter. Consequently, these terms are viewed as being synonymous.

developmental phenomenon that is determined by the degree of approval or disapproval that children perceive in achievement situations. When children succeed and receive approval, strong perceptions of competence are developed, and they expect to perform well and persist longer in situations when failure does occur. When continual failure is experienced, however, little competence is developed, and the children expect to perform poorly and experience anxiety and shame when failing. Thus, Harter's theory has important implications for adult leaders involved in children's sport.

Unfortunately, Harter's theory has not received extensive empirical testing in the athletic domain. However, some indirect support exists for its contentions. Smith, Smoll, and Curtis (1979) examined the relationships between various coaching behaviors and self-esteem in Little League Baseball players (ages 10 to 15). Their results revealed significant correlations between the degree of technical athletic instruction exhibited by the coach and various measures of self-esteem. Additionally, significant relationships existed between positive coaching orientations (the degree to which coaches gave encouragement and positive reinforcement) and athletic self-esteem. Similarly, McGowan, Jarman, and Pedersen (1974) found that seventh-grade boys who participated in an endurance training program, which was designed to ensure success for all participants, showed a positive increase in self-concept over an 18-week training program. In contrast, no significant self-concept changes were evident in a control group. Thus, these studies demonstrate that the social environments in which the children participate have an important influence on self-concept development.

The critical component in developing self-confidence in young athletes, then, is ensuring that they have positive experiences and improve their skills. Adult leaders involved in youth sport must plan and implement specific strategies to provide for positive experiences and success for young athletes. Several strategies are readily available to accomplish this objective (Gould 1982). First, adult leaders can develop self-confidence in young athletes by holding both formal and informal discussions. In these meetings, the meaning of success, the proper way to view mistakes and losses, and the need to set individual, realistic goals should be emphasized. Second, adult leaders must serve as positive role models by extolling and exhibiting confidence, emotional control, and a positive attitude. Additionally, coaches can use contemporary college and professional athletes as role models by selecting quotes and stories about how these outstanding athletes often lost and made mistakes early in their careers but were able to overcome these setbacks by setting realistic goals and working hard. Third, coaches must continually emphasize the positive approach to coaching outlined in this chapter and examined in detail in the next chapter. Constant criticism, sarcasm, and yelling only frustrate the young athlete and deteriorate her fragile self-image. Fourth, parents must be informed of adult leaders' attempts to foster psychological development in young athletes, because some parents set unrealistic goals, place undue emphasis on winning, and make pessimistic or sarcastic remarks about the young athletes. When this happens, the coach's effort to develop self-confidence is often undermined. Finally, developing confidence is a long-term, continuous process that requires continual planning and emphasis if adult leaders are to be successful in achieving this objective.

SUMMARY

An area of considerable concern for those interested in children's sport is the effect that athletic participation has on the psychosocial development of the young athlete. Sport participation affects the young athlete's view of competition, level of motivation, degree of competitive stress experienced, sportsmanlike attitude and behavior, and feelings of self-competence. More important, participation in youth sport programs can have both beneficial and detrimental effects on psychosocial development. The critical component in determining whether beneficial or detrimental ramifications occur is the quality of the adult leaders supervising the young athlete. Adult leaders involved in these programs must plan, develop, and implement specific strategies designed to foster psychosocial growth in the young athlete.

REFERENCES

Alderman, R. B., & Wood, N. L. An analysis of incentive motivation in young Canadian athletes. *Canadian Journal of Applied Sport Sciences,* 1976, **1**(2), 169-176.

Alley, L. E. Athletics in education: The double-edged sword. *Phi Delta Kappan*, 1974, **56**, 102-105, 113.

Berryman, J. W. The rise of highly organized sports for preadolescent boys. In R.A. Magill, M. J. Ash, & F. L. Smoll (Eds.), *Children in sport: A contemporary anthology.* Champaign, Illinois: Human Kinetics, 1978.

Brugel, B. A. The self-concept of eight- and nine-year-old boys participating in a competitive baseball league. Unpublished master's thesis, Pennsylvania State University, 1972.

Casady, M. The tricky business of giving awards. *Psychology Today*, 1974, **8**(4), 52.

Coleman, J. S. *Youth: Transition to adulthood.* Chicago: University of Chicago Press, 1974.

Feltz, D. Athletics in the status system of female adolescents. *Review of Sport and Leisure,* 1978, **3**, 98-108.

Gill, D. L., Gross, J. D., & Huddleston, S. Motivation in youth sports. In G. C. Roberts & D. M. Landers (Eds.), *Psychology of motor behavior and sport—1980.* Champaign, Illinois: Human Kinetics, 1981.

Gould, D. *Motivating young athletes.* East Lansing, Michigan: Youth Sports Institute, 1979.

Gould, D. Sportsmanship: Building character or characters? In V. Seefeldt, F. L. Smoll, R. E. Smith, & D. Gould, *A winning philosophy for youth sports programs.* East Lansing, Michigan: Youth Sports Institute, 1981.

Gould, D. Fostering psychological development in young athletes: A reaction. In T. Orlick, J. T. Partington, & J. H. Salmela (Eds.), *Mental training for coaches and athletes.* Ottowa, Ontario: Coaching Association of Canada, 1982.

Gould, D. Sport psychology in the 1980s: Status, direction and challenge in youth sports research. *Journal of Sport Psychology,* 1982, **4**, 203-218.

Gould, D., Feltz, D., & Horn, T. Reasons for attrition in competitive youth swimming. *Journal of Sport Behavior,* 1982, **5**, 155-165.

Gould, D., Feltz, D., Weiss, M., & Petlichkoff, L. Participation motives in competitive youth swimmers. In T. Orlick, J. T. Partington, & J. H. Salmela (Eds.), *Mental training for coaches and athletes.* Ottowa, Ontario: Coaching Association of Canada, 1982.

Griffin, L. E. *Why children participate in youth sports.* Paper presented at the American Alliance of Health, Physical Education and Recreation National Conference, Kansas City, Missouri, 1978.

Halliwell, W. Intrinsic motivation in sport. In W. F. Straub (Ed.), *Sport psychology: An analysis of athlete behavior.* Ithaca, New York: Mouvement Publications, 1978.

Hanson, D. L. Cardiac response to participation in little league baseball competition as determined by telemetry. *Research Quarterly,* 1967, **38**, 384-388.

Harter, S. The development of competence motivation in the mastery of cognitive and physical skills: Is there still a place for joy? In G. C. Roberts & D. M. Landers (Eds.), *Psychology of motor behavior and sport—1980.* Champaign, Illinois: Human Kinetics, 1981.

Joint Legislative Study Committee. *Joint legislative study on youth sports programs: Phase I report.* East Lansing, Michigan: Youth Sports Institute, State of Michigan, 1976.

Joint Legislative Study Committee. *Joint legislative study on youth sports programs: Phase II report.* East Lansing, Michigan: Youth Sports Institute, State of Michigan, 1978a.

Joint Legislative Study Committee. *Joint legislative study on youth sports programs: Phase III report.* East Lansing, Michigan: Youth Sports Institute, State of Michigan, 1978b.

Kistler, J. W. Attitudes expressed about behavior demonstrated in certain specific situations occurring in sports. *National College Physical Education Association for Men Proceedings,* 1957, **58**, 55-58.

Kohlberg, L. Stage and sequence: The cognitive developmental approach to socialization. In D. A. Goslin (Ed.), *Handbook of socialization: Theory and research.* Chicago: Rand McNally, 1969.

Lowe, R., & McGrath, J. E. *Stress, arousal and performance: Some findings calling for a new theory.* Project report, AF 1161-67, AFSOR, 1971.

Magill, R. A., & Ash, M. J. Academic, psycho-social and motor characteristics of paticipants and non-participants in children's sport. *Research Quarterly,* 1979, **50**, 230-240.

Martens, R. *Sports competition anxiety test.* Champaign, Illinois: Human Kinetics, 1977.

Martens, R. *Joy and sadness in children's sports.* Champaign, Illinois: Human Kinetics, 1978a.

Martens, R. Kid's sports: A den of iniquity or land of promise? In R.A. Magill, M. J. Ash, & F. L. Smoll (Eds.), *Children in sport: A contemporary anthology.* Champaign, Illinois: Human Kinetics, 1978b.

Martens, R., Christina, R., Harvey, J. S., & Sharkey, B. J. *Coaching young athletes,* Champaign, Illinois: Human Kinetics, 1981.

Martens, R., & Gould, D. Why do adults volunteer to coach children's sports? In G. C. Roberts & K. M. Newell (Eds.), *Psychology of motor behavior and sport—1978.* Champaign, Illinois: Human Kinetics, 1979.

Maul, T., & Thomas, J. R. Self-concept and participation in children's gymnastics. *Perceptual and Motor Skills,* 1975, **41**, 701-702.

McAfee, R. A. Sportsmanship attitudes of sixth, seventh and eighth grade boys. *Research Quarterly,* 1955, **26**, 120.

McGowan, R. W., Jarman, B. O., & Pedersen, D. M. Effects of a competitive endurance training program on self-concept and peer approval. *Journal of Psychology,* 1974, **86**, 57-60.

Nelson, L. L., & Kagan, S. Competition: The star-spangled scramble. *Psychology Today*, 1971, **5**, 53-56, 90-91.

Ogilvie, B. C., & Tutko, T. A. Sport: If you want to build character try something else. *Psychology Today,* 1971, **5**, 61-63.

Orlick, T., & Botterill, C. *Every kid can win.* Chicago: Nelson-Hall, 1975.

Orlick, T. D., McNally, J., & O'Hara, T. Cooperative games: Systematic analysis and cooperative impact. In F. L. Smoll & R. E. Smith (Eds.), *Psychological perspectives in youth sports.* Washington, D.C.: Hemishere, 1978.

Passer, M. W. Psychological stress in youth sports. In R. A. Magill, M. J. Ash, & F. L. Smoll (Eds.), *Children in sport: A contemporary anthology.* (2nd ed.) Champaign, Illinois: Human Kinetics, 1982.

Pierce, W. J., & Stratton, R. K. Perceived sources of stress in youth sport participants. In G. C. Roberts & D. M. Landers (Eds.), *Psychology of motor behavior and sport—1980.* Champaign, Illinois: Human Kinetics, 1981.

Pooley, J. C. *Drop-outs from sport: A case study of boys' age-group soccer.* Paper presented at the American Alliance for Health, Physical Education, Recreation and Dance National Conference, Boston, April 1981.

Roberts, G. C. Children in competition: A theoretical perspective and recommendations for practice. *Motor Skills: Theory Into Practice*, 1980, **4**, 37-51.

Roberts, G. C., Kleiber, D. A., & Duda, J. L. An analysis of motivation in children's sport: The role of perceived competence in participation. *Journal of Sport Psychology,* 1981, **3**, 206-216.

Sapp, M., & Haubenstricker, J. *Motivation for joining and reasons for not continuing in youth sports programs in Michigan.* Paper presented at the American Alliance for Health, Physical Education, and Recreation National Conference, Kansas City, Missouri, April 1978.

Scanlan, T. K., & Passer, M. W. Factors related to competitive stress among male youth sports participants. *Medicine and Science in Sports,* 1978, **10**, 103-108.

Scanlan, T. K., & Passer, M. W. Source of competitive stress in young female athletes. *Journal of Sport Psychology,* 1979, **1**, 151-159.

Sherif, C. W. The social context of competition. In D. M. Landers (Ed.), *Social problems in athletics.* Urbana, Illinois: University of Illinois Press, 1976.

Sherif, M., & Sherif, C. *Social psychology.* New York: Harper & Row, 1969.

Simon, J. A., & Martens, R. Children's anxiety in sport and nonsport evaluation activities. *Journal of Sport Psychology,* 1979, **1**, 151-159.
Skubic, E. Emotional responses of boys to little league and middle league competitive baseball. *Research Quarterly,* 1955, **26**, 342-352.
Smith, M. D. "Significant others' " influence on the assaultive behavior of young hockey players. *International Review of Sport Sociology,* 1974, **31**, 45-56.
Smith, M. D. The legitimation of violence: Hockey players' perceptions of their reference groups' sanctions for assault. *Review of Canadian Sociology and Anthropology/Canadian Review Sociology and Anthropology,* 1975, **12**.
Smith, M. D. Social learning of violence in minor hockey. In F. L. Smoll & R. E. Smith (Eds.), *Psychological perspectives in youth sports.* Washington, D.C.: Hemisphere, 1978.
Smith, R. E., Smoll, F. L., & Curtis, B. Coach effectiveness training: A cognitive-behavioral approach to enhancing relationship skills in youth sport coaches. *Journal of Sport Psychology,* 1979, **1**, 59-75.
Thomas, J. R. Attribution theory and motivation through reward: Practical implications for children's sports. In R. A. Magill, M. J. Ash, & F. L. Smoll (Eds.), *Children in sport: A contemporary anthology.* Champaign, Illinois: Human Kinetics, 1978.
Veroff, J. Social comparison and the development of achievement motivation. In C. P. Smith (Ed.), *Achievement-related motives in children.* New York: Russell Sage, 1969.

SUGGESTED READINGS

Undergraduate Students

General

Martens, R. *Joy and sadness in children's sport.* Champaign, Illinois: Human Kinetics, 1978.
Martens, R., Christina, R. W., Harvey, J. S., & Sharkey, B. J. *Coaching young athletes.* Champaign, Illinois: Human Kinetics, 1981.
Martens R., & Seefeldt, V. (Eds.), *Guidelines for children's sports.* Washington, D.C.: American Alliance for Health, Physical Education, Recreation and Dance, 1979.
Seefeldt, V., Smoll, F. L., Smith, R. E., & Gould, D. *A winning philosophy for youth sports programs.* East Lansing, Michigan: Youth Sports Institute, 1981.
Thomas, J. R. (Ed.) *Youth sports guide for coaches and parents.* Washington, D.C.: AAHPERD Publications, 1977.

Competition

Martens, R. *Joy and sadness in children's sport.* Champaign, Illinois: Human Kinetics, 1978.
Nelson, L. L., & Kagan, S. Competition: The star-spangled scramble. *Psychology Today,* 1972, **5**, 53-56, 90-91.
Sherif, C. W. The social context of competition. In D. Landers (Ed.), *Social problems in athletics.* Champaign, Illinois: University of Illinois Press, 1976.

Motivation

Gould, D., & Weiss, M. *Motivating young athletes.* East Lansing, Michigan: Youth Sports Institute, 1980.
Halliwell, W. Intrinsic motivation in sport. In W. F. Straub (Ed.), *Sport psychology: An analysis of athlete behavior.* Ithaca, New York: Mouvement Publications, 1978.
Orlick, T., & Botterill, C. *Every kid can win.* Chicago: Nelson-Hall, 1975.
Roberts, G. C. Children in competition: A theoretical perspective and recommendation for practice. *Motor Skills: Theory Into Practice,* 1980, **4**(1), 37-51.

Weinberg, R. S. Why kids play or do not play organized sports. *Physical Educator*, 1981, **38**(2), 71-76.

Competitive Stress

Gould, D. Psyching-up or psyching-out: Understanding the arousal-performance relationship. In D. Gould & M. Weiss (Eds.), *Motivating young athletes*. East Lansing, Michigan: Youth Sports Institute, 1980.
Passer, M. W. Psychological stress in youth sports. In R. A. Magill, M. J. Ash, & F. L. Smoll (Eds.), *Children in sport*. (2nd ed.) Champaign, Illinois: Human Kinetics, 1982.

Psychosocial Development Through Sport

Feltz, D., & Weiss, M. Developing self-efficacy through sport. *JOPERD*, 1982, **53**(3), 24-26, 36.
Gould, D. Sportsmanship: Building "character" or "characters." In V. Seefeldt, F. L. Smoll, R. E. Smith, & D Gould (Eds.), *A winning philosophy for youth sports programs*. East Lansing, Michigan: Youth Sports Institute, 1981.
Martens, R. Kids' sports: A den of iniquity or land of promise? In R. A. Magill, M. J. Ash, & F. L. Smoll (Eds.), *Children in sport: A contemporary anthology*. Champaign, Illinois: Human Kinetics, 1978.

Graduate Students

General

Gould, D. Sport psychology in the 1980s: Status, direction and challenge in youth sports research. *Journal of Sport Psychology*, 1982, **4**, 203-218.
Magill, R. A., Ash, M. J., & Smoll, F. L. (Eds.) *Children in sport*. (2nd ed.) Champaign, Illinois: Human Kinetics, 1982.
Martens, R. *Joy and sadness in children's sports*. Champaign, Illinois: Human Kinetics, 1978.
McPherson, B. D. The child in competitive sport: Influence of the social milieu. In R. A. Magill, M. J. Ash, & F. L. Smoll (Eds.), *Children in sport*. (2nd ed.) Champaign, Illinois: Human Kinetics, 1982.
Seefeldt, V., & Gould, D. *Physical and psychological effects of athletic competition on children and youth*. Washington, D.C.: ERIC Clearinghouse on Teacher Education, 1980.
Smoll, F. L., & Smith, R. E. *Psychological perspectives in youth sports*. Washington, D.C.: Hemisphere, 1978.

Competition

Scanlan, T. K. Antecedents of competitiveness. In R. A. Magill, M. J. Ash, & F. L. Smoll (Eds.), *Children in sport*. (2nd ed.) Champaign, Illinois: Human Kinetics, 1982.
Scanlan, T. K. Social evaluation: A key developmental element in the competition process. In R. A. Magill, M. J. Ash, & F. L. Smoll (Eds.), *Children in sport*. (2nd ed.) Champaign, Illinois: Human Kinetics, 1982.
Sherif, C. W. The social context of competition. In D. Landers (Ed.), *Social problems in athletics*. Urbana, Illinois: University of Illinois Press, 1976.

Motivation

Dweck, D. Learned helplessness in sport. In C. H. Nadeau, W. R. Halliwell, K. M. Newell, & G. C. Roberts (Eds.), *Psychology of sport and motor behavior—1979*. Champaign, Illinois: Human Kinetics, 1980.
Martens, R. The uniqueness of the young athlete: Psychologic considerations. *The American Journal of Sports Medicine*. 1980, **8**(5), 382-385.
Orlick, T., & Botterill, C. *Every kid can win*. Chicago: Nelson-Hall, 1975.
Passer, M. W. Children in sport: Participation motives and psychological stress. *Quest*, 1981, **33**, 231-234.

Thomas, J. R., Gallagher, J. D., & Thomas, K. T. Developmental memory factors in children's perception of sport. In R. A. Magill, M. J. Ash, & F. L. Smoll (Eds.), *Children in sport*. (2nd ed.) Champaign, Illinois: Human Kinetics, 1982, 219-234.

Weinberg, R. S. Why kids play or do not play organized sports. *Physical Educator*, 1981, **38**(2), 71-76.

Competitive Stress

Passer, M. W. Psychological stress in youth sports. In R. A. Magill, M. J. Ash, & F. L. Smoll (Eds.), *Children in sport*. (2nd ed.) Champaign, Illinois: Human Kinetics, 1982.

Scanlan, T. K., & Passer, M. W. Sources of competitive stress in young female athletes. *Journal of Sport Psychology*, 1979, **1**, 151-159.

Simon, J. A., & Martens, R. Children's anxiety in sport and nonsport evaluative activities. *Journal of Sport Psychology*, 1979, **1**(2), 160-169.

Psychosocial Development Through Sport

Feltz, D., & Weiss, M. Developing self-efficacy through sport. *JOPERD*, 1982, **53**(3), 24-26, 36.

Harter, S. The development of competence motivation in the mastery of cognitive and physical skills: Is there still a place for joy? In G. C. Roberts & D. M. Landers (Eds.), *Psychology of sport and motor behavior—1980*. Champaign, Illinois: Human Kinetics, 1981.

Zaichkowsky, L. D., Zaichkowsky, L. B., & Martinek, T. J. Moral development. In L. D. Zaichkowsky, L. B. Zaichkowsky, & T. J. Martinek (Eds.), *Growth and development*. St. Louis: Mosby, 1980.

12

Improving the Quality of Coach-Player Interaction

Frank L. Smoll
Ronald E. Smith

The two previous chapters focused on participatory patterns in children's sport programs and the psychosocial impact of these programs. Clearly, millions of youngsters have been attracted to organized athletics, and these programs have become firmly entrenched in our social and cultural milieu. Not only has there been tremendously rapid growth in highly structured, adult-supervised athletic programs, but also there is no reason to anticipate a decline. Furthermore, the psychological concomitants of participation are significant factors affecting youngsters' development.

In spite of the establishment of children's sport as a social institution of major import, many critics claim that organized athletics place excessive physical or psychological demands or both on children, and that athletics are conducted primarily to satisfy the self-serving interests of parents and coaches. Devereux (1978) suggests that children would benefit far more if adults simply left them alone to participate in self-organized activities. Our position is that sports are neither universally good nor bad for youngsters. Although some of the criticisms are well founded and constructive, we believe that sport has a strong, positive potential for achieving important educational objectives. Thus, the issue is not whether children's sport should exist—it is inevitable and will continue to grow—but rather how to increase the likelihood of a favorable outcome.

A basic rationale for adult-supervised children's sport is that coaches can play an important role in teaching skills, transmitting desirable values and attitudes, and serving as positive adult models. In fact, virtually unanimous agreement exists that the nature of the relationship between coach and player is a primary determinant of the ways in which children are ultimately affected by their participation in organized athletic programs (Smoll, Smith, and Curtis 1977; Martens 1978; Smith, Smoll, Hunt, Curtis, and Coppel 1979; Seefeldt and Gould 1980). Coaches not only occupy a central position in the athletic setting, but also their influence can extend into other areas of the child's life as well. For example, because of the high frequency of single-parent families, coaches frequently occupy the role of a substitute parent. The manner in which coaches structure the athletic situation, the goal priorities they establish, and the ways in which they relate to their players can markedly influence the likelihood that the outcomes of participation are favorable for children.

Most children receive their first, and in many cases their only, supervised athletic experience in programs that relatively untrained, amateur coaches administer. Because the vast majority of volunteer coaches have positive and desirable motives for coaching (Smith, Smoll, and Curtis 1978; Martens and Gould 1979), we can assume that their limitations as coaches result primarily from both a lack of information and a lack of awareness of how they affect their players. Therefore, our efforts in contributing to the betterment of children's sport have been devoted to the development and assessment of a training program designed to enhance the ability of coaches to relate more effectively to their young athletes. To accomplish this, we completed a two-phase research project over a seven-year period. This chapter thus includes (1) an overview of the Phase I research in which a large-scale study related specific coaching behaviors to players' attitudes toward their coach, teammates, themselves, and other aspects of their sport involvement, and consideration of how characteristics of the children, such as their ages and levels of self-esteem, affected their responses to specific coaching practices, (2) a discussion of our research-derived coaching guidelines, (3) recommendations for enhancing implementation of the guidelines, (4) a description of Phase II, which involved developing and conducting a psychologically oriented training program for coaches and then measuring the ways in which the program affected coaches' behaviors and the sport-related attitudes and self-esteem of youngsters who played for them, and (5) consideration of various avenues for making coach training programs available on a wide-scale basis.

PHASE I: THEORETICAL ORIENTATION AND BASIC RESEARCH

The impetus for our work arose from the fundamental assumption that a training program should be based on empirical evidence rather than on intuition or on what we assume on the basis of athletic folklore. However, at the time our project began, there was no existing scientific foundation on which to base a psychologically oriented training program. Therefore, our approach to developing research-derived behavioral guidelines for coaches was based on the measurement of relationships between antecedents (i.e., coach behaviors) and their consequences.

Conceptual Model and Research Paradigm

Phase I was guided by an information-processing model of coach-player relationships (Smoll, Smith, Curtis, and Hunt 1978), which is schematically presented in the following simplified diagram:

Coach behaviors ⟶ Player perception and recall ⟶ Players' evaluative reactions

A major tenet of this model is that coaching behaviors do not directly affect children's evaluative reactions (attitudes) toward the coach and other aspects of their athletic experience. Rather, players' evaluative reactions are mediated by their perception and recall of the coach's behaviors. In a sense, the youngsters serve as a filter whose cognitive and affective processes mediate between the coach's behaviors and the attitudes and reactions that they ultimately evoke. Therefore, if we wish to understand how coaching behaviors affect players' reactions, we need to take into account the mediating processes that occur in the players.

The research paradigm that the mediational model suggests prompted us to measure and define relationships existing between each of the three major components of the model. Thus, we measured actual coaching behavior, player perception and recall of the behaviors, and the children's affective responses to the total situation. We also measured coaches' recall of their own behavior. This is an important variable, because it indicates the extent to which the coaches are aware of what they do.

Method

Measurement of Coaching Behaviors

The Coaching Behavior Assessment System (CBAS) was developed to permit the direct observation and coding of coaches' behavior during practices and games (Smith, Smoll, and Hunt 1977). Both the measurement approach and the behavioral categories of the CBAS are an outgrowth of social learning theory (Mischel 1973, Goldfried and Sprafkin 1974). The 12 CBAS categories (Table 12.1), though empirically derived, tap behavioral dimensions that have been shown to affect both children and adults in a variety of nonathletic settings (Bales and Slater 1955).

The CBAS was developed over several years. Initially, soccer coaches were observed during practice sessions and games to determine the classes of behaviors that occurred. The observers carried portable tape recorders and essentially recorded an independent play-by-play of the coaches' behaviors using a time-sampling procedure. The behavior descriptions were transcribed, their contents analyzed, and then combined to develop an initial set of scoring categories from which the present system eventually evolved. Subsequent use of the system in observing and coding the behaviors of basketball, baseball, and football coaches indicated that: (1) the scoring system is sufficiently comprehensive to incorporate the vast majority of coaching behaviors, (2) the system can discern individual differences in behavioral patterns, and (3) the coding system can be used easily in field settings.

The CBAS encompasses two major classes of behaviors. *Reactive* behaviors are responses to immediately preceding player or team behaviors, whereas the coach initiates *spontaneous* behaviors, which are not a response to an immediately preceding event. These classes are roughly analogous to the distinction between elicited behaviors (responses to identifiable stimuli) and emitted behaviors (behaviors that do not have clear-cut antecedents). As shown in Table 12.1, reactive behaviors are responses to either desirable performances, mistakes, or misbehaviors on the part of players, while the spontaneous class is subdivided into game-related and game-irrelevant behaviors that the coach initiates. The system thus involves basic interactions between the situation and the coach's behavior. The situation-behavior linkage inherent in the system undoubtedly contributes to the high interobserver reliability that has been obtained.

In using the CBAS, observers station themselves at a point from which they can observe the coach in an unobtrusive manner. Typically, coaches are observed for several games before actual research data are collected in order to reduce possible reactivity effects (i.e., behavioral changes that the presence of an observer causes). Observers do not introduce themselves to the coach, nor do they indicate in any way that they will be observing him. Observations are recorded by writing the behavioral codes (e.g., R, P, TIM) on code sheets designating specific activity intervals (e.g.,

Table 12.1. Response Categories of the Coaching Behavior Assessment System

Class I: Reactive Behaviors	
Responses to desirable performance	
Reinforcement (R)	A positive, rewarding reaction (verbal or nonverbal) to a good play or good effort
Nonreinforcement (NR)	Failure to respond to a good performance
Responses to mistakes	
Mistake-contingent encouragement (EM)	Encouragement given to a player following a mistake
Mistake-contingent technical instruction (TIM)	Instructing or demonstrating to a player how to correct a mistake
Punishment (P)	A negative reaction (verbal or nonverbal) following a mistake
Punitive technical instruction (TIM+P)	Technical instruction following a mistake given in a punitive or hostile manner
Ignoring mistakes (IM)	Failure to respond to a player mistake
Response to misbehavior	
Keeping control (KC)	Reactions intended to restore or maintain order among team members
Class II: Spontaneous Behaviors	
Game related	
General technical instruction (TIG)	Spontaneous instruction in the techniques and strategies of the sport (not following a mistake)
General encouragement (EG)	Spontaneous encouragement that does not follow a mistake
Organization (O)	Administrative behavior that sets the stage for play by assigning, e.g., duties, responsibilities, positions
Game irrelevant	
General communication (GC)	Interactions with players unrelated to the game

half innings, quarters) as the behaviors occur. The CBAS data may be used in a number of ways, including the percentage of behaviors across all observations (games) falling within each coding category and the rate of behaviors in each category per unit time. We have found the percentage measure to be more useful when studying baseball coaches and the rate per unit time more useful in basketball studies.

Research has shown that well-trained observers can achieve high levels of reliability among their ratings when using the CBAS; reliability coefficients ranging from the high .80s to the mid .90s are typically obtained (Smith et al. 1977). The 31 trained undergraduates who served as observers in the Phase I study exhibited a high degree of accuracy (M = 97.8% agreement with expert scoring) in coding videotaped samples of coaching behavior, and assessment of reliability among raters in field settings yielded a mean reliability coefficient of .88.

The Phase I research involved 51 male coaches in three Little League Baseball programs in Seattle. With his written consent, each coach was observed and his behaviors coded during at least three games ($M = 3.96$ games). An average of 1122 behaviors were coded for each coach during the course of the season, thus permitting the development of a behavioral profile for each coach.

Measuring perceptions and attitudes. Several self-report measures were developed to assess coaches' beliefs, attitudes, and perceptions. These were combined into a questionnaire that the coaches completed at the end of the season. Coaches' self-perception of their behaviors was of primary importance. This was assessed by describing and giving examples of the 12 CBAS behaviors and asking coaches to indicate on a seven-point scale—ranging from "almost never" to "almost always"—how often they engaged in the behaviors in the situations described.

The children's data were collected at the end of the season in personal interviews that lasted approximately 30 min. A total of 542 players (ages 8 to 15 years) were interviewed, representing 83% of the youngsters who played for the 51 coaches. Among the data collected during the interviews were the children's perceptions and recall of how their coach behaved, and their evaluative reactions to him and to other aspects of their organized athletic experience. To measure perception and recall of the coach's behavior, the player was given a verbal description and examples of each of the 12 CBAS behaviors and then indicated how frequently his coach engaged in each behavior on a seven-point scale ranging from "never" to "almost always." A series of questions was also presented to the child to provide measures of the player's attitudes toward the coach, toward teammates, and toward the athletic experience as a whole. These questions included specific queries on how much the child liked the sport of baseball, how much the child enjoyed playing for the coach, how much he would like to play for the coach again, how well the players on the team got along with one another, and other questions of a similar nature. Finally, the child completed several personality measures, including measures of athletic and general self-esteem (a modified form of the Coopersmith [1967] inventory). This permitted a determination of the role of personality variables in children's reactions to particular kinds of coaching behaviors as well as assessment of postseason differences in these measures for children exposed to different kinds of coaches.

Results

In Phase I, we determined what coaches were doing, what they thought they had done, what the children thought the coaches had done, and how the children felt about their experience and about themselves. These variables were analyzed as a total system, and clear-cut relationships were found between coaching behaviors and children's perceptions and attitudes. Our focus in this section is on results that bear most directly on the intervention program designed to assist coaches in creating more positive athletic experiences for youngsters. A more complete presentation of results appears elsewhere (Smith et al. 1978).

Coaches' Behaviors and Self-Perceptions

Examination of the distribution of behaviors within the CBAS categories indicated that the rates per 100 behaviors for general technical instruction, general encouragement, and reinforcement were 27.3, 21.4, and 17.1, respectively. The next highest rates occurred for organization (8.4%) and general communication (6.1%). Nearly two-thirds of the behaviors fell within the three instructional and supportive categories. By way of contrast, the frequency of punitive behaviors was relatively low in comparison with other categories (punishment, 1.8% and punitive technical instruction, 1.0%), but about 20% of the observed mistakes were responded to with either punishment or punitive technical instruction.

An important issue concerns the degree of accuracy with which coaches perceive their own behavior. Correlations between CBAS-observed behaviors and coaches' ratings of how frequently they performed the behaviors were generally low and nonsignificant. The only significant correlation occurred for punishment (r = .45). Thus, self-perceptions of coaches show correspondence with externally observed behaviors only for punitive behaviors. Coaches apparently have limited awareness of how frequently they engage in other forms of behavior.

Player Perceptions of Coaching Behaviors

Correlations between the mean behavioral ratings of each team and the observed CBAS behaviors of the 51 coaches yielded significant coefficients for punishment (r = .54), punitive technical instruction (r = .45), mistake-contingent technical instruction (r = .45), mistake-contingent encouragement (r = .31), and general communication (r = .26). None of the coefficients for the other categories exceeded .20. Thus, players most accurately perceived punitive behaviors, reactions to mistakes, and game-irrelevant communicative behaviors of the coaches.

Correlations between players' perceptions of their coaches' behaviors and the coaches' self-perceptions were low and generally nonsignificant. The highest correlation again occurred for punishment (r = .26), but the relationship was even lower than when the coaches' self-ratings of their behavior were correlated with the CBAS punishment score. Clearly, there was little correspondence between the way coaches viewed themselves and how their players perceived them. Indeed, the players' perceptions tended to be more accurate in that they correlated more highly with CBAS-observed scores. The potential importance of increasing coaches' awareness of how they behave was thus determined to be a key to changing their behaviors.

Observed Behaviors and Player Attitudes

As shown above, our data provide little support for the charges of children's sport critics that coaches engage in highly frequent hostile and punitive behaviors. In fact, we have found that rewarding and encouraging responses are far more common. Perhaps this is one reason why the overwhelming majority of the children interviewed expressed favorable attitudes toward their coaches. Fewer than 7% of the players evaluated their coach below the neutral points ("neither like nor dislike") on either liking for the coach or desire to play for him again. This does not mean that unfortunate coaching practices do not exist, but it does suggest that the vast majority of coaches related to their players in a favorable manner.

Factor analysis of the CBAS behaviors indicated that the observed behaviors were patterned along meaningful dimensions. We therefore compared the attitudes of children who played for coaches whose behavioral profiles were at extreme ends of the behavioral dimensions. The results indicated that coaches oriented toward technical instruction were evaluated more positively than were coaches who engaged in more general encouragement and general communication. Players who played for the technically instructive coaches also evaluated their teammates and the sport more positively. Furthermore, coaches scoring high on the supportive behaviors of reinforcement and mistake-contingent encouragement were evaluated more positively by their players. Finally, players evaluated their teammates and the sport more positively if they played for coaches who gave high levels of reinforcement and support.

Coaching Behavior and Children's Self-Esteem

The results of the behavioral data clearly indicated that coaches who fell at the technically instructive and supportive ends of the statistically independent behavioral dimensions were evaluated more favorably by their players. In addition, other analyses showed that players with low self-esteem were affected more by differences on these coaching behavior dimensions than were players higher in general self-esteem.

Also of interest were relationships between coaching behaviors and players' self-esteem scores obtained after the season ended. On the instructional behavioral dimension, a significantly lower mean self-esteem rating of baseball ability was found for players for the technically instructive coaches, but no difference was found in general self-esteem. Apparently, an emphasis on technical instruction makes players more aware of their skill limitations than does a nontechnical orientation.

The reinforcement-support coaching dimension was unrelated to postseason baseball self-esteem, but a significant difference was found in general self-esteem scores. Youngsters who played for coaches who gave high levels of reinforcement and mistake-contingent encouragement had higher general self-esteem scores at the end of the season. While the absence of preseason measures precluded the assessment of self-esteem changes over the season, the fact that player assignment to teams was a basically random process suggests the possibility that certain coaching behaviors may affect levels of self-esteem. These data provided the first evidence linking coaching behaviors to children's self-esteem.

Player-Perceived Behaviors and Attitudes Toward Coaches

The correlations between the players' perceptions of their coaches' behaviors and their subsequent attitudes were generally much higher than were the observed behavior-attitude relationships. This finding is consistent with the mediational model, in that players' evaluative reactions to their coaches' behaviors were indeed mediated by cognitive and perceptual processes. More specifically, significant positive correlations were found for both technical instruction and both of the encouragement categories, while punishment and punitive technical instruction correlated negatively with measures of attraction toward the coach.

Another analysis indicated that the best-liked coaches were rated as giving more frequent reinforcement, mistake-contingent encouragement, general encouragement, and mistake-contingent technical instruction, and as engaging in more organization and keeping control behaviors. The least popular coaches were rated as more frequently engaging in punishment and punitive technical instruction following mistakes. Thus, the relationships between player-perceived coach behaviors and attraction toward the coach are substantial and meaningful.

The Role of Winning

A somewhat surprising finding was that the team's won-lost record was essentially unrelated to how well preadolescent children liked the coach and how strongly they desired to play for the coach in the future. In discussing this result with coaches, many believe that their personal popularity hinges on their won-lost record. Our data indicate that how the coach relates to players is far more important than the won-lost record. Another interesting finding related to winning was that players on winning teams thought that their parents liked the coach more and that the coach liked them more than did players on losing teams. This is an interesting commentary on children's perceptions of adult values; winning made little difference to the children, but they knew that it was important to the adults. Winning assumes greater importance beyond age 12, although it continues to account for less attitudinal variance than coaches' behaviors.

GUIDELINES FOR RELATING EFFECTIVELY TO CHILD ATHLETES

The data obtained in Phase I provided some initial scientific information on coach-player relationships. From this empirical data base, we derived behavioral guidelines designed to help coaches relate more effectively to child athletes. The series of coaching dos and don'ts are based primarily on (1) a conception of success, or winning, as consisting of giving maximum effort (Smoll and Smith 1981) and (2) a positive approach to social influence that involves the use of reinforcement and encouragement while discouraging the use of punishment and criticism (Smoll et al. 1977, Smoll and Smith 1979).

A Healthy Philosophy of Winning

An important issue requiring clarification is the distinction between youth and professional models of sport. Children's sport is believed to provide an educational medium for the development of desirable psychosocial characteristics, such as cooperation, independence, leadership, sportsmanship, achievement motivation, self-assertiveness, and coping skills. These programs are viewed as miniature life situations in which children can learn to cope with realities they will face in later life. Furthermore, participation in organized sport programs affords opportunities for continued refinement and expansion of the child's motor skills as well as for promoting health and fitness. Thus, children's sport provides a setting within which an educational process can occur. On the other hand, professional sport constitutes a huge commercial enterprise in which financial success is paramount. Such success depends heavily on a product orientation, namely, winning. Thus, the notion of sport for education versus sport as part of the entertainment industry constitutes different philosophies.

The conventional concept of success in sport involves achieving a victorious outcome. Unfortunately, some children's coaches get caught up in a "winning is everything" philosophy, and may temporarily lose sight of other important objectives and values of their program. This is not to say that coaches should not try to build winning teams, but that sometimes winning becomes more important to the coach than it is to the players. When winning games becomes the sole or primary goal in children's sport, youngsters can be deprived of important opportunities to develop their skills, to enjoy participation, and to grow as people.

In light of the educational potential of sport, we believe that children can learn from both winning and losing. For this to occur, winning must be placed in a *healthy* perspective. We have therefore developed a four-part philosophy of winning designed to maximize young athletes' enjoyment of sport and their chances for deriving the positive benefits of participation:

1. *Winning is not everything, nor is it the only thing*. Young athletes cannot possibly learn from winning and losing if they think the only objective is to beat their opponents. Although winning is an important goal, it is not the most important objective. Children should leave a program having enjoyed the relationships with their coach and teammates, feeling better about themselves, having improved their skills, and looking forward to

future sport participation. When this happens, something far more important has been accomplished than a winning record or a league championship.

2. *Failure is not the same thing as losing*. Players should not view losing as a sign of failure or as a threat to their personal value. Children should be taught that losing a game is not a reflection of their own self-worth.
3. *Success is not synonymous with winning*. Thus, neither success nor failure need depend on the outcome of a contest or on a won-lost record. Winning and losing pertain to the outcome of a contest, whereas success and failure do not.
4. *Children should be taught that success is found in striving for victory.* The important concept is that success is related to effort. In presenting a *Bill of Rights for Young Athletes*, Martens and Seefeldt (1979) stated that "children do not have a right to success in sports—this must be earned. They do have a right to an equal opportunity to *strive* for success." The only thing players have complete control over is the amount of effort they give. They have only limited control over the outcome that is achieved. Youngsters should be taught that they are never "losers" if they give maximum effort.

A major source of athletic stress is fear of failure. Knowing that making mistakes or losing a game while giving maximum effort is acceptable to the coach removes an important source of pressure from the child. Moreover, coaches who apply this same standard of "success" to themselves are less likely to define their own adequacy in terms of their won-lost record, and are more likely to focus on the more important children's sport goals of participation, skill development, and just plain fun. They are also less likely to experience stress of their own when their teams are not winning. When winning is kept in perspective, the child comes first and winning is second (Martens and Seefeldt 1979). In this case, the most important coaching product is not a won-lost record—it is the quality of the experience provided for the players.

Behavioral Guidelines

Tharp and Gallimore (1976) reported a behavioral analysis of former UCLA basketball coach John Wooden, and used the data as a basis for recommendations for teachers. Similarly, although our focus is on coaching, the principles presented here can be applied in any leadership situation, particularly those involving teaching motor skills to youngsters.

Like other kinds of human interaction, coaching and teaching involve people trying to influence others in desired ways. The key distinction made within our behavioral guidelines is that of *positive* versus *negative* approaches to influencing behavior. The positive approach entails the use of reinforcement and encouragement in an attempt to strengthen desired behaviors and motivate players to perform them. The negative approach uses various forms of punishment in an attempt to eliminate undesirable behaviors. The motivating factor here is fear, and we believe that the negative approach produces stress, decreases enjoyment of the sport situation, and produces dislike for the coach.

Reacting to Player Behaviors and Game Situations

Good plays—using "reinforcement power." Our concern with influencing players' behavior in a desirable way involves the process of learning. *Learning* refers to a relatively permanent change in behavior that occurs as a result of experience, that is, behavior changes that result from interaction with the environment, excluding change brought about from maturation, fatigue, drugs, and the like. The three major types of learning are classical conditioning, instrumental or operant conditioning, and observational learning (modeling) (Smith, Sarason, and Sarason 1982). According to the law of effect, which is the cornerstone of operant conditioning, people tend to repeat behaviors that produce positive outcomes and not to repeat those that produce neutral or negative results. In this context, reinforcement refers to any event occurring after a behavior that affects the probability that the behavior will occur in the future. In other words, positive reinforcement is any stimulus or event that increases the frequency of a behavior it follows, or more exactly, on which it is made contingent. Examples of positive reinforcement within the behavioral repertoire of coaches include both verbal praise and nonverbal forms of communication, such as a pat on the back, a smile, clapping, and a friendly nod. Although the term *reward* is often used as if it were synonymous with positive reinforcement, in many instances material rewards (e.g., candy, trophies, money) do not serve to strengthen behavior.

1. *Be liberal with reinforcement.* In our Phase I research, the single most important difference between coaches to whom players responded most favorably and those to whom they responded least favorably was the frequency with which they reinforced desirable behaviors. Reinforcement should not be restricted to learning and performance of sport skills. Rather, it should also be liberally applied to strengthen desirable psychosocial behaviors (e.g., teamwork, leadership, sportsmanship). Coaches should look for positive things, and reinforce them, so that they will increase. We are not advocating a sickeningly sweet approach with which there is a danger of losing credibility. When sincerely given, reinforcement does not spoil youngsters—it gives them something to strive for.
2. *Have realistic expectations and consistently reinforce achievement.* Expectations should be geared to individual ability levels. For some players, merely running up and down the field or court without tripping is a significant accomplishment deserving of praise. For those who are more skilled, expectations should be set at appropriately higher levels.

   The principle concerning consistency of reinforcement is particularly true during the early part of the learning process. When new skills are being taught, continuous reinforcement (i.e., reinforcement after each desired response) should be given. More specifically, during the initial stages of learning, continuous reinforcement should be given for any sign of improvement or progress toward the ultimate objective. However, once skills are well-learned, a partial reinforcement schedule is more effective in maintaining motivation and producing higher resistance to extinction (i.e., gradual disappearance of a learned response that occurs when there is no reinforcement). A variable schedule of partial reinforcement is most effective. This means that reinforcement is neither given after a fixed number of responses or after a fixed time interval. In variable schedules, the required number of responses or the time interval varies around an average. The selective administration of reinforcement thus requires thorough knowledge of sport skills teaching-learning progressions, sensitivity to individual differences in players' levels of abilities and learning rates, and use of good judgment in applying reinforcement.
3. *Give reinforcement to desirable behavior as soon as it occurs.* Immediate reinforcement is more potent in its effects than is delayed reinforcement, but even delayed reinforcement is better than none at all.
4. *Reinforce effort as much as results.* This guideline has direct relevance to developing a healthy philosophy of winning. To put this philosophy into practice, coaches should tell

players that their efforts are valued and appreciated and support the verbalization with action (i.e., reinforcement). Players' efforts should not be ignored or taken for granted. As stated earlier, players have complete control over how much effort they make, but they have only limited control over the outcome of their efforts. By looking for and reinforcing players' efforts, adult leaders can thereby encourage players to continue or increase their output.

Reacting to mistakes. Many athletes are motivated to achieve because of a positive desire to succeed. They appear to welcome pressure and to peak under it. Unfortunately, many others are motivated primarily by fear of failure, and consequently they dread critical game situations and the possibility of failure and disapproval. Fear of failure can harm performance, and it detracts from the enjoyment of competing. We believe that the manner in which coaches react to players' mistakes can play a prominent role in either creating or combating fear of failure.

A typical attitude about mistakes is that they are totally bad and must be avoided at all costs. Rather than focusing on the negative aspects of mistakes, coaches must recognize that mistakes are not only inevitable but also that they have a positive side. Mistakes should be viewed as the *stepping stones to achievement* in that they provide the information necessary to help improve performance. By communicating this concept to players in word and action, coaches can help players to accept and learn from their mistakes. In addition, coaches should deal honestly and openly with their own mistakes. When a coach has the confidence and courage to admit to players that she made a mistake, this provides a valuable model conducive to developing a sense of tolerance for human error and ultimately to reducing fear of failure. The positive approach is designed to create positive motives to achieve rather than fears of failure.

1. *Give encouragement immediately after a mistake.* Players know when they make a poor play and often feel embarrassed about it. This is the time they are in most need of encouragement and support from their coach.
2. *If the player knows how to correct the mistake, encouragement alone is sufficient.* Telling a player what he already knows may be more irritating than helpful, and coaches should not overload athletes with unnecessary input. If the coach is not sure if the player knows how to correct the mistake, she should ask the athlete for verification.
3. *When appropriate, give corrective instruction after a mistake, but always do so in an encouraging and positive way.* In line with the positive approach, mistakes can be golden opportunities to provide corrective instruction. Three keys to giving mistake-contingent technical instruction include knowing (1) *what* to do—the technical aspects of correcting performance, (2) *how* to do it—the teaching-learning approach, and (3) *when* to do it—timing. Many players respond best to immediate correction, and instruction is particularly meaningful at that time. However, some players respond much better to instruction if the coach waits for some time after the mistake when the player can respond in a more objective fashion.

   When correcting mistakes, a three-part instructional approach is recommended: (1) Start with a *compliment* (e.g., "Way to hustle. You really ran a good pattern!"). This is intended to reinforce a desirable behavior and create a respective attitude on the part of the player. (2) Give the *future-oriented instruction* (e.g., "If you follow the ball all the way into your hands, you'll catch those just like a pro does"). Emphasize the desired positive outcome rather than the negative one that just occurred. (3) End with another *positive* statement (e.g., "Hang in there. You're going to get even better if you work hard at it!"). This "sandwich" approach (two positive communications wrapped around the instruction) is designed to make the player positively self-motivated to perform correctly rather than negatively motivated to avoid failure and disapproval.

4. *Do not punish when things go wrong.* Punishment is any consequence that decreases the future occurrence of a behavior that it follows. Punishment can be administered in either of two forms: (1) by doing something adverse such as painful physical contact or verbal reprimands and (2) by taking something that is valued away from the player, or more technically, by removing positive reinforcers that are customarily available to an individual such as privileges, social interactions, or possessions. With respect to the first form, in a sport context, punishment is not just yelling at players; it can be any form of disapproval, tone of voice, or action. Constant use of this form of punishment leads to resentment of the coach and is a probable factor contributing to the athletic dropout rate.

   Distinguishing between punishment and negative reinforcement is important. In operant conditioning, negative reinforcement is anything that serves to increase a behavior that results in its removal. Thus, negative reinforcement increases a response that enables an individual to escape or avoid the reinforcer, whereas punishment simply decreases the response on which it is contingent (Smith, Sarason, and Sarason 1982).
5. *Do not give corrective instruction in a hostile or punitive way.* Although a coach may have good intentions in giving instruction, this kind of negative communication is more likely to increase frustration and create resentment than to improve performance.

Misbehaviors, lack of attention—maintaining order and discipline. Problems of player misbehavior during games and practices can indeed become serious. In dealing effectively with this, coaches should recognize that youngsters want clearly defined limits and structure. They do not like unpredictability and inconsistency, nor do they like it when a coach plays the role of a policeman or enforcer. Thus, the objective is to structure the situation in a way that the coach can avoid having to use the CBAS behavior category of keeping control.

1. *Maintain order by establishing clear expectations and a "team rule" concept.*
2. *Involve players in formulating behavioral guidelines and work to build team unity in achieving them.*
3. *Strive to achieve a balance between freedom and structure.*

   These guidelines promote a cooperative approach to leadership in that players are given a share of the responsibility for determining their own governance. The rationale for this approach is that people are more willing to live by rules (1) when they have a hand in formulating them and (2) when they have made a public commitment to abide by them. Considerable empirical support for this rationale exists in the social psychology literature.

   Team rules should be developed early in the season. In helping players to share responsibility for formulating rules, the coach should (1) explain why team rules are necessary (e.g., they keep things organized and efficient, thereby increasing the chances of achieving individual and team objectives), (2) explain why the team rules should be something that they can agree on as a group (e.g., they are their rules, and it is their responsibility to follow them), (3) solicit suggestions and ideas, and listen to what players say to show that their ideas and feelings are valued, (4) incorporate players' input into a reasonable set of rules (they should provide structure and yet not be too rigid), and

(5) discuss the kinds of penalties that will be used for breaking of team rules (here again, players should participate in determining the consequences to follow rule violations). The advantage of this approach is that it places the responsibility where it belongs—on the players themselves. Thus, when someone breaks a team rule, it is not the individual's versus the coach's rules, but the breaking of their own rules.

4. *Emphasize that during a game, all members of the team are part of the game, even those on the bench.* This rule can play an important role in building team cohesion and mutual support among teammates.
5. *Use reinforcement to strengthen team participation and unity.* By strengthening desirable behaviors, coaches can help to prevent misbehaviors from occurring. In other words, coaches can prevent misbehaviors by using the positive approach to strengthen their opposites.

Dealing with team rule violations requires that the coach do the following:

1. *Allow the player to explain her actions.* There may be a reasonable cause for what the player did or did not do, and lines of communication should be kept open.
2. *Be consistent and impartial.* In other words, avoid showing favoritism by treating *all* players equally and fairly.
3. *Do not express anger and a punitive attitude.*
4. *Do not lecture or embarrass the player.*
5. *Focus on the fact that a team policy has been broken, placing the responsibility on the player.* This should be done without degrading the individual. The coach should simply remind the player that a rule was violated that he had agreed to follow, and because of that, a penalty must be paid. This focuses the responsibility where it belongs—on the player—and helps to build a sense of personal accountability and responsibility.
6. *When giving penalties, it is best to deprive children of something they value.* For example, participation can be suspended temporarily by having the player sit off to the side ("time out").
7. *Do not use physical measures that could become adverse by being used to punish (e.g., running laps, doing push-ups).* To have beneficial physical activities become unpleasant because they have been used as punishment is not educationally sound.

Spontaneous, Self-Initiated Coaching Behaviors

Getting positive things to happen demands that the coach encourage the players in certain ways.

1. *Set a good example of behavior.* Observational learning (modeling), which is based on watching and imitating others, is a particularly important form of learning for children. Most players have a high regard for their coach, and consequently they are likely to emulate their coach's behaviors and deal with sport situations in similar ways. Players probably learn as much from what their coach does as from what she says. Because of this, coaches should portray a role model worthy of respect from players, officials, parents, and other coaches as well.
2. *Encourage effort and do not demand results.* This is another guideline that is pertinent to the healthy philosophy of winning. Most young athletes are already motivated to develop

their skills and play well. By appropriate use of encouragement, a coach can help to increase their natural enthusiasm. If, however, youngsters are encouraged to strive for unrealistic standards of achievement, they may feel like failures when they do not reach the goals. Therefore, coaches should base encouragement on reasonable expectations. Again, encouraging effort rather than outcome can help to avoid problems.

3. *In giving encouragement, be selective so that it is meaningful.* In other words, coaches should be supportive without acting like cheerleaders.
4. *Never give encouragement or instruction in a sarcastic or degrading manner.* Even if a coach does not intend the sarcasm to be malicious, youngsters sometimes do not understand the meaning or intent of this type of communication. They think that the coach is amusing others at their expense, resulting in irritation or frustration or both.
5. *Encourage players to be supportive of each other, and reinforce them when they do so.* Encouragement can become contagious and contribute to building team cohesion. Coaches should communicate the enthusiasm they feel, which then carries over to their players. The best way to do this is by presenting an enthusiastic coaching model.

Creating a good learning atmosphere. Young athletes expect their coaches to help them satisfy their desire to become as skilled as possible. Therefore, coaches must establish their teaching role as early as possible. In doing this, they should emphasize the fun and learning parts of sport, and let their players know that a primary coaching goal is to help athletes develop their athletic potential.

Individual attention is another essential component of a positive learning environment. During each practice or game, every youngster should be recognized at least once. Those players who usually get the most recognition are the stars or those who are causing problems. Average players need attention as well. A good technique is for coaches occasionally to keep a count of how often they talk with each player to make sure that their personal contact is being appropriately distributed.

1. *Always give instruction positively.* Coaches should emphasize the good things that happen if players do things right rather than focusing on the negative things that occur if they do not. As we noted earlier, this approach motivates players to make desirable things happen rather than building fears of making mistakes.
2. *When giving instructions, be clear and concise.* Young athletes have a short attention span, and in addition, they may not be able to comprehend the technical aspects of skill performance in great detail. Coaches should therefore provide simple yet accurate teaching cues, using as little verbalization as possible.
3. *Show players the correct technique.* Coaches should demonstrate or model skills being taught. If they cannot perform the skill correctly, they can use accomplished players for demonstration purposes. A proper teaching sequence to follow includes (1) introducing a skill via demonstration, (2) providing a verbal explanation that is clear and concise, and (3) having the players actively practice the skill. Because of the way in which children respond to instructional efforts, the following Chinese proverb applies: "I hear and I forget. I see and I remember. I do and I understand."
4. *Be patient and do not expect or demand more than maximum effort.* Acquisition of sport skills does not occur overnight. The gradual learning process is characterized by both overt manifestations of improvement and plateaus in which change is not readily dis-

cernible. Not only must coaches be persistent but also players must be convinced to persevere and continue to give their best.

When an athlete has had a poor practice or a rough game, the youngster should not go home feeling bad, but should get some kind of support from the coach—a pat on the back, a kind word (e.g., "Hey, we're going to work that out. Everyone has days like that sometimes."). Players should not leave feeling alienated from the coach or feeling like a loser.

5. *Reinforce effort and progress.* Again, the foundation of the positive approach is the extensive administration of reinforcement for effort as well as for desirable motor performance and psychosocial behavior.

RECOMMENDATIONS FOR ENHANCING IMPLEMENTATION OF THE COACHING GUIDELINES

Although the guidelines presented above are rather basic, a thorough understanding of them is a prerequisite for their effective use. In addition, several issues concerning communication skills and self-awareness are germane to the successful implementation of the guidelines.

Communicating Effectively

Everything we do communicates something to others. Because of this, coaches should develop the habit of asking themselves (and, at times, their players) how their actions are being interpreted, and then evaluate if they are communicating what they intended.

Effective communication is a two-way street. By keeping the lines of interaction open, coaches can be more aware of opportunities to have a positive impact on players. Fostering two-way communication does not mean that players are free to be disrespectful toward the coach. Rather, it is an open invitation for players to express their views (both positive and negative) with the assurance that they will be heard. Furthermore, by presenting a model of an attentive listener, coaches can hope to improve the listening skills of their players.

Effective communication also is based on viewing a team as made up of unique individuals, and then responding to them accordingly. For example, a youngster who has low self-confidence may be devastated (or positively affected) by something that has no impact whatever on a player with high self-esteem. By improving their sensitivity to the individual needs of their players, coaches can be more successful. The ability to read players and respond to their needs is characteristic of effective youth coaches.

Increasing Self-Awareness and Compliance with the Guidelines

An important aspect of self-awareness pertains to insight into how we behave and come across to others—knowing what we do and how others perceive what we do. One of the striking findings from our Phase I research was that coaches had limited awareness of how frequently they behaved in various ways. Indeed, players' perceptions of their coaches' behaviors were more accurate than the self-ratings that the coaches made. Thus, for successful implementation of coaching guidelines, attempts should be made to increase both the coaches' awareness of what they are doing and their motivation to comply with the behavioral guidelines. Two behavioral change techniques are recommended in this regard, namely, behavioral feedback and self-monitoring (Smoll and Smith 1980).

Of the two procedures, *behavioral feedback* is clearly the more difficult to implement. This procedure requires that a means be developed for assessing overt behaviors and transmitting them to the coach. Although it is highly desirable to obtain unobtrusive behavioral ratings as a basis for feedback (which was actually done in our Phase II research described below), this is often impossible because of practical considerations. As an alternative, developing procedures that allow coaches to obtain feedback from their assistants appears possible. Coaches can be encouraged to work with assistants as a team and share descriptions of each others' behaviors. They can then discuss alternate ways of dealing with difficult situations and players, and prepare themselves for dealing with similar situations in the future. This requires an open relationship between coaches, a willingness to exchange feedback that may not always be positive, and a sincere desire to improve the ways in which they relate to children. Other feedback procedures include soliciting input from the players themselves, and provision of feedback by a league committee.

Self-monitoring (systematically observing and recording one's own behavior) can not only be an effective procedure for increasing self-awareness of behaviors and their antecedents and consequences but also may be an effective behavior-changing procedure in itself (Kazdin 1974, Thoresen and Mahoney 1974). A self-monitoring form should be easy to complete and done regularly after practices and games to achieve optimal results. Furthermore, self-monitoring should be restricted to desired behaviors in light of evidence that tracking of undesired behaviors can be detrimental to effective self-regulation (Gottman and McFall 1972, Cavior and Marabotto 1976, Kirschenbaum and Karoly 1977). A sample form is presented in Figure 12.1. Besides increasing their awareness of what they are doing, completing the form is also a means of reminding coaches of recommended behaviors.

PHASE II: TESTING A PSYCHOLOGICALLY ORIENTED COACH TRAINING PROGRAM

The guidelines presented above are the heart of a three-hour training program that we call Coach Effectiveness Training (CET). We thought it was important not only to develop CET on the

Complete this form as soon as possible after a practice or game. Not only think about what you did but also consider the kinds of situations in which the actions occurred and the kinds of players who were involved.

1. Approximately what percentage of the time they occurred did you respond to good players with reinforcement? ____________.
2. Approximately what percentage of the time they occurred did you respond to mistakes or errors with each of the following communications?
   A. Encouragement only ____________.
   B. Corrective instruction given in an encouraging manner ____________.
   (sum of A plus B should not exceed 100%)
3. About how many times did you reinforce players for effort, complying with team rules, encouraging teammates, showing "team spirit," and other behaviors? ________.
4. Might you do anything differently if you had a chance to coach this practice or game again? If so, briefly explain. ______________________________
____.

Figure 12.1. A brief form for self-monitoring of desirable coaching behaviors.

basis of sound evidence but also to measure its effects on coaches and the youngsters who play for them. In Phase II of our research project, we attempted to modify coaching behaviors and evaluated the success of the intervention program.

Method

Thirty-one Little League Baseball coaches were randomly assigned to an experimental (training) group or to a no-treatment control group. All of the coaches were involved in a program for children between 10 and 15 years of age. The experimental group coaches participated in a preseason CET program designed to assist them in relating more effectively to children. The intervention program was conceptualized within a cognitive-behavioral framework (cf. Bandura 1977). Behavioral guidelines were presented both verbally and in written materials given to the coaches. The verbal presentation was supplemented with actual demonstrations of how to behave in desirable ways (i.e., modeling).

In addition to the information modeling portion of the CET program, behavioral feedback and self-monitoring procedures were employed to increase the coaches' self-awareness and to encourage compliance with the coaching guidelines. These methods, singly and in combination, have proved to be effective behavioral change procedures in a variety of intervention contexts (Gottman and McFall 1972, McFall and Twentyman 1973, Edelstein and Eisler 1976). To provide behavioral feedback, 16 observers trained in the use of the CBAS observed experimental group coaches for two complete games. Behavioral profiles for each coach were derived from these observations and were then mailed to the coaches so that they were able to see the distribution of their own behaviors. Also, coaches were given brief self-monitoring forms that they completed immediately after the first ten games of the season. On these forms, they indicated approximately what percentage of the time they engaged in the recommended guideline behaviors in relevant situations.

The effects of the experimental CET program were measured by essentially repeating the Phase I procedures. Behavioral profiles were developed by observing experimental and control coaches during four complete games. At the end of the season, a total of 325 players were interviewed to obtain player data—82% of those who played for the experimental and control coaches. The experimental and control coaches were then compared on all of the behavioral and player measures.

Results

On both behavioral measures and in players' perceptions of their coaches' behaviors, the trained coaches differed from the controls in a manner consistent with the behavioral guidelines. They gave more reinforcement and encouragement and were less punitive than the controls. The behavioral differences were reflected in their players' attitudes as well, despite the fact that the average won-lost records of the two groups of coaches were quite similar. Trained coaches were liked better and were rated as better teachers of baseball skills, and players on their teams liked one another more. Perhaps more importantly, children who played for the trained coaches exhibited a significant increase in general self-esteem as compared with scores obtained a year earlier; control group children did not show such an increase. Finally, the greatest differences in players' attitudes toward trained as opposed to control coaches were found among children with low self-esteem. This was also encouraging, since the child with low self-esteem is probably in greatest need of a positive athletic experience. Such children apparently respond favorably to coaches who adopt the guidelines, and they exhibit an increase in their feelings of self-worth (Smith, Smoll, and Curtis 1979).

With respect to the psychological concomitants of children's sport, the results obtained from the experimental training program indicated that coaches can be trained to relate more effectively to their players. Measures of player performance were not among the dependent variables included in our research. However, other behavioral investigations have shown that reinforcement that was systematically applied in sport settings resulted in enhanced skill acquisition and performance. Specifically, dramatic improvements in performance have been reported for youth and adult athletes (football, gymnastics, tennis, and swimming) whose coaches applied procedures emphasizing manipulation of reinforcement contingencies and the systematic use of corrective instruction and feedback (Rushall 1975, Komaki and Barnett 1977, Allison and Ayllon 1980).

Future Directions

CET began with Little League Baseball, but is now being offered for other sports as well. Workshops have been presented to soccer, football, basketball, bowling, swimming, wrestling, and hockey coaches. Our experience in offering CET has shown that most coaches not only are committed to providing a positive experience for youngsters but also are willing to spend time to acquire additional information and to take advantage of workshops. Coaches in youth organizations such as the Boys' and Girls' Clubs, the YMCA, the United States Soccer Federation, and the Catholic Youth Organization are participating in CET.

Because of the ever-expanding nature of organized children's sport and because most programs are staffed with untrained volunteers, the need for training programs is obvious. Likewise, the large turnover rate in coaches from year to year ensures a continuing need. Canada, England, Australia, and other countries have national delivery systems for training coaches at all levels of amateur sport. Unfortunately, this is not the case in the United States. However, if the need for large-scale dissemination is to be met, the number of competent trainers must be increased. A realistic and promising approach is to train children's sport administrators at the local level to conduct highly structured coach-training programs.

This approach has been taken in the American Coaching Effectiveness Program (ACEP) (Martens 1981), which was developed under the auspices of the Office of Youth Sports at the University of Illinois. The ACEP curriculum consists of a sport-specific part that is designed to help coaches understand (1) how to teach the basic skills of the sport in an appropriate learning sequence, (2) the basic strategy of the sport and how to teach the strategy appropriate to the skill level and age of the athletes, and (3) the rules of the sport and how to officiate. The sports medicine part of the curriculum helps coaches to understand (1) a philosophy of coaching—coaching objectives and a philosophy of winning, (2) sport psychology—communication and motivation techniques, (3) sport pedagogy—planning and teaching sport skills and strategy, (4) sport physiology—conditioning, nutrition, and weight control, and (5) sports medicine—prevention, treatment, and rehabilitation of athletic injuries. Although the ACEP instructional staff is available to conduct workshops for local programs, a major goal is to teach children's sport administrators to conduct coaching workshops. At an ACEP leadership seminar, administrators are provided with the knowledge and resources (e.g., instructor's manuals and films) necessary to return to their own community and conduct coach-training programs. A similar educational model has been adopted by the Youth Sports Institute at Michigan State University. Such efforts may greatly enhance the dissemination of coach-training programs, the need for which is becoming increasingly urgent.

SUMMARY

In this chapter, we described the major procedures and results of a research and intervention program conducted in a naturalistic setting. It is an example of the manner in which psychological research can have a direct and immediate application to improving the quality of experiences that children receive during sport participation. Our project was conducted in two phases. In Phase I, the behaviors of coaches were observed and coded for an entire Little League Baseball season, and then players were interviewed after the season was over. The results provided strong evidence of specifiable relationships between coach behaviors and children's reactions to their athletic experiences. In Phase II, research-derived behavioral guidelines were incorporated in a cognitive-behavioral Coach Effectiveness Training (CET) program for coaches. After conducting an experimental training program with a group of coaches, we then measured the ways in which this program affected the coaches' behaviors and the attitudes of their players. The results indicated that coaches can benefit from a psychologically oriented program intended to improve the manner in which they relate to their players.

The behavioral guidelines for coaches are placed in a goal context of increasing positive coach-player and player-player interaction, developing team cohesion, and developing in players a positive desire to achieve rather than a fear of failure. Basically, the guidelines stress the desirability of a positive approach to influencing children. This approach emphasizes (1) the liberal use of reinforcement for effort as well as for performance, (2) giving encouragement after mistakes, and (3) the desirability of giving techanical instruction in an encouraging and supportive fashion. When technical instruction is given after a mistake, the guidelines recommend first complimenting the player for something done correctly, then giving the corrective instruction, focusing on the positive things that will happen in the future if the instruction is followed rather than the negative consequences of the mistake. A decrease in the use of punitive behaviors is encouraged. Recommendations are included on how to avoid having to reprimand players continually for misbehaviors and breaking of team rules. This is partly accomplished by establishing team rules early and, in line with the positive approach, reinforcing compliance with them. Reinforcement is also recommended as a means of establishing and strengthening encouragement and support among teammates.

Implementation of the coaching guidelines can be enhanced by applying some basic principles and procedures relative to communication skills and self-awareness. Several key issues underlying effective communication were addressed. Consideration was then given to the importance of self-awareness and the ways in which behavioral feedback and self-monitoring can be used to make coaches aware of what they are doing and to increase children's motivation to comply with the behavioral guidelines.

The relationship-oriented approach to coaching is complemented by a healthy philosophy of winning, which stresses giving maximum effort in striving for excellence. If young athletes are well trained, give maximum effort, and have a positive motivation to achieve rather than performance-disrupting fears of failure, winning takes care of itself within the limits of their abilities. They also are more likely to develop their athletic potential in an enjoyable rather than in a stressful sport environment.

REFERENCES

Allison, M. G., & Ayllon, T. Behavioral coaching in the development of skills in football, gymnastics and tennis. *Journal of Applied Behavioral Analysis,* 1980, **13**, 297-314.

Bales, R. F., & Slater, P. Role differentiation in small decision-making groups. In P. Parson & R. F. Bales (Eds.), *Family, socialization, and interaction process.* Glencoe, Illinois: Free Press, 1955.

Bandura, A. *Social learning theory.* Englewood Cliffs, New Jersey: Prentice-Hall, 1977.

Cavior, N., & Marabotto, C. M. Monitoring verbal behaviors in a dyadic interaction. *Journal of Consulting and Clinical Psychology,* 1976, **44**, 68-76.

Coopersmith, S. *The antecedents of self-esteem.* San Francisco: Freeman, 1967.

Devereux, E. C. Backyard versus Little League Baseball: The impoverishment of children's games. In R. Martens (Ed.), *Joy and sadness in children's sports.* Champaign, Illinois: Human Kinetics, 1978.

Edelstein, B. A., & Eisler, R. M. Effects of modeling and modeling with instructions and feedback on the behavioral components of social skills. *Behavior Therapy,* 1976, **7**, 382-389.

Goldfried, M. R., & Sprafkin, J. N. *Behavioral personality assessment.* Morristown, New Jersey: General Learning Press, 1974.

Gottman, J. M., & McFall, R. M. Self-monitoring effects in a program for potential high school dropouts: A time series analysis. *Journal of Consulting and Clinical Psychology,* 1972, **39**, 273-281.

Kazdin, A. E. Self-monitoring and behavior change. In M. J. Mahoney & C. E. Thoresen (Eds.), *Self-control: Power to the person.* Monterey, California: Brooks/Cole, 1974.

Kirschenbaum, D. S., & Karoly, P. When self-regulation fails: Tests of some preliminary hypotheses. *Journal of Consulting and Clinical Psychology,* 1977, **45**, 1116-1125.

Komaki, J., & Barnett, F. T. A behavioral approach to coaching football: Improving the play execution of the offensive backfield on a youth football team. *Journal of Applied Behavior Analysis,* 1977, **10**, 657-664.

Martens, R. (Ed.) *Joy and sadness in children's sports.* Champaign, Illinois: Human Kinetics, 1978.

Martens, R. American coaching effectiveness program. *Sportsline,* 1981, **3**(4), 2-3.

Martens, R., & Gould, D. Why do adults volunteer to coach children's sports? In G. C. Roberts & K. M. Newell (Eds.), *Psychology of motor behavior and sport—1978.* Champaign, Illinois: Human Kinetics, 1979.

Martens, R., & Seefeldt, V. *Guidelines for children's sports.* Washington, D.C.: American Alliance for Health, Physical Education, Recreation and Dance, 1979.

McFall, R. M., & Twentyman, C. T. Four experiments on the relative contributions of rehearsal, modeling, and coaching to assertion training. *Journal of Abnormal Psychology,* 1973, **81**, 199-218.

Mischel, W. Toward a cognitive social learning reconceptualization of personality. *Psychological Review,* 1973, **80**, 252-283.

Rushall, B. S. Applied behavior analysis for sports and physical education. *International Journal of Sport Psychology,* 1975, **6**, 75-88.

Seefeldt, V., & Gould, D. *Physical and psychological effects of athletic competition on children and youth.* Washington, D.C.: ERIC Clearinghouse on Teacher Education, 1980.

Smith, R. E., Sarason, I. G., & Sarason, B. R. *Psychology: The frontiers of behavior.* (2nd ed.) New York: Harper & Row, 1982.

Smith, R. E., Smoll, F. L., & Curtis, B. Coaching behaviors in Little League Baseball. In F. L. Smoll & R. E. Smith (Eds.), *Psychological perspectives in youth sports.* Washington, D.C.: Hemisphere, 1978.

Smith, R. E., Smoll, F. L., & Curtis, B. Coach effectiveness training: A cognitive-behavioral approach to enhancing relationship skills in youth sport coaches. *Journal of Sport Psychology,* 1979, **1**, 59-75.

Smith, R. E., Smoll, F. L., & Hunt, E. A system for the behavioral assessment of athletic coaches. *Research Quarterly,* 1977, **48**, 401-407.

Smith, R. E., Smoll, F. L., Hunt, E., Curtis, B., & Coppel, D. B. Psychology and the Bad News Bears. In G. C. Roberts & K. M. Newell (Eds.), *Psychology of motor behavior and sport—1978.* Champaign, Illinois: Human Kinetics, 1979.

Smoll, F. L., & Smith, R. E. *Improving relationship skills in youth sport coaches.* East Lansing, Michigan: Michigan Institute for the Study of Youth Sports, 1979.

Smoll, F. L., & Smith, R. E. Developing a healthy philosophy of winning in youth sports. *A winning philosophy for youth sports programs.* East Lansing, Michigan: Michigan Institute for the Study of Youth Sports, 1981.

Smoll, F. L., & Smith, R. E. Techniques for improving self-awareness of youth sports coaches. *Journal of Physical Education and Recreation,* 1980, **51**, 46-49, 52.

Smoll, F. L., Smith, R. E., & Curtis, B. Coaching roles and relationships. In J. R. Thomas (Ed.), *Youth sports guide for parents and coaches.* Washington, D.C.: American Alliance for Health, Physical Education, and Recreation, 1977.

Smoll, F. L., Smith, R. E., Curtis, B., & Hunt, E. Toward a mediational model of coach-player relationships. *Research Quarterly,* 1978, **49**, 528-541.

Tharp, R. G., & Gallimore, R. What a coach can teach a teacher. *Psychology Today,* 1976, **9**, 75-78.

Thoresen, C. E., & Mahoney, M. J. *Behavioral self-control.* New York: Holt, Rinehart and Winston, 1974.

SUGGESTED READINGS

Undergraduate Students

Martens, R. (Ed.) Coaches—Do they build character or "characters?" *Joy and sadness in children's sports.* Champaign, Illinois: Human Kinetics, 1978.

Martens, R., & Seefeldt, V. *Guidelines for children's sports.* Washington, D.C.: American Alliance for Health, Physical Education, Recreation and Dance, 1979.

Smith, R. E., Sarason, I. G., & Sarason, B. R. Learning: Principles and applications, Frontiers of applied psychology (section on psychological applications in sports). *Psychology: The frontiers of behavior.* (2nd ed.) New York: Harper & Row, 1982.

Tharp, R. G., & Gallimore, R. What a coach can teach a teacher. *Psychology Today,* 1976, **9**, 75-78.

Graduate Students

Allison, M. G., & Ayllon, T. Behavioral coaching in the development of skills in football, gymnastics and tennis. *Journal of Applied Behavioral Analysis,* 1980, **13**, 297-314.

Komaki, J., & Barnett, F. T. A behavioral approach to coaching football: Improving the play execution of the offensive backfield on a youth football team. *Journal of Applied Behavior Analysis,* 1977, **10**, 657-664.

Smith, R. E., Smoll, F. L., & Curtis, B. Coaching behaviors in Little League Baseball. In F. L. Smoll & R. E. Smith (Eds.), *Psychological perspectives in youth sports.* Washington, D.C.: Hemisphere, 1978.

Smith, R. E., Smoll, F. L., & Curtis, B. Coach effectiveness training: A cognitive-behavioral approach to enhancing relationship skills in youth sport coaches. *Journal of Sport Psychology,* 1979, **1**, 59-75.

Smith, R. E., Smoll, F. L., & Hunt, E. A system for the behavioral assessment of athletic coaches. *Research Quarterly,* 1977, **48**, 401-407.

Smoll, F. L., & Smith, R. E. Psychologically oriented coach training programs: Design, implementation, and assessment. In C. H. Nadeau, W. R. Halliwell, K. M. Newell, & G. C. Roberts (Eds.), *Psychology of motor behavior and sport—1979.* Champaign, Illinois: Human Kinetics, 1980.

Smoll, F. L., Smith, R. E., Curtis, B., & Hunt, E. Toward a mediational model of coach-player relationships. *Research Quarterly,* 1978, **49**, 528-541.

Laboratory 5 from Chapter 14 should be used at the completion of this chapter.

PART IV

Issues and Examples in Motor Development Research

This final part is designed for graduate students. Chapter 13 describes some of the theoretical and methodological problems involved in studying motor skill development in children, especially one phenomenon—that older children catch on to the cognitive aspects of the research setting more quickly than do younger children. This results in better performance for older children. Chapter 13 thus discusses appropriate theory on how to select age groups for study. It considers age differences in kinesthetic sensitivity, treatment consistency, outliers in data, appropriate statistical analyses, sampling problems, and age group language problems.

Chapter 14 provides five laboratory experiences in motor development. The laboratory studies cover the areas of body dimensions (Chapter 1), children and exercise (Chapter 2), throwing patterns (Chapter 3), memory for movement (Chapter 4), and observing children and coaches in sport (Chapter 12).

13

Planning "Kiddie" Research: Little "Kids" but Big Problems[1]

Jerry R. Thomas

Motor development emerged as an area of study in the 1930s with the research efforts of Bayley (1936), McGraw (1935), Wild (1937), and several others. Up until the 1970s, these research efforts were basically descriptions of two types: milestones at which certain movement patterns emerged or changed (e.g., running, throwing) and the age levels associated with typical motor performances (e.g., how much faster do eight-year-olds run than six-year-olds?). These studies described what the typical performances and forms were for children at various ages across the preschool and elementary school years. Some of these studies were cross sectional in design (looked at children of different ages at one point in time), while others were longitudinal in nature (observed the same children over several years).

Many types of phenomena can be studied developmentally (e.g., changes with age in strength, cardiovascular fitness, mechanics of movement). These changes can be described as they change across ages, or specific treatments can be applied to evaluate their differential effects across ages. This chapter is specifically concerned with learning and performance experiments as applied to motor development. For the past ten years, an increasing number of scholars have been doing research about how children learn and perform motor skills.

The intent of this chapter is to present a model that will identify sources of variation in developmental learning and memory research. Then using this model and empirical evidence from the developmental literature (both motor and cognitive), several valid methodological issues in this research are discussed. Also some proposed solutions for the planning of developmental studies are offered.

1. This chapter was developed from a paper presented at the Physical Education Measurement Symposium, Houston, October 1980.

A PROCESSING MODEL FOR MOTOR DEVELOPMENT

Information processing is the most widely used theory in both cognitive and motor learning research. Also, a substantial body of knowledge from developmental psychology uses a processing approach. However, only in recent years has a developmental processing view of motor skill acquisition been used (Wade 1977, Kerr 1980, Thomas 1980).

Figure 4.1 (page 92) is a developmental model of information processing, and is used as part of the basis for methodological concerns in this chapter (refer to Chapter 4 for a more complete discussion). The factors that develop across childhood are the control processes used in short-term store (STS), the contents of long-term store (LTS), and the effective direction of attention.

Figure 13.1 provides a look at the sources of natural (as opposed to treatment) variation that occur across age that affect the variability in motor performance (as opposed to an accuracy estimate of performance). Note that between-subject variation about an accuracy score increases across age groups, that is, the standard deviation (SD) of an accuracy score (e.g., CE, |CE|, AE)[2] is typically greater for a group of nine-year-olds when compared with a group of six-year-olds. However, individual children become increasingly consistent in their own performances as they get older, that is, the variation in a child's score about his own mean performance (an individual's VE, which is the SD of CE) will be greater at six than nine years of age. Finally, the average of ($\bar{X}$) an age group's within-subject variability ($\bar{X}$ of VE) decreases with increasing age, that is, the $\bar{X}$ of VE for a group of six-year-olds is greater than for that of nine-year-olds.

Interage variation ($\bar{X}$ of an age group's VE) is particularly interesting in its step decreases. Both the cognitive and motor development literature suggest that the step decrease (labeled A in Figure 13.1) results from the use of spontaneous rehearsal strategies around 6 to 7 years of age. The step decrease (labeled B) results from memory organization (use of grouping and recoding), which begins to be used around 10 to 11 years of age. Both of these control processes result in greater consistency of motor performances (or a stronger memory trace).

From the models presented in these two figures, several methodological considerations emerge. Three are of particular interest:

1. How are age groups selected for study?
2. Are there age differences in speed of processing?
3. Are there age differences in perception of movements? Are they just noticeable differences (JND) or different limens?

SELECTING AGE GROUPS FOR RESEARCH

How an age group should be selected has never been examined or explained by theories. Typically, researchers have used whatever age groups they could obtain. Even when age was thought about, frequently the plan was only guesswork (i.e., "Let's try every two years"). One

2. Constant error (CE) is a subject's average of several scores that vary around a target taking the sign ± into account. For example, a subject is asked to walk 10 m on a line and then repeat this four more times—the result is five estimates of 10 m. Some of these estimates are too short (–), while others are too far (+). The average of the five trials is CE. If CE is calculated and then the sign ± is disregarded for a subject, the measure is absolute CE (|CE|). The standard deviation (SD) for a subject's CE score represents variability about that score and is called variable error (VE). If the sign is dropped on each of the five trials before averaging, the measurement is called absolute error (AE).

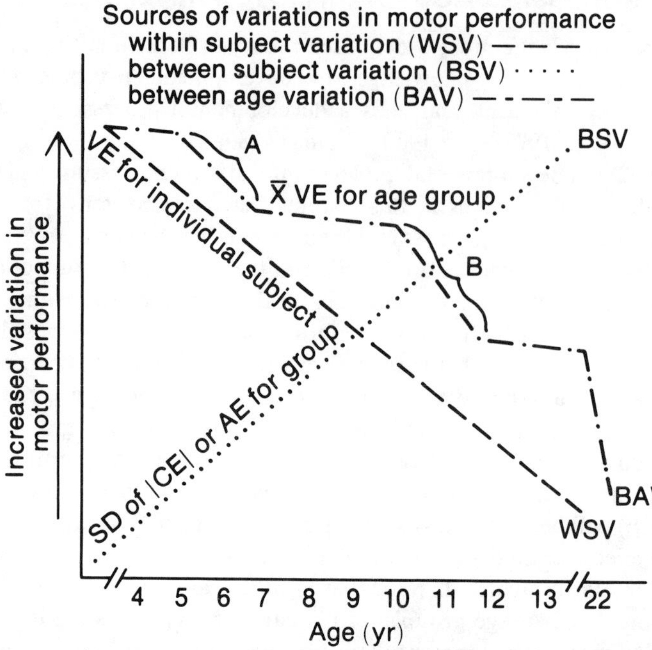

Figure 13.1. Developmental model of motor performance. (A, effects of beginning of spontaneous rehearsal; B, effects of beginning of memory organization; SD, standard deviation; |CE|, absolute constant error; AE, absolute error; $\bar{X}$, mean; VE, variable error.)

viewpoint holds that to ensure significant differences, age groups should be spread far apart. In practice, however, few researchers select age groups based on any theoretical rationale.

For example, using the models presented earlier as well as models from memory development literature, key points on which to base age group selections for developmental studies can be determined. Developmental processing theory identifies the ages of six to seven years as an important point in development (Thomas 1980). At these ages, children begin to use spontaneous rehearsal processes. That is, before this age they are able to rehearse, but do not do so spontaneously. After this age, they use rehearsal strategies without having to be reminded to do so. Flavell (1977) referred to this as a production mediation deficiency.

Around 10 to 11 years of age, a considerable increase in the use of effective rehearsal strategies is evident. When a 7-year-old is given a list of words, one at a time, to remember, he rehearses as shown in Figure 13.2. Given the same word list, an 11-year-old uses the rehearsal strategy shown on the right side of Figure 13.2. Thus, the 7-year-old simply repeats the stimulus word over and over, while the 11-year-old enters several previously given words in the increasing rehearsal list. At recall, the 11-year-old is able to remember more words, owing to a more sophisticated rehearsal strategy.

Cognitive rehearsal of cues for movements and the parts of complex movements are processed in the same way. In fact, some evidence in motor development is available (Gallagher 1980).[3] Thus,

3. Gallagher, J. D., & Thomas, J. R. Rehearsal strategy effects on developmental differences for recall of a movement series. *Research Quarterly for Exercise and Sport*, 1984, in press.

Word List	7-Year-Old	11-Year-Old
Red	Red, red, red	Red, red, red
Blue	Blue, blue, blue	Red, blue, red, blue
Green	Green, green, green	Red, blue, green, red, . . .
Yellow	Yellow, yellow, yellow	Red, blue, green, yellow, . . .
White	White, white, white	Red, blue, green, yellow, white, . . .

RECALL

Figure 13.2. Age differences in spontaneous rehearsal strategies.

when researchers are interested in developmental differences in children's ability to use rehearsal in the skill acquisition process, they should consider appropriate selection of age groups. One strategy is to select age groups as depicted in Table 13.1. This change in rehearsal strategy has been demonstrated to be responsible for a substantial portion of the age-related performance changes (Winther and Thomas 1981). Figure 13.3 shows what happens when younger children are forced to use the strategies that older children and adults use, or when older children and adults are forced to use the strategies of younger children. The performance of the younger children is facilitated by the adultlike strategy, while the older children's and adults' performance is depressed by use of the less sophisticated strategy. The rehearsal conditions were patterned after the word list rehearsal strategies depicted in Figure 13.2. That is, the less sophisticated (seven-year-old) strategy is to stay at the end point of a movement for a 8-sec rehearsal period for each of several movements. The adult strategy is to rehearse previously presented movements during the 8-sec rehearsal period. Performance at recall was significantly affected. Incidentally, our organization of these strategies is accurate. Note that a self-determined strategy group was included. Not only was their performance similar to what we had proposed for the less or more sophisticated strategy, but also we found from questioning the subjects that they used the age-appropriate strategy.

Similar findings from another study (Winther and Thomas 1981) are reported in Figure 13.4. When children were taught to use a relevant label, in this case a clockface, for recalling two-dimensional movements, the kindergartners' performance became similar to the fifth graders who used an irrelevant label, in this case animal names. The fifth graders' performance became more similar to that of the adults. Giving the younger children a relevant way to encode the position of the movement facilitated recall.

Thus, when planning a study on motor development involving either memory or learning, considerable theoretical and empirical rationale exists for the process of selecting age groups at key points in development. The same rationale applies to the study of any phenomenon in a cross-sectional design.

Consider Processing Speed in Developmental Learning Studies

In motor learning studies, a number of repeated trials on the motor task typically are performed, and knowledge of results (KR) is given on some schedule between trials. The time between trials is called the *intertrial interval*, and is divided as shown in Figure 13.5. Most typically, the intertrial interval is held constant (e.g., 10 sec), with KR provided after a delay (e.g., 4 sec). This means that after Trial X ends, 4-sec pass and KR is provided; then 6 sec pass and Trial

Table 13.1. Age Groups for Rehearsal Studies

5-year-olds	Do not typically use rehearsal spontaneously
7-year-olds	Beginning of spontaneous use of rehearsal strategies
11-year-olds	Use of more sophisticated rehearsal strategies
Adults	Constant comparison group

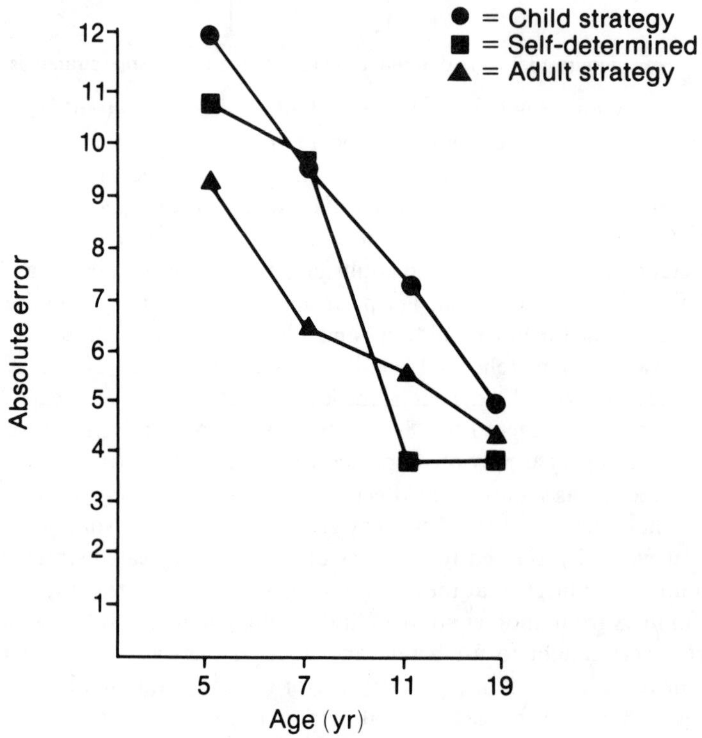

Figure 13.3. Differences in use of strategy across age (from Gallagher 1980).

X + 1 begins. Thus, the subject is given 6 sec to process the KR, including making any needed corrections in the movement plan for the next trial.

This design (or some variation of it) presents no problems for intra-age group comparisons. However, when hypotheses are tested across age groups, the post-KR interval becomes important. Numerous reviews (Elliot 1972; Wickens 1974; Chi 1976, 1977; Thomas 1980; Chi and Gallagher 1982) all report processing speed (especially speed of encoding) to be an age-related phenomenon (i.e., younger children have a slower processing speed when compared with older children and adults). Thus, a cross-age design that holds a relatively short post-KR interval constant produces significant differences that are due to deficits in the processing speed of the younger age group or groups. Figure 4.3 (page 94) clearly demonstrates this phenomenon from one of our studies (Gallagher and Thomas 1980). Note how the younger children's performance improves as the

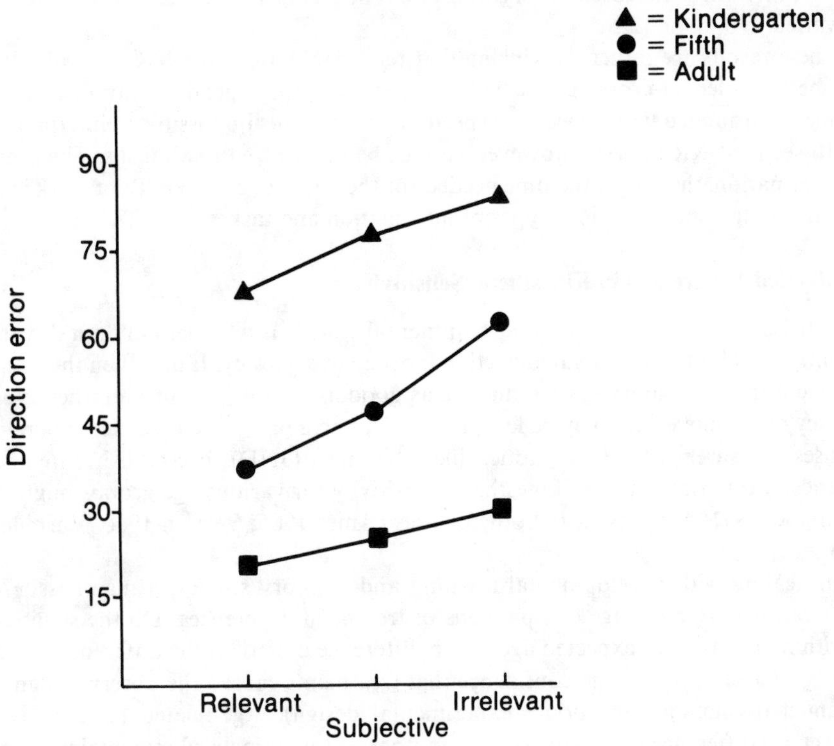

Figure 13.4. Age differences in use of labels for remembering location. (Reprinted with permission from Winther, K. T., and Thomas, J. R. Developmental differences in children's labeling of movement. *Journal of Motor Behavior,* 1981, **13**, 77-90, a publication of the Helen Dwight Reid Educational Foundation.)

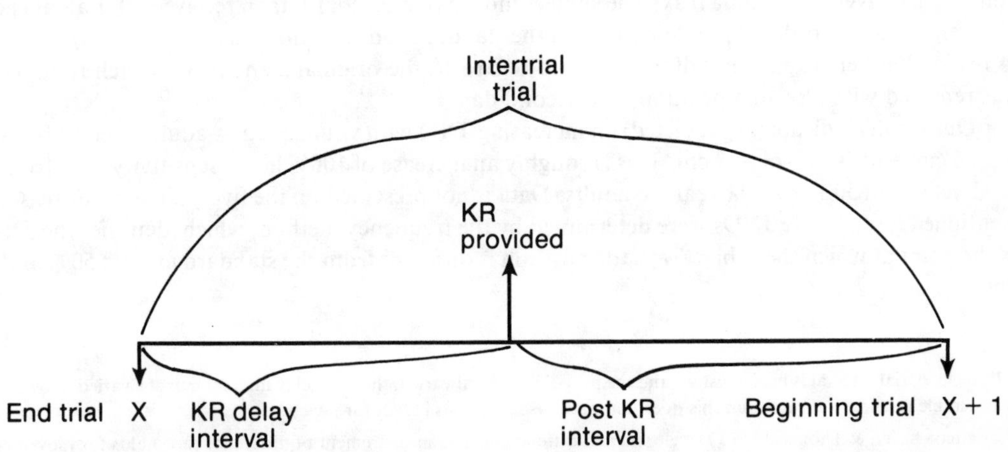

Figure 13.5. Division of the intertrial interval in motor learning studies. (KR, knowledge of results.)

post-KR interval is increased. Everything else is held constant[4] except the post-KR interval, which was varied to 3, 6, or 12 sec.

These results are rather convincing that reasonably long post-KR intervals (10 sec or longer) must be provided in cross-age learning studies or the independent variable being manipulated becomes confounded with processing speed, making results impossible to interpret. The suggestion of a 10-sec post-KR interval, however, cannot be generalized to all tasks. The more complex the KR information, the longer the time needed for the younger children. Pilot work is the only way to make this judgment for various types of information and tasks.

Age-Related Differences in Kinesthetic Sensitivity

One issue of vital concern in developmental studies is whether children of various ages have equivalent levels of sensitivity in detecting movement accuracy. If not, then their representation of movement in the memory system may be as good as an adult's, but kinesthetic sensitivity to the accuracy of the movement may be less precise. This area of research is called *differences thresholds*, and uses measurements of just noticeable differences (JND) to establish difference limens. The existence of differing levels of kinesthetic sensitivity for various age groups might be anticipated, since these JNDs are present for other senses (Ames 1966, Vernon 1966, Vurpillot 1974, Bower 1978).

In dealing with developmental learning and memory studies, a major issue is whether the reader can believe cross-age comparisons of treatment differences. Do the significant differences fall within or outside of expected age group difference limens? If the differences are larger than the age-related JNDs, then some confidence that treatments caused the observed significant effects is warranted (assuming appropriate experimental design). Age-related research is not available, however, on difference limens for various motor tasks used in developmental memory and learning studies. Briefly, data are presented from one or our recent studies[5] in this area.

In this study, 12 children in each of four age groups were used—5, 7, and 11 years, and adults. These age groups were selected to correspond to the previously presented age criteria relative to the development of rehearsal strategies. Subjects received 140 trials for each of two days on a two-dimensional lever positioning task. The subject moved to a standard, then received 20 trials at each of seven randomly ordered positions around the standard (one position was the standard) and had to respond either "same" or "different" (with regard to the original standard) on each trial. This was repeated with a second position on a second day.

Our results indicate (as predicted) an increasing JND with younger age—adults, 3 cm; 11-year-olds, 6 cm; and 7-year-olds, 9 cm. This is roughly an increase of 100% in the sensitivity level from 7 to 11 years and 50% from 11 years to adults. Data is not presented on the five-year-olds for reasons mentioned later. These JNDs were determined by the frequency method, which identifies the JND as the point at which the subject says the position is different from the standard at least 50% of the time.

4. If the intertrial interval is held constant and the post-KR interval varied, the KR delay interval must be varied. However, considerable research indicates that this does not matter (see Thomas [1980] for review).

5. Thomas, K. T., & Thomas, J. R. Developmental differences: The measurement of difference thresholds for movement location. Paper presented at Computer Workshop and Measurement Symposium, Rice University, Houston, Texas, October 1980.

These data suggest that for a two-dimensional lever positioning task, the difference between 7-and 11-year-olds or 11-year-olds and adults should exceed 3 cm in order to be attributed to some factor other than increased sensitivity to position location. If the 7-year-olds are to be compared with the adults, differences should exceed 6 cm.

Figure 13.4 includes data in which three different types of labels are used with 5-year-olds, 11-year-olds, and adult subjects. While the age groups are not identical, the task is, and the application of an age-group JND could be approximated. In making between-age comparisons, a typical finding for a significant difference in this study is that 10% to 15% of the between-age difference is attributable to difference limens. Thus, the differences are not due (in major part) to differences in kinesthetic sensitivity, but represent other between-age factors (e.g., in this study, encoding and rehearsal differences among the age groups).

While the above application is approximate, if the general finding of increased sensitivity for movement location between these ages is correct, a more accurate estimate of between-age differences due to other factors could be made. A considerable number of JND studies would need to be conducted before any standard could be accepted across tasks. The results of the JND study with kindergarten subjects were not mentioned because we found some rather interesting data that raise several methodological issues. There seemed to be three major questions:

1. What should be done with a subject who makes an all "same" or all "different" response?
2. What should be done for a JND when the 50% different criterion is reached at one point but performance falls below that for a point farther from the standard?
3. What should be done if the JND is "0"?

Making an all "same" or "different" response is a strategy that young subjects used. That they did not understand "same" or "different" was not the problem, because we established before testing that they did understand. Some five-year-olds seem to use this strategy to obtain the correct answer at least part of the time. Subjects who respond in this way should be eliminated from the study.

The criterion for establishing the JND is the first point at which 50% or more responses are "different." Yet some of the younger children reached this criterion at one distance from the target (e.g., 3 cm) but then failed to reach the 50% criterion at 6 cm. None of the 11-year-olds or adults exhibited this pattern. We decided that the JND should be established at the point where none of the "more distance" responses fall below the 50% "different" criterion. Logically, a JND could not exist at 3 cm that was not detectable at 6 cm.

The third issue is what to do when the 50% criterion is at "0" JND. The JND cannot be "0." Whether a subject with this characteristic should be eliminated, or whether we should use the next JND that meets all criteria, is debatable. If the sample size can stand the loss, the subject should probably be eliminated.

AGE-RELATED EMPIRICAL ISSUES IN METHODOLOGY

The previously presented considerations have been closely tied to developmental information-processing theory. Several less theoretical issues are of importance in motor development studies. These concerns and proposed solutions are my own, based on numerous individual research studies and relevant literature from various areas in methodology. There will certainly be other solutions besides the ones identified here. My major concern is that the issues be thought through in research planning, and that the experimenter make a decision about them (even if that decision is to do nothing). The purpose is to eliminate post hoc methodological blame for unexpected results. Too many studies already exist in which the discussion is based on "things I should have done differently." This explanation is basically one of poor planning and lack of pilot work. This section identifies many of the planning issues that are of special concern in developmental studies. *Nothing can substitute for trying out the methods* (including the statistical analysis) *of a proposed study*.

Procedures

The issue of individual differences (both within and between subjects) in cross-age research has been discussed. Recall that within-subject differences are likely to decrease with increased age, but between-subject differences increase. Thus, estimates of performance such as variable error (VE, the variation about a subject's $\overline{X}$ performance on several trials) decrease from early childhood through the teen years. However, the standard deviation of age group performance measures increases across childhood. This leads to a number of considerations about treatments for experimental groups.

Treatment Consistency

Since within-subject variability is already large for younger children, the appropriate and consistent application of the treatments is essential. One of the most important factors is making sure young subjects (this also applies to any subject) understand what is expected of them. Frequently, younger subjects need more practice trials. Be certain that they understand what to do at least as well as the older subjects do. Otherwise, treatment differences occur due to the more rapid comprehension of the older children. This issue may also involve the level of language used. Nothing is wrong with taking more time and using different words to explain what the younger child is to do. This applies to the treatment procedures as well as to learning the purpose of the task used to obtain the dependent measure.

Occasionally, a child is encountered who fails to understand what to do no matter how well the experimenter explains. If this occurs in only isolated instances, eliminate the child from the study and randomly select a replacement. If many of the children fail to understand, the problem lies with the explanation.

Attention and motivation also are factors that affect the length of treatment and testing sessions. Frequently, multiple trials are needed in memory and learning studies. An attempt should be made to make the experimental session interesting. For instances, in our research we frequently use a ballistic linear movement task in which the object is to learn to move a specified distance in a certain time (e.g., 40 cm in 400 msec). Recently we mounted a toy airplane on top of the handle the child was to grasp. The child also wore earphones delivering white noise. The child was told that the task was to learn to move the airplane at the correct takeoff speed (in this case, 40 cm in 400 msec), with KR (amount too fast or slow) provided after each trial. With this technique, five to seven-year-old children's interest was maintained over 40 acquisition and 20 retention trials.

Sometimes a young child's attention cannot be maintained regardless of the conditions. If the child has lost attention on the task so that performance is seriously affected, then:

1. Begin again if the procedure allows this to be done without destroying the nature of the experiment, or

2. Randomly select a replacement for the child in the study.

Failing to consider these factors in the treatment and testing session or sessions results in both within- and between-subject variability being further inflated. In addition, some of these variables can create artificial differences between age groups.

Measurement Issues

There are more measurement issues than could possibly be listed here, but one or two are particularly important in developmental studies. Already mentioned were the wide and inconsistent variances in scores (both within and between subjects) that frequently occur in developmental research. The question then is how the researcher can determine if an observation in a data set is outside reasonable limits.

These extreme scores are frequently referred to as *outliers*, which are defined as "extreme, unusual, unexpected, and seemingly unrepresentative observations or elements in data sets" (Fisher 1980). Only researchers who look carefully at the distribution of scores in their data are even concerned about outliers or any other characteristics of the data set. The hope is that all researchers are concerned about the score distributions. Outliers become a difficult decision for typical research studies because the number of subjects per group is usually small, and no one wants to reduce the *N* even further. Recall that first, if the data point is a real outlier, it is unrepresentative and should be eliminated. Second, all statistical tests of group differences involve some estimate of true variance divided by error variance. Since outliers increase the group variance, they inflate the error variance, thus reducing the chances of obtaining significant differences.

Outliers are easy to get in data sets from children. Already suggested was that the outliers be eliminated during the testing process if possible (i.e., if a child's performance has been seriously affected by loss of attention, either the testing should begin again or the child should be replaced in the study). What happens, however, if an extreme score is missed during testing but discovered when examining the data distribution? The application of an outlier test is suggested.

A good deal of thought is necessary in making decisions about outliers. For instance, formulation of a distribution model gives some basis for determining outliers. Sometimes outliers may be the value of greatest interest to the observer, frequently indicating successful "treatment." How can treatment effects be determined from deviant scores? To answer these theoretical questions here would be difficult, and some could not be answered. Readers who want a considerably more detailed discussion of outliers should read Barnett and Lewis (1978).

Fisher (1980) says that "regardless of whether the researcher views the presence of extreme values with gloom or glee, he or she still faces the issue of outlier definition." This decision is purely subjective, as an outlier test is usually not applied unless the experimenter is suspicious of some of the data points.

A number of outlier tests exist (Barnett and Lewis [1978] list 17 distinct, useful tests, which, with variations and special cases, can be expanded to 60 tests) that can be classed into six categories. A general notion underlying most of these tests is that the sample contains, at most, one or two potentially deviant data points. The procedures for dealing with these observations can be classed as either block or consecutive techniques, both of which present problems. The *block technique* involves identifying outliers (usually one or more) and applying an outlier test to that block of observations. The problem is that the potential outliers have to be labeled subjectively by the experimenter to identify the block to be tested. *Consecutive procedures* involve applying an outlier test to the most divergent data point. If it is significant, then the test is applied to the next most divergent point, and so on, until one is not significant. The problem here is called *masking*, and is created because outlier tests contrast the divergent point with some estimate of the variance or spread of the rest of the data. If a second data point is nearly as deviant as the first one, the error term of the outlier test is inflated, and the first point may not be declared an outlier.

Thus, a good deal of subjectivity is involved in both selection and application of outlier tests. I do not have any solutions except to note a few of these points:

1. Outliers are likely to exist in development data sets, especially with younger children who have attention problems.
2. Experimenters should carefully review data distributions to identify these potential deviant data points.
3. Experimenters should then make some type of logical decision about what to do.
4. Barnett and Lewis (1978) or Fisher (1980) should be read for a greater understanding.

Analysis

Already evident from a previous section of this chapter is the fact that the variation about the age-group mean is likely to increase with age. Equal variances among groups is a basic assumption for all analysis of variance techniques. Moderate violations of this assumption do not appear to have a serious effect on the F statistics (Winer 1971). For example, Winer (1971) gives the case in which the variance ratios are 1, 2, 3, with $N = 5$ per group, which results in less than a 1% error in the level of a significance toward rejecting the null hypothesis more frequently. Recent evidence (Hakstian, Roed, and Lind 1979) indicates that multivariate techniques are also robust with regard to this assumption. Even in developmental studies, relatively few cases are encountered in which one age group variance was twice or three times another age group's. When this problem is found, a square root transformation has generally solved it (Winer 1971). This issue further supports the need to examine data carefully before grinding out analysis procedures. Researchers are encouraged to run the data description programs available on most computer systems and to examine all appropriate characteristics prior to all other statistical manipulation of the data set.

One final point about statistical analysis of developmental studies should be made. Most of the experiments (and their hypotheses) are developed around anticipated age by treatment interactions (i.e., the effectiveness of the treatment is expected to vary according to the subject's age). Statistical interactions are rather elusive. They are extremely difficult to replicate; in fact, a former colleague in educational research at Florida State University declares he has never been able to replicate one in 30 years of research. While I am more optimistic than that, the interpretation of interactions must be done carefully; most helpful is when the actual differences are large, reliable, produced for more than one dependent measure and experiment, and consistent with theory and previous data. The effects should certainly be present in the overall hypothesis test (e.g., the multivariate test) before follow-ups on separate, dependent measures are considered.

Common Methodological Problems

In research, I have consistently encountered some methodological problems in motor development studies that are rather practical in nature but can seriously alter results. The first is a sampling problem. All researchers need the subject's permission for participation in an experiment. In studies of children, parental permission for the child to participate must be obtained. Our parents' agreement rate was running about 35% to 40% when we began to realize many of the letters were not getting home (or back to us). By adding a statement asking that parents return the signed letter whether or not the child could participate, we found that when a second letter was needed because the first one had not gotten home (or back), our agreement rate increased to more than 70%.

A second problem involves what teachers tell the students or the students tell each other about the study. The influence teachers can have on the students in studies is amazing. We have had teachers tell the children they would have to participate in the study during their recess time if they did not behave. This creates considerable anxiety and resentment on the part of the children. One teacher helped us by assuring her children they would not be tested during recess. Some teachers fail to understand the purposes of the research and badly distort what happens to the child. Our experience indicates that a good investment of time is to explain personally what the teacher is to tell the children about the experiment, including things not to say.

Children definitely discuss the experiment with each other, particularly children who have been tested with those yet to be tested. This is a strong argument against the use of intact groups. Even when children within a classroom are randomly assigned to the various treatments, the problem remains. Under these circumstances, the child may get incorrect information that may predispose her to behave in certain ways. The best way to handle the situation is to tell all the children that they will be doing several different things, and not to think they will do exactly what another child does. Also helpful is to use only a few children from each classroom, but this frequently is not possible.

Not only are motor performance scores sometimes different for boys and girls but also the use of cognitive strategies differ. This is all evidence of the more rapid maturation of females. Either controlling for gender differences by using only one sex in the study or splitting on this factor to test for significant differences is suggested. If differences are not significant, experimenters frequently collapse their design across the gender factor to increase power.

In the first part of this chapter, some theoretical bases for selection of age groups in experiments was provided. The researcher should also define the allowable age range for an age group a priori. Normally, a 12-month range may be used (e.g., to select six-year-olds, use children from five-years, seven-months old to six-years, six-months old. If grade level rather than age is used, some children in the sample may be substantially outside the desired age range. This is likely to increase the within-age (age group) variation for memory and learning studies, which reduces the power of the statistical test.

When trying to study the cognitive processes associated with motor performance and motor learning, the experimenter infers what processes have been operating in memory. To verify this, researchers should question the children about what they did or thought. These results can be used to support reasoning about the processes that were operating during performance or learning. Researchers should be aware, however, of how questions are worded. Closed statements such as "I tried to remember both movements and put them together" have the advantage of being easily scoreable (e.g., Likert scale), but are severely limiting to responses. Open questions such as "How did you remember where to move?" offer a wide variety of responses, but are difficult to score. Also, the language level and syntax used in statements are important. Young children give vague responses anyway, and if the experimenter's language or syntax confuses them, the results are meaningless.

Many of the concerns expressed in this section come from a researcher's lack of knowledge about kids. I always have reservations about studies from researchers who have used children as subjects just for a special instance in their research. These researchers generally know little about children, and I always wonder how they have anticipated and solved the many problems inherent in developmental research. Collecting valid, reliable data with young children is no easy task.

SUMMARY

Theoretical knowledge, empirical findings, and experience with children are all necessary to plan motor development research. The experiment or experiments should evaluate several issues carefully:

1. Is the research based on a sound theoretical framework? Is this theory, along with empirical evidence, used for selecting the age levels to be studied?
2. When planning developmental studies involving memory for movement or learning, are important variables considered, such as age differences in processing speed or difference limens or both?
3. Are appropriate methodological issues taken into account, such as:
   a. Age level variability of between- and within-subject age groups?
   b. Some a priori system during testing and analysis to deal with extreme performance scores (outliers)?
   c. Careful evaluation of the data and its distribution prior to statistical analysis?
   d. Thoughtful consideration of age by treatment interactions, since they are usually the focus of developmental research?
4. Does the experimenter really understand children, and is this reflected in all aspects of the planning of the research?

Children are not "little people" who have been reduced from 5 to 6 ft to 3 to 4 ft in size. They truly think and behave in different ways, requiring appropriate adjustments in theory and research methodology to accommodate these differences.

REFERENCES

Ames, L. B. Verbal and motor responses to perceptual stimuli throughout the life span. In A. H. Kidd & J. L. Rivoire (Eds.), *Perceptual development in children.* New York: International Universities Press, 1966.

Baley, N. The development of motor abilities during the first three years: A study of sixty-one infants tested repeatedly. *Monographs of the Society for Research in Child-Development,* **1**, 1935.

Barnett, V. & Lewis, T. *Outliers in statistical data.* New York: Wiley, 1978.

Bower, T. G. Perceptual development: Object and space. In E. C. Carterette & M. P. Friedman (Eds.), *Handbook of perception.* Vol. III. New York: Academic Press, 1978.

Chi, M. Age differences in the speed of processing: A critique. *Developmental Psychology,* 1977, **13**, 543-544.

Chi, M. Short-term memory limitations in children: Capacity or processing deficits. *Memory & Cognition,* 1976, **4**, 559-572.

Chi, M. & Gallagher, J. D. Speed of processing: A developmental source of limitation. *Topics in Learning & Learning Disabilities,* 1982, **2**, 23-32.

Elliott, R. Simple reaction time in children: *Journal of Experimental Child Psychology, 1972,* **23**, 540-557.

Fisher, P. O. An investigation of outlier definition and the impact of the masking phenomenon on several statistical outlier tests. Unpublished doctoral dissertation, Florida State University, 1980.

Flavell, J. H. What is memory development the development of? *Human Development,* 1971, **4**, 225-286.

Gallagher, J. D. Adult-child motor performance differences: A developmental perspective of control processing deficits. Unpublished doctoral dissertation, Louisiana State University, 1980.

Gallagher, J. D. & Thomas, J. R. Effects of varying post-KR intervals upon children's motor performance. *Journal of Motor Behavior,* 1980, **12**, 41-46.

Hakstian, A. R., Roed, J. D. & Lind, J. D. Two-sample T^2 procedure and the assumption of homogeneous covariance matrices. *Psychological Bulletin,* 1979, **86**, 1255-1263.

Kerr, B. The cognitive/information processing approach to age related differences in performance. Paper presented at NASPSPA, Boulder, Colorado, May 1980.

McGraw, M. *Growth: A study of Johnny and Jimmy.* New York: Appleton-Century, 1935.

Thomas, J. R. Acquisition of motor skills: Information processing differences between children and adults. *Research Quarterly for Exercise and Sport,* 1980, **51**, 158-173.

Vernon, M. D. Perceptions in relation to cognition. In A. H. Kidd & J. L. Riviore (Eds.), *Perceptual development in children.* New York: International Universities Press, 1966.

Vurpillot, E. The developmental emphasis. In E. C. Carterette & M. P. Friedman (Eds.), *Handbook of perception.* Vol. 1. New York: Academic Press, 1974.

Wade, M. G. Developmental motor learning. In J. Keogh & R. S. Hutton (Eds.), *Exercise and sport sciences reviews.* Vol. 4. Santa Barbara, California: Journal of Publishing Affiliates, 1977.

Wickens, C. C. Temporal limits of human information processing: A developmental study. *Psychological Bulletin,* 1974, **81**, 739-755.

Wild, M. *The behavior pattern of throwing and some observations concerning its course of development in children.* Doctoral dissertation, University of Wisconsin, 1937.

Winer, B. J. *Statistical principles in experimental design.* (2nd ed.) New York: McGraw-Hill, 1971.

Winther, K. T. & Thomas, J. R. Developmental differences in children's labeling of movement. *Journal of Motor Behavior,* 1981, **13**, 77-90.

14

Laboratory Experiences in Motor Development[1]

Jerry R. Thomas

This chapter is designed to provide concrete experiences for concepts presented in several of the chapters. Many additional laboratory experiences could be developed, but the number presented here should be adequate to bring the student into several data collection situations with children. On occasion a laboratory may not work perfectly because of the tremendous variability in children and atypical performances (or children) may be selected. If each student does the laboratory individually, the majority of results should be as predicted. The class instructor may want to put all the data together to get a more representative picture of the proposed effect.

Figure 14.1 provides a suggested report form for the laboratories. The student should read the appropriate chapter in the text carefully prior to collecting the data for a specific laboratory. In addition, the instructor should go over the data collection procedures in class and allow each student to practice before testing the children.

The hands-on experience with children not only demonstrates the appropriate concepts but also provides valuable experience in understanding children's behavior.

LABORATORY 1: BODY DIMENSIONS AND MOTOR PERFORMANCE

Both Malina and Newell (Chapters 1 and 5) discuss the importance of the effects of body size on motor performance, particularly how size changes with growth, especially during puberty. Malina also mentions the gender differences in growth. The purpose of the laboratory is to measure the age and gender differences in body proportions and to think about how the changes in these proportions affect performance.

1. I wish to thank Scotty Powers for developing the lab "Children and Exercise" and my wife, Kathi, for her many suggestions on the other four labs.

I. General Information
  A. Student's name
  B. Name of lab
  C. Purpose of lab
  D. Description of situation
    1. Source of subjects
    2. Age in months of children
    3. Sex of children
    4. Description of testing conditions
II. Tests
  A. Name of test
  B. Brief description
    1. Testing area (layout or equipment)
    2. Type of test
    3. Validity and reliability of test (if known)
    4. Suitable age range for test
    5. Description of norm procedures
III. Children Tested
  A. Individual scores by age, sex, condition, etc.
  B. Mean scores by age, sex, condition, etc.
  C. Comparisons
    1. To norms
    2. By age, sex, condition, interactions, etc.
  D. Comments on individual children
IV. Results
  A. Appropriate tables
  B. Appropriate figures
V. Answer Questions From Specific Lab
VI. Other Comments (e.g., testing problems, problems with children)

Figure 14.1. Format for laboratory report.

Procedures

Select four 6-, 10-, and 14-year-old children ($N = 12$), two boys and two girls at each age level. Required is a steel tape calibrated in centimeters. Have each child stand straight (without shoes) with their back to a wall and measure their standing height to the nearest centimeter. Then have each child sit in a straightback chair and measure sitting height (seat of chair to top of head) to the nearest centimeter. The child must sit straight and slide completely back into the chair.

Results

Create a proportion of sitting height/standing height for each child. Multiply this by 100, and the result is the percentage of total height represented by sitting height. Subtracting this percentage from 100% yields the percentage of total height made up by the legs. Now do the following with this data:

1. Average the scores for sitting height percentages for the two boys and two girls at each age level.
2. Do the same for the percentage of the body the legs make up.
3. Plot two graphs of these data points, placing percentages for sitting height on the Y axis for one graph and percentages for the legs on the Y axis of the other. Put age (6, 10, 14) on the X axis and use "X" to mark data points for boys and "O" for girls.

Answer the following questions about your data:

1. Describe the characteristics of the two graphs plotted, considering age changes, gender differences, and effects of puberty.
2. What effect might the changes in leg length and trunk length have at each age for boys and girls on motor skills such as running speed and floor exercises in gymnastics?

REFERENCES

Malina, R. Chapter 1.
Newell, K. Chapter 5.

LABORATORY 2: POWER AND MUSCULAR STRENGTH: SEX AND AGE DIFFERENCES[2]

Power and muscular strength influence success in many athletic endeavors. Power is defined as work performed over time, while muscular strength is defined as the maximal amount of force that a muscle group can exert during a single contraction. Prior to puberty, girls often exhibit qualities of strength and power that are similar to their male counterparts. However, after puberty, girls are less powerful or strong than males owing to lower levels of endogenous androgens (primarily testosterone). The purpose of this laboratory is to compare power and muscular strength of boys and girls both before and after puberty.

The *objectives* of this laboratory are:

1. To experience the use of two measures of power and muscular strength
2. To compare power and muscular strength of boys and girls at various ages

Procedures

Muscular strength of the groups of prepubescent and postpubescent boys and girls will be measured using a grip dynamometer and a leg extension tensiometer (or Cybex, Universal Gym, etc.). The measure of muscular power will be a simple vertical jump test.

Common to any measure of strength or power should be a series of light to moderate warm-up contractions that precede the actual test. These warm-up exercises should involve the same movement pattern as required by the strength or power test. When using dynamometers and cable

2. This laboratory was modified from *Experiences in work physiology* by R. Byrd & S. Powers, Minneapolis: Alpha Editions, Burgess Publishing Company, 1981.

tensiometers, isolation of the muscle group from influence of other body parts is important, and standardization of joint angles in question is critical. The mean of three trials of the strength measures and the vertical jump should be recorded for each subject. The means and standard deviations of all three trials should be tabulated for both boys ($\bar{X}$ m) and girls ($\bar{X}$ f) according to their age groups.

Results

Strength measures		Absolute values			Per kilogram of body weight		
Method	Measurement	$\bar{X}$ m	$\bar{X}$ f	m/f	$\bar{X}$ m	$\bar{X}$ f	m/f
Dynamometer	Grip strength						
Tensiometer (Cybex)	Leg extension						

Power measure	Inches above reach	
Vertical jump	$\bar{X}$ m	$\bar{X}$ f

Answer the following questions about your data:

1. Discuss the differences in muscular strength between sexes relative to age.
2. Explain the differences in the male/female (m/f) ratio in strength between absolute strength and that relative to body size. What role does fat play in the above ratios?
3. How does the increase in body fat in girls after puberty affect the sex differences seen in the vertical jump?

REFERENCES

Brown, C. H., & Wilmore, J. H. The effects of maximal resistance training on the strength and body composition of women athletes. *Medicine and Science in Sports,* 1974, **6**, 174-177.

Campbell, C. J., Bonen, A., Kirby, R. L., & Belcastro, A. N. Muscle fiber composition and performance capacities of women. *Medicine and Science in Sports,* 1979, **11**, 260-265.

Cheek, D. B. Muscle cell growth in children. In D. B. Cheek (Ed.), *Human growth.* Philadelphia: Lea & Febiger, 1968.

Rodahl, L. Physical work capacity. *American Medical Association Archives of Environmental Health,* 1961, **2**, 499-510.

LABORATORY 3: CHILDREN'S THROWING PATTERNS

Frequently teachers fail to realize that children change their overarm throwing patterns depending on how they are asked to throw. For example, asking young children to throw for accuracy frequently results in the use of a dartlike throwing movement. While the movement results in increased accuracy for short throws with light objects, learning this movement is not useful for such skills as throwing baseballs and footballs. The purpose of this laboratory is to demonstrate the changes that occur in young children's throwing motions depending on how they are asked to throw.

Procedures

Select four 7-year-old children, two boys and two girls. Equipment needed includes a 2 × 2-ft piece of posterboard, 10 used tennis balls, and an area at least 10 × 20 yd with a wall at one end. Draw a picture of Snoopy or some other cartoon figure on the posterboard and place it on the wall about head height for the children. Have the child stand behind a line 20 ft from the picture of Snoopy, and put the 10 tennis balls in a box beside the child. Ask the child to throw the balls one at a time at Snoopy, trying to hit him. Do this for each child, then move the throwing line back to 36 ft and take down the picture of Snoopy. Tell the child to stand behind the line and throw the ball as hard as she can against the wall.

Results

Note the following characteristics of the children's performances in the two tasks:

1. Consider the first trial practice.
2. For the next three trials on each task, watch the child's arm and shoulder action.
3. For the next three trials, note the child's pelvic rotation.
4. For the last three trials, watch the child's feet.

Answer the following questions about the children's performance:

1. What, if any, obvious differences do you see in the three movement components (arm and shoulder, hip, and feet) between the two tasks?
2. What, if any, differences do you see between the boys and girls? Describe the differences, using the components and tasks as the basis for description.
3. Use Roberton's description (Chapter 3) to aid your laboratory write-up.

REFERENCES

Roberton, M. A. Chapter 3.

LABORATORY 4: CHILDREN'S MEMORY FOR MOVEMENT

When location and distance information about a movement are both available, children use locations to make decisions about movements in their environment. However, sometimes movements must be made using distance judgments rather than locations. For instance, if a child is to run a pass pattern (e.g., a 10-yd square out) in flag football, how does he remember the distance to run before making the 90-degree cut? The yard markers are undependable, as the ball may be located anywhere on the field. Consider also how a swimmer doing the 50-m backstroke in a 25-m pool knows when to make a flip turn. The obvious answers for an adult are for the football player to count steps and for the swimmer to count strokes. However, this strategy is not so obvious to the young child. The purpose of this laboratory is to demonstrate the increasing use of a spontaneous memory strategy as children mature.

The objectives of this laboratory are:

1. To observe the spontaneous development across age of a step-counting strategy to remember the distance jogged

2. To compare the effects on performance when a step-counting strategy is induced
3. To become familiar with ways of estimating error scores and their meanings

Procedures

Cut four strings 50 m long and place them on a flat surface on the playground as shown in Figure 14.2. The start and finish points are marked on the criterion (A) and reproduction (B1, B2, B3) strings. Put colored golf tees into the ground to mark the distances of 15, 25 and 35 m on the criterion. Put a tee in the ground (hidden down in the grass so the child cannot see it) at 15 m on string B3, at 35 m on B2, and at 25 m on B1. Select 12 children, four each at ages 6, 9, and 12 years. Two children at each age are placed in the strategy group and two in the no-strategy group. Take the children (one at a time) in the no-strategy group and tell them, "We are going to run down this string [criterion] until I say stop. Then we'll go to one of the other strings [reproduction], and you will try to run the same distance we did the first time." For children in the strategy group, say the same as above, but ask, "How can you remember the distance you will run?" If the child says that she will count her steps and then run the same number the second time, then say, "Good. Do that to help you remember." If she does not say that she will count her steps, then say, "Why don't you count your steps the first time and then run the same number on the other string?"

All children should be tested as follows:

1. Have them run 25 m on the criterion string and then run their estimate of that distance on string B1.
2. Have them run 35 m on the criterion string and then run their estimate of that distance on string B2.

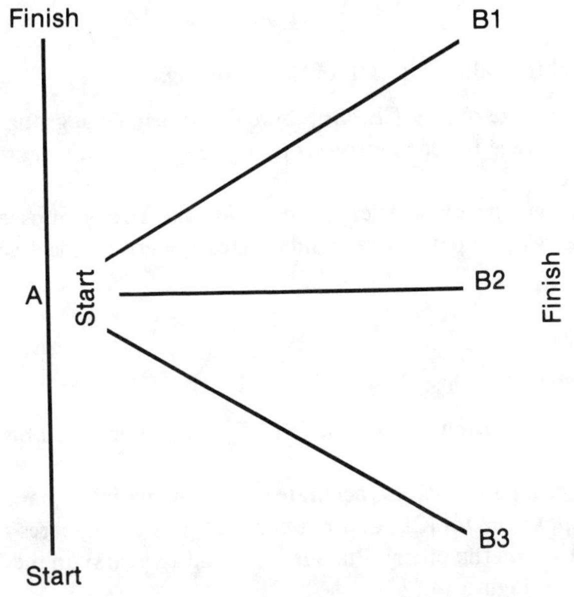

Figure 14.2. Playground layout for jogging task.

3. Have them run 15 m on the criterion string and then run their estimate of that distance on string B3.
4. Use a block to mark where the child stops on the B strings.
5. After the child has three trials, measure the distance between his estimate (location of the block) and the criterion distance (where the golf tee was placed on the B strings) for each trial and record the error in centimeters. Use a minus (−) to denote an underestimate and a plus (+) for an overestimate.
6. Ask each child in the control group what they did to remember the distance. Write down their responses.

Obtain four types of error scores for each child:

1. Absolute error (AE)—average the three scores for each child, disregarding the sign (+ or −).
2. Constant error (CE)—average the three scores for each child, but use the sign of each score (+ or −); the average will now have a sign (+ or −), depending on whether the negative or positive scores are larger.
3. Absolute constant error (|CE|)—do as in 2, but once the average of the three scores (using the sign) is obtained, drop the sign.
4. Variable error (VE)—calculate the standard deviation (SD) of CE for each subject,

$$\text{VE} = \text{SD of CE} = \sqrt{\frac{\sum(\text{X} - \bar{\text{X}})^2}{N-1}}$$

where $\sum$ = sum, X = a CE score, $\bar{\text{X}}$ = average CE for that child, and N = number of trials (three here).

Using the data, find the values for each of the following:

1. Calculate the average of AE, CE, |CE|, and VE for each age group (6, 9, and 12 years).
2. Calculate the average for each error score of the strategy (disregard age of child) and the no-strategy groups.
3. Calculate the average of each error score for the two groups at each age level: the 6-year-old strategy group, the 6-year-old no-strategy group, the 9-year-old strategy group, and so on.

Results

Answer the following questions:

1. Are the younger children less accurate (|CE|) and more variable (VE) than the older children?
2. Is the strategy group more or less accurate (|CE|) and variable than the no-strategy group?
3. Draw two graphs (one for |CE| and one for VE). Put error scores on the Y axis (|CE| on one graph and VE on the other). Put age (6, 9, and 12 years) on the X axis. Do the graphs look like those in Figure 14.3?

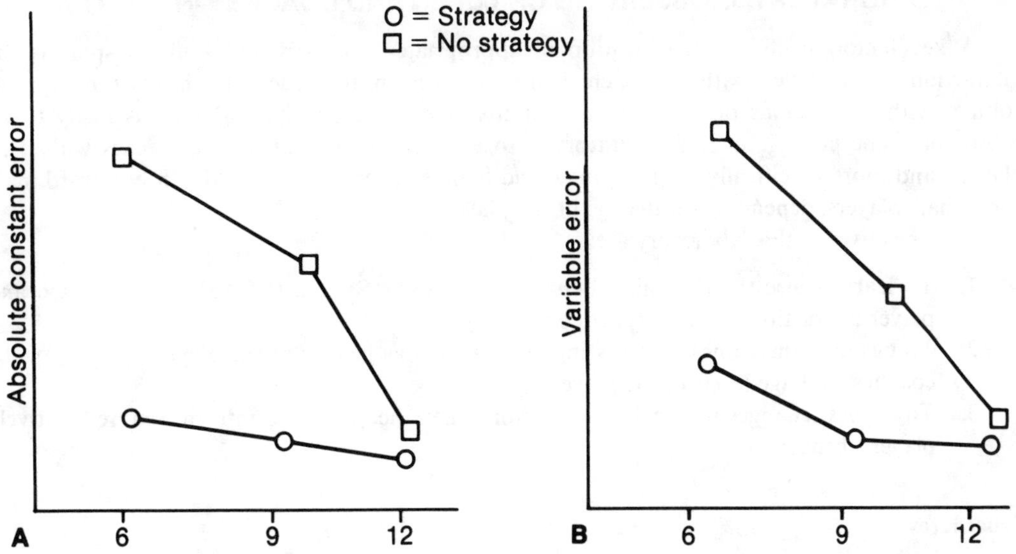

Figure 14.3. Predicted outcome of jogging laboratory.

The plots in Figure 14.3 are called interactions. These interactions show that as children get older, the strategy and no-strategy groups become more similar. The student's graph should look something like this (note that |CE| and VE values on the Y axis are not included here, but students' graphs will show them). What do these results mean? If the student has trouble figuring this out, then rereading Chapter 4 and reading the references listed for this laboratory will help.

4. Look at the CE error score. Did the subjects (on the average) undershoot the longer jog and overshoot the shorter jog? This has commonly been called the "range effect."
5. AE is a composite error score. It is not particularly useful, although AE is frequently reported. What do the AE means look like when graphed?
6. By age level, tally the responses on how the children in the no-strategy group told how they remembered. Are the responses more strategic (showed the children used a plan to remember) for the older children when compared with the younger ones? How does this relate to the children's performances shown in the graph of the interaction?
7. What do the results tell about how children of different ages remember movements?
8. What do these findings suggest to elementary school physical education teachers about teaching?

REFERENCES

Thomas, J. R. Chapter 4.

Thomas, J. R. Acquisition of motor skills: Information processing differences between children and adults. *Research Quarterly for Exercise and Sport,* 1980, **51**, 158-173.

Thomas, J. R., Thomas, K. T., Lee, A. M., Testerman, E., & Ashy, M. Age differences in use of strategy for recall of movement in a large scale environment. *Research Quarterly for Exercise and Sport,* in press.

LABORATORY 5: OBSERVING CHILDREN AND COACHES IN SPORT

A key factor in children's education in appropriate behaviors and skills in sport is the interaction of the players with the coach. During the season, the coach may have as much close contact with a player as do the player's parents. Thus, the coach's influence is likely to be substantial. The purpose of this laboratory is to evaluate the interaction of coaches with their players, and more specifically, to see if male and female coaches behave differently toward male and female players, depending on the age of the players.

The objectives of this laboratory are:

1. To learn to use the Coaching Behavioral Analysis System (CBAS) to code coach and player interaction during a sport contest
2. To evaluate the games, contrasting factors such as gender of the players, gender of the coaches, and age levels of the players
3. To suggest changes in coaching behavior, where necessary, to influence more positively players' behaviors

Procedures

Three factors need to be considered in this laboratory experience: the gender of the coach, the gender of the player, and the age of the player. First, select one of these factors to hold constant (e.g., use only one gender of coach, one gender of players, or one age group of players). Students will use two levels of the other two factors. For example, if the student decides to watch only female coaches, then four games should be selected. Two of the games should be with younger age groups (one with male players and one with female players) and two with an older age group (one with male players and one with female players). This would result in a design as depicted in Figure 14.4.

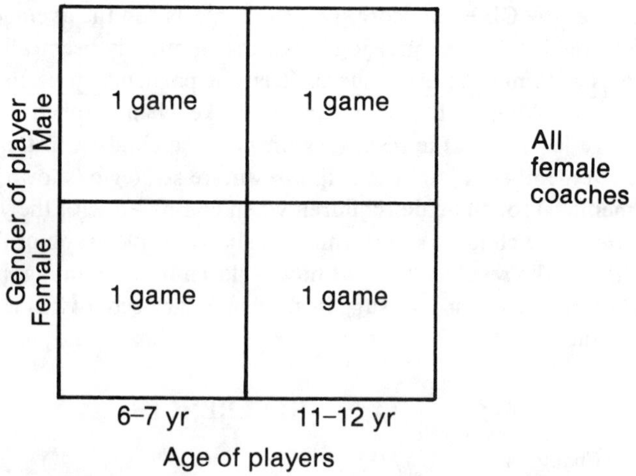

Figure 14.4. Sample of coach and player characteristics to be chosen; all female coaches is the constant.

Students are to use the CBAS developed by Smoll and Smith (1977) to code the coach-player interaction. Tables 14.1 and 14.2 and Figure 14.5 explain this system and provide a sample score sheet for baseball or softball. The CBAS can also be used with other team sports.

When students go over this exercise in class, several examples in each category of the CBAS should be mentioned so that students are sure which types of behaviors go in each. I suggest that students practice on at least one game and have a question and answer session in class before coding four games. This small amount of practice will not produce high reliability or objectivity among raters, but the purposes of the laboratory will be served.

Results

Do the following with the data:

1. Sum the frequencies in each subcategory (e.g., positive reinforcement or reward (R)).
2. Sum the frequencies in the categories (e.g., responses to desirable performances).
3. Sum the frequencies for reactive behaviors and spontaneous behaviors.
4. Add together reactive and spontaneous behaviors for the total number of behaviors coded.
5. Convert all sums obtained in 1, 2, and 3 to percentages by dividing each sum by the total number of behaviors coded.
6. Draw bar graphs to represent data for each game.

Answer the following questions (questions will differ slightly depending on the factor selected to hold constant):

1. Are age differences in the percentages of behaviors evident:
   a. For spontaneous versus reactive?
   b. By category?
   c. By subcategory?
2. Are differences in coaches' behavior toward male and female players evident in any category or subcategory?
3. Do female coaches treat male and female players differently according to age levels in any category or subcategory?
4. List other interesting things observed, such as:
   a. Parents' behaviors
   b. Information about players and coaches on the other teams
   c. Whether behaviors appeared to vary depending on how far ahead or behind the team being observed was
   d. Any other pertinent information

REFERENCES

Smoll, F. L. & Smith, R. E. Chapter 12.

Smoll, F. L. et al. Toward a mediational model of coach-player relationships. *Research Quarterly,* 1978, **49,** 528-541.

Smith, R. E. et al. A system for the behavioral assessment of athletic coaches. *Research Quarterly,* 1977, **48,** 401-407.

Table 14.1. Coaching Behavior Assessment System (CBAS)[a]

Class I. Reactive Behaviors
- A. Desirable performance
  - 1. Positive reinforcement (R)
  - 2. Nonreinforcement (NR)
- B. Responses to mistake/errors
  - 3. Mistake-contingent encouragement (EM)
  - 4. Mistake-contingent technical instruction (TIM)
  - 5. Punishment (P)
  - 6. Punitive TIM (TIM + P)
  - 7. Ignoring mistakes (IM)
- C. Responses to misbehaviors
  - 8. Keeping control (KC)

Class II. Spontaneous Behaviors
- A. Game-related behaviors
  - 9. General technical instruction (TIG)
  - 10. General encouragement (EG)
  - 11. Organization (O)
- B. Game-irrelevant behavior
  - 12. General communication (GS)

[a] *Two major classes of behaviors in the CBAS—reactive behavior*: responses to immediately preceding player or team behaviors; *spontaneous behavior*: behaviors that are initiated by the coach and are not a response to an immediately preceding event.

Table 14.2. The 12 Behavioral Categories of the (CBAS)[a]

I. Reactive behaviors
 A. Responses to desirable performances
  1. *Positive reinforcement or reward (R)*—A positive reaction by the coach to a desirable performance by one or more players; may be either verbal or nonverbal (e.g., congratulating a player or a pat on the back after a good play)
  2. *Nonreinforcement (NR)*—A failure to reinforce a positive behavior; the coach fails to respond (e.g., a player gets a base hit and the coach shows no reaction)
 B. Reactions to mistakes
  3. *Mistake-contingent encouragement (EM)*—Encouragement of a player by a coach following a mistake
  4. *Mistake-contingent technical instruction (TIM)*—Telling or showing a player who has made a mistake how to make the play correctly. This requires that the coach instruct the player in some specific way (e.g., showing a player how to field the ball after an error is made)
  5. *Punishment (P)*—A negative response by the coach following an undesirable behavior; may be either verbal or nonverbal. (e.g., making a sarcastic remark to a player who has just struck out or the coach waving in disgust after an error)
  6. *Punitive (TIM) (TIM + P)*—Sometimes TIM + P occur in the same communication. When a coach gives TIM in a punitive or hostile manner, P is also scored (e.g., coach yells angrily, "How many times do I have to tell you to catch the ball with two hands!")
  7. *Ignoring mistakes (IM)*—A lack of response, either positive or negative, to a mistake on the part of a player or the team
 C. Responses to misbehaviors
  8. *Keeping control (KC)*—Responses that are designed to maintain order, usually caused by unruly behavior or inattentiveness

II. Spontaneous behaviors
 A. Game-related behaviors
  9. *General technical instruction (TIG)*—A communication that provides instruction relevant to techniques and strategies of the sport to foster the learning of skills and strategies for game situations. Message must clearly be one of instruction, not elicited by an immediate preceding mistake (e.g., telling a player how to bat, telling the fielder which base to throw to)
  10. *General encouragement (EG)*—Encouragement that does not immediately follow a mistake; not a response to a specific action by a player. It relates to future hopes rather than to behaviors of the past (e.g., come on team, get some more runs)
  11. *Organization (O)*—Behavior directed at administrative organization, not intended to influence play immediately (e.g., reminding the players of the batting order, reassigning positions, announcing substitutions)
 B. Game-irrelevant behavior
  12. *General communication (GS)*—Interactions with players that are unrelated to game situations or team activities (e.g., joking with players)

[a]This is an expansion of Table 12.1 (page 240) by Smoll and Smith.

Game Evaluation Form

Name of evaluator ______________ Team outcome: W or L or T

Team being evaluated ______________ Opponent ______________

Date ________ Location ________ Length on game (Time) ________

Players
Male ________
Female ________
Mixed ________

Coach: M or F
Age of players ________
T-Ball, BB, SB, CP

BEHAVIORS	INNINGS 1	2	3	4	5	6
I. Reactive (Total)						
A. Desirable performance (Total)						
1. Positive reinforcement						
2. Nonreinforcement						
B. Mistakes/errors (Total)						
3. Mistake-contingent encouragement						
4. Mistake-contingent technical instruction						
5. Punishment						
6. Punitive mistake-contingent technical instruction						
7. Ignoring mistakes						
C. Misbehaviors (Total)						
8. Keeping control						
II. Spontaneous (Total)						
A. Game-related (Total)						
9. General technical instruction						
10. General encouragement						
11. Organization						
B. Game-irrelevant (Total)						
12. General communication						

Comments:

Figure 14.5. Game evaluation form.

Index

Student Survey

Jerry R. Thomas, Editor

MOTOR DEVELOPMENT DURING CHILDHOOD AND ADOLESCENCE

Students, send us your ideas!

We want to know how well this book served you and what can be done to improve it for those who will use it in the future. By completing and returning this questionnaire, you can help us to develop better textbooks. We value your opinion and want to hear your comments. Thank you.

Your name (optional)________________________ School______________

Your mailing address____

City____________________ State______________ ZIP______________

Instructor's name (optional)____________________ Course title______________

1. How does this book compare with other texts you have used? (Check one)

   ☐ Superior ☐ Better than most ☐ Comparable ☐ Not as good as most

2. Circle those chapters you especially liked:

   Chapters: 1 2 3 4 5 6 7 8 9 10 11 12 13 14

   Comments:

3. Circle those chapters you think could be improved:

   Chapters: 1 2 3 4 5 6 7 8 9 10 11 12 13 14

   Comments:

4. Please rate the following (check one for each):

	Excellent	Good	Average	Poor
Logical organization	( )	( )	( )	( )
Readability of text material	( )	( )	( )	( )
General layout and design	( )	( )	( )	( )
Match with instructor's course organization	( )	( )	( )	( )
Illustrations that clarify the text	( )	( )	( )	( )
Up-to-date treatment of subject	( )	( )	( )	( )
Explanation of difficult concepts	( )	( )	( )	( )
Selection of topics in the textbook	( )	( )	( )	( )

OVER, PLEASE

5. List any chapters that your instructor did not assign. ________________________________

____

6. What additional topics did your instructor discuss that were not covered in the text? ______

____

7. Did you buy this book new or used? ☐ New ☐ Used

Do you plan to keep the book or sell it? ☐ Keep it ☐ Sell it

Do you think your instructor should continue to assign this book? ☐ Yes ☐ No

8. After taking the course, are you interested in taking more courses in this field? ☐ Yes ☐ No

Are you a major in physical education? ☐ Yes ☐ No

9. GENERAL COMMENTS:

May we quote you in our advertising? ☐ Yes ☐ No

Please remove this page and mail to:

Mary L. Paulson
Burgess Publishing Company
7108 Ohms Lane
Minneapolis, MN 55435

THANK YOU!